# TRANSNATIONAL PATRIOTISM IN THE MEDITERRANEAN, 1800–1850

T0355302

Praise for *Transnational Patriotism in the Mediterranean, 1800–1850*

'This book breaks new ground between transnational intellectual history, biography and cultural history and even suggests—rather unassumingly—a different way of writing history; it is bound to travel well and will accompany many who delve into the history of the Adriatic Sea.'

*(Sakis Gekas, H-Soz-u-Kult)*

'To say that this book makes significant contributions to a number of historiographical themes is probably an understatement...a book that has transgressed a number of scholarly boundaries and that has already become a reference book for the history of the region. This work is useful not just for specialists in the field (and for relevant university courses), but also for all those who want to enhance their knowledge of modern Europe, and of the processes through which the modern world emerged.'

*(Michalis Sotiropoulos, Reviews in History)*

'A pioneering contribution to our general understanding of early Mediterranean and European liberalism, patriotism and nation-building; it is also a refreshing methodological renovation of the way to approach history.'

*(Rolf Petri, History: The Journal of the Historical Association)*

# Transnational Patriotism in the Mediterranean, 1800–1850

## *Stammering the Nation*

KONSTANTINA ZANOU

# OXFORD
## UNIVERSITY PRESS

Great Clarendon Street, Oxford, OX2 6DP,
United Kingdom

Oxford University Press is a department of the University of Oxford.
It furthers the University's objective of excellence in research, scholarship,
and education by publishing worldwide. Oxford is a registered trade mark of
Oxford University Press in the UK and in certain other countries

First published 2018
First published in paperback 2023

Published in the United States of America by Oxford University Press
198 Madison Avenue, New York, NY 10016, United States of America

British Library Cataloguing in Publication Data
Data available

Library of Congress Cataloging in Publication Data
Data available

ISBN 978–0–19–878870–6  (Hbk.)
ISBN 978–0–19–888510–8  (Pbk.)

To my parents, Christos and Kate

# *Acknowledgements*

Every book is a solitary voyage as much as it is a collective endeavour. In the almost ten years since I first set out on this voyage, I have been joined by numerous companions. Completing it enables me, happily, to record my gratitude for the abundant support, both material and moral, that I received along the way.

Financial support was generously provided by a research grant from the Research Promotion Foundation of Cyprus (National Framework Programme for Research and Technological Development 2008–2011/DIDAKTOR Programme), a Fulbright Fellowship at the Center for European and Mediterranean Studies and the Remarque Institute at New York University, an Advanced Academia Fellowship for International Scholars at the Centre for Advanced Study Sofia, a Centenary Bursary Award by the British School at Athens, and a Lenfest Junior Faculty Development Grant by Columbia University.

Earlier versions of selected parts of this book were 'tried out' on audiences in a variety of venues in North America and Europe. I thank the organizers and the participants at these lectures, conferences, and seminars for their stimulating engagement with the topic and for their refinement of my arguments through the astute comments and criticisms that they have offered. Let me list those venues here: the Modern Greek Seminar at Columbia University; the Modern Greek and 'Mediterranean Topographies' Seminar at the University of Michigan; the History department at the University of Miami; the History department at the University of California, San Diego; the History department at York University, Toronto; the Centre for Advanced Studies Sofia, Bulgaria; the conference '(Trans)nationality and cultural asymmetry in the humanities, social sciences and politics, 19th and 20th centuries' at the Department of History and Civilization, European University Institute, Florence; the conference 'Revolutions in the Balkans: Revolts and Uprisings in the Era of nationalism (1804–1908)' at Panteion University, Athens; the Modern Greek Studies Seminar at King's College, London; the conference 'Re-imagining Political Communities in the Mediterranean: Peoples, Nations, and Empires in the Age of Democratic Revolution' at Columbia University; the Institute for Mediterranean Studies, Rethymno, Crete; the Modern Greek Seminar at the University of Oxford; the British School at Athens; the seminar 'Chrétiens, Romains, Hellènes: Discours identitaires et transferts culturels' at the École des Hautes Études en Sciences Sociales (EHESS), Paris; the Séminaire d'Histoire Comparée du Centre de Recherche en Histoire Européenne Comparée (CRHEC) at the Université Paris-Est Créteil, Val de Marne, Paris; the conference 'Philhellenism and European Identity' at the University of Cyprus; the workshop '1821: What made it Greek? What made it Revolutionary?' at the Jordan Center for the Advanced Study of Russia, New York University; and, finally, the Institut für Griechische und Lateinische Philologie, Freie Universität, Berlin.

I was privileged to work in various archives and libraries. I would like to thank the employees of the Biblioteca Nazionale Centrale, Florence; the Gabinetto Scientifico Letterario G. P. Vieusseux, Florence; the Biblioteca Riccardiana, Florence; the Biblioteca della Scuola Normale Superiore, Pisa; the Biblioteca dell'Accademia delle Scienze, Turin; the Archivio di Stato, Milan; the Biblioteca Ambrosiana, Milan; the Biblioteca Trivulziana, Milan; the Archiginnasio di Bologna–Biblioteca Comunale, Bologna; the Biblioteca di Storia Moderna e Contemporanea, Rome; the Biblioteca Marciana, Venice; the Benaki Museum, Athens; the Gennadius Library, Athens; the General State Archives, Athens; the General State Archives, Corfu; the Bibliothèque de Port-Royal, Paris; the Bibliothèque de l'Arsenal–Bibliothèque nationale de France, Paris; the Bibliothèque Victor Cousin–Bibliothèque de la Sorbonne, Paris; the Bibliothèque de l'Institut de France, Paris; and, finally, the Bibliothèque Publique et Universitaire, Geneva. Bertrand and Michelle Bouvier were extremely kind in helping me delve into the archives of the latter and Grégoire Bron was the best company and host I could hope for. My special thanks go to the Diocese of Corfu, and particularly to the Bishop of Corfu Nektarios, for granting me access to the precious Mustoxidi Papers. Christos Desyllas and Konstantinos Thymis, both employees of the diocese and fellow historians, were particularly helpful and welcoming during my stay there.

I am endlessly indebted to Antonis Liakos, my teacher, friend, and mentor. For many years, he has been an indispensable guide and inspiration. I am grateful also to Maurizio Isabella, my colleague and dear friend, with whom I have worked closely and learned how to write Mediterranean history. They both read the manuscript in its different stages and offered valuable feedback.

Over the years, I have benefited from the ideas, guidance, and criticism of many teachers, colleagues, and friends. Joanna Innes, Mark Philp, Eduardo Posada Carbo, and their 'Re-imagining Democracy in the Mediterranean, 1750–1860' project offered a valuable platform to test my ideas and to learn from others. Dominique Kirchner Reill and Michael T. Bernath, during a discussion at the University of Miami, inspired the subtitle of this book. Vassilis Lambropoulos was the first to point out that I should envisage the biographies of Foscolo, Kalvos, and Solomos as being in so many respects conjoined. Peter Mackridge, Thomas Gallant, Yianni Kotsonis, Ada Dialla, Lucien Frary, Mark Mazower, and Karen Emmerich read the manuscript in its entirety, or else selected parts of it, and ventured shrewd observations that saved me from myself on multiple occasions. Martin Thom not only did much to improve the quality of my English, but also offered astute comments and suggestions.

Many friends have accompanied me with their love and intellectual engagement throughout this long journey. Yiannis Papadakis, Christodoulos Panayiotou, Karen Emmerich, Kyriakos Pachoulides, Hara Kouki, Daphne Lappa, Michalis Sotiropoulos, Kostis Kornetis, Raluca Grosescu, Sakis Gekas, Maya de Leo, Silvia Rosa, Eleni Liarou, Maria Anestopoulou, Mariamargherita Scotti, Alessio Petrizzo, Alkis Hadjiandreou, Andreas Onoufriou, Magda Egoumenides, Andry Panayiotou, all supported me and discussed with me aspects of the book. Niyazi Kizilyürek showed me what it means to be a transnational patriot.

My graduate students at the Italian Department of Columbia University, where I have had the good fortune to be based in the last two years, have offered different and unexpected perspectives when the book was nearing completion. I thank them, as I thank my colleagues at the Italian Department (and other departments) at Columbia University for being so welcoming and supportive.

At Oxford University Press, I thank Robert Faber for embracing my book proposal and offering me a contract and Cathryn Steele for guiding me through the process of delivery. They were both always warmly responsive and helpful. I should also thank the three anonymous reviewers, who read the book with care and offered valuable insights.

My final words of thanks here are for my family. My father, Christos Zanos, who has been also my main interlocutor during all these years, has taught me how to combine history with the magic world of theatre and, what is most important, how to put meaning into words. My mother, Kate, and my sister, Eleni Zanou, have offered me their unconditional love and generosity and taught me how to impart feeling to what I do. I can scarcely find the words to express my deep gratitude to all of them for looking after me in times of anxiety and frustration, but also for sharing with me the immense joy of this life.

New York, January 2018

# *Contents*

# List of Illustrations

# List of Abbreviations

| | |
|---|---|
| BAM | Biblioteca Ambrosiana di Milano |
| BAST | Biblioteca dell'Accademia delle Scienze di Torino |
| BCNF | Biblioteca Nazionale Centrale di Firenze |
| BM | Benaki Museum, Athens |
| BnF-BA | Bibliothèque nationale de France-Bibliothèque de l'Arsenal |
| BpuG | Bibliothèque publique et universitaire de Genève-Département de Manuscrits |
| BRF | Biblioteca Riccardiana di Firenze |
| BTM | Biblioteca Trivulziana di Milano |
| BVC-BS | Bibliothèque Victor Cousin-Bibliothèque de la Sorbonne |
| FE | Ugo Foscolo, *Epistolario*, edited by Plinio Carli, Giovanni Gambarin, Francesco Tropeano, Mario Scotti (Florence, 1949–94), 9 vols |
| GSA-A | General State Archives, Athens |
| HMC: MP | Holy Metropolis of Corfu: Mustoxidi Papers |

# Note on Transliteration

In most cases I have transliterated Greek words into the Roman alphabet. In doing so, I have followed by and large the example set by Peter Mackridge in his *Language and National Identity in Greece, 1766–1976* (Oxford, 2009), whereby the transliteration reproduces the Greek letters rather than the pronunciation, placing emphasis on the visual image of the word rather than on its sound.

So, except for those occasions when authors use specific transliterated versions of their names, I have normally transliterated:

αι as ai (pronounced *e*)
αυ as av or af according to the pronunciation in each particular case
β as b (pronounced *v*)
γγ as gg
γι as gi
γκ as nk
ει as ei (pronounced *i*)
ευ as ev or ef according to the pronunciation in each particular case
η as i
θ as th
μπ as mp (pronounced *mb* or *b*)
ντ as nt (pronounced *nd* or *d*)
ξ as x (pronounced *x*)
οι as oi (pronounced *i*)
ου as ou (pronounced *u*)
σ as s or ss according to the pronunciation in each particular case
υ as y (pronounced *i*)
φ as f, but as ph in words with the component 'philo-' (philhellenism, Philiki, Philomousos, Philorthodox, Philologikos) and in standardized names or terms (Cephalonia, autocephalous, Ephor, klephtic, Phanariots, Nicephorus, Philostratus, Photius, Sophia)
χ as ch, not h
ω as o

This book is populated by transnational and multi-lingual characters who had different names in each of their languages and cultural settings. In most cases, I have opted for the Italian variant, or for the name which the characters themselves used for longer periods in their lives and by which they signed most of their writings and other documents. I have respected the practice of some of these characters in their use of different versions of their names during different phases of their lives or in their different publications. Nevertheless, in order to facilitate things for the reader, in the bibliography I have adopted a more standardized version of each of these names, adding also in parentheses the specific version that was used on each occasion. Where some of the better-known figures are concerned, I have used the English variant of their name (e.g. Kapodistrias, Ignatius, Koraes). I have done the same with place names.

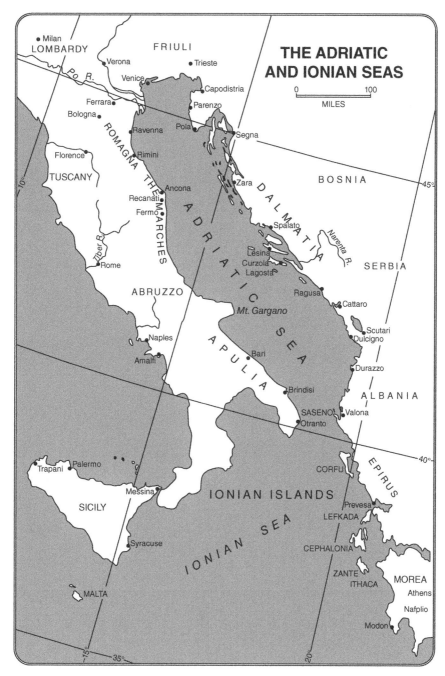

**Figure 1.** Map of the Adriatic and Ionian Seas

# Introduction

## Personal Stories in a Vanishing World

The 1797 carnival in Venice was, for those who remembered it in retrospect, among the most delightful and captivating in the whole of its history. *It was singularly lively*, wrote one of those who took part in it. *The entertainment was a veritable frenzy, a continuous Bacchanalia. The whole night long a vigil, a banquet, a feast. From the cafés to the theatres, from the theatres to the foyers, and then back to the cafés again, nor was there any thought of going to bed before the cock announced the new day.*[1] Neither this eye-witness nor any other could have imagined that this would be the last ever carnival to be staged in the Venetian Empire's glorious capital. Only three months later, when the Doge and his Great Council were forced to turn power over to Napoleon and to his rampant revolutionary army, the once powerful and 'serene' Venetian Republic silently shut its eyes.

This story starts when the Republic of Venice ends. It is, in a certain sense, a story of the ruins of the Serenissima. It narrates the lives of men (and a few women) of letters and politics, who lived along the shores of the Adriatic during the first half of the nineteenth century, when the region was transformed from a 'Venetian lake' into a battlefield between old and new imperial powers and emerging nationalisms and nation-states. It is a book about people trying to reinvent themselves in times of perpetual crisis and change. These were intellectuals and politicians born within empires but confronted with the emerging vocabulary of nationalism, much of which they themselves had forged. The focal point of this story is the borderland between the collapsing Venetian imperial world, the changing Ottoman world, and the ascendant, emerging national worlds of Italy and Greece. These nationalisms developed within the context of four other empires: the Napoleonic, Russian, British, and Habsburg. Much of this story was played out in the southeastern corner of the Adriatic Sea, more specifically on an insular extension of the Greek peninsula, the seven Ionian Islands, during their slow transformation from being a periphery of the Venetian Republic to a region of the Greek nation-state.

At its broadest, this is a history of the processes by which premodern, multi-ethnic empires were replaced by modern nation-states—'perhaps the most momentous

---

[1] Mario Pieri, *Della vita di Mario Pieri corcirese scritta da lui medesimo* (Florence, 1850), vol. I, pp. 36–7. See also Pier-Alessandro Paravia, 'Gli ultimi giorni della Repubblica di Venezia, frammento storico', in idem, *Memorie veneziane di letteratura e di storia* (Turin, 1850), p. 294.

but least widely understood development in modern history', as one scholar has observed.[2] In the Adriatic, as elsewhere in the world, this transition amounted to the dissolution of a common regional space and to the shattering of its centuries-old cultural continuum. It involved a shift in political and cultural geographies. In the case of most of the Ionians described in this book, for example, loyalties shifted from the centre that Venice used to be to the centre that Athens was now becoming, while there was a liminal phase during which the statelet of the Ionian Islands was configured as an autonomous space protected by colonial empires. The long transition from a world of empires to a world of nation-states also brought about the radical transformation of the concept of 'patria', from a cultural and local community into a political and national entity. Furthermore, it meant the gradual reconceptualization of language, which was transformed from an index of social mobility into an attribute of national identity. On the whole, this transition and the processes that it entailed led to the total restructuring of space and to the tracing of new boundaries between homelands and languages: in the world that was now emerging, a world of mutually exclusive nationalisms, the Adriatic Sea was slowly being transformed 'from a bridge into a border'.[3]

Along with geopolitics, people also changed. The book investigates the different ways in which a number of individuals experienced historical transformation. It explores how historical developments changed their lives by redirecting their mobilities, recasting their patriotisms, refashioning their sense of belonging, and reshaping their political, cultural, and ideological options. The written traces these men and women left behind, the correspondence, diaries, autobiographies, published books, and manuscripts which I have explored, attest to a sense of dislocation and fragmentation fostered by the reframing of identities in a rapidly altering post-Venetian Adriatic. In most cases, they reflect how these former Venetian subjects were transformed, by turns, into Ionian 'citizens' who were the subjects of great empires (Napoleonic, Russian, or British), Italian patriots, transnational liberals or revolutionaries, exiles, and Greek nationals. These were all individuals bearing a surplus of meaning, able to assume ever new identities and contexts.

Drawing on recent works in 'global microhistory' and historical biography, this book takes as its starting point modest, humble lives in order then to pull back and survey the grander, more sweeping historical changes. In other words, it combines microhistory with macrohistory so as to look at the big picture through the small details.[4] By focusing on the intimate craving of these individuals to attain stability and a sense of belonging in a period when all the known social, political, and cultural certainties were shifting like tectonic plates beneath their feet, I will try to

---

[2] David Armitage, *Foundations of Modern International Thought* (Cambridge, 2013), p. 191.

[3] To borrow Dominique Kirchner Reill's apt expression in her *Nationalists Who Feared the Nation: Adriatic Multi-Nationalism in Habsburg Dalmatia, Trieste, and Venice* (Stanford, Calif., 2012), p. 8.

[4] Francesca Trivellato, 'Is There a Future for Italian Microhistory in the Age of Global History?', *California Italian Studies* 2/1 (2011): <https://escholarship.org/uc/item/0z94n9hq>; John-Paul A. Ghobrial, 'The Secret Life of Elias of Babylon and the Uses of Global Microhistory', *Past and Present* 222 (2014), pp. 51–93; A. Woollacott, D. Deacon, and P. Russell (eds), *Transnational Lives: Biographies of Global Modernity, 1700–Present* (London and New York, 2010).

offer a human and personal reading of the large-scale historical processes at work in a febrile age. It is my firm conviction that biography is not only a way of reviving the 'human dramas that make history come alive', but also of revealing what was possible and what was not.[5]

So, history in this book becomes personal. It also becomes embodied. In its pages, we will come across dead bodies that were exhumed and reburied, saints' relics that were borne in solemn processions through the streets, itinerant individuals who expressed a devout wish to be buried in the 'patria' they had left behind, embalmed corpses that were venerated, blood that was collected on account of its purportedly miraculous powers, skulls that were studied for their secrets. It is all about embodying abstract ideas, and especially embodying the patria. One of the minor characters in this story, Ioannis Zampelios, an Ionian playwright, lover of freedom, and fervent Greek patriot, beautifully encapsulates this phenomenon when he writes in his autobiography (1844?) that *during the Greek Revolution, specifically in its second year, he was in so inflamed and heated a state that for a whole month he risked falling into insanity, and for that reason he had to be locked up.*[6] At a time when doctors composed medical treatises on the *maladie démocratique* as a new form of madness, sensing patriotism on one's own skin was not so strange a thing.[7]

## Stammering the Nation

In this book we will also meet people stammering, more often metaphorically rather than literally. The book borrows its subtitle from a letter written in 1795 by Ugo Foscolo, Italy's foremost poet at that date, when he was still an Ionian adolescent making his first, faltering steps into Italian letters. *Udrò da voi i precetti di una lingua che con gran fatica ho studiato, e che al presente τραυλίζω*, he wrote to his teacher in a hybrid Italo-Greek (I shall hear from you the precepts of a language that I studied with great difficulty, and for the moment I only stammer).[8] The 'stammering' metaphor was dear to him as it was to several of the characters encountered in this book. Time and again, they employed it in order to denote their difficulties in carving out a space for themselves in between patrias, and in living bilingualism and multi-patriotism.

Placed in the title, 'stammering' encompasses the first awkward attempts made by these intellectuals and politicians to articulate the vocabulary of the nation. It is also a reference to the central place that language occupies in this book. Its characters were all individuals who began their intellectual life writing in one language (be it Italian, Greek, or French) and then had to reinvent themselves as representatives of

---

[5] Tonio Andrade, 'A Chinese Farmer, Two Black Boys, and a Warlord: Towards a Global Microhistory', *Journal of World History* 21/4 (2011), p. 574.

[6] [Anonymous], 'Aftobiografia Io. Zampeliou' (The autobiography of Ioannis Zampelios), *Armonia* 3 (1902), p. 231.

[7] Carl Theodor Groddeck, *De la maladie démocratique, nouvelle espèce de folie* (Paris, 1850). See Laure Murat, *The Man Who Thought He Was Napoleon: Toward a Political History of Madness* (Chicago, 2014), p. 183.

[8] FE, vol. 1, p. 20.

a different nationality. The more language came to be connected to the nation and the more it gained in symbolic validity, the more these individuals felt the discrepancy between their language and their patriotism. In addition, many of the characters who populate this book were engaged in the heated linguistic battles that took place in those years regarding the forging of one single national language from the variety of different dialects spoken in former multi-ethnic and multi-lingual imperial areas. The Greek and Italian linguistic battles thus feature here, through the lives of intellectuals who participated in both of these zones of cultural conflict, intrinsically interconnected as they were.

## CHARACTERS

### Transnational Lives in the Age of Nationalism

But who exactly were these individuals? The cast of characters includes, first of all, some Ionian and Dalmatian intellectuals and politicians, who subsequently became the 'fathers' of the Greek or Italian nations, namely Ugo Foscolo, Andreas Kalvos, Dionysios Solomos, Ioannis Kapodistrias, and Niccolò Tommaseo. Second, a group of Ionian, Dalmatian, Greco-Italian, Greco-Russian, and other peoples of the Adriatic diasporas, all men and women of letters and politics who remained relatively or completely unknown. Let me list their names in order of appearance: Isabella Teotochi-Albrizzi, Giorgio Mocenigo, Spiridione Naranzi, Andrea Mustoxidi, Bishop Ignatius, Alexandre and Roxandra Stourdza, Spyridon Destunis, Mario Pieri, Maria and Spiridione Petrettini, Constantine Polychroniades, Angelica Palli, Andrea Papadopoulo Vretto, Spiridione Vlandi, Giovanni and Spiridione Veludo, Bartolommeo Cutlumusiano, Antimo Masarachi, Pier-Alessandro Paravia, and Emilio Tipaldo. These, the principal characters in our stories, are accompanied by countless others who appear in secondary roles: mainstream figures on the Italian literary stage (especially in Venice, Milan, Florence, Turin, and Naples), individuals from the Italian liberal or revolutionary world, Napoleonic and former Napoleonic officers and trans-Mediterranean revolutionaries, Italo-Albanian diaspora literati, British philhellenes and colonialists, yet other Ionian and Greek men of letters, German philologists, and French and Swiss liberals.

This study summons up an entire lost world. It reconstructs an intellectual universe that existed between the two shores of the Adriatic but which has all but disappeared from the historical record. Most of the literati involved in this world fell victim to the separation of historical writing into distinct national schools, which developed from the mid-nineteenth century. The fact that they wrote mainly in Italian meant that they did not fit into the Greek national narrative. On the other hand, their espousal of Greek nationalism led to their being expunged from Italian national history. They have thus slipped into oblivion. Even those who were not forgotten and managed to enter the 'pantheon of national founding fathers' did so after being purged of their more 'embarrassing' aspects. Some of them were Hellenized or Italianized and were studied as 'national poets' and intellectuals

(Foscolo, Solomos, Kalvos, Tommaseo). One of their number, Kapodistrias, was commemorated as the founder of a nation-state and studied as a political actor within a national context. Even so, these individuals have only rarely been seen for what they were: figures oscillating between the world of the former imperial Venetian realm and the world of nations that was dawning; between old and new empires and nation-states; between two or more patrias, languages, and cultures. The aim of this book is to return to the stage of history the world of these individuals, a world characterized by multiple cultural, intellectual, and political affiliations that have since been elided by the conventional narrative of the formation of nation-states.

All of the leading characters in this book were individuals who for most of their lives resided outside of their homelands, in one or more of the old and new empires and states. They were men and women whose lives transcended narrowly bounded geographical, religious, and linguistic areas, and who moved at will across the Mediterranean and the Balkans, between East and West. In a certain sense, then, this is a history of diasporas. Usually, when we encounter this label, we think of organized communities abroad, often presented as pieces of national life scattered here and there, in places far away from the national core. One part of the book builds indeed on an important historiographical tradition of this kind on Greek migration and diaspora communities.[9] However, on the whole, the book understands diasporas not as extensions of the homeland, but as sites where collective or individual consciousnesses were originally shaped, as diasporas-in-the-making. Instead of being an emblem of the unity of a dispersed people with an imagined homeland as a point of reference, diasporas become here an expression of diversity, of a multiplicity of loyalties and belongings. Movement is treated in this book not as an exception, but as the rule: Greeks and Italians (and most peoples for that matter) always circulated, created networks, and settled in certain places—and these places, these flows, became by turns their homes. By following, in addition, recent historiographical developments, which approach the topic through the lens of transnationalism and trans-imperialism, the book sees the itinerant people of the diasporas as in-between figures and frontier intellectuals, acting and living at the fringes of languages and cultures.[10] It was often through this distance, I argue, that

---

[9] Artemis Xanthopoulou-Kyriakou, *I elliniki koinotita tis Benetias (1797–1866): dioikitiki kai oikonomiki organosi, ekpaideftiki kai politiki drastiriotita* (The Greek community of Venice (1797–1866), administrative and economic organization, educational and political activity) (Thessaloniki, 1978); Olga Katsiardi-Hering, *I elliniki paroikia tis Tergestis, 1751–1830* (The Greek community of Trieste, 1751–1830) (Athens, 1986), 2 vols; Despina Vlami, *To fiorini, to sitari kai i odos tou kipou: Ellines emporoi sto Livorno, 1750–1868* (The forint, the wheat and the garden road: Greek merchants in Livorno, 1750–1868) (Athens, 2000); Vassilis Kardasis, *Diaspora Merchants in the Black Sea: The Greeks in Southern Russia, 1775–1861* (Lanham, Md, 2001).

[10] Maurizio Isabella and Konstantina Zanou (eds), *Mediterranean Diasporas: Politics and Ideas in the Long Nineteenth Century* (London, 2016); Bernard Heyberger and Chantal Verdeil (eds), *Hommes de l'entre-deux: parcours individuels et portraits de groupes sur la frontière de la Méditerranée (XVIe–XXe siècle)* (Paris, 2009); Natalie Rothman, *Brokering Empire: Trans-Imperial Subjects between Venice and Istanbul* (Ithaca, NY, 2012); Dimitris Tziovas (ed.), *Greek Diaspora and Migration since 1700* (London, 2009).

individuals first developed new notions of nationhood or empirehood, sometimes combining them with other allegiances.[11]

Despite their differences, the characters who populate these stories are viewed as sharing one basic feature, namely, transnational patriotism—loyalties suspended between or across Venice, Italy, the Ionian Islands, Greece, and the Russian, British, and Ottoman empires—accompanied at the same time by a constant, nagging feeling of estrangement from these patriotisms and a sense of being 'away' and 'outside'. Sometimes they described themselves as exiles, even if they hardly moved or, if they did, followed the very same routes that countless generations of Venetian Adriatic provincials had taken before them. It was the geographies around them that were now moving. In other words, the delineation and consolidation of new frontiers (cultural, national, linguistic, and religious) transformed many of these individuals, even the most immobile, into liminal beings, obliged to live in the margins of new empires and nation-states which now came to be seen as separate and distinct.[12] But there was something else in play too. Customary trajectories of mobility were now read through the lens of exile, because of a growing fashion in Neoclassical and Romantic letters for connecting this theme to the emerging idea of the nation. Foscolo was one of the first to forge a link between the two, and later to turn his own life into both an experience and a fiction of exilic patriotism.[13] Indeed, the boundaries between fiction and reality were often confounded in the lives under examination in this book. As much as they were lives spent in writing fiction, they could also at times become fictional lives.

By studying Foscolo, Kalvos, and Solomos, emblematic poets of Italy and Greece, a part of this book aspires to be a contribution to the histories of Italian and Greek literature. Unlike most histories of the kind, however, which presuppose that national traditions already existed, here literary figures and traditions are explored in their making. The book studies the process by which the works of Solomos and Kalvos gave birth to the field of modern Greek literature, while those of Foscolo became foundational for the Italian Risorgimento, and it endeavours to unearth, at the same time, the literary universe of the Ionian Islands in the immediate post-Venetian period, an Italian-speaking tradition obscured by the creation of the Greek canon of national literature and the establishment of Athens as a literary centre. By approaching these poets, first and foremost, as historical figures before they ever became national symbols, I try to reconstruct their views of the world,

---

[11] Engseng Ho, 'Empire through Diasporic Eyes: A View from the Other Boat', *Society for Comparative Study of Society and History* 46/2 (Apr. 2004), pp. 210–46; Benedict Anderson, 'Long-Distance Nationalism', in idem, *The Spectre of Comparisons: Nationalism, Southeast Asia and the World* (London and New York, 1998), pp. 59–74.

[12] Dominique Kirchner Reill, 'Away or Homeward Bound? The Slippery Case of Mediterranean Place in the Era before Nation-States', in Isabella and Zanou (eds), *Mediterranean Diasporas*, pp. 135–52.

[13] Maurizio Isabella, 'Exile and Nationalism: The Case of the Risorgimento', *European History Quarterly* 36/4 (2006), pp. 493–520; Konstantina Zanou, 'Nostalgia, Self-Exile and the National Idea: The Case of Andrea Mustoxidi and the Early-19th-Century Heptanesians of Italy', in A. Aktar, N. Kızılyürek, and U. Özkırımlı (eds), *Nationalism in the Troubled Triangle: Cyprus, Greece and Turkey* (London and New York, 2009).

their bicultural imperial subjectivity between Venice and the Ionian Islands, their transnational patriotism between Italy and Greece, and their multiple cultural and political options, not excluding loyalty to the Napoleonic and British empires. I thus hope to challenge established views on the idealized 'nationality' of these poets and to question some of the teleologies of the national literary canons. In addition, my book aims to open a field of research for historians which, save for a couple of recent, groundbreaking studies, has been the exclusive preserve of literary theorists.[14]

## SETTING

### Modern History in the Mediterranean

Since itinerant lives elude boundaries, the geographical setting of this story is not easy to define. The world I am writing about encompasses the Mediterranean, and more specifically the Ionian Islands, the Italian peninsula (Venice, Milan, Turin, Florence, Pisa, Livorno, and Naples), Greece (Nafplio, Aegina, Athens), and the Ottoman Empire (Epirus, Constantinople, Smyrna, but also Bucharest); it stretches all the way to the Russian Empire and the Black Sea (St Petersburg, Odessa), spanning also the British Empire (London), the Habsburg Empire (Vienna), France (Paris), and Switzerland (Geneva). Giving it life and meaning are our main characters and countless others who feature in their stories. The messy fluidity of their lives shows just how interconnected history is.

Entangled histories of the kind cannot be written unless we adopt a regional framework. This is a story that can be told only if we open up our gaze to the Mediterranean Sea, to the empires that it nurtured during the first half of the nineteenth century, and to the connections that it engendered. It is a central contention of this book that there is a whole world in the margins of the various territories, an entire universe of the 'in-between', which goes missing if we stick to conventional national and state divisions of historical writing. In adopting the Mediterranean as a category of historical analysis, the book does indeed join forces with a growing body of literature intent upon showing that the area continues to be a relevant framework even after 1800, when all political action seems to be transferred to the Atlantic, and when nation-states allegedly fragmented the landscape. More specifically, it is in sympathy with works that study the trans-Mediterranean circulation of people and ideas and which approach the sea as a zone of intellectual communication, and as a theatre of transnational, trans-imperial, and colonial experience.[15] By so doing, it also adopts a view of the Mediterranean as an open and malleable space, much larger than its geographical bounds suggest. As the

---

[14] Dimitris Arvanitakis, *Ston dromo gia tis patrides: i 'Ape Italiana', o Andreas Kalvos, i istoria* (On the road to the patrias: The 'Ape Italiana', Andreas Kalvos and history) (Athens, 2010); Eugenio Biagini, 'Liberty, Class and Nation-Building: Ugo Foscolo's "English" Constitutional Thought, 1816–1827', *European Journal of Political Theory* 5/34 (2006), pp. 34–49.

[15] Isabella and Zanou (eds), *Mediterranean Diasporas*; Julia Clancy-Smith, *Mediterraneans: North Africa and Europe in an Age of Migration, c.1800–1900* (Berkeley, 2010); Manuel Borutta and Sakis Gekas (eds), 'A Colonial Sea: The Mediterranean, 1798–1956', special issue of the *European Review of*

book shows, the flux of peoples, cultures, and ideas was such that the basin's borders could at times be reckoned to extend as far as the Black Sea or Latin America.

With the exception of a couple of studies (which have been for this book deeply inspirational), the post-Venetian Adriatic has never been treated by historians as a whole.[16] Surveys of the history of the area usually treat the events of the nineteenth century, and particularly the different revolutions and nation-state-building processes, on a national or subnational scale, only rarely delving into their inner interconnectedness. When a more regional or international framework is adopted, this is habitually one that looks to Europe (especially France and England) and, in the case of Greece, sometimes to the Ottoman Balkans.[17] Historians in Italy and Greece have stubbornly refused to turn their gaze to their Mediterranean neighbours and to examine the links created between the sea's various shores.[18] One of the purposes of this book is precisely to geographically relocate our view of Greece and Italy and of their modern histories. Instead of an approach that sees historical phenomena as a radiation between western Europe and its periphery, it proposes a new geography of different traditions and conjunctures between the Mediterranean, northern Europe, the Ottoman world, and the Russian Empire. As regards the latter in particular, the book is concerned to present the various ways in which Russia entered the Mediterranean not only by conquest and colonization, but also by opening up career opportunities for the region's merchants, artisans, and intellectuals, and to show how its religious, cultural, and at once national and imperial policy encountered the fluidity of Mediterranean modes of belonging and created new ones in its turn.

Viewing Italian and Greek history through the lens of a shifting maritime periphery offers the historian at least three major advantages. First of all, it helps to dispense with the once-dominant notion (still widespread among Mediterranean and Balkan scholars) that the countries of south-eastern Europe lagged behind on most factors measurable on a graph of modernization. Italy and Greece feature here, instead, not as the historical product of the incomplete diffusion of Enlightenment ideals and modernization processes from western Europe to its south-eastern periphery, but rather as a result of a Mediterranean geography of the 'in-between', where different traditions from East and West met and conversed, thereby producing 'alternative and indigenous modernities'.[19]

---

*History-Revue européenne d'histoire* 19/1 (2012); Ilham Khuri Makdisi, *The Eastern Mediterranean and the Making of Global Radicalism, 1860–1914* (Berkeley, 2010).

[16] Kirchner Reill, *Nationalists Who Feared the Nation*; Francesco Bruni and Chryssa Maltezou (eds), *L'Adriatico: incontri e separazioni (XVIII–XIX secolo)* (Venice, 2011). See also some parts of Pierre Cabanes et al., *Histoire de l'Adriatique* (Paris, 2001).

[17] Frederick Anscombe, 'The Balkan Revolutionary Age', *The Journal of Modern History* 84 (2012), pp. 572–606; Sukru Ilicak, 'A Radical Rethinking of Empire: Ottoman State and Society during the Greek War of Independence 1821–1826' (Ph.D. dissertation, Harvard University, 2011); and various chapters in Antonis Anastasopoulos and Elias Kolovos (eds), *Ottoman Rule and the Balkans, 1760–1850: Conflict, Transformation, Adaptation* (Rethymno, 2007).

[18] Exceptions are the important works by Antonis Liakos and Gilles Pécout: Antonis Liakos, *L'unificazione italiana e la Grande Idea: ideologia e azione dei movimenti nazionali in Italia e in Grecia, 1859–1871* (Florence, 1995); Gilles Pécout, 'Pour une lecture méditerranéenne et transnationale du Risorgimento', *Revue d'histoire du XIXe siècle* 44 (2012), pp. 29–47.

[19] Lucien J. Frary, *Russia and the Making of Modern Greek Identity, 1821–1844* (Oxford, 2015), p. 13.

Second, the Mediterranean perspective reveals new connections and suggests different genealogies as far as the history of nationalisms and revolutions is concerned. Take for example the constitutional revolts of 1820 and 1821 in southern Europe and the Ottoman Empire. By adopting a southern European and Mediterranean regional framework, historians have recently approached these events as connected and interrelated phenomena. They have demonstrated that it was not only the reactionary powers of the Restoration that tended to see the Portuguese, Neapolitan, Sicilian, Piedmontese, and Greek revolts of 1820 and 1821 as a direct continuation of the Spanish rising (1820), but also liberals and revolutionaries throughout Europe, the Mediterranean, and Latin America. By studying the circulation of people, political ideas, and revolutionary practices between the Mediterranean shores and across the Atlantic, these historians have shown, not only the transnational nature of patriotism and liberalism in the 1820s, but also the central place that the Spanish constitution (Cadiz 1812) occupied in these events. They have thus largely jettisoned the once dominant notion that the age of revolutions was exclusively defined by the French 1789.[20]

Finally, the Mediterranean framework enables the historian to view Greek and Italian histories in relation to the old empires and new colonial powers which established a presence in the region during the first half of the nineteenth century. More specifically, it encourages a reading which takes into account the changes and connections brought about by the Napoleonic Mediterranean Empire (1798–1814); the new ideas, hopes, and trajectories created by Russian encroachment upon the eastern Mediterranean (1770–1856) and the Ionian Islands (1800–7); the different political options and commercial routes produced by the gradual creation of Britain's Mediterranean Empire (starting in 1806); the geopolitical and ideological changes precipitated by Austria's acquisition of Adriatic territories (since 1815), as well as by the restoration of the Bourbons in southern Italy (1815). At the same time, a regional reading offers access to the ways older empires and their geographies, whether they had disappeared from the political map (like the Venetian Republic) or not (like the Ottoman Empire), persisted in defining people's movements and mental framework for many years to come.

## QUESTIONS OF INTELLECTUAL HISTORY

This is not only a history of intellectuals and politicians, however. It is also intellectual history (in the sense of history of ideas) and history of political thought. By questioning a series of dualisms, between empire and nation, religion and the Enlightenment, revolution and counter-revolution, East and West, I hope to

---

[20] Maurizio Isabella, *Risorgimento in Exile: Italian Émigrés and the Liberal International in the Post-Napoleonic Era* (Oxford, 2009); idem, 'Entangled Patriotisms: Italian Liberals and Spanish America in the 1820s', in Matthew Brown and Gabriel Paquette (eds), *Connections after Colonialism: Europe and Latin America in the 1820s* (Tuscaloosa, Ala., 2013), pp. 87–107; idem and Zanou (eds) *Mediterranean Diasporas*; Richard Stites, *The Four Horsemen: Riding to Liberty in Post-Napoleonic Europe* (Oxford, 2014).

challenge some of the most enduring stereotypes of European intellectual history regarding the Napoleonic and post-Napoleonic eras.

## Nation and Liberty within Empires

A major purpose of the book is to recover the forgotten realities and lost possibilities obscured by what was to come. In other words, it aims to contest teleological narratives of the emergence and triumph of nation-states. By imagining the epoch in which these people lived as a transitional period with an open and unknown future, and by describing the different political options available at the time, I endeavour to show that on various occasions nationhood and empire were not mutually exclusive, and that the nation-state was not the most obvious solution either. For people like Kapodistrias, who before becoming the first governor of Greece, served Russia in various diplomatic roles (not least as its Foreign Minister) and envisaged for a period a Russian-protected statelet in the Ionian Islands, or for Foscolo and other Ionian liberals, who in 1815 supported the islands' annexation to the British Empire, the nation, being in its early stages of life, could exist only as a sub-unit within an imperial, hierarchical system of rule. The binary division between 'nation' and 'empire' seems to be redundant here, in that many liberals at the time saw self-rule as compatible with acceptance of an overlordship, insofar as, of course, civil and political rights were guaranteed for the population. As we shall see, indeed, what was in question in the case of the post-Venetian Ionian Islands, in both their phases as a 'semi-protectorate' of Russia (1800–7) and Britain (1815–64) respectively, was some form of self-rule within larger, layered systems of imperial rule.

It is not only through a dichotomy between nation and empire that we are used to reading the history of nationalism, but also between liberalism and conservatism, revolution and counter-revolution, and religion and the Enlightenment. I shall demonstrate, however, that the political outlook of the intellectuals and political thinkers encountered in this book did not fit neatly into these distinctions. Like most of their contemporaries, these people were trying to make sense of the changes they were living through by combining elements of the old and familiar with the new and unfamiliar. They were, therefore, experimenting with new forms of imperial nationalism, but also of conservative liberalism and religious Enlightenment. We tend to forget just how deeply anti-revolutionary the times were in which these men and women lived. The excesses of the French Revolution and the Napoleonic Wars were deeply traumatizing for a European society which was now concerned more with *preventing* revolution than with promoting it. Recent studies on liberalism point out, indeed, that during the first half of the nineteenth century the term tended to imply a centrist doctrine that opposed the revolutionary spirit in all its forms and promoted gradual political reforms.[21] In this sense, my book argues, conservative politicians such as Kapodistrias fell within—and

---

[21] Lucien Jaume, *L'Individu effacé ou le paradoxe du libéralisme français* (Paris, 1997); Aurelian Craiutu, *Liberalism under Siege: The Political Thought of the French Doctrinaires* (Lanham, Md, 2003).

not outside, as is usually assumed—the spectrum of liberal politics. For these people, who were situated midway between revolution and reaction, there was only one solution that could safeguard societies against both: constitutions. Not all societies, they did of course believe, were to have them. It was their conviction that certain societies were readier than others, depending largely on the degree of 'enlightenment' of each population.

On the other hand, scholars now argue that during the first half of the nineteenth century, especially in southern Europe and the Russian Empire, rather than rejecting religion, liberals strove to achieve an accommodation between constitutional culture and enlightened forms of religiosity.[22] One chapter of this book indeed examines the way in which, during the years around the Congress of Vienna (1814–15), which is to say when Russia's influence on European politics reached its zenith, a contingent of European conservative liberals who were attached to the tsarist court, including Kapodistrias and other diaspora Greeks, was led to believe that nationalisms could exist and even thrive within a renewed Christian ecumene. For these men, the treaty of the Holy Alliance (1815) offered a new framework for the development of a liberal and national society based on the solid foundations of religion. Despite their disappointment in 1822 at the transformation of the Holy Alliance into a militaristic establishment espousing an absolutist politics, and at Russia's disavowal of the Greek revolution, these men nonetheless never abandoned the imperial, ecumenical, and religious framework of their political world view and remained loyal to Orthodoxy as the foundation of their national agenda, even when later (some of them) came to lead the Greek nation-state.

On the whole, the book aspires to offer a contribution to the field of the history of nationalism. While accepting the basic premises of the theories of nationalism as these were shaped in the works of historians like Eric Hobsbawm, Benedict Anderson, and Miroslav Hroch during the 1980s and 1990s, it also goes one step further.[23] This is a transnational history of nationalism, which incorporates the lessons learned by historians after the global turn, and which places emphasis on the way national consciousness was created as a transitional and diasporic phenomenon, *combining* rather than *opposing* forms of modernity and tradition, nation and empire, revolution and reaction, independence and subjection, liberalism and conservatism, and enlightenment and religion.[24]

---

[22] Maurizio Isabella, 'Citizens or Faithful? Religion and the Liberal Revolutions of the 1820s in Southern Europe', *Modern Intellectual History* (published online: January 2015), pp. 1–24: <http://dx.doi.org/10.1017/S147924431400078X>.

[23] Eric Hobsbawm, *Nations and Nationalism since 1780* (Cambridge, 1992); Benedict Anderson, *Imagined Communities: Reflections on the Origin and Spread of Nationalism* (London, 1983); Miroslav Hroch, *Social Preconditions of National Revival in Europe: A Comparative Analysis of the Social Composition of Patriotic Groups among the Smaller European Nations* (New York, 1985). See Umut Özkirimli, *Theories of Nationalism: A Critical Introduction* (Basingstoke, 2000).

[24] John Breuilly, 'Hobsbawm and Researching the History of Nationalism', in J. H. Arnold, M. Hilton, and J. Ruger (eds), *History after Hobsbawm: Writing the Past for the Twenty-First Century* (Oxford, 2018), pp. 76–95; Jürgen Osterhammel, 'Nationalism and Globalization', in John Breuilly (ed.), *The Oxford Handbook of the History of Nationalism* (Oxford, 2013), pp. 694–709.

## The Multiple Greek Enlightenments

A related intellectual question the book attempts to revise is our understanding of the modern Greek Enlightenment and the origins of the Greek nation-state. The conventional view of these phenomena is filtered through the scheme and genealogy of the so-called 'Neohellenic Enlightenment', a tradition which dominates Greek intellectual historiography and connects the birth of Greek nationalism and the Greek state with the ideas of the Paris-based intellectual Adamantios Koraes (1748–1833), attributing a central place in it to the heritage of the French Revolution and the radical and secular tradition of the Enlightenment. The Ecumenical Patriarchate of Constantinople, and its diehard resistance to the ideas of nationalism and liberalism, also features in this picture. Its open war against Koraes and other fathers of the 'Neohellenic Enlightenment' certainly offered convincing enough evidence to interpret the development of Greek national consciousness as a clash between religion and secularism and between East and West. However, as this book will show, this is only a partial reading of the phenomenon.

I will attempt to revise some basic premises of this tradition in two ways. First of all, I will engage with the more recent scholarship on religion and the Enlightenment, which depicts their relationship as far more complex and intricate than had once been supposed. The Enlightenment, these scholars argue, was not at war with Christianity, but rather was *within* it. It was, in most cases, a 'Christian Enlightenment'. What is more, scholars over the past few years have been 'pluralizing' the phenomenon, discovering its regional and national variations across Europe and beyond. The Enlightenment is no longer described as a single and unified francophone phenomenon with anti-Christian and anti-Church characteristics.[25] Likewise, I will attempt to turn our gaze away from the one, all-encompassing 'Neohellenic Enlightenment', towards a more fragmented and complex view of what I see as the multiple Ottoman, Venetian, and Mediterranean Enlightenments of the Greek world, some of which differed to some degree from the others.[26]

Second, by showing that there were other important sites of Greek Enlightenment thought besides the Orthodox Academies and Paris, I hope to reframe the spatiality of the Greek Enlightenment and to reveal the importance of the Russo-Mediterranean dimension. The reconstruction of diasporic intellectual

---

[25] Helena Rosenblatt, 'The Christian Enlightenment', in Stewart J. Brown and Timothy Tackett (eds), *The Cambridge History of Christianity*, vol. 7: *Enlightenment, Reawakening and Revolution 1660–1815* (Cambridge, 2006), pp. 283–301; Eric Palmer, 'Less Radical Enlightenment: A Christian Wing of the French Enlightenment', in Steffen Ducheyne (ed.), *Reassessing the Radical Enlightenment* (London, 2017), pp. 197–222; Knud Haakonssen, *Enlightenments and Religions* (Athens, 2010); David Sorkin, *The Religious Enlightenment: Protestants, Jews, and Catholics from London to Vienna* (Princeton, 2008); Ulrich L. Lehner, *The Catholic Enlightenment: The Forgotten History of a Global Movement* (Oxford, 2016); Francesca Bregoli, *Mediterranean Enlightenment: Livornese Jews, Tuscan Culture, and Eighteenth-Century Reform* (Stanford, Calif., 2014).

[26] For the Ottoman Enlightenment, see Harun Küçük, 'Natural Philosophy and Politics in the Eighteenth Century: Esad of Ioannina and Greek Aristotelianism at the Ottoman Court', *Journal of Ottoman Studies* 41 (2013), pp. 125–58; Molly Greene, *The Edinburgh History of the Greeks, 1453 to 1768: The Ottoman Empire* (Edinburgh, 2015), pp. 192–213. On the Septinsular Enlightenment, Paschalis M. Kitromilides, 'Eptanisiakos diafotismos: ta oria tis idiomorfias' (Septinsular Enlightenment: the limits of its specificities), *VII Panionian Conference, Proceedings* (Athens, 2004), vol. I, pp. 241–57.

trajectories between the Ionian Islands, Italy, and Russia, trajectories which developed far from the Parisian nuclei of Greek thought and the democratic ideological tradition of the French Revolution, allows the historian to tell a markedly different story about the Greek diasporas and their Enlightenments, one which, in terms of the circulation of ideas, is less obviously derived from the West and offers a more polycentric account, geographically and intellectually, of the origins of Greek nationalism and of the Greek state.

## HISTORICAL OVERVIEW

A historical overview of the major events setting the scene is in order at this point. The reader should be aware however that, if, for the sake of clarity, events are depicted here as distinct and coherent, in reality they were much more messy, complicated, and entangled—and this is indeed how they are treated in the body of the book.

### Ionian Islands

The seven Ionian Islands (or *Eptanisa*), in the south-eastern corner of the Adriatic Sea (Corfu, Zante, Lefkada, Cephalonia, Ithaca, Cythera, and Paxi), are found in a location where empires meet (Figures 1, 2). Part of the ancient Greek world, they followed a profoundly different historical path from the rest of the Ottoman Greek lands when they were conquered by the Venetians in the fourteenth century. The Lion of St Mark, Venice's emblem, standing half on water and half on land, placed his front paws here, and stayed for four whole centuries. This long period of partial or total Venetian rule (from 1386 until 1797, when the islands were liberated by the advancing French democratic army) transformed the Ionian archipelago into a culturally Italian region. Yet, despite its high degree of cultural, political, and economic unity, the Venetian Adriatic was also a space of ethnic, religious, and linguistic diversity. Venice's colonial system allowed for many local differences to exist.[27] In the Ionian Islands, the local aristocracy of the cities, educated at the universities of Padua, Pavia, and Pisa, spoke the Italian language, while the peasantry still used the local Greek idiom. Likewise, the world of the countryside remained Orthodox, whereas the religion of the upper echelons in the towns and the official religion of the state was Catholicism. From the beginning of the eighteenth century onwards, however, the Orthodoxy of the inhabitants served more and more to differentiate them from their Venetian rulers and created links instead with their coreligionists from Russia, who started to offer Ionians career opportunities as public servants and in trade.

The Russian presence became more intensely felt in this part of the world during the Russo-Ottoman war of 1768–74. It was then that the Russian fleet sailed for

---

[27] Frederic C. Lane, *Venice: A Maritime Republic* (Baltimore and London, 1973); Eric R. Dursteler (ed.), *A Companion to Venetian History, 1400–1797* (Leiden and Boston, 2013).

**Figure 2.** The Venetian Adriatic (1587), a 'Sea of intimacy', was imagined very differently from the way we see it today. 'Map of Italy, the Ionian islands and continental Greece', in Jean Zuallart, *Il devotissimo viaggio di Gerusalemme fatto, & descritto in sei libri dal Sig. Giovanni Zuallardo* [1587]. American School of Classical Studies at Athens, Gennadius Library.

the first time in Mediterranean waters, briefly occupying several Aegean islands and, in 1770, fomenting a major but unsuccessful Greek revolt in the Ottoman Peloponnese, precisely on the shores facing the Ionian Islands. These Russian activities formed part of a grander vision entertained by the Tsarina Catherine the Great of conquering the Ottomans and founding a great Orthodox Christian empire centred on Constantinople. This dream was abruptly interrupted, however, by the Revolutionary and Napoleonic Wars, which transformed the Mediterranean into a theatre of conflict between Britain and France. Napoleon's seizure of the Ionian Islands in 1797, his expedition to Egypt in 1798 and the consequent British takeover, as well as the opportunistic diplomatic games that he played with Ali Pasha of Yiannina (a powerful albeit rebellious local Ottoman ruler in Epirus, not far removed from the Ionian Islands), convinced Russia to set its differences aside and to enter into an alliance with the Ottoman Empire. By 1799, the combined forces of the two powers took control of the seven islands, a garrison ideally placed to prevent the spread of revolutionary ideas in the Balkans. The outcome of this occupation was the 'Septinsular Republic', a constitutional aristocratic, semi-independent statelet, which united the islands in a federation under the sovereignty of the Porte and the direct political and military protection of Russia. On the islands' new flag the Lion of St Mark appeared now as hanging in the air against a blue background with a Gospel in its paw instead of the sword.

Confessional affinities were indeed more important in the new setting than geographical contiguity. The Russian-protected state would last only seven years (1800–7). In 1806, the Russo-Ottoman alliance collapsed and war once again broke out between the two powers. Following the reverses in Europe, the new Tsar, Alexander I, made his peace with Napoleon at Tilsit in 1807 and sealed it by ceding the Ionian Islands to imperial France.[28]

The fall of Napoleon marked yet another phase in the history of the Ionian Islands. By a treaty signed in Paris in 1815, Britain—which since 1810 had gained possession of all the Ionian Islands (except Corfu which was taken over only in 1814)—was officially proclaimed the protecting power of the islands, which were now united to form an 'independent' state, known as the United States of the Ionian Islands (1815–64). The Mediterranean Pax Britannica (depicted on the islands' new flag by Britain's blue ensign, which framed now the Russian version of the Lion of St Mark) promised a new era of imperial liberal reforms, which were to grant 'freedom' and 'independence' to the territories under its aegis.[29] Nevertheless, the Ionian constitution which was drafted in 1817 provided only a semblance of autonomous local rule, while in reality it vested all power in the hands of the British colonial administration, establishing a system of unrestricted colonial despotism. As colonial officers with different political views succeeded each other to the post of Lord High Commissioner on the islands, periods of autocracy and oppression were followed by intervals of relatively more enlightened administration and benign, liberal rule. Things became particularly critical after 1821, when the outbreak of the Greek revolution led thousands of Ionian islanders to cross over to the Ottoman continent, and, despite Britain's declared neutrality, to join the rebellion. A wave of constitutional reforms in 1848, which granted freedom of the press, local control of the state finances, and free elections, did nothing to allay popular unrest (manifested earlier that year by a peasant uprising in the poorest of the seven islands, Cephalonia). The growing financial deficit of the Ionian state, especially since the 1840s, and the increasing demands for unification with Greece voiced by a new political party, the Radical-Unionists (*Rizospastai*), which grew in numbers and importance in the 1850s, rendered the islands ungovernable and eventually impelled Britain to cede the region to the Kingdom of Greece (1864).[30]

## Napoleonic and Restoration Italy

Before 1796 the Italian peninsula numbered more than ten independent states, including duchies, kingdoms, maritime empires, tiny principalities, and city-republics. Less than eighty years later, it comprised only one state extending from

---

[28] Thomas W. Gallant, *The Edinburgh History of the Greeks, 1768 to 1913: The Long Nineteenth Century* (Edinburgh, 2015), pp. 2–23.

[29] Robert Holland, *Blue-Water Empire: The British in the Mediterranean since 1800* (London, 2013).

[30] Sakis Gekas, *Xenocracy: State, Class and Colonialism in the Ionian Islands, 1815–1864* (New York and Oxford, 2017); Lauren Benton and Lisa Ford, *Rage for Order: The British Empire and the Origins of International Law, 1800-1850* (Cambridge, Mass., and London, 2016), pp. 102–116; Thomas W. Gallant, *Experiencing Dominion: Culture, Identity, and Power in the British Mediterranean* (Notre Dame, Ind., 2002).

Sicily to Turin and Venice. This whole transformation—including the periods of Jacobin and Napoleonic rule, the Restoration regimes, and the Italian Wars of Independence—is known as the *Risorgimento*, implying the 'revival' of the Italian nation. Until the late eighteenth century there was no such thing as 'Italian nationalism'. Whereas among the educated classes across the peninsula there had been a sense of sharing a common Italian literary tradition, the patriotism of the general populace was confined to their states, cities, or even villages, while the language of the Church and the universities was Latin. Everything else, from spoken dialects to printed newspapers, and from academies to arts, was locally based.

Napoleon, as general of the Directory, invaded northern Italy in 1796. While he conceded the area of Veneto to the Austrians by the Treaty of Campo Formio (1797), in the rest of the Italian peninsula he established a series of republics: in northern Italy, the Cispadane and the Transpadane Republics, united in 1797 as the Cisalpine Republic; in central Italy, the Roman Republic; and in southern Italy, the Neapolitan Republic. France's losses in the War of the Second Coalition in 1799 marked the end of the Italian so-called 'Revolutionary Triennium' (1796–9) and, amid popular counter-revolutions, these republics collapsed. However, Napoleon soon regained control of the peninsula when he defeated Austria at the Battle of Marengo (1800). By 1805, the French had gained possession of the whole Italian mainland—in the only areas which rested outside their control, Sicily and Sardinia, the Bourbon and the Savoy royal families (the former rulers of, respectively, the kingdoms of Naples and Piedmont) took refuge under the protection of the British navy. Under Napoleon (1801–14), the Italian peninsula was divided into three territorial units: Piedmont and a large part of central Italy, including Rome, were directly annexed by France. An 'Italian Republic' was created in the north-east, which, after Napoleon's self-proclamation as French Emperor and his triumph against his enemies at Austerlitz, was enlarged to include Veneto and was renamed as the 'Kingdom of Italy' (1805–14). The Kingdom of Naples extended to the south and had been ruled since 1808 by Napoleon's brother-in-law, Joachim Murat.[31]

The reader must already feel puzzled by all these names and territorial readjustments. Imagine how the contemporary inhabitants of the Italian peninsula felt. This was indeed the greatest upheaval experienced by Italians since at least the sixteenth century. And it left an indelible mark on the years that followed. To begin with, continuous territorial changes worked to undermine the sense of history and of regional distinctions, on which the former rulers had built their legitimacy. 'This drastic and repeated refashioning of state boundaries', it has been observed, 'made it difficult to regard the eighteenth-century political map of the peninsula, or anything like it, as sacred'.[32] Second, the French states, and especially the kingdoms of Italy and Naples, prepared some of the ground for the development of a more

---

[31] Michael Broers, *The Napoleonic Mediterranean: Enlightenment, Revolution and Empire* (London, 2017); Antonino De Francesco, *L'Italia di Bonaparte: politica, statualità e nazione nella penisola tra due rivoluzioni, 1796–1821* (Milan, 2011).

[32] Derek Beales and Eugenio F. Biagini, *The Risorgimento and the Unification of Italy* (London and New York, 2002 [1971]), p. 26.

uniform, national identity. The vision of Italy becoming an independent state was further enhanced by the experience of constitutional rights (however brief it was), the spread of revolutionary ideas and secret societies, and the introduction of a new political vocabulary, bringing words like 'nation' and 'fatherland' into public debate.[33]

The collapse of the Napoleonic Empire, sealed by the Congress of Vienna (1814–15), once again marked the end of one period and the beginning of another. What came to be known as the Restoration—aptly characterized by one historian as the 'Recuperation'—reorganized the geopolitical map of Europe and put legitimate dynasties back on their thrones after a long revolutionary period, which was henceforward seen as a mere parenthesis in the natural course of European history.[34] In the Italian peninsula, which was now divided into eight different states, the Restoration was strictly defined and controlled by the Habsburg Empire (represented at the Congress of Vienna by the omnipotent Austrian Chancellor, Clemens von Metternich). Under the terms of the Vienna treaty, Lombardy and Veneto were annexed to Austria. The areas of central Italy (Tuscany, Modena, and Parma), were restored as duchies and were ruled by members of the Habsburg dynasty. The Papal States, including Rome, were returned to the Pope, while the Kingdom of Naples, with the island of Sicily, was returned (as the 'Kingdom of the Two Sicilies') to its former Bourbon absolute rulers. Both these states contracted defensive alliances with Austria. The only Italian state to remain relatively independent from Austrian control was the Kingdom of Sardinia (or Piedmont), which was intended to serve as a 'buffer state' between the Habsburg Empire and France, and was ruled by the Savoy monarchy.

It was Austria's intention to expunge from the peninsula, and from Europe in general, all ideas connected to liberalism, nationalism, and revolution. And yet, these were precisely the ideas that flourished during those years. Their first significant expression was the wave of constitutional revolts, organized mostly by former Napoleonic officers and members of secret societies, which shook southern Europe in 1820–1 (Spain, Portugal, Naples, Sicily, Piedmont, and Greece). These revolts were, with the exception of Greece, swiftly suppressed by the Austrian army and a period of harsh political reaction followed throughout the peninsula bringing with it the proscription of most of the revolutionary leaders.[35] Another wave of failed rebellions came in 1831–2, this time affecting above all the Papal States and the central Italian duchies, and a yet more important one in 1848–9. The latter, coordinated chiefly by a younger generation of Italian and transnational revolutionaries inspired by the democratic-radical teachings of Giuseppe Mazzini, saw uprisings in Palermo, Naples, Rome, Bologna, Florence, Livorno, Turin, Milan, and Venice, joined by a chain of revolutionary upheavals throughout Europe, from Paris to Vienna, and from Budapest to Berlin. In Italy, these revolts forced the kings to grant liberal constitutions almost everywhere and established short-lived

---

[33] David Laven and Lucy Riall (eds), *Napoleon's Legacy: Problems of Government in Restoration Europe* (Oxford and New York, 2000); Lucy Riall, *Risorgimento: The History of Italy from Napoleon to Nation State* (London, 2009).
[34] Stites, *The Four Horsemen*, p. 4.     [35] Isabella, *Risorgimento in Exile*.

republics in Venice, Milan, Tuscany, and Rome, which were, however, soon crushed by foreign military intervention.[36]

At the same time, a different trend of Italian nationalism and liberalism, more religious and moderate, was growing among Italian elites. Inspired by the election in 1846 of an allegedly liberal Pope, Pius IX, these forces were led by Piedmont, whose King Carlo Alberto, seemingly endorsing nationalist aspirations, declared war on Austria in 1848. The war resulted in a crushing defeat for Italians and the King was forced to abdicate his throne in favour of his son, Vittorio Emanuele II. Nonetheless, Italian moderate liberals, joined by a section of the democrats, started to see in Piedmont's leadership, in its monarchy and army, the only way to throw out the Austrians and unite the peninsula. The fact that it was the only one of the Italian states to keep its 1848 constitution, and that a new, relatively liberal, government was elected there in 1849, convinced many that a compromise between royal authority and liberal reforms was possible. Camillo Benso di Cavour, the state's Prime Minister since 1852, played a crucial role in asserting Piedmontese power both within Italy and abroad. Among his achievements was Piedmont's last minute entrance into the Crimean War (1853–6) on the side of the Franco-British powers, which prevailed over Russia, and his success at bringing the 'Italian Question' onto the table of the peace negotiations that followed. In 1859, he also signed an alliance with France, and their combined forces entered into war against Austria, which they quickly won. Lombardy was ceded to the winners, while in 1860 plebiscites were held in the central Italian states, resulting in an overwhelming vote in favour of Piedmontese rule. Democratic agitation beyond Piedmont's control, led by Giuseppe Garibaldi, the most popular symbol of the Italian Risorgimento and global icon of liberty, pushed in favour of continuing the war against Austria and extending it to the Papal States. With that in mind, Garibaldi landed in Sicily with his legendary 'Thousand' (volunteers) and in the space of six months he overthrew the Bourbon kingdom and set out to liberate Rome, only to be halted by the Piedmontese troops. In the meantime, plebiscites were held in southern Italy and Sicily in favour of annexation to Piedmont. In 1861, Italy was formally united with Victor Emmanuel II as its first king and Turin as its capital city. Thanks to favourable international circumstances the new state gained Veneto in 1866 and Rome in 1870.

## The Greek Revolution and the Creation of the Greek State

When Alexandros Ypsilantis, an Ottoman Christian officer in Russian service, and his multi-ethnic army of volunteers raised in March 1821 the banner of revolt against the Ottoman Empire in the Danubian Principalities (today's Romania), no one at the time could ever have imagined that this would be the beginning of a protracted and bloody war that would result in the foundation of the modern state of Greece about a decade later. Although Ypsilantis and his 'Sacred Battalion' (a body of about 500 volunteers, including many Greek students enrolled in European universities) were soon tragically defeated, and harsh reprisals against the

---

[36] Michael Rapport, *1848: Year of Revolution* (New York, 2010).

Christians followed throughout the empire (including the exemplary execution of Grigorios V, the Orthodox Patriarch of Constantinople who, ironically, was an opponent of the revolution), simultaneously a new rebellion broke out in the south-western corner of the empire, the Peloponnese. Prepared largely through the conspiratorial activities of the *Philiki Etairia* (Friendly Society), one of the many secret societies that had sprung up in the Greek diaspora centres of southern Russia and the Balkans, the Peloponnese rebellion soon made rapid strides. The Greek forces, a combination of local chieftains, primates, priests, peasants, *klepths* (brigands), and *armatoles* (ethnic Greeks serving the Ottoman militia but blending occasionally with the resistance), were able to capture many of the major Ottoman strongholds in the Peloponnese and establish a foothold in mainland Greece as well. As several of the Aegean islands one after the other also threw in their lot with the insurrection, victories on land were soon coupled with successes at sea. Despite the political rifts and local antagonisms between the various revolutionary factions, the insurgents managed to gather in a National Congress (Epidaurus, December 1821), where they declared their independence, promulgated a constitution, and created a republican provisional government.

Like every war, this one too was characterized by terrible bouts of violence and bloodshed. The combination of irregular bands of brigands craving booty and oppressed Christian peasants eager for revenge, on the one side, and an imperial army made up of irregular groups led by chieftains who were called on to take up arms to suppress the revolt on the promise of looting, on the other side, was a lethal one. It is estimated that, in the period between 1821 and 1823, the casualties were in aggregate of the order of 50,000, mostly unarmed non-combatants. The death rate only further increased when, in 1823, a war within the war, this time between different revolutionary fractions, erupted. In 1824, and while one after another the revolutionaries' military gains of the previous three years had begun to be reversed, and Mahomet Ali of Egypt, after coming to terms with the Sultan, had deployed his western-style army to suppress the revolt, the Great Powers decided to intervene on behalf of the insurgents. The protracted disruption of their economic interests in the eastern Mediterranean, their mutual distrust in front of an Ottoman Empire suffering permanent political instability, as well as the international visibility and popular support the Greek revolution had gained, informed their decision. An agreement between Britain and Russia in 1826, which stipulated that Greece should become an autonomous state within the empire and tributary to the Porte, was followed by a treaty between Britain, Russia, and France one year later, which called for an immediate armistice between the contending parties, promised Great Power protection, and authorized the dispatching of a joint fleet to guarantee the peace. The Battle of Navarino (in south-western Greece), which took place in October 1827, between the combined Great Power forces and the Ottoman fleet, witnessed the destruction of the latter and determined the outcome of this prolonged war.[37]

---

[37] Thomas W. Gallant, *Modern Greece* (London, 2001), pp. 16–26; idem, *The Edinburgh History of the Greeks*, pp. 51–106; Petros Pizanias (ed.), *The Greek Revolution of 1821: A European Event* (Istanbul, 2011).

An important part of the Greek revolution's story is philhellenism. The Ypsilantis march and its collapse, combined with tales about the bishops and guerrilla chiefs of the Morea (Peloponnese), joined later by Lord Byron's sacrifice in besieged Missolonghi and Santorre di Santarosa's martyrdom on the island of Sphacteria, made the Greek revolt a *cause célèbre* in Europe and elsewhere, leading to the establishment of philhellenic committees from Paris to London and New York. Hundreds of philhellene volunteers began to make their way to the beleaguered country, eager to assist its cause. Among the former Napoleonic soldiers, professional revolutionaries, political refugees, religious zealots, university graduates, and adventurers, many went there with Pausanias and Plato under their arm. The Greek war of independence touched a chord in western Europe, not only because of its evocation of the glory of ancient Hellas, but also because of its universalistic message on liberty. It would in the end prove to be the first major successful war of independence by a subject population against an imperial power since the American Revolution of 1776.[38]

By the spring of 1828 a free Greece had thus been established. The exact boundaries, nature, and disposition of the new state remained, however, to be determined. In the meantime, the revolutionaries had elected by means of a National Assembly an internationally acclaimed figure, Ioannis Kapodistrias, to be their President (1827–31). Faced with a number of daunting problems (a war which was in reality still ongoing, a devastated countryside, a completely destroyed economy, uncertain frontiers, thousands of orphans—to list just a few), Kapodistrias made some attempts at introducing reforms (land redistribution, the levying of new taxes, the creation of a regular army, the centralization of the administration), which were nevertheless unsuccessful. His political ideology of a gradual and moderate liberalization of society, and his decision to 'temporarily' suspend the constitution and rule by executive degree, cost him a great deal of support, and in the end his life. After his assassination by members of the political opposition, in October 1831, the country slipped once again into civil war.

The protective powers, Britain, France, and Russia, decided to intervene once more and 'save' the country from chaos and anarchy. By the London Convention of May 1832, they agreed to make the 17-year-old Prince Otto of Bavaria the monarch of Greece. It was not clear, however, if Otto would govern as an absolute or a constitutional king. Yet the three-man regency made up of Bavarian court officials, which ruled the country until Otto's coming of age (1833–5), did indubitably make no mention of political rights. As a matter of fact, the Kingdom of Greece ceased to be an absolute monarchy only in 1843, when a bloodless revolt took place in Athens constraining the King to grant a constitution. Among the noteworthy developments of this period was also the creation of a separate Greek national Church in 1833 (autocephalous), which broke once and for all the new

---

[38] Roderick Beaton, *Byron's War: Romantic Rebellion, Greek Revolution* (Cambridge, 2014); David Roessel, *In Byron's Shadow: Modern Greece in the English and American Imagination* (Oxford, 2002); Enrica Lucarelli and Caterina Spetsieri Beschi (eds), *Risorgimento greco e filellenismo italiano: lotte, cultura, arte* (Rome, 1986); William St Clair, *That Greece Might Still Be Free: The Philhellenes in the War of Independence* (Oxford, 1972).

polity's ties with the Ecumenical Patriarchate of Constantinople. A pivotal point in Greece's political history was, finally, the outbreak of the Crimean War, when Otto hoped that Greek participation on the side of the Russians might present an opportunity to gain further territorial possessions, thus fostering his programme of the 'Great Idea' (*Megali Idea*), a plan to reconquer the so-called 'unredeemed lands' of the former Byzantine Empire. After a humiliating occupation of the Piraeus (the major Greek port) by French and British forces, which had in the meantime entered the war on the side of the Ottoman Empire, in May 1854, Otto was obliged to give up his grandiose imperial plans.

This brief account of key facts in three different but intersecting geographical settings (the Italian peninsula, the Greek peninsula, and their Adriatic and Ionian intermediate space) sketches the general—although not exhaustive—background where the individual stories in this book unfold. It remains now to see what kind of stories these are.

## STRUCTURE

### A Historical Drama in Four Acts

The book is divided into four parts and an epilogue. These contain six quite different stories, which, though circling the same theme, also follow their own individual trajectories. While writing this book, I came to think of it in terms of a multi-part film, whose autonomous but converging acts evolve in a cinematic sequence. Characters who appear as protagonists in one part may appear again in secondary roles in another. In following the example set by another scholar, I render the words of the characters and their contemporaries in italic type, and without quotation marks, in an effort to integrate their perspective seamlessly into the story and to render the narrative itself more intimate and direct.[39] One can certainly read each of the parts of this book separately (although the individual chapters are not intended to be entirely freestanding). Taken together, however, they also create a whole which is larger than the sum of its individual parts.

A word about the sources I have used may be clarificatory here. Since the book engages with diverse questions and themes in many locations, it takes advantage of a wide array of sources in various genres and languages (including Italian, French, Greek, and English). In addition to the burgeoning scholarly literature in different languages on the period, documents from archives in Corfu, Athens, Florence, Milan, Turin, Venice, Rome, Livorno, Paris, and Geneva, some published but most unpublished, provide the bulk of source material for my story. My lack of knowledge in Russian is to a large degree compensated by the fact that most of the diplomatic and private life described in this book was conducted in French or Italian.

---

[39] Martha Elizabeth Hodes, *The Sea Captain's Wife: A True Story of Love, Race, and War in the Nineteenth Century* (New York and London, 2007).

Part I (Chapters 1–3) is the story of three poets, Foscolo, Kalvos, and Solomos, who set off from the same Ionian island, Zante, within twenty years of each other, and ended up becoming the 'national poets' of two different countries, Italy and Greece. I investigate the reasons behind these men's different choices regarding language, poetry, and, finally, national consciousness, and explore the way they experienced transition from local patria to national patria(s) and from imperial centres to national centres, and vice versa. I focus also on the increasing importance of exile and nostalgia in their refashioning of themselves as patriots, and of the new Neoclassical and Romantic poetic idols, namely Vittorio Alfieri and Lord Byron, in shaping their view of the poet's role and 'mission'. On the whole, I see these three thematic biographies as the three stages of the transition from the common Venetian imperial Adriatic space to the fragmented, modern, multinational, and multi-state setting of the region.

Part II (Chapters 4–7) introduces Russia to the scene. Here I explore Kapodistrias's life in conjunction with a set of other biographies, devoted to his friends and collaborators in the Ionian Islands and Russia during the first three decades of the nineteenth century. My aim is to unravel a particular intellectual geography that was formed between Italy, the Ionian Islands, the Danubian Principalities, and Russia, and to show the peculiar brand of Orthodox Enlightenment, imperial nationalism, and conservative liberalism that these lives in conjunction created. The basic premise here is that Russia's political and military conduct in the Mediterranean, and particularly in the Ionian Adriatic during the first decades of the nineteenth century, had a strong impact on the way Enlightenment, liberal, and national ideas were developing in the area and fostered trends of thought to which historians have paid scant attention.

Part III (Chapters 8–9) is about forgotten lives and their memories. Based on two selected examples of autobiographical writing in the Ionian space, I unearth here a set of obscured biographies. Chapter 8 tells the story of Mario Pieri and of certain other Ionian and Greco-Italian diaspora intellectuals with whom he was connected. Drawing from both his unpublished diary and his published autobiography, it recounts the adventures of a man who felt that he lived his life 'out of place', remaining perpetually suspended between the Italian and the Greek culture. By following Pieri's steps from Russian-controlled Corfu to Napoleonic and Habsburg Padua, Treviso, and Venice, and from there to Restoration Florence and back to British-controlled Corfu, I study the way this ex-Venetian subject and transnational patriot came to see himself as a Greek through his involvement in Italian, and more specifically Tuscan philhellenism, investigating at the same time some of the major tropes of this movement. I hope thus to tell something about the perceptions of the war from a position far removed from the theatre of battle, as well as of the impact that the Greek revolution and the European philhellenisms had on the peoples of the 'Greek diasporas', reshaping even the very meaning of this notion.

Chapter 9 narrates the life of another forgotten individual, Andrea Papadopoulo Vretto, through his autobiographical manuscript. A student of medicine in Naples, a man of letters and archaeologist in Lefkada, a librarian and bibliographer in Corfu, a pharmacist and entrepreneur of culture in Nafplio, a diplomat and translator in St Petersburg, a Greek consul in Ottoman Varna and later in Venice, Papadopoulo Vretto lived, to say the least, a mobile life. His memoirs reflect the 'big' geopolitical changes that affected the lives of the Ionians of his generation and attest to the intricate interconnectedness of these geopolitical phenomena through the trajectories of individuals who moved across the Mediterranean and the Balkans, between East and West. By illuminating the activities of this itinerant and adventurous man, the chapter aspires, in addition, to offer a contribution to a number of issues in intellectual history, such as the creation of Albanian nationalism in the diasporic centres of southern Italy, the rise of interest in archaeology in the British Mediterranean, as well as the emergence of the modern Greek bibliographic tradition. It also provides insight into the consolidated links between Greece and Russia throughout the 1830s and illustrates the way Orthodox ecumenism was reshaped within the Greek kingdom.

Part IV (Chapters 10–12) tells the story of a largely forgotten Corfiot who was famous in his own lifetime, Andrea Mustoxidi, and of his circle of Greco- and Dalmato-Venetian intellectuals. Chapter 10 provides insight into Mustoxidi's biography, focusing in particular on the way this scholar inserted himself into the Italian and European intellectual scene with works on philology and history inspired by Neoclassicism and philhellenism. It also unearths the unknown adventure of this man's involvement in Russian diplomacy and the 1821 revolution in Piedmont, as well as his subsequent transformation from a Russian diplomat into a Greek minister (the first 'Ephor' for culture and education in Greece) and into a liberal politician in the British Ionian Islands. By so doing, the chapter also studies the educational programme of Kapodistrias's government, as well as the adventure of liberal politics in the British Mediterranean Empire. In following Mustoxidi's slow transition from Italian to Greek letters, Chapter 11 adds to the wider story the endeavours of a group of Ionian and Dalmatian intellectuals who were living in the decrepit embrace of the Greek community of Venice during the first half of the nineteenth century. By mapping out their lives, the chapter examines these men's bicultural existence and transnational patriotism, and investigates their intellectual work. Orchestrated largely by Mustoxidi, as Chapter 12 shows, these figures carried out an ambitious programme to rehabilitate the most neglected areas of the Greek national ideology of the time, the 'dark' centuries of Byzantine and medieval history and popular tradition (especially folk songs), thus placing emphasis on the historical 'continuity'—rather than the 'revival'—of the Greek nation.

The book closes with an epilogue, which recounts the story of Mustoxidi's clash with the celebrated Dalmato-Venetian intellectual Niccolò Tommaseo, who had lived as an exile on the Ionian Islands since 1849. The reason for this disagreement was the gradual replacement of Italian with Greek as the official language of the Ionian state in the early 1850s, a process that Mustoxidi supported but in which Tommaseo discerned xenophobic, and more particularly anti-Italian, dimensions. The Crimean War created additional tension on the islands, widening the gap between Christian Orthodox and Catholics in the region. The conflict between these two intellectuals is seen in this book as symbolically marking the end of the 'transnational patriotism' moment in the Adriatic, a declaration of the irreversible dissolution of its common Venetian cultural space. The de-Venetization, Hellenization, and Orthodoxization of the Ionian Islands signified the completion of the transition process from empires to nation-states and the passing to an era of more distinct and solidified national consciousnesses in the region.

# PART I

# ONE ISLAND, THREE (TRANS)NATIONAL POETS

## INTRODUCTION

### Embodying the Nation

On 8 June 1871, a telegram arrived at the offices of the Italian ministry of education: *Ugo Foscolo has returned to Italy. The disinterment was done; the corpse was found in a state of perfect preservation in two cases well conditioned, authenticity is fully established; Minister Cadorna and a good number of Italians were present.* The telegram was sent from Chiswick, a village near London, to where an Italian delegation was sent to retrieve the body of the Zakynthian poet, who had lain there since 1827 (see Figure 3). Within a few days, the mortal remains of Foscolo were transferred to Florence. An Italian anthropologist and doctor was given permission to examine the skull in order to establish scientifically what the physical characteristics of a genius were.[1] After that, the remains were reburied in the Pantheon of Santa Croce Church between the tombs of Italy's classic poets Dante and Alfieri. Unlike the poet's burial in England, which was attended by no more than five people—and most of them his impoverished fellow exiles—the ceremony in Florence was performed with all due solemnity and pomp and in the presence of a huge throng. After all, the newly established Italian state was burying its national poet. Senators, ministers, consuls, priests, and local dignitaries came in great numbers to Santa Croce, yet there was one glaring absence: the Greek ambassador to Italy. Greece lodged a protest because the poet was a native, or so it claimed, of the recently annexed Ionian Islands, and therefore belonged to Greece.[2]

At about the same date, in 1869, another Zakynthian poet, Andreas Kalvos, drew his last breath in Louth, Lincolnshire, 230 km north-east of London, offering

---

[1] Paolo Mantegazza, 'Il cranio di Ugo Foscolo', *Archivio per l'antropologia e la etnologia* 1/3 (1871), pp. 301–6; 'Modello in gesso del cranio di Ugo Foscolo' (1871), in Gianfranca Lavezzi (ed.), *'Amate palesamente e generosamente le lettere e la vostra nazione': Ugo Foscolo nell'ateneo pavese, catalogo della mostra documentaria etc.* (Pavia, 2009), p. 106.

[2] Pellegrino Artusi, *Vita di Ugo Foscolo* (Florence, 1878), pp. 259–74; Francesca Irene Sensini, 'Niccolò Ugo Foscolo in Grecia: prolegomena', *Cahiers d' études italiennes* 20 (2015), pp. 201–15.

**Figure 3.** Exhumation of the remains of Ugo Foscolo in the cemetery of Chiswich, 1871 (photo credit Fratelli Caldesi). Archivio del Museo Centrale del Risorgimento di Roma: MCRR Cassetta XIX(43).

Greece the chance to take revenge (albeit belatedly): almost one century later, in 1960, and on the initiative of the Greek ambassador to Britain and Nobel laureate Giorgos Seferis, Kalvos's corpse was disinterred from England and transferred to Greece. It was received with honours (see Figure 4) and buried in a church graveyard in Zante. That was not the end, however, of the poet's postmortem journey. In 1968, during the dictatorship of the Greek colonels, his corpse was exhumed once more and transferred amidst drum rolls to a mausoleum, there to lie for all eternity alongside another of Greece's national poets, Dionysios Solomos.

Solomos was the third Zakynthian poet to be disinterred and reburied in about the same period. In 1865—that is one year after the annexation of the Ionian Islands to Greece—his corpse was exhumed from Corfu, where death had found him, and transported to his native island, where the aforementioned mausoleum was erected in his honour. In that same year, the first two stanzas of his lengthy *Hymn to Liberty* (written back in 1823 and set to music some years later) were officially proclaimed the national anthem of Greece. Unlike the two other poets, Solomos's first burial had itself been a grandiose affair. When he died in 1857, the Ionian Parliament declared a day of public mourning; the theatre of Corfu was shut down and the Carnival festivities were interrupted. His burial was performed by all the priests of Corfu together and was attended by vast crowds of

**Figure 4.** Reception of the remains of Andreas Kalvos and of his wife, Charlotte Augusta Wadams, in Zante, 1960 (photo credit Fanis Dafnos). Museum of D. Solomos and Eminent People of Zakynthos.

mourners, while several poems and obituaries were published in honour of Greece's greatest poet.[3]

The political lives of these three dead bodies, and, more precisely, their function in embodying the nation, is, I believe, a fitting introduction to the protagonists of the first three chapters of this book: Ugo Foscolo (1778–1827), Andreas Kalvos (1792–1869), and Dionysios Solomos (1798–1857).[4] All three were important poets of the early nineteenth century, all born in Zante within a few years of each other, and all in due course declared 'national poets'—national, though, in relation to two different countries. How and why these men, in such a narrow span of time, took such different routes as regards cultural and political belonging and national consciousness, and what this tells us about their intellectual production, the world in which they lived, and the wider issues of their epoch, are questions that Chapters 1–3 explore.

It is certainly hard to talk about these three poets without touching a chord with those who attended an Italian or a Greek school. It is hard to credit just how deeply embedded these figures are in the national imaginaries of Italy and Greece. Foscolo

---

[3] Theodosis Pylarinos, 'O thanatos tou D. Solomou' (The death of D. Solomos), *Periplous* 46–7 (July 1998–Feb. 1999), pp. 203–19.

[4] I borrow the definition given by Katherine Verdery in her *The Political Lives of Dead Bodies: Reburial and Postsocialist Change* (New York, 1999).

for the Italians, as Solomos and Kalvos for the Greeks, are not just *any* poets; they are emotionally charged *ideas* and symbols connected to identity. It is almost impossible to approach these three poets as anything other than 'national poets'. In Italy—where no one has heard of Solomos or Kalvos—Foscolo has countless streets and schools named after him. His stanzas are memorized by schoolchildren and are recited in national celebrations. Foscolo is considered to be one of the principal protagonists of the Risorgimento and, more than any of his contemporaries, became the poet laureate of united Italy, the Dante of the modern era. Thanks to the monumentalizing work of Giuseppe Mazzini first and of Francesco De Sanctis later, Foscolo's work was very early given a prominent place in the histories of Italian literature, becoming an integral part of the canon of *italianità*, the essence of Italian national identity.[5] If in the nineteenth century his figure came to be associated with the actual 'moral existence of the nation', Foscolo has ever since then been viewed through all kinds of political and ideological lenses: liberal, socialist, nationalist, Marxist, and even fascist.[6] Only recently, and thanks to the work of a new generation of literary theorists and historians, has the poet been restored to his original historical context and judged critically in relation to a set of scholarly questions. First of all, a number of new literary biographies of Foscolo tend to emphasize, rather than to ignore, the poet's Zakynthian origins and his double consciousness as an Italian and a Greek. In these biographical specificities scholars recognize now some of the most enriching elements of the poet's oeuvre.[7] Second, recent historians addressing the construction of the Italian 'national canon', and the prominent place that the 'myth of exile' had in the national imaginary, have stressed Foscolo's originality in combining the themes of 'romantic love' and 'love for the nation' and his emblematic self-fashioning as a sorrowing 'exiled patriot'.[8] Finally, intellectual historians and historians of political thought have revisited Foscolo's poetry and political prose, studying it in relation to a current in Mediterranean liberalism and patriotism which was transnational and connected to the British Empire.[9] All these approaches have historicized the poet, viewing him also as an

---

[5]  Giuseppe Mazzini, 'A chi legge', preface to Ugo Foscolo, *Scritti politici inediti: raccolti a documentarne la vita e i tempi* (Lugano, 1844), pp. vii–xxxix; Francesco De Sanctis, 'Ugo Foscolo poeta e critico', *Nuova Antologia* 17/6 (1871), pp. 253–82. See Christian Del Vento, *Un allievo della rivoluzione: Ugo Foscolo dal 'noviziato letterario' al 'nuovo classicismo' (1795–1806)* (Bologna, 2003), pp. 3–9; Maurizio Isabella, 'Exile and Nationalism: The Case of the Risorgimento', *European History Quarterly* 36/4 (2006), pp. 495–6.

[6]  For an account see Del Vento, *Un allievo della rivoluzione*, pp. 10–27.

[7]  Maria Antonietta Terzoli, *Foscolo* (Rome and Bari, 2000); Manlio Pastore Stocchi, '1792–1797: Ugo Foscolo a Venezia', in idem and G. Arnaldi (eds), *Storia della cultura veneta*, vol. VI: *Dall'età napoleonica alla Prima Guerra Mondiale* (Vicenza, 1986), pp. 21–58; Raffaele Morabito, 'Ugo Foscolo', in N. Borsellino and W. Pedullà (eds), *Storia generale della letteratura italiana*, vol. VII: *L'Italia romantica il primo Ottocento* (Milan, 2004), pp. 119–204.

[8]  Maurizio Isabella, 'Exile and Nationalism', pp. 493–520; Alberto M. Banti, *La nazione del Risorgimento: parentela, santità e onore alle origini dell'Italia unita* (Turin, 2000); Paul Ginsborg, 'Romanticismo e Risorgimento: l'io, l'amore e la nazione', in *Storia d'Italia*, Annali 22; idem and Alberto M. Banti (eds), *Il Risorgimento* (Turin, 2007), pp. 5–67.

[9]  Eugenio Biagini, 'Liberty, Class and Nation-Building: Ugo Foscolo's "English" Constitutional Thought, 1816–1827', *European Journal of Political Theory* 5/34 (2006), pp. 34–49; Maurizio Isabella, *Risorgimento in Exile: Italian Émigrés and the Liberal International in the Post-Napoleonic Era*

intellectual and a transnational patriot who contributed with his work and his life to the formation of Italian nationalism and global liberalism.

For all the attention that Foscolo has attracted in Italy, in Greece he has remained largely unknown. Only in a narrow circle of Zakynthian literati and local Ionian patriots were voices from time to time raised against the original appropriation of his corpse and memory by the Italian state. Their leading representative, Spyridon De Biasi, dedicated his efforts to writing treatises about Foscolo's role in promoting the Greek national cause and, more generally, about his essential 'Greekness'. He even persuaded the municipality of Zante to buy the birthplace of the poet and turn the house into a museum, of which he became the president.[10] Half-Italian and half-Greek himself, De Biasi expressed the hope that the inauguration of the museum in 1887 would prove to be 'a real celebration of Greco-Italian friendship'.[11] As a matter of fact, Foscolo's memory survived in Zante more as a reminder of the peculiar mixture of Greco-Italian culture that characterized the Ionian Islands and still perplexed De Biasi's generation, rather than as a symbol of Greek national consciousness. The only occasion when Foscolo was discussed as a 'Greek national poet' was indeed when another Ionian, the historiographer Spyridon Zampelios, proposed in 1859 that he replace Solomos as Greece's 'national poet'—a proposal reflecting an intra-Ionian dispute between the author and Solomos's followers.[12]

That the person who delivered Foscolo's funeral oration in Zante was in fact Solomos, Foscolo's 'Greek counterpart', is only one of history's many ironies.[13] Solomos, indeed, has been as revered in Greece as Foscolo has been in Italy. The countless streets named after him (forty-six in the greater Athens area alone), the film and television representations of the poet, his depiction on banknotes and stamps, the theatrical performances or settings of his work to music, the celebrations of anniversaries of his birth and death, the erection of public statues and the ubiquity of his name in school curricula, all clearly attest to Solomos's consecration as a national poet.[14] It is only since the late 1980s that scholarship on Solomos has

(Oxford, 2009), esp. pp. 70–5; idem, 'Liberalism and Empires in the Mediterranean: the View-Point of the Risorgimento', in Silvana Patriarca and Lucy Riall (eds), *The Risorgimento Revisited, Nationalism and Culture in Nineteenth-Century Italy* (London and New York, 2012), pp. 232–54; Del Vento, *Un allievo della rivoluzione.*

[10] Spyridon De Biasi, *O Ougos Foskolos kai i elliniki epanastasis* (Ugo Foscolo and the Greek revolution) (Zante, 1890); idem, *Ta apokalyptiria tis anathimatikis plakos epi tis genethliou oikias Ougou Foskolou* (The unveiling of the voting stone on the birth-house of Ugo Foscolo) (Zante, 1892). Along the same lines also was a later publication of Foscolo's poem *Dei Sepolcri* in Greek, which was accompanied by a text entitled 'The Greek soul of Foscolo' and signed by Spyros Minotos (Athens, 1927). The biography of Foscolo by Marinos Sigouros (Athens, 1915) is along the same lines.

[11] Letter to Domenico Bianchini, in Theodosis Pylarinos and Panagiota Tzivara, 'Foskoliana ergobiografika: oi epistoles tou Spyridona de Biasi pros ton Domenico Bianchini' (The letters of Sp. De Biasi to D. Bianchini), in *X Panionian Conference: Proceedings*, forthcoming. The museum was destroyed by the earthquake that struck the southern Ionian Islands in 1953.

[12] Spyridon Zampelios, *Pothen i koini lexis 'Tragoudo'? Skepseis peri ellinikis poiiseos* (Where does the vernacular word 'Sing' come from? Thoughts on Greek poetry) (Athens, 1859), pp. 55–88.

[13] Dionisio Solomos, *Elogio di Ugo Foscolo*, edited by Carlo Brighenti (Turin, Milan, and Florence, 1934) (pronounced in 1827 and first published in Corfu, 1859).

[14] Giorgos Veloudis, *O Solomos ton Ellinon, ethniki poiisi kai ideologia: mia politiki anagnosi* (Solomos of the Greeks, national poetry and ideology: a political reading) (Athens, 2004).

acquired a more detached and critical colour: a generation of scholars trained in philology, literary theory, and cultural studies, and working mainly outside Greece, have drawn attention to the poet's Greco-Italian bilingualism (diglossia), the fragmentary and incomplete nature of his poetry, the posthumous construction of his poems through editorial revision, and the fashioning of his image as 'national'. It is on these studies that the present chapter builds, hoping however to add a more distinctly historical perspective.[15]

If Solomos's beatification had started already during the last years of his life, Andreas Kalvos was, for his part, a 'belated national poet'. Before 1889, when he was discovered by the Athenian poetic establishment through a lecture delivered by Kostis Palamas, one of Greece's major poets, Kalvos was known only in Zante—and again through the indefatigable Spyridon De Biasi.[16] But it was only during the twentieth century, especially in the inter-war and post-war years, that Kalvos would emerge as an emblematic poet in Greek national consciousness. Since then several men of letters, not least among them two Nobel laureates, the poets Odysseas Elytis and the afore-mentioned Giorgios Seferis, have written at length about his poetic production.[17] Despite the years of neglect, Kalvos became a deeply revered figure, so much so that in 1979 his (Greek only) poems, prefaced by an introduction hailing him as the poet of Greek freedom, were published by the then President of the Greek Republic, Konstantinos Tsatsos, and were distributed gratis to all secondary schools.[18] However, right from the outset, some critics had discerned inconsistencies in Kalvos's poetic language, and were alert to the problems raised by claiming him as a 'national poet': 'the gaps [in Kalvos's poetry]', Seferis wrote, 'are as disconcerting as the staggering of a strict and formal man'.[19] Indeed, since the 1990s and especially after 2000, philologists and historians alike have been more and more concerned to scrutinize Kalvos's bicultural formation, his Italian literary background, and the presence of Italian

[15] Vassilis Lambropoulos, *Literature as National Institution: Studies in the Politics of Modern Greek Criticism* (Princeton, 1988), pp. 66–99; Peter Mackridge, 'Dionisio Salamon/Dionysios Solomos: Poetry as a Dialogue between Languages', *Dialogos* 1 (1994), pp. 59–76; Giannis Dallas, 'O Solomos anamesa se dyo glosses: i amfidromi dokimasia tis poiitikis ideas' (Solomos between two languages), *I lexi* 142 (Nov.–Dec. 1997), pp. 688–703; Afroditi Athanasopoulou, 'To problima tis diglossias: i periptosi tou Solomou' (The problem of diglossia: the case of Solomos) (Ph.D. dissertation, University of Crete, 1999); Vangelis Calotychos, *Modern Greece: A Cultural Poetics* (Oxford and New York, 2003), pp. 73–87; Karen Van Dyck, 'The Language Question and the Diaspora', in Roderick Beaton and David Ricks (eds), *The Making of Modern Greece: Nationalism, Romanticism, and the Uses of the Past (1797–1896)* (London, 2009), pp. 189–98; Karen Emmerich, ' "A genre mixed, but valid": Dionysios Solomos's *The Free Besieged* and its Posthumous Editorial Forms' (unpublished chapter from a book in progress on editorial practice and the material construction of modern Greek poetry).

[16] Spyridon de Biasi, *I Lyra tou Andrea Kalvou* (The 'Lyra' of Andreas Kalvos) (Zante, 1881). Kostis Palamas's lecture was published in instalments in the periodical *Estia* (26 Nov.–10 Dec. 1889).

[17] Vasilis Letsios, 'Elytis, Kalvos, Solomos: mia synomilia me prosdokies' (Elytis, Kalvos, Solomos: a conversation with expectations), *Ionios logos* 4 (2013), pp. 213–26; Giorgos Seferis, 'Apories diabazontas ton Kalvo' (Questions while reading Kalvos), 'Prologos gia mia ekdosi ton Odon' (Introduction to a publication of the Odes), and 'Kalvos, 1960', in idem, *Dokimes*, edited by G. P. Savvides (Athens, 1981), vol. I: *1936–1947*, pp. 56–63, 179–210 and vol. II: *1948–1971*, pp. 112–35 respectively.

[18] Konstantinos Tsatsos, 'Kalvos, o poiitis tis ideas' (Kalvos, the poet of the ideal), introduction to the so-called Kalvos's *Omnibus Work* (but in reality including only his 24 Greek odes) distributed to secondary schools (Athens, 1979).

[19] Seferis, 'Kalvos, 1960', p. 113.

Neoclassicism and Romanticism in what was perceived otherwise to be a poetry inspired directly by ancient Greek models.[20] Of particular importance, in this respect, are a number of recent historical studies, which examine Kalvos's early life as a poet, a philologist, an Italian patriot, an exile, and a carbonaro, attempting to reconnect him with the historical specificities of his time.[21]

Part I of this book tells the story of the three poets, its purpose being to explore through the intricate detail of their biographies the vast geopolitical transformations, the great changes afoot in the Mediterranean world which they had known. These three biographies, taken together, may perhaps illuminate the processes under way on a macrohistorical level in the Adriatic region at the end of the eighteenth and during the first decades of the nineteenth century. These processes involved the total or partial dismemberment of three empires (the Venetian, the Habsburg, and the Ottoman), the emergence of three others (the Napoleonic, the Russian, and the British), and the rise within these empires of a series of distinct nationalisms that would eventually be crystallized in separate nation-states. By combining poetry, politics, and biography, the following chapters reconstitute the process by which the Ionian Islands, once an eastern periphery of the Venetian Republic and an immediate satellite of Venice, became first an autonomous statelet protected by great empires, and finally a western province of the Greek nation-state. They do so by exploring the impact of these wider geopolitical developments on the lives and choices of the three men, and by examining the way the large-scale events of their times (the creation of the Napoleonic states in Italy, the French occupation of the Ionian Islands, the proclamation of the Septinsular Republic under Russo-Ottoman protection, the incorporation of the Ionian Islands within the British Empire, the outbreak of the Greek revolution, and the revolutionary tumult in Naples, Sicily, and Piedmont) entered their ordinary, workaday lives and reshaped them. They investigate the way in which these poets experienced the transition from the local patria to the national patria(s) and from the imperial centres to the national centre, and vice versa. They focus also on the increasing importance of exile and nostalgia in their refashioning of themselves as patriots, and of the new Neoclassical and Romantic poetic idols, namely Alfieri and Byron, in conditioning their view of the poet's role and 'mission'. In addition, this part of the book studies the process by

[20] Nasos Vagenas, 'Scholia ston Kalvo' (Comments on Kalvos), *Parnassos* 14/3 (1972), pp. 453–65; idem, 'Paramorfoseis tou Kalvou' (Contortions of Kalvos), *To dentro* 71–2 (Sept.–Oct. 1992), pp. 123–39; Mario Vitti, *O Kalvos kai i epochi tou* (Kalvos and his times) (Athens, 1995); Giannis Dallas, *Solomos kai Kalvos: dyo antizyges poiitikes tis epochis, philologika dokimia* (Solomos and Kalvos: two poetic counterparts of the time, philological essays) (Athens, 2009); Athina Georganta, *Ta thavmasia nera, Andreas Kalvos: o romantismos, o Byronismos kai o kosmos ton karmponaron* (The exquisite waters, Andreas Kalvos: Romanticism, Byronism and the world of the carbonari) (Athens, 2011); Michail Paschalis, *Xanadiabazontas ton Kalvo: o Andreas Kalvos, i Italia kai i archaiotita* (Rereading Kalvos: Andreas Kalvos, Italy and antiquity) (Herakleion, 2013).

[21] Dimitris Arvanitakis, *Ston dromo gia tis patrides: i 'Ape Italiana', o Andreas Kalvos, i istoria* (On the road to the patrias: the 'Ape Italiana', Andreas Kalvos and history) (Athens, 2010); Andreas Kalvos, *Allilografia* (Correspondence), edited by Dimitris Arvanitakis and Lefkios Zafeiriou (Athens, 2014), 2 vols. But also the older K. Porfyris, *O Andreas Kalvos karmponaros: i mystiki diki ton karmponaron tis Toskanis* (Andreas Kalvos carbonaro: the secret trial of the Tuscan carbonari) (Athens, 1992 [1975]).

which the works of Solomos and Kalvos gave birth to the field of modern Greek literature, while those of Foscolo became foundational for the Italian Risorgimento, and endeavours, at the same time, to shed light on the literary universe of the Ionian Islands of the immediate post-Venetian period, an Italian-speaking tradition obscured by the creation of the Greek canon of national literature and the establishment of Athens as a literary centre.

Since the three chapters of Part I of this book are organically bound to each other and followed by a unique conclusion, the reader is advised to read them together rather than separately.

# 1

## Ugo Foscolo

### A Life of Stammering in Exile

#### FOSCOLO'S LINGUISTIC AND
#### LITERARY LANDSCAPE

Ugo Foscolo was born, not as 'Ugo' but as 'Nicolaos' (or Niccolò), one winter's day in 1778. Zante, the place of his birth, belonged for almost four centuries to the Venetian Republic, being one of the most remote regions of the empire and essentially, after the fall of Crete and the Morea (1715), its southernmost territory. In the 'intimate' world of the Venetian Adriatic (see Figure 2), with all its political unity, interconnectivity, and shared experience, there was still leeway for a large degree of autonomy at the local level.[1] As long as residents paid taxes and obeyed the rules of the mercantile colonial system of the *Dominante* (which obliged them to sell their goods only to Venice), they were free to deal with local affairs more or less as they wished.[2] In such a remote corner of the empire, where metropolitan control was lax, political and judicial power was in effect in the hands of a local aristocracy, whose corrupt and violent rule suffered few checks from the central authorities. This aristocracy, despite being predominantly Orthodox Christian, conducted its official business in the Venetian dialect, which was also the empire's language of trade, law, education, and high culture. Routine, day-to-day affairs were transacted in the local Greek language, the dialect of the peasantry and the lower echelons of society. Rather than being ethnic, the frontier between languages in this diglossic environment was social. The local Greek used in Zante, just one among the various Greek dialects spoken then across the Ottoman and Venetian worlds, was of course colloquial and unstandardized. But such was also the Italian spoken by the Zakynthian bilingual aristocracy: the so-called *dialetto corcirese* (originating in Corfu, but used nearly everywhere on the Ionian Islands) consisted of an odd mixture that included archaic Venetian words, no longer featuring in the metropolitan language, and certain Greek syntactical features.[3]

---

[1] The Adriatic has been labelled a 'sea of intimacy' by Predrag Matvejević in his *Mediterranean: A Cultural Landscape* (Berkeley, 1999), p. 14.

[2] Benjamin Arbel, 'Venice's Maritime Empire in the Early Modern Period', in Eric R. Dursteler (ed.), *A Companion to Venetian History 1400–1797* (Leiden and Boston, 2013), pp. 125–253.

[3] Niccolò Tommaseo, 'Dialetto corcirese', in idem, *Il secondo esilio: scritti di Niccolò Tommaseo concernenti le cose d'Italia e d'Europa dal 1849 in poi* (Milan, 1862), pp. 168–70; Manlio Cortelazzo, 'Il dialetto corcirese per Niccolò Tommaseo', in T. Agostini (ed.), *Daniele Manin e Niccolò Tommaseo: cultura e società nella Venezia del 1848* (Ravenna, 2000), pp. 323–7; Tzortzis Ikonomou, 'Il dialetto corcirese: dialetto veneto e lingua italiana nelle Isole Ionie', in Giovanni Ruffino and Mari D'Agostino

On Zante, as on all the other Ionian Islands, there were no schools or universities, libraries or printing presses. It was only with the arrival of the French Jacobins that the first publishing house was established on Corfu (1798), while Zante acquired its own only in 1810, under the military occupation of the British. From 1778, when the last public school of Corfu had shut down, and until 1802, when Ioannis Kapodistrias in his capacity as Minister of Education of the Septinsular Republic founded a new one, there were no public institutions of elementary education anywhere on the islands. Children were taught the rudiments of Italian, Greek, Latin, and arithmetic by private tutors, most often Catholic or Orthodox priests.[4] In exchange, Venice offered access—at any rate to those who could afford it—to the illustrious universities of the metropole and of the Italian hinterland, namely in Padua, Pavia, and Bologna. As for the less privileged among its Ionian subjects, they could always cross the Adriatic and go to the metropole as immigrants, in search of a better life.[5]

In terms of literary production, the Ionian Islands had nothing remarkable to show either. It was not until the end of the eighteenth century, when education started spreading to wider sectors of society, that the first signs of any literary activity appeared on the islands. This activity was undertaken, of course, in Italian. It was through their studies in Italy and their readings of Italian books that a generation of Ionian aristocrats discovered, towards the end of the eighteenth century, their poetic predilections and their inclination towards Greek antiquity. This is probably the reason they never appear in surveys of modern Greek literature. Figures such as Antonio Trivoli Pieri (1766–99), a composer of Arcadian verses and admirer, from his solitary Corfiot retreat, of Italy's foremost poet at that date, Melchiorre Cesarotti;[6] Niccolò Delviniotti (1777–1850), a jurist who studied at the universities of Padua and Pavia, wrote both Greek and Italian patriotic poems (all in Italian verse), published a translation of the *Odyssey*, and composed *visioni* in the manner of Dante;[7] Demetrio Arliotti (1777–1860), a philo-Jacobin who frequented

(eds), *Storia della lingua italiana e dialettologia* (Palermo, 2010), pp. 459–76; Konstantinos E. Soldatos, 'I ethniki glossa eis tin Eptanison' (The national language on the Ionian Islands), *Kerkyraika chronika* 13 (1967), p. 86; Emanuele Banfi, 'Dinamiche linguistiche nell'area Adriatica tra i secoli XVIII–XIX: tra diglossie, bilinguismi e ricerca di lingue nazionali', in Francesco Bruni and Chryssa Maltezou, *L'Adriatico: incontri e separazioni (XVIII–XIX secolo)* (Venice, 2011), pp. 39–93.

[4] Mario Pieri, *Della vita di Mario Pieri corcirese scritta da lui medesimo* (Florence, 1850), vol. I, p. 19; Giuseppe Pecchio, *Vita di Ugo Foscolo* (Milan, 1851), pp. 9–10; Panagiota Tzivara, *Scholeia kai daskaloi sti venetokratoumeni Kerkyra (16os–18os aionas)* (Schools and teachers in Corfu in the Venetian period, 16th–18th centuries) (Kavala, 2003).

[5] Manlio Pastore Stocchi, 'Moralità e costume nei letterati delle province adriatiche e ioniche', in Filiberto Agostini (ed.), *L'area alto-adriatica dal riformismo veneziano all'età napoleonica* (Venice, 1998), pp. 91–101.

[6] Antonio Trivoli Pieri, *Poesie* (Venice, 1800 [posthumous]); Mario Pieri, 'Elogio di Antonio Trivoli Pieri', in idem, *Tributo all'amicizia, con vari componimenti in verso* (Verona, 1806), pp. 7–63.

[7] Niccolò Tommaseo, 'Della civiltà ionia e di Niccolò Delviniotti', *Archivio storico italiano* 2/1 (1855), pp. 65–88; Spyridon De Biasi, 'Eptanisioi poiitai: Nikolaos Delbiniotis' (Ionian poets: Niccolò Delviniotti), *Nea zoi* 5/58 (1909), pp. 310–17; Tzortzis Ikonomou, 'In cerca della musa italiana: Niccolò Delviniotti e la poesia ionia in italiano', in Bruni and Maltezou (eds), *L'Adriatico: incontri e separazioni*, pp. 221–38; Vittorio Volpi (ed.), *Odissea di Omero: traduzione di Niccolò Delviniotti corcirese* (Iseo 2005 [1843]).

Venetian literary salons and published Italian poems and the first biography of
Kapodistrias;[8] or Pier Antonio Bondioli (1765–1808), who was among Cesarotti's
favourite disciples and later a professor of medicine at the University of Bologna,
have all slipped into oblivion.[9] Yet, these—along with some others whom we
shall encounter later in this book—were the people who made up the Ionian literary universe of Foscolo's time. In the arid intellectual landscape of the Ionian
Islands of the turn of the century, these men published journals (as soon as the
first publishing houses were established), founded philological societies, and met
to discuss their readings of Dante, Petrarch, Tasso, and Metastasio, or of Anacreon
and Homer in Italian translations, and to share their admiration of Italy's living
poets—besides Cesarotti, Vincenzo Monti, Giuseppe Parini, Ippolito Pindemonte,
and, of course, Vittorio Alfieri.[10] Completely immersed in the universe of Venetian
and more widely Italian letters as these figures were, they nevertheless had, like every-
body on the Ionian Islands, a vague sense of being 'Greek', of obscurely belonging
to the greater Greek space: *Born in this dark corner of modern Greece... I made so
bold as to consider myself a Priest of the Muses*, were the words used by Trivoli Pieri
to preface his collection of Italian poems.[11] This sense of 'Greekness' was prompted
not only by the language of the Orthodox Church, but also by the islands' ancient
ruins, their geographical proximity to the Greek mainland, and, of course, by the
spoken idiom of the peasantry and its folktales and popular songs.[12]

Yet the language of poetry could not help but be Italian. *In barbarous Greece one
cannot study anything else but Greek; hence for a good number of years I bided my time*,
Delviniotti wrote in a letter to Foscolo in 1809, enclosing with it his collection of
poems (which featured an ode to the beauty of the Greek language and to the need
to restore it—written, of course, in Italian).[13] All this may raise eyebrows today,
but it was completely comprehensible at the time. For, what was the field of modern
Greek literature when these people turned their hand to poetry? Against the rich
landscape of the Italian literature of the *Settecento* and early *Ottocento*, with its
many academies and journals and with an established poetic tradition that went
back to the great Italian writers of the *Trecento* and the *Quattrocento*, Greek literature had as yet almost nothing to offer in terms of poetic models. Apart from
the seventeenth-century Cretan dialectal narrative poetry (notably the romance
*Erotokritos*, published somewhat later, in 1713, and itself influenced by Ariosto's

---

[8] Demetrio Arliotti, 'Inno alla luna', *Nuovo giornale de' letterati di Pisa* 46 (1839), pp. 174–5;
idem, *La vita di Giovanni Conte Capodisria* (Corfu, 1859); Michail Lascaris, 'Demetrio Arliotti,
1777–1860', *Kerkyraika chronika* 8 (1960), pp. 62–3.

[9] Mario Pieri, 'Elogio di Pier Antonio Bondioli', in idem, *Operette varie in prosa* (Milan, 1821),
pp. 289–327; Claudio Chiancone, *La scuola di Cesarotti e gli esordi del giovane Foscolo* (Pisa, 2012),
pp. 123–7.

[10] Journals include the *Gazzetta urbana* (1802–3), *Monitore Settinsulare* (1803–5), *Mercurio
letterario* and *Foglio estemporaneo* (1805–7). See Ntinos Konomos, *Eptanisiakos typos, 1798–1864* (The
press on the Ionian Islands, 1798–1864), special issue of *Eptanisiaka fylla* 5 (1964), pp. 38–43.

[11] Quoted in Ikonomou, 'In cerca della musa italiana', p. 223.

[12] Dimitris Arvanitakis, 'Glossa kai ethniki taftotita sto Ionio kata ton 19o aiona' (Language and
national identity on the Ionian Islands in the nineteenth century), *Ta istorika* 46 (2007), pp. 15–24.

[13] FE, vol. 5, pp. 220–1 and Niccolò Delviniotti, 'Alla lingua greco volgare', in idem, *Poesie* (Corfu,
1809), p. 52.

*Orlando furioso*) and the klephtic songs of the area of Epirus facing the Ionian Islands (which indeed Foscolo recalls having sung),[14] the rest of the cultural production in Greek—what is sometimes known as the 'Neohellenic Enlightenment' of the eighteenth century—concerned philosophical and scientific prose and works of educational proselytization, which had nothing to do with literature as such.[15] One could counter that towards the end of the century some Phanariots (a Christian elite that managed to acquire wealth and leading positions in the Ottoman Empire) in the salons of Constantinople, like Athanasios Christopoulos, started composing Arcadian verses in Greek, while in Vienna the revolutionary Rigas Velestinlis published a Greek translation of Metastasio's *Olimpiade* (1797) and composed his *Thourios* (a patriotic battle-hymn), which in 1798 would be printed in Corfu and be sung wherever Greek was spoken.[16] But these stimuli were either too distant or too weak and too much overshadowed by the grandeur of Italian literature to attract the attention of the literati of a Venetian province. It is true that Mario Pieri—another of Foscolo's Ionian contemporaries—testifies to having read *Erotokritos* as a child; but it was the reading of Metastasio that changed his life.[17]

Accounts of modern Greek literature start instead with a group of poets who have been labelled, quite teleologically, '*Prosolomikoi*' ('pre-Solomians', i.e. those preceding Solomos). These were mostly Zakynthian and Foscolo's somewhat older contemporaries, who wrote verses in the local Greek idiom and translated Italian works of literature into Modern Greek. Almost all of them were Orthodox clerics, hence their deeper knowledge of the Greek language. They were also republicans and endorsed the French revolutionary cause. Men like Nicolaos Koutouzis (1741–1813) or Antonios Martelaos (1754–1819)—the latter being the most noted among this group and, as one story has it, Foscolo's tutor in childhood—developed a sense of Greek patriotism which transcended Zante and the Ionian Islands to embrace the wider Greek space. After the arrival of the French and the Russians, their cultural patriotism took on a political colouring: *Our Islands are an enviable | State. But the rest | of our patria is enslaved. | Yet I have hopes | to see, before I die, | Greece as a great State*—read one of Martelaos's poems written around 1800.[18] Martelaos was particularly inspired by Rigas Velestinlis and he composed, on the model of the latter's *Thourios*, a Greek version of the *Marseillaise*. He also wrote pro-Napoleonic verses, which he dedicated, in 1797, to his 'student Nicolaos Foscolo'. Martelaos was indeed the first to claim that Foscolo was Greek. When in 1807 he read the latter's poem *Dei Sepolcri* (Sepulchres), he is said to have exclaimed: *They vainly want to*

---

[14] 'Sometimes we sing Greek songs and polyphony in the manner of the Albanians—those arias that are at once barbaric and impassioned' (1808). In FE, vol. 2, pp. 551–2. See also [Anonymous], 'Aftobiografia Io. Zampeliou' (The autobiography of Ioannis Zampelios), *Armonia* 3 (1902), p. 228.

[15] G. P. Henderson, *The Revival of Greek Thought (1620–1830)* (Albany, NY, and New York, 1970); Paschalis Kitromilides, *Enlightenment and Revolution: The Making of Modern Greece* (Cambridge, Mass., and London, 2013).

[16] Mario Vitti, *Istoria tis ellinikis logotechnias* (History of modern Greek literature) (Athens, 2003), pp. 150–9. Konomos, *Eptanisiakos typos*, pp. 16–17.

[17] Pieri, *Della vita*, vol. I, pp. 18, 23. On Pieri see Chapter 8 of this book.

[18] Faidon Mpoumpoulidis, *Prosolomikoi* (The pre-Solomians) (Athens, 1966–97), 5 vols; Theodosis Pylarinos, *Eptanisiaki Scholi* (The Heptanesian School) (Athens, 2003), pp. 19–33.

*make you a Frank, | while the Sepulchres cry out that you are Greek.*[19] Apart from a developed sense of Greek patriotism, which, in combining French republican values with Orthodoxy, produced a particular local culture of oral compositions in Modern Greek, this group of poets is worth mentioning also for another reason: their work as translators. Ioannis Kantounis's (1731–1817) translation of Metastasio's *Artaserse* and Demetrios Gouzelis's (1774–1843) adaptation of Tasso's *Gerusalemme liberata* show that, its Greek cultural patriotism notwithstanding, this group's cultural references remained embedded within the wider framework of Italian literature familiar to the Ionian Islands at this date.[20]

## A LIFE OF STAMMERING IN EXILE

Let us go back now to Nicolaos Foscolo. Born to a Greek Orthodox Zakynthian mother and a Venetian Catholic father from an impoverished family which had been living for several generations on the eastern peripheries of the empire, Foscolo seemed to epitomize by birth the interconnected universe situated between the two shores of the Venetian Adriatic. As a child of a mixed marriage, he took the religion of his father and, despite the insistent demands of his Orthodox relatives, he was never re-baptized into Orthodoxy (as was then the usual practice for children of mixed marriages on the Ionian Islands).[21] When he was 7 his family moved to Spalato, in Dalmatia (present-day Split in Croatia), where his father succeeded his grandfather as a doctor in the city's military hospital. However, only three years later his father died and Nicolaos, who was thus orphaned at the age of 10, was sent back to Zante, where he was placed in the care of an aunt. In 1793, at the age of 15, he left his native island once and for all, in order to move with his mother and siblings to Venice.[22] This definitive separation from his native place was later to acquire almost mythical dimensions in the poet's imagination and in his poetry. As we will see, in Foscolo's self-narration, the departure from Zante came to signify the symbolic beginning of a life construed in terms of a sequence of exiles without end.

The first years in Venice, his 'adopted patria' as he used to call it, were very difficult for the young Nicolaos, not least because he was poor. *He lived with his widowed mother and I think also with his brother and with a sister, in Campo delle Gatte, one of the filthiest quarters of that magnificent city*—wrote his friend Pieri—*in a house, or rather a shack, so wretched that there was no glass in the windows but only*

[19] Spyridon De Biasi, 'Eptanisioi poiitai: Antonios Martelaos' (Ionian poets: Antonios Martelaos), *Nea zoi* 5/59 (1909), pp. 354–68.

[20] *I Ierousalim Eleftheromeni, poiima iroikon tou Torkouatou Tassou... metafrasthen... para tou Dimitriou Gouzeli Zakynthiou* (Gerusalemme liberata, a heroic poem by Torquato Tasso... translated... by Demetrios Gouzelis the Zakynthian) (Venice, 1807); Theodosis Pylarinos, 'O *Artaxerxis* tou Petrou Metastasiou, metafrasmenos stin aploelliniki apo ton prosolomiko Ioanni Kantouni (1731–1817)' (Metastasio's *Artaserse* translated into Modern Greek by the pre-Solomian Ioannis Kantounis (1731–1817)), *Parabasis* 10 (2010), pp. 377–9.

[21] Marinos Sigouros, *Ougos Foskolos (biografiki Meleti)* (Ugo Foscolo: a biographical study) (Athens, 1915), pp. 10–11.

[22] Bruno Rosada, *La giovinezza di Niccolò Ugo Foscolo* (Padua, 1992), pp. 1–26.

*cloth coverings.*[23] As if his poverty was not burden enough, the modest origins of the boy could be seen also in the way he talked. When Foscolo arrived in Italy he could speak only the Zakynthian Greek dialect and, probably, a broken Venetian idiom (the *dialetto corcirese*), inherited by his father's family. The Greek passages from the letters to his mother, even those of a later date, are indicative of the kind of language that Foscolo spoke as a child.[24] Of course, he was taught some elementary Italian during his short stay in Spalato. As he would write some time later, *Young as I am, born in Greece, educated among Dalmatians, I have been stammering for only four years in Italy.*[25] The 'stammering' metaphor was dear to him and he would use it often. For example, in a letter of those days to Cesarotti, who was soon to become his guide in the world of poetry, Foscolo would say: *I shall hear from you the precepts of a language that I studied with great difficulty, and for the moment I only stammer.* The phrase is much more telling in the original because written in a hybrid Italo-Greek: *udrò da voi i precetti di una lingua che con gran fatica ho studiato, e che al presente* τραυλίζω. It is interesting also that it is in fact the word 'stammer' that comes across into Greek, exemplifying the very point the young man is concerned to make.[26]

However difficult they were, these early years in Venice were also formative. *I had barely a smattering of Latin, and was wholly ignorant of Tuscan when I came from Greece into Italy*—Foscolo would recall some years later—*but those first years of my youth though surrounded by much wretchedness were nonetheless illuminated by the Muse, and my intellect was as it were steeped in poetry, and with all my soul I abandoned myself to it.*[27] Under the guidance of his Venetian teachers, and especially of the director of the Marciana Library, the deeply learned Jacopo Morelli, and of course of the most revered of Venice's living poets, Cesarotti, the provincial orphan gradually discovered his literary and cultural universe: Latin and ancient Greek writers (mainly Homer), the French Enlightenment, Christian texts, European literature (notably Shakespeare, Goethe, Ossian, Thomas Gray, Edward Young— all in Italian translation), and Italian classics (namely Dante, Petrarch, Tasso, Alfieri, Parini, and Monti). *At the age of sixteen the desire to study erupted*—Foscolo confessed several years later.[28] And he did so in an incredibly assiduous fashion. His so-called '*piano di studi*' (plan of studies), a detailed list of the readings and of the writing exercises accomplished or to be accomplished by the young man in 1796, shows Foscolo's determination to make his way in the world of letters. It also attests to a learning project typical of the model of education received in Venice, and especially in the avant-garde Paduan school of Cesarotti, of the Neoclassical and pre-Romantic decades.[29]

---

[23] Pieri, *Della vita*, vol. I, p. 39.    [24] FE, vol. 4, p. 65; vol. 6, pp. 131, 237.

[25] Introduction to the ode *A Bonaparte liberatore* (1797). In *Edizione nazionale delle opere di Ugo Foscolo*, vol. 2: *Tragedie e poesie minori*, edited by Guido Bézzola (Florence, 1961), p. 331.

[26] FE, vol. 1, p. 20. On the 'stammering' metaphor see also Terzoli, *Foscolo*, pp. 169–70.

[27] *Della poesia lucreziana* (1802–1803). In Stocchi, '1792–1797: Ugo Foscolo a Venezia', p. 26.

[28] In Carlo Dionisotti, 'Venezia e il noviziato di Foscolo', in idem, *Appunti sui moderni, Foscolo, Leopardi, Manzoni e altri* (Bologna, 1988), p. 37.

[29] Dionisotti, 'Venezia e il noviziato di Foscolo', pp. 33–53; Chiancone, *La scuola di Cesarotti*, pp. 218–63; Terzoli, *Foscolo*, pp. 4–7; Stocchi, '1792–1797: Ugo Foscolo a Venezia', pp. 30–1.

Young Foscolo's literary apprenticeship was mostly served in the intellectual salon of Isabella Teotochi-Albrizzi (1760–1836), a beautiful and learned Corfiot woman, who played an active role in the literary scene of the capital. Yet another representative of Foscolo's Ionian 'lost' generation, Teotochi-Albrizzi was born to a Greek Corfiot father and a Venetian mother. Married (twice) to Venetian noblemen who were high-ranking officers or state functionaries, Isabella spent her life in Venice, where she became a cultural mediator, a woman of letters, and a *salonnière*. Her salon was the meeting point between the last representatives of the Venetian Enlightenment (including Foscolo's mentor, Morelli) and the new literati and artists of the Neoclassical and pre-Romantic coteries (such as Cesarotti, the tragedian Pindemonte, and the renowned sculptor Antonio Canova). Numerous foreign intellectuals, travellers, devotees of the Grand Tour, and diplomats gathered there too—famously, Lord Byron called her '*la Staël veneziana*' (the Venetian Madame de Staël).[30] As an author, Teotochi-Albrizzi made something of a name for herself by writing about her famous friends. Her works thus include a collection of written portraits of her guests and interlocutors (entitled *Ritratti*), but also a voluminous description of the sculptures of Canova.[31] Isabella's leading position in Venetian intellectual sociability, her broad education, and great beauty could not but captivate the young Ionians, who flocked to her salon in search of conversation, contacts, inspiration, and cultural protection. Isabella was happy to become their patron, their Muse, and also, occasionally, their lover. It was, indeed, looking into her eyes that Foscolo discovered his first love. At least this is what his numerous letters to her attest, which again contain some of the most interesting hybrid Italo-Greek: *addio addio Kardiamu* (goodbye goodbye my heart); *addio psichimu kai agapimu* (goodbye my soul and my love); *cai seli su ipò opos se agapao me olinmou tin psichinmu* (and I will tell you that I love you with all my heart); *cai egò se agapao polì, sebbene voi den me agapas ti potes* (and I love you very much, even if you do not love me at all)—are all phrases which mix Italian words with Greek Zakynthian dialect features (written in Latin characters), to reveal the curious linguistic and cultural universe of the two correspondents.[32]

Foscolo was thus slowly initiated into love, but also into poetry. His solid training in Italian letters started to produce fruit and he began to compose his own verses, which he sent out to friends and to literary journals, signing them now with

[30] Vittorio Malamani, *Isabella Teotochi Albrizzi: i suoi amici, il suo tempo* (Turin, 1882); Cinzia Giorgetti, *Ritratto di Isabella: studi e documenti su Isabella Teotochi Albrizzi* (Florence, 1992); Adriano Favaro, *Isabella Teotochi Albrizzi: la sua vita, i suoi amori e i suoi viaggi* (Udine, 2003); Marianna D'Ezio, 'Isabella Teotochi Albrizzi's Venetian Salon: A Transcultural and Transnational Example of Sociability and Cosmopolitanism in Late Eighteenth- and Early Nineteenth-Century Europe', in Ileana Baird (ed.), *Social Networks in the Long Eighteenth Century: Clubs, Literary Salons, Textual Coteries* (Cambridge, 2014), pp. 175–98.

[31] Isabella Teotochi-Albrizzi, *Ritratti* (Brescia, 1807 [revised and republished in 1808, 1816 and 1826]); idem, *Opere di scultura e di plastica di Antonio Canova* (Florence, 1809) [published posthumously in English as *The Works of Antonio Canova in Sculpture and Modelling* (London, 1849, 2 vols)]. See also Niccolò Barozzi (ed.), *Lettere d'illustri italiani ad Isabella Teotochi-Albrizzi* (Florence, 1836).

[32] FE, vol. 2, pp. 116, 121, 129, 132 respectively. See also Giuseppe Chiarini, *Gli amori di Ugo Foscolo nelle sue lettere* (Bologna, 1892), pp. 14ff.; Gilberto Pizzamiglio, 'Ugo Foscolo nel salotto di Isabella Teotochi-Albrizzi', *Quaderni Veneti* 2 (1985), pp. 49–66.

his new and *more Italian* name, 'Ugo'.[33] In 1797, at only 18 years of age, he wrote *Tieste* (Thyestes), a Neoclassical tragedy inspired by the style and themes of Alfieri, which debuted with great success on the Venetian stage. Tragedy-writing was considered to be the most sublime form of composition, while *Alfierismo*, the love of all things linked to the Piedmontese dramatist and poet Vittorio Alfieri (1749–1803) and to his anti-tyrannical and libertarian stance, was in vogue; and young Foscolo seemed to be adept at both.[34]

But in the damp alleys of Venice and in its libraries, cafés, and intellectual salons, the young Zakynthian not only discovered love and poetry; he also discovered politics. These were the days when Napoleon crossed the Alps, bringing to the Italian peninsula the principles of the French Revolution, and delivering the final blow to the already crumbling Venetian Republic. By the time the *Serenissima* collapsed, Foscolo had become a convinced Jacobin.[35] Involved as he was in the republican patriotic circles of the capital, he welcomed with enthusiasm the provisional Venetian Democratic Municipality which replaced the Doge's aristocratic *Gran Consiglio* after the latter's abdication in May 1797. Hoping that Napoleon would help the Venetian nation to restore its venerable traditions of republican liberty, Foscolo participated in the Patriotic Association of Public Instruction, which was founded in those days with a view to fostering the values of freedom and equality.[36] These were times of excitement and change not only for Venice, but for the whole of the Italian peninsula and the Adriatic. As Napoleon's army marched back and forth through the Italian states and the ex-Venetian provinces, the wind of revolution blew everywhere. Foscolo enlisted as a volunteer in the republican army encamped before Bologna, while at the same time he penned patriotic poems, including a famous ode to *Bonaparte liberatore*. The creation of the French-protected 'Jacobin' republics in central and northern Italy (the Cispadane Republic, and later the Cisalpine Republic), along with Napoleon's promises that he would secure Italian independence, raised hopes among patriots and intellectuals alike that the Italian peninsula (or at least part of it) would be transformed into a nation on the model of revolutionary France.[37] Foscolo shared these hopes: *[I may have been born in Greece]*—the young Zakynthian confessed in his introduction to the ode to *Bonaparte liberatore*—, *[but] the lofty genius of Liberty that inflames me and renders me a Free Man and Citizen of a Fatherland not touched by chance but chosen,*

---

[33] In private letters, especially to members of his own family, he continued to use his original name, or sometimes even both: '*Ugo, cioè Niccolò*' (Ugo, that is Nicolaos). (Ntinos Konomos), 'Dyo simeiomata anekdota tou Ougou Foskolou' (Two unpublished notes of Ugo Foscolo), *Eptanisiaka fylla* 14 (Feb. 1949), p. 222. Artusi, *Vita di Ugo Foscolo*, p. 10.

[34] Rachel A. Walsh, *Ugo Foscolo's Tragic Vision in Italy and England* (Toronto, 2014), pp. 25–46; Giuseppe Nicoletti, 'Alfierismo mediato e controcorrente nel *Tieste* foscoliano', in idem, *La memoria illuminata: autobiografia e letteratura fra Rivoluzione e Risorgimento* (Florence, 1989), pp. 131–45; Franco Fido, 'La tragedia nell'età giacobina e napoleonica', in Borsellino and Pedullà (eds), *Storia generale della letteratura italiana*, pp. 115–17.

[35] Del Vento, *Un allievo della rivoluzione*, p. 33; Pieri, *Della vita*, vol. I, pp. 45–6.

[36] Xavier Tabet, 'Foscolo et la révolution vénitienne', in Enzo Neppi (ed.), *Ugo Foscolo, l'Italie et la révolution française* (Grenoble, 2004), pp. 37–64.

[37] Antonino De Francesco, *L'Italia di Bonaparte: politica, statualità e nazione nella penisola tra due rivoluzioni, 1796–1821* (Milan, 2011), pp. 3–34.

*gives me the rights of an Italian.*[38] The hopes of the Venetian patriots were, however, soon to be dashed, when news arrived of the Treaty of Campo Formio (October 1797), a settlement between France and Austria which handed Veneto over to the Habsburg Empire. Devastated by the turn of events, Foscolo, like several other liberal patriots, retreated to Milan, the then capital of the Cisalpine Republic and the sole remaining stronghold of those who still envisioned a nationwide political emancipation. In Milan and in other parts of the 'liberated' Italian territories, where he stayed during the revolutionary and Napoleonic years, Foscolo developed a cultural programme for the Italian democratic nation, engaging in military and journalistic activity and becoming, along with the celebrated Milanese poet Vincenzo Monti, the first genuinely 'Italian intellectual'.[39] In addition, the young Zakynthian applied for 'Italian citizenship', to which, because he was recognized as a Venetian refugee from the circumstances created by the Treaty of Campo Formio, he was judged eligible.[40] It was in this context, then, that Foscolo's cultural identity turned political, and *quel grecotto* (that little Greek guy)—as a Venetian police report read—became Italian.[41] He not only became Italian; he became at once Italian and a refugee.

Nationality, indeed, came for Foscolo together with exile. And this is the way that he perceived and expressed it in the work that did the most to ensure him a place in the Italian pantheon of letters. I refer here to his best-seller *Le ultime lettere di Jacopo Ortis* (The last letters of Jacopo Ortis), undoubtedly the most popular novel of the Italian Risorgimento, which Foscolo first published in 1798 and then redrafted and republished several times, updating it according to historical developments in the period up until 1817.[42] *Ortis* was an epistolary novel, written on the model of Rousseau's *La Nouvelle Héloïse* (1761) and Goethe's *The Sorrows of Young Werther* (1774). It recounts the adventures and travails of Jacopo, a young man forced into exile by a double disenchantment: the loss of his *patria*, Venice, which is occupied by the Austrians, and the loss of his beloved, Teresa, who is destined by her father to marry a marquis, a man far richer than Jacopo. This mixture of 'unhappy love' (*amore infelice*), at once political and romantic, engenders sentiments of great distress and disquiet for the protagonist who decides, by the end of the novel, to commit suicide. This seemingly simple formula enabled Foscolo to do, in reality, something extremely elaborate. First, he managed to marry the themes of romantic love and love for the *patria* in a unique ensemble, which made his novel easily digestible and thus immensely popular. The romanticization of individual love and the depiction of it as tragic and dramatic was a constant

---

[38] In *Edizione nazionale delle opere di Ugo Foscolo*, vol. 2, p. 331.

[39] Roberto Pertici, 'Appunti sulla nascita dell' "intellettuale" in Italia', postface to Christophe Charle, *Gli intellettuali nell'Ottocento* (Bologna, 2002), pp. 314–15.

[40] Del Vento, *Un allievo della rivoluzione*, pp. 70–3.

[41] In Del Vento, *Un allievo della rivoluzione*, p. 69.

[42] Christian Del Vento, 'Il mito di Foscolo e il modello dell'*Ortis*', in C. Gigante and D. Vanden Berghe (eds), *Il romanzo del Risorgimento* (Brussels, 2011), pp. 13–27.

characteristic of pre-Romantic and Romantic literature, but the connecting of it to collective feelings of patriotism, and especially to the nation, was due to Foscolo.[43]

Second, Foscolo forged one of the most powerful myths of the Italian Risorgimento, the 'myth of exile'. His novel belonged, in actual fact, to a venerable tradition within Italian letters dealing with this same theme. The 'myth of exile' consisted in the almost paradoxical idea—present in, among others, Dante and Alfieri—according to which, in certain political circumstances, men can preserve their patriotism only by abandoning their patria. What Foscolo did was to take this essentially republican idea and to make it national: whereas previously the link between exile and freedom was based on the dictum 'there is no patria without citizens', in Foscolo it became 'there is no patria without people'. He married this theme with the national preoccupations of his time, suggesting that wherever people cannot freely express their national spirit, they have no real homeland. This results in men, even those who never leave home, feeling as if they were in eternal exile. The protagonist of his novel personifies, in fact, the perpetual and desperate sense of loss and homelessness (*a-patria*): *exiled, poor, unknown to all mankind, or I fail to find a homeland as I look inside myself* are phrases uttered again and again by Jacopo Ortis.[44] As has been aptly argued, the 'myth of exile' escaped gradually from the sphere of literature and gained a firm foothold in the Italian collective imaginary. Thanks to Foscolo and to certain patriots and intellectuals who followed after him, exile and its predicaments (loss, homelessness, abandonment, and nostalgia) came to occupy a central place among the rhetorical motifs of the national-patriotic discourse of the Risorgimento, becoming one of the foundational myths of Italian nationalism.[45]

What made Foscolo's novel even more appealing was the fact that there was a strong autobiographical element in it. Not only did Foscolo invent Ortis, he also *became* him. In order to express the hopes and fears of an entire generation of disillusioned Italian patriots, he literally chose the road of exile himself: after years of disappointment and wandering during the Napoleonic Wars through various cities of Italy and France, in 1815, when the Austrians occupied what had remained of the kingdom of northern Italy, he refused to swear allegiance to the occupying power and decided to leave, intending never to come back. After one year of hiding in Switzerland (where he used, among others, the fake name 'Jacopo Ortis'), he settled in London, where he lived out the remaining ten years of his life, thus concluding the last episode of what had become by now an emblematic and almost

[43] Ginsborg, 'Romanticismo e Risorgimento: l'io, l'amore e la nazione', pp. 8, 18–19; Alberto M. Banti, *L'onore della nazione: identità sessuali e violenza nel nazionalismo europeo dal XVIII secolo alla Grande Guerra* (Turin, 2005), pp. 199–200.

[44] Ugo Foscolo, *Last Letters of Jacopo Ortis* (London, 2002), pp. 71, 111 respectively.

[45] Maurizio Isabella, 'Exile and Nationalism', pp. 493–520; idem, 'Esilio', in A. M. Banti, A. Chiavistelli, L. Mannori, and M. Meriggi (eds), *Atlante culturale del Risorgimento: lessico del linguaggio politico dal Settecento all'Unità* (Rome and Bari, 2011), pp. 65–74; Konstantina Zanou, 'Nostalgia, Self-Exile and the National Idea: The Case of Andrea Mustoxidi and the Early-19th-Century Heptanesians of Italy', in A. Aktar, N. Kızılyürek, and U. Özkırımlı (eds), *Nationalism in the Troubled Triangle: Cyprus, Greece and Turkey (New Perspectives on South-East Europe)* (New York, 2009), pp. 98–111.

fictional life of never-ending exiles.[46] *I chose Exile*—he stated in the pages of a work that he drafted during those first days in Switzerland, and which, more than any other perhaps, expressed his definitive estrangement from Italian affairs.[47] He was disappointed not only by Bonaparte and by the French, who had betrayed the last vestiges of republican and liberal aspirations, but also by the Italians, who had proved unworthy of political independence: *Italians, you no longer have a history*—reads one of the harsher versions of that manuscript.[48] By that time, *a-patria* had become one of the central motifs of Foscolo's itinerant existence: *What then of the patria?... Heaven has not granted me one, indeed, it instructed fortune to cast me into the world like a dice.*[49]

## THE MANY PATRIAS OF FOSCOLO

When Foscolo was asked in 1823 to say where he came from, he answered that he was *Greco di nascita, nativo di Zante, Veneziano di diritto e suddito dell'Inghilterra* (Greek by birth, a native of Zante, Venetian by law, and an English subject).[50] Forlorn and stateless as he had felt after his repeated disappointments with all things Italian, it seems nonetheless that during the years of his British exile the Italian expatriate dug out a series of patrias and belongings both old and new.

To begin with, he rediscovered Zante and the Ionian Islands. As we have seen, Foscolo's early and radical separation from his native place had transformed Zante into a literary 'topos', symbol of an impossible and utopian return: *No, I'll not land upon your sacred shore, | Zante, ever again!... You will have nothing left you but the verse | Your child sings, O my mother's land! My doom | Is exile and an unwept sepulchre*—reads the beginning of one of his most famous sonnets, entitled precisely *A Zacinto* (To Zante) and written in 1803, when the poet was in self-imposed exile from Venice to Milan.[51] The thought of finding refuge in Zante often returned to his mind as a consolation in times of trouble. In a letter of 1813 to his student and friend Andreas Kalvos—who, as we will see, shared the same sort of 'literary nostalgia' for that place—Foscolo confessed: *At the first opportunity I shall take ship to our islands like a fugitive Ulysses. There I shall settle my own and my family's business affairs such as they are... In my maternal Zante I shall find more peace and wield a freer pen and I will use the years of youth to finish some dozen tragedies.*[52]

[46] Morabito, 'Ugo Foscolo', p. 121; Carlo Dionisotti, 'Foscolo esule', in idem, *Appunti sui moderni*, pp. 55–77; Eric Reginald Vincent, *Ugo Foscolo: An Italian in Regency England* (Cambridge, 1953).

[47] Ugo Foscolo, 'Della servitù dell'Italia', in *Edizione nazionale delle opere di Ugo Foscolo*, vol. 8: *Prose politiche e letterarie dal 1811 al 1816*, edited by Luigi Fassò (Florence, 1972), p. 156.

[48] Foscolo, 'Della servitù dell'Italia', p. 162.

[49] From his unpublished work *Il sesto tomo dell'io* (The sixth volume of I), a fragmentary pseudo-autobiography that he drafted in 1799–1800. Ugo Foscolo, *Il sesto tomo dell'io*, edited by V. Di Benedetto (Turin, 1991), p. 19.

[50] In N. Katramis, 'Ougos Foskolos' (Ugo Foscolo), *Pandora* 282 (15 Dec. 1861), p. 442.

[51] Ugo Foscolo, *Sepulchres and Other Poems*, translated by J. G. Nichols (London, 2009), p. 15; Clauco Cambon, *Ugo Foscolo, Poet of Exile* (Princeton, 2014), pp. 21–2.

[52] In Vincent, *Ugo Foscolo: An Italian in Regency England*, p. 107. See also Kalvos, *Allilografia*, vol. I, p. 123.

Foscolo's nostalgia for Zante was also real, however. And it became less markedly poetical and more concrete with the establishment of the British protectorate over the Ionian Islands in 1815. By the Treaty of Paris of that year, Britain—which since 1810 had gained possession of all the Ionian Islands (except Corfu which was taken over only in 1814)—was officially proclaimed the protecting power of the islands, which were now united to form an 'independent' state, known as the United States of the Ionian Islands. It was indeed as a subject of this statelet protected by the British Empire that Foscolo obtained his passport to travel as an exile to England in 1816. In London, his Ionian British patriotism was only strengthened, since he became closely involved in certain Liberal-Whig circles, which saw the British control of the Ionian Islands as an occasion to experiment with new forms of government that could combine imperial protection with the principles of liberty. Foscolo took a lively interest in these discussions and voiced his views in a set of private memoranda (1817), where he argued for the creation of a confederal state of the Ionian Islands, which would be placed under British protection but granted a liberal constitution—only to see his hopes dashed once again, when the constitution which was conceded to the Ionian Islands later that year was little more than a formal recognition of the British High Commissioner's despotic power.[53]

Nonetheless, Foscolo's desire to return to Zante grew stronger, especially as news of the death of his mother and the small estate that she left behind on the island reached his ears in 1817. In addition, among the liberal circles of London, he had made the acquaintance of a philhellene scholar and linguist, Frederick North, Lord Guilford, who had conceived a plan to found a university in the British protectorate of the islands. Like many other Ionian intellectuals, Foscolo thought that Guilford's university might offer him the opportunity to settle permanently in the Ionian Islands—*my only asylum*, as he said in a letter to him. With this purpose in mind, or so it would seem, he also penned a memorandum on the state of public education on the islands.[54] Yet his plans were thwarted by the Austrian police, which in 1817 sent a note to the British authorities of Corfu warning about the dangers to the whole area posed by a possible return of the intractable exile.[55] So, while in due course Guilford's university was founded, Foscolo was not destined to benefit by it.

Nevertheless, Foscolo's Ionian patriotism continued to deepen as his disappointment with Britain grew. In 1819, the Zakynthian exile turned his attention to the unhappy story of the small town of Parga. Located on the coast of Epirus opposite the Ionian Islands, Parga had belonged to Venice along with the rest of the Ionian

---

[53] Ugo Foscolo, 'Stato politico delle Isole Ionie' and 'Come ottenere modifiche alla costituzione delle Isole Ionie', in idem, *Prose politiche e apologetiche (1817–1827)*, vol. I: *Scritti sulle Isole Ionie e su Parga*, edited by Giovanni Gambarin (Florence, 1964), pp. 3–37 and 44–55. See Biagini, 'Liberty, Class and Nation-Building', pp. 34–49; Maurizio Isabella, *Risorgimento in Exile: Italian Émigrés and the Liberal International in the Post-Napoleonic Era* (Oxford, 2009), pp. 70–1.

[54] FE, vol. 7, pp. 165–7. Idem, 'Mémoire sur l'éducation publique aux Isles Ioniennes', in idem, *Prose politiche e apologetiche*, vol. I, pp. 38–43. See Vincent, *Ugo Foscolo: An Italian in Regency England*, pp. 110–11.

[55] Polychronis K. Enepekidis, *Korais—Koumas—Kalvos—An. Gazis—Ougos Foskolos... etc.* (Athens, 1967), pp. 135–49.

area, with which it had long-standing economic and cultural ties. In 1800, when the Ionian Islands were declared a Russo-Ottoman protectorate, their mainland dependencies, including Parga, were placed under the direct rule of the Porte. However, the city became a garrison for French, and from 1814 onwards, for British troops. It was only in 1819 that Britain decided to comply with the treaty of 1800 and hand Parga over to Ali Pasha. The surrender, though, of a Christian town to a man already notorious for his massacres of Christian populations was to become a humanitarian issue, especially as the Christian inhabitants of Parga—who at one time or another had begged in vain for their city to be annexed to the Ionian Islands— started abandoning their homes en masse rather than submit to the Ottoman regime. The Parga affair outraged European public opinion and caught the attention of several politicians, intellectuals, and artists, who gave speeches, wrote memoranda, composed poems, or painted pictures in support of the Pargiots' cause. In the mouths of men like Foscolo and other Ionian expatriates (Ioannis Kapodistrias and Andrea Mustoxidi being some of them) or the Lombard exile Giovanni Berchet, the vicissitudes of that small town were soon to be turned into a powerful tool of philhellenic propaganda and of the cause of liberty of the southern European peoples in general.[56] Foscolo set to work to stir up his friends in and out of the British Parliament on this question. Supported by documents provided by Kapodistrias— with whom he organized a common political strategy on the affair—he also wrote fervent articles supporting the Pargiots' demand to be annexed to the Ionian Islands.[57] So, through these experiences Foscolo, like many other expatriate Ionians, became a philhellene and discovered not only his Ionian belonging but also his Greekness.

It is no surprise, then, that Greece features among the patrias of Foscolo's later years. Once his application to obtain permission to settle in the Ionian Islands had been rejected by the British authorities (which, after the Parga affair, suspected him of being a Russian agent), Foscolo indeed came up with a new idea: to go and fight for the liberation of Greece and to become a citizen of the newborn country. In the letter that he addressed to a member of the Greek revolutionary government in 1824—written entirely in his own peculiar idiomatic Greek—he claimed that he wanted to go and live amongst his Greek 'fellow-citizens' and even give his life in the struggle for the liberation of the country. The condition was that, since he would lose his British Ionian citizenship (because he would break the declared neutrality of the Ionian Islands in the context of the Greek revolution) and since, as a result,

[56] [Andrea Mustoxidi], *Exposé des faits qui ont précédé et suivi la cession de Parga* (Paris, 1820); Giovanni Berchet, *I profughi di Parga* (poem, 1821), in idem, *Poesie*, edited by Egidio Bellorini (Bari, 1941), pp. 3–5. See Natale Caccia, 'L'episodio di Parga in alcuni componimenti poetici francesi e inglesi', in *Studi sul Berchet, pubblicati per il primo centenario della morte* (Milan, 1951), pp. 389–417; Caterina Spetsieri Beschi, 'Il filellenismo italiano nelle arti figurative', in idem and Enrica Lucarelli (eds), *Risorgimento greco e filellenismo italiano: lotte, cultura, arte* (Rome, 1986), pp. 120–7.
[57] Ugo Foscolo, 'On Parga', *Edinburgh Review* 32/64 (Oct. 1819), now in idem, *Prose politiche e apologetiche*, vol. I, pp. 65–102; Kostas Kairofylas, 'Kapodistrias kai Foskolos' (Kapodistrias and Foscolo), *Imerologion tis Megalis Ellados* 8/8 (1929), pp. 161–86. For an account of Foscolo's activities in regard to Parga see Isabella, *Risorgimento in Exile*, pp. 70–7; Vincent, *Ugo Foscolo: An Italian in Regency England*, pp. 111–15.

he was going to forfeit the property he held in Zante, the Greek authorities should recognize him as a citizen and offer him a job.[58]

Nobody knows what happened to Foscolo's application to become Greek. It was probably lost somewhere among the warring factions of the revolutionary government during the Greek civil war. What we do know is that a couple of years later, in 1826, the exiled poet addressed another letter to a relative in Zante, in which he assured him that he would soon return to his native island to be buried *under Greek soil.*[59] This was only a few months before death found him in Chiswick, by no means old (he had not even turned 50), poor, exhausted by an advanced oedema, and harried by his creditors, though endeavouring to escape their attentions by living under yet another assumed name. Foscolo breathed his last in 1827, in the arms of his 20-year-old daughter, whose very existence had only recently been revealed to him. He never returned to Zante; he never returned to Italy; he never returned to Greece. Having passed, as he did, from the Venetian Zakynthian to the Italian patria, and from there back to the British Ionian and then to the Greek patria, Foscolo's transnationalism was condemned to remain forever unfulfilled and utopian.

---

[58]  FE, vol. 9, pp. 381–3. This is the second of only two known letters drafted by Foscolo entirely in Greek. The first was addressed to a committee of Pargiots (1818) and, interestingly, was signed using the Greek transliteration of his Italian name, Ούγων Φώσκολος. See Kairofylas, 'Kapodistrias kai Foskolos', pp. 163, 169.

[59]  To Dionisio Bulzo. In De Biasi, *O Ougos Foskolos kai i elliniki epanastasis*, pp. 34–5.

# 2

# The Staggering of Andreas Kalvos

## THE MULTIPLE LIVES OF CALBO/KALVOS

I will now turn to the second character in our story, Andreas Kalvos—who was not actually born as 'Andreas Kalvos', but as 'Andrea Calbo': this is the name that his family used, even when they wrote it in Greek (*Κάλμπο*). He was born to Greek Ionian parents from noble Zakynthian and Corfiot families in 1792, that is, fourteen years after Foscolo. When he was born, the Venetian Republic had not yet collapsed. But when he reached 5 he could probably already hear the singing of the *Marseillaise* outside his Zakynthian window. He could no doubt see the people planting the 'Tree of Liberty' in the central square of the island, or declaiming the *Thourios* of Velestinlis, one of the very first Greek patriotic poems, as I have said, printed in those years in the newly established publishing house of the Ionian Islands. Nevertheless, by the time little Andrea turned 7, Zante was already part of the Septinsular Republic under a joint Russo-Ottoman protectorate. He was not destined to see so very much in Zante, because in 1802, when he was 10, his parents separated and his father took his two sons and moved to Livorno, where Andrea's uncle was established as a consul. It was there then, in that Italian port of Tuscany, with its prosperous and deep-rooted Greek community, that little Andrea, amidst economic and family difficulties, would be taught his first letters. As in the case of Foscolo, the early separation from Zante transformed that place into a mythical and nostalgic 'topos' in Calbo's imagination, standing in his poetry as the symbol of an ever-distant patria: *O, beloved land, | o, wondrous isle, | Zante, you who gave me | life, and Apollo's | golden gifts… May fate not | decree my grave abroad; | death is sweet | only when we sleep | in our land*—read some of his most famous verses, in fact written long afterwards, in 1824, when the poet was in exile from Florence to Geneva.[1]

If for Foscolo the pivotal year was 1797, when Napoleon entered Italy and the Adriatic, sealing their fates once and for all, for Calbo it was 1812 and 1817 that loomed large: these were the dates when he met Foscolo and when their paths diverged. The two met in Florence and the by then famous Zakynthian took a liking to this young man who, as he put it, *knows Italian like a Tuscan, and some French and Greek.*[2] So he decided to take him under his wing, as his amanuensis and student. The 20-year-old provincial and self-educated boy could hardly have

---

[1] Ode 'The Patriot'. In Andreas Kalvos, *Odes*, translated by George Dandoulakis (Nottingham, 1998), p. 18.
[2] FE, vol. 4, p. 382.

hoped for a better turn of events. Under his celebrated compatriot's guidance—on long walks in the hills of Florence, one of Foscolo's happiest places of exile—young Andrea studied the ancient Greek and Latin languages, read the Italian and French classics, transcribed texts, and helped Foscolo with his translations of Sicilian poetry. He even started composing his own verses and writing his first Neoclassical and Alfierian tragedies, thus following in the footsteps of his illustrious teacher: a hymn to Napoleon (written in 1811 but later, naturally, repudiated) was followed by an *Ode to the Ionians* (1814)—where Ionian *amor patrio* mingled with a vague Italian and ancient Greek patriotism, vouchsafed the young man's fervent anti-tyrannical stance and love for freedom—and by the tragedy *Teramene* (Theramenes), which was unsuccessfully submitted to a competition at the Crusca Academy (1813).[3] The apprenticeship with Foscolo was so enriching that in spring 1816 Calbo took his *trunk full of books* and followed his teacher into exile in Switzerland and, after some months, in England.[4] The idyll with Foscolo did not last, however. The end of summer 1816 found the two in London, and sadly estranged. We do not know the reasons for this breach, but it must have been violent and traumatic, since from that moment on, teacher and student never exchanged another word.

Thus, in the winter of 1817, without even realizing quite how, Calbo found himself in London, without a job, and alone. Thanks mainly to Foscolo, he gained access to the Liberal-Whig circles of the capital, and there he found students prepared to pay for private lessons in Italian, French, and Modern Greek. Among his students were British and Italian orientalists, Hellenists, antiquarians, and philhellenes, as well as a member of Parliament, Charles Monck, whom Calbo helped to compile an English–Modern Greek dictionary (despite his obvious shortcomings in Modern Greek).[5] For the purposes of these lessons he started composing his voluminous handbook *Italian Lessons* which, besides an Italian grammar and translation exercises, contained a tragedy by Alfieri, extracts from Tasso, Ariosto, Petrarch, and Dante, and alongside all these, without undue modesty, a new tragedy written by Calbo himself (the *Danaidi*).[6] He was also allegedly preparing a Modern Greek–English dictionary (which however never saw the light of day), while at the same time he wrote a Modern Greek grammar.[7] Aside from teaching, Calbo also frequented certain circles of Italian exiles, who were admirers of the British system of government and with whom the Zakynthian published a

---

[3] Camillo Antona-Traversi, *Una lettera inedita di Ugo Foscolo e una canzone inedita di Andrea Calbo* (Rome, 1884); Georgios Zoras, 'Andreou Kalvou, Odi eis Ionious' (Andrea Calbo, Ode to the Ionians), *Nea estia* 21/248 (15 Apr. 1937), pp. 564–75; Dimitris Arvanitakis, 'O *Thiramenis* tou Andrea Kalvou: ena athelito work in progress' (The *Theramenes* of Andrea Calbo: an unintended work in progress), *Ta istorika* 29/57 (Dec. 2012), pp. 345–66.

[4] Andreas Kalvos, *Allilografia* (Correspondence), edited by Dimitris Arvanitakis and Lefkios Zafeiriou (Athens, 2014), vol. I, pp. 196 and 108 respectively.

[5] These are obvious in the correspondence he maintained with his students in Modern Greek. For example, Kalvos, *Allilografia*, vol. I, p. 297. See also Nasos Vagenas, 'Paramorfoseis tou Kalvou' (Contortions of Kalvos), *To dentro* 71–2 (Sept.–Oct. 1992), p. 136.

[6] Andrea Calbo, *Le Danaidi* (London, 1818).

[7] It was included in Frederick Nolan, *A Harmonical Grammar of the Principal Ancient and Modern Languages*, Part I (London, 1822).

journal called *L'ape italiana*.[8] As far as his personal education was concerned, it appears that during these same years Calbo started reading a variety of modern Greek books, which were in the course of being printed around this date or earlier in north Italy and in central Europe—such as the *Ellinikon Lexikon* (Greek Dictionary) by Anthimos Gazis (1809–16), the history of the Peloponnesian War by Thucydides translated into Modern Greek by Neofytos Doukas (1805–6), a Greek translation of the New Testament (dated much earlier, in 1638), and William Martin Leake's *Researches in Greece* (1814), to mention just a few.[9] What is more important, in the same period the young Zakynthian read Byron, certainly *Childe Harold's Pilgrimage*, but possibly also other poems with Greek and oriental subjects, such as *The Giaour, The Bride of Abydos*, or *The Corsair*, which had been printed only a few years before and had made their author famous overnight. We should indeed bear in mind that philhellenism loomed large in these years in Britain, as did the cult of Byron, and with it the emergence of a new image of Greece and of its modern inhabitants. It was in fact in 1817 that the British Museum welcomed the Parthenon marbles, while shortly afterwards the Parga affair would outrage those in liberal and philhellenic circles—not least Sir Charles Monck, the student of Calbo and the friend of Foscolo, who in May 1819 brought up the question in the House of Commons.[10]

It is within this cultural climate then, that we have to imagine the young Andrea Calbo, who had apparently gained sufficient popularity among the intellectual circles of London to be invited to deliver a series of public lectures in 1818 and 1819 in the city's famous Argyll Rooms. The lectures, which were reported extensively in the press, concerned the subject of the modern Greek language and its relation to the ancient Greek pronunciation. More specifically—and as a press article informed the public—*[Calbo's] object was to show that though the purity of the tongue has been debased, the pronunciation remains the same as in the most classic times.*[11] Ideas about the continuity of ancient Greek with the modern Greek language were then commonplace among Greek diaspora intellectuals and philhellenes, but Calbo was among the first to specifically claim that the pronunciation in classical times (that is, from the fifth century to the death of Alexander in 323 BCE) was identical to that to be found in the modern period. Calbo joined the cohort of authors arguing that the Greek language had survived uninterrupted from ancient times to the present, thus proving an identity between ancient and modern Greeks and the integrity of the language currently spoken.[12] By so doing, he also entered

---

[8] Dimitris Arvanitakis, *Ston dromo gia tis patrides: i 'Ape Italiana', o Andreas Kalvos, i istoria* (On the road to the patrias: the 'Ape Italiana', Andreas Kalvos and history) (Athens, 2010).

[9] See the letter of his bookseller in Kalvos, *Allilografia*, vol. I, pp. 258–9.

[10] On the impact of Byron on Kalvos see Athina Georganta, *Ta thavmasia nera, Andreas Kalvos: o romantismos, o Byronismos kai o kosmos ton karmponaron* (The exquisite waters, Andreas Kalvos: Romanticism, Byronism and the world of the carbonari) (Athens, 2011); On *Byromania*: Frances Wilson (ed.), *Byromania: Portraits of the Artist in Nineteenth- and Twentieth-Century Culture* (New York, 1999); David Roessel, *In Byron's Shadow: Modern Greece in the English and American Imagination* (Oxford, 2002); Antoine Lilti, *The Invention of Celebrity, 1750–1850* (Cambridge, 2017), pp. 219–23.

[11] *New Monthly Magazine and Universal Register* (July 1818), p. 548.

[12] Indicatively, Enrico Mayer [Ellenofilo], 'Cenni sulla lingua romaica', *Antologia* 4 (Oct.–Dec. 1821), pp. 438–54; Andrea Mustoxidi, 'Alcune considerazioni sulla presente lingua de' Greci', *Antologia* 17 (Jan.–Mar. 1825), pp. 44–73.

the hotly contested linguistic disputes, in which Greek and Italian men of letters were alike engaged. Following the line of Panagiotis Kodrikas, an Athenian-born Phanariot and secretary in the Ottoman embassy in Paris who had just published a *Study of the Common Hellenic Dialect* (1818), Calbo argued that the traditional written language used by the Christian Orthodox Church hierarchy and the Phanariots, handed down as it had been from generation to generation, and elevated above all local dialects, was the best kind of written Greek then available, and accepted as such by the whole nation.[13] He thereby also built upon an argument drawn from Dante but further refined by several Italian intellectuals during the heated linguistic battles of Italy in the first decades of the nineteenth century, according to which the national language can be found, not in the spoken and territorially confined dialects, but in the written word of the great authors and in the living language of the political institutions. As we will have the chance to see also in Chapter 10, the Greek and Italian language questions—which were not only philological and literary issues, but more especially social and national ones—though they addressed different problems, nevertheless shared certain features and were intertwined in the writings of a number of Ionian intellectuals and Italian philhellenes.[14]

It was at this point then, in 1819, that Calbo decided to write his first poem in Greek. The initial verses of the poem, which he signed now as *Ανδρέας Κάλβος Ιωαννίδης, Ζακύνθιος* (Andreas Kalvos of Ioannis, Zakynthian)—hellenizing thus not only his name but also that of his father—are indicative of his decision: *In solemn duty, yet in fearful awe, | For the first time I make my fingers fall | Across the silver strings of the cithara, | Legacy of my fathers.*[15] The ode was accompanied by a letter (in Greek) to Lord Guilford, to whom the poem was dedicated, along with the wish that his lordship enjoy a safe voyage to the Ionian Islands. That was the year when Guilford was appointed as the chancellor of the Ionian Academy (to be opened some years later, in 1824, on Corfu) and Kalvos, just like Foscolo, hoped to be allowed to play a part in its founding—with a far greater measure of success than his former teacher, as we shall see below.[16] So, it was there, in London, and in his mid-twenties, that Kalvos decided to become a Greek poet: after rejecting Foscolo, discovering modern Greek literature, listening to the promptings of *Byromania* and of British philhellenism, and resting his hopes on the creation of the first Greek university in his native land.

---

[13] Kalvos, *Allilografia*, vol. II, pp. 142–50; K. Th. Demaras, 'Gyro ston Kalvo kai ton Kodrika (scholiasmena keimena)' (On Kalvos and Kodrikas (commentated texts)), in idem, *Ellinikos romantismos* (Greek Romanticism) (Athens, 1982), pp. 116–29; Peter Mackridge, *Language and National Identity in Greece, 1766–1976* (Oxford, 2009), pp. 133–42.

[14] Dimitris Arvanitakis, 'Scholia gia tis proypotheseis tou solomikou *Dialogou*' (Comments on the prerequisites of Solomos's *Dialogue*), in Giorgos K. Myaris (ed.), *Dionysios Solomos (150 chronia apo ton thanato tou poiiti)* (Nicosia, 2011), pp. 101–50. On the Italian language question see Stefania De Stefanis Ciccone, *La questione della lingua nei periodici letterari del primo Ottocento* (Florence, 1971).

[15] Andreas Kalvos Ioannidis, *Elpis Patridos: odi en ti ton nyn Ellinon dialekto* (Hope of the Patria, ode in the language of modern Greeks) (London, 1819), cordially translated by Nick Moschovakis.

[16] Kalvos, *Allilografia*, vol. II, pp. 150–1, 180–1; Arvanitakis, *Ston dromo gia tis patrides*, pp. 176–9.

The rest of the story is more or less predictable. In two years, the Greek revolution would break out. Kalvos, in the following years (1823–6) an exile first in Geneva and then Paris—and we will see below why—was actively involved in the philhellenic movement. In Geneva he met distraught refugees arriving from Wallachia after the unsuccessful initial outbreak of the Greek revolution in the Danubian Principalities, even as, in shock and disbelief, news of the death of Lord Byron in Missolonghi reached his ears. In that same year (1824) he published the first of the two collections of his Greek odes, ten out of the twenty masterpieces that earned him a place among Greece's pantheon of poets. Entitled *I lyra* (The Lyre), the publication—which was soon translated and published in French—included an ode *To the Sacred Band* (the contingent of Greek revolutionaries in Wallachia), one *To Parga*, another *To Chios* (which had suffered the notorious massacre), and one *To Liberty*.[17] In Paris, where he moved later that year, Kalvos kept up his philhellenic and liberal activity, writing for, among others, some of the most popular French journals. In an article that he penned in 1825 for the *Globe*, where he expressed his disappointment at Italy's apparent incapacity to win independence, he set the parameters of what he now thought was the poet's mission: to promote social and political values by means of a poetry which was militant and patriotic.[18] As a matter of fact, his second collection of odes, entitled *Ta lyrika* (The Lyrics) and published in Paris in 1826, began with a dedication to General Lafayette—the hero of revolutionary transnationalism and symbol of global freedom of those years—and included poems of a patriotic, liberal, and philhellenic character (among others, an ode on the death of Lord Byron), all written in a committed and 'serious tone' (*ton sérieux*—to use Kalvos's own words from his article in the *Globe*).[19]

However, there was something still torturing the Italian, now Greek poet: *I feel bitterness at not having been able up until now, and perhaps not in the future, to serve my patria*—wrote Kalvos to a friend in Greece in 1825. *I assure you, my worthy friend, that I would willingly have served as an ordinary soldier. Whenever I hear that a foreigner is setting out for Greece, my heart bleeds. I hardly dare to say that I am Greek, lest I am asked the question that would devastate me so: why do I too not go and share in the dangers afflicting my patria?*[20] As I will show also in Chapter 8 of this book, the revolution in Greece caused similar disquiet to a number of Ionian diaspora intellectuals, who now identified themselves as Greeks. Sometimes these questions—more often voiced in Italian than in Greek, as in Kalvos's letter—were

---

[17] Andreas Kalvos Ioannidis, Zakynthios, *I lyra* (Geneva, 1824). The French translation: *La Lyre patriotique de la Grèce, odes traduites du Grèc moderne de Kalvos de Zante; par Stanislas Julien* (Paris, 1818).

[18] C** de Zante [Andreas Kalvos], 'Il poeta di teatro | Le Poète de théâtre. Par F. Pananti', *Le Globe* 160 (20 Sept. 1825), p. 1. On this see Mario Vitti, *O Kalvos kai i epochi tou* (Kalvos and his times) (Athens, 1995), pp. 91–111. On the modern notion of 'poetry's mission', crafted by Romantic and liberal poets at the beginning of the nineteenth century, see Paul Bénichou, *The Consecration of the Writer, 1750–1830* (Lincoln, Nebr., and London, 1999), esp. pp. 189–90, 218ff., 336–9.

[19] It was a bilingual edition (French–Greek) and included also some poems by Athanasios Christopoulos: *Kalvou kai Christopoulou, Lyrika* (in French: *Odes nouvelles de Kalvos de Zante, suivies d'un choix des poésies de Chrestopoulo, traduites par l'auteur des Helléniennes, P. de C. (J. P. G. Pauthier)*) (Paris, 1826).

[20] Kalvos, *Allilografia*, vol. II, p. 313.

left unanswered: they remained disturbing aspects of lives which were irrevocably unfolding elsewhere. Kalvos's case, however, was different. Unlike Foscolo, the Zakynthian poet was given a real chance to go and fight in Greece. In 1826 he was sent there as a delegate of the philhellenic committee of Paris. He arrived in Nafplio in June of that year, but instead of staying to fight *as an ordinary soldier*, he preferred to head to the Ionian state, where he could do what he knew best, namely, teach Italian. What remain from the two months or so that Kalvos spent in Greece are only a couple of reports on the fortunes of the revolution that he submitted to the *Revue encyclopédique*, which, however, went missing.[21] Kalvos spent the next twenty-five years of his life as a professor of Italian philology and philosophy on Corfu, sharing his time between the Ionian Academy (where he was successful in obtaining a post in 1827) and his private classroom.[22]

## THE 'STAGGERING OF A STRICT AND FORMAL MAN'

*The gaps [in Kalvos] are as disconcerting as the staggering of a strict and formal man*— Seferis wrote. There are indeed in Kalvos's biography some details which do not fit into the story of a national poet's life. The first is the fact that even after his initiation into Greek poetry, Kalvos continued to write and publish works in Italian. This is the case with the Alfierian tragedy *Ippia* (Hippias), which he drafted in 1820–1, but it is also true of an unfinished tragedy named by researchers *Abantida* (Abantidas), which according to some chronologies was penned in the same period. On the other hand, his earlier tragedy *Danaidi*, initially published in 1818, was republished in 1820 and signed with his Italian name, Andrea Calbo.[23]

But what is more important, so far as the transnational patriotic principles that inspired Kalvos and several other intellectuals of his generation are concerned, is another biographical detail: in March and April 1821, when, that is, the revolts of Naples and Piedmont were being suppressed and the revolution in the Morea was just beginning, Kalvos was not in Greece alongside the insurgents, nor did he show any intention of being so. He was in Florence, where he was put on trial as a member of the Italian carbonari, a clandestine association which fought for the liberation of Italy and, with it, for the rest of the world. It was in his quality as a carbonaro that Kalvos was sent into exile in Geneva—the centre, besides, of the international carboneria at the time. It is even more telling that one year after his expulsion from Florence, in 1822, Kalvos submitted a petition to the Tuscan authorities asking to be permitted to return to Tuscany which, *despite being born in Zante*, he *considered to be his patria*. In other words, it was from the viewpoint of a

[21] Kalvos, *Allilografia*, vol. II, pp. 326–43.

[22] Georgios Typaldos-Iakobatos, *Istoria tis Ioniou Akadimias* (History of the Ionian Academy), edited by Sp. Asdrachas (Athens, 1982), pp. 57–8.

[23] It was included in Andrea Calbo, *Italian Lessons in Four Parts* (London, 1820). Lefkios Zafeiriou, *O bios kai to ergo tou Andrea Kalvou (1792–1869)* (The life and works of Andreas Kalvos) (Athens, 2006), p. 66; Michail Paschalis, *Xanadiabazontas ton Kalvo: o Andreas Kalvos, i Italia kai i archaiotita* (Rereading Kalvos: Andreas Kalvos, Italy and antiquity) (Herakleion, 2013), p. 171.

Tuscan, and more broadly an Italian, exile that Kalvos composed in Geneva, in the space of two short years, his Greek national odes. Had he not been denied re-entrance into Tuscany, some scholars have commented, Kalvos might not have become a Greek poet.[24]

Another 'detail' in Kalvos's biography which has been perplexing researchers is the fact that from the moment that the poet set foot in the Ionian Islands, that is from 1826 and until his death (for a total of forty-three years), he never wrote a piece of poetry again, Greek or Italian—or at least this is what the findings suggest. In addition, in 1852, when he was already 60 years old, Kalvos decided to board a ship and leave the Ionian Islands once and for all. At an age at which people often repatriate, Kalvos chose to expatriate once more. This time he headed for London, where he married a British woman some twenty years his junior, with whom he opened a girls' school and settled down.[25] In England he spent the remaining eighteen years of his life, without ever—as far as we know—writing a single letter to his friends in Italy, in Greece, or in the Ionian Islands. Death found him in Louth, where he had moved with his wife some years earlier. He was buried according to the rite of the Anglican Church, to which he had apparently converted. *Andrew Kalvo* was a *Professor of Languages and Mathematics*, his death certificate declared. Nobody remembered him as an Italian or a Greek poet. *Maybe Kalvos wanted, after all, to burn all bridges behind him*—Seferis's insightful pen commented; *maybe he wanted to be left alone to die in that green graveyard of St Margaret's.*[26]

[24] Nasos Vagenas, 'Mia eftichis aporripsi' (A happy rejection), *To Bima* newspaper (18 June 2006); See also Kalvos, *Allilografia*, vol. II, pp. 282–92. On the trial of Kalvos as a carbonaro see Porfyris, *O Andreas Kalvos karmponaros*.

[25] Lefkios Zafeiriou, 'Charlotte Augusta Kalvo (Wadams) kai Andreas Kalvos apo tin Kerkyra sto Londino kai sto Louth: nea stoicheia' (Charlotte Augusta Kalvo (Wadams) and Andreas Kalvos from Corfu to London and Louth: new elements), *Porfyras* 147–8 (Apr.–Sept. 2013), pp. 43–53.

[26] Giorgos Seferis, 'Kalvos, 1960', in idem, *Dokimes*, edited by G. P. Savvides (Athens, 1981), vol. II: *1948–1971*, p. 129.

# 3

## Dionysios Solomos
### A Life in Translation

## A LIFE IN TRANSLATION

Let us go now to the last figure to feature in this story, Dionysios Solomos—who was not actually born as 'Dionysios Solomos', but as 'Dionisio Salamon'.[1] We are now in 1798 and in a world that differed profoundly from the one into which Foscolo had been born twenty years before. The *Serenissima* was already a thing of the past and people in Zante were celebrating Napoleon's triumphs in the Adriatic and the radical break with their old world. Of course, some things could not change so easily. Venice had left its enduring legacies on the islands, especially as regards language, law, and education. Old cultural geographies persisted as well-to-do families continued to send their sons to Italy for their studies and Italian continued to be the dominant language of culture. Italian remained the de facto language of administration and justice for at least another half-century. Despite consecutive declarations in the constitutions that regulated the political status of the Ionian Islands every time they passed to a new ruler in the immediate post-Venetian period (the French constitution of 1799, the 1803 Russian constitution, and the 1817 constitution under the British—all, save the first, drafted in Italian), the law proclaiming Greek to be the official language of the state was applied fully only in the second half of the century.[2] In the courts the use of Greek became obligatory only in 1836, while the juridical codes continued to be drafted in Italian until 1851. Only in 1849 did Greek replace Italian in administrative matters and in legal process, while until 1848 the dominant language of the parliamentary sessions was Italian.[3] And even then, some people had difficulty coping with the

---

[1] I borrow for the subtitle of this chapter the definition by Isabelle de Courtivron in her (ed.), *Lives in Translation: Bilingual Writers on Identity and Creativity* (London, 2003).

[2] Peter Mackridge, 'Peri boulis kai gerousias: o Platon Petridis kai i "neoelliniki" metafrasi tou ioniou syntagmatos tou 1817' (On parliament and senate: Platon Petridis and the translation into 'Modern Greek' of the 1817 Ionian Constitution), in St. Kaklamanis, Al. Kalokairinos, and D. Polychronakis (eds), *Logos kai chronos sti neoelliniki grammateia (18os–19os aionas)* (Word and time in modern Greek literature (18th–19th centuries)) (Herakleion, 2015), pp. 157–70.

[3] Peter Mackridge, 'Venise après Venise: Official Languages in the Ionian Islands, 1797–1864', *Byzantine and Modern Greek Studies* 38/1 (Mar. 2014), pp. 68–90; Konstantinos E. Soldatos, 'I ethniki glossa eis tin Eptanison' (The national language on the Ionian Islands), *Kerkyraika chronika* 13 (1967); Theodosis Pylarinos, *Glossikos patriotismos: oi agones gia tin kathierosi tis glossas tou ellinikou laou ktl.* (Linguistic patriotism: the battles for the establishment of the language of the Greek people etc.) (Corfu, 2013).

new regulations: this was the case with a Zakynthian deputy who, in one of the last sessions of the 1848 parliamentary season, excused himself for making a speech in Italian, because *although he ardently desires the general extension of the national language, he unfortunately confesses his inability to speak it freely, since he has had no cause to practise it.*[4] Andrea Mustoxidi, by then one of the Ionian state's most prominent politicians, had solid grounds then in 1839 to complain that *The citizen sees himself dragged before the courts, accused, defended, judged over matters of substance, condemned where life and liberty are at stake in a language that he does not know, and through laws that have never even been translated. And why? Because a portion of those who enjoy a monopoly over public affairs, a residue or emanation of Venetian education, speak the language of Harlequin and Pantaloon. And for thirty who stammer Italian, we sacrifice national honour, and the interests of almost two hundred thousand men.*[5] As we will see again in the epilogue of this book, proposals about language were also a way of challenging the local Venetian social order and of redefining the relations of the islands with the opposite shore of the Adriatic.

Among those few who were still *stammering Italian* was certainly Dionisio Salamon (and Mustoxidi likewise). All but four of the surviving letters in Salamon's hand, dating to various periods of his life, were composed in Italian, including (curiously) those addressed to his illiterate Greek mother. Moreover, in complete disregard for Greek orthographical rules, these few Greek letters follow a phonetic and colloquial writing.[6] Dionisio was the son of an aged Greek Zakynthian count and a much younger plebeian woman who had served as the countess's maid before becoming the count's wife. When he was 9 his father died and the boy was placed in the custody of his private tutor, an exile from Cremona, in northern Italy, who in 1808 returned to his country and was instructed to take Dionisio with him. So, young Salamon went to school at Venice and Cremona and took up higher studies at the University of Pavia. During the same period, he started shyly to compose his first verses in Latin and Italian, which were assigned to him as educational exercises by his teachers, who professed astonishment at their brilliance. These early poems were mostly imitations of the religious verses of Vincenzo Monti and Alessandro Manzoni, by then two of Italy's leading poets and authors, with whom young Salamon soon became acquainted. In the Milan of the post-Napoleonic years, then under Austrian occupation, Salamon also had the chance to follow closely the intense controversy between Classicists and Romanticists and to become friends with one of the key figures of the Romantic circle, Giuseppe Montani.[7]

---

[4] From the parliamentary proceedings. In Mackridge, 'Venise après Venise', p. 86. See also Nikolaos Pantazopoulos, 'Ethniko fronima, glossa kai dikaio sto Ionio kratos prin tin ensomatosi' (National spirit, language, and law in the Ionian state before incorporation), in Panagiotis Moschonas (ed.), *To Ionio kratos, 1815–1864* (The Ionian state, 1815–1864) (Athens, 1997), pp. 364–5.

[5] Andrea Mustoxidi, *Sulla condizione attuale delle Isole Ionie: promemoria presentato in agosto 1839 etc.* (London, 1840), pp. 8–9.

[6] Dionysios Solomos, *Allilografia* (Correspondence), edited by Linos Politis (Athens, 1991), pp. 101, 116, 118, 119. Linos Politis, 'I grafi kai i orthografia tou Solomou' (Solomos's writing and orthography), in idem, *Gyro sto Solomo: meletes kai arthra (1938–1982)* (Around Solomos: studies and articles (1938–1982)) (Athens, 1995), pp. 47–57.

[7] Louis Coutelle, *Formation poétique de Solomos (1815–1833)* (Athens, 1977), pp. 11–26.

It was Montani who encouraged him to stay in the Ionian Islands when Dionisio, upon his graduation in 1818, went back to Zante for what he thought would be a short vacation: *Goodbye then, my dear Dionisio, goodbye! You at least will see again a patria, one that can truly call itself such; even though the external protection is almost a cloak of servitude. But in the end the laws are yours, the arms are yours and the government is yours; once rights have been recognized you will reawaken virtue*—Montani wrote to him, in a passage implying a reference to the recently founded 'independent' Ionian state under British protection. In connecting poetry with patriotism, he exhorted the aspiring poet to stay in the Ionian Islands and to try to become useful to his country: *Patriotism will be a sublime inspiration to you, and the better poet you are, the better citizen you will be and will regard yourself as being.*[8] It is little wonder perhaps that Salamon stayed forever on the Ionian Islands—undertaking only one trip in his life (and this was when he left Zante to go and settle on Corfu in 1828).

The first years in Zante were spent between acts of Ionian patriotism—Salamon's name features on the list of Zakynthian notables who in 1821 signed a petition calling for liberal reforms from the British government—and intellectual sociability. Salamon was soon incorporated into a circle of Zakynthian intelligentsia who passed whole afternoons improvising poetry in Italian. One fruit of these gatherings was the only book of his poems ever printed during his lifetime, *Rime improvvisate*, a collection of Italian-language sonnets supposedly sent to press by his friend Lodovico Strani (1822). The collection was preceded by a letter of dedication to Ugo Foscolo, where the author (allegedly Strani) urged the famous Zakynthian to encourage Salamon *to spare no pains in studying ancient Greek in order to draw from it greater riches of language, so that by so doing, by writing the mother tongue, he will be more ours than you yourself are.* At the same time, he asked the celebrated poet to excuse the young Zakynthian for still writing poetry in Italian and explained that, while he did that *in order to please his circle of friends*, in the meantime he *devotes himself to forming the modern Greek Language.*[9]

In fact, from his return to Zante onwards, Salamon tried now and then to write poems in Greek. It appears, however, that it was only in 1823 that he consciously decided to become a Greek (and actually a national) poet, repositioning himself so that he was no longer on the eastern periphery of the Italian world but rather on the western periphery of the Greek world. It took him a long time to get this far. This was indeed a very slow process, a gradual transformation which is highlighted in the successive variations of his own name—from the Italian 'Dionisio Salamon', to the semi-Hellenized 'Dionisio Solomòs' (from 1828 onwards in the letters he wrote in Italian), to the Greek 'Διονύσιος Σολωμός' (Dionysios Solomos), with which he published his Greek works beginning with the *Hymn to Liberty*.[10]

There were various reasons for Solomos's decision to reinvent himself as a Greek poet. First and foremost, the outbreak of the Greek revolution and, especially,

---

[8] Solomos, *Allilografia*, p. 455.

[9] Conte Dionisio Salamon Zacintio, *Rime improvvisate* (Corfu, 1822), preface.

[10] Peter Mackridge, 'Dionisio Salamon/Dionysios Solomos: Poetry as a Dialogue between Languages', *Dialogos* 1 (1994), pp. 60–1.

the terrible shadow it cast on Zante. Solomos saw the wretched refugees from Missolonghi arriving on the island and felt the earth trembling under his feet from the cannonades of the first siege of the city in 1822. No wonder that he dedicated some of his later Greek masterpieces, such as the *Free Besieged* and the *Woman of Zakynthos*, to that very subject. What is more, when Solomos was in Zante, Byron made a brief visit to the Ionian Islands on his way to Greece. There is no evidence that the two met (Byron stayed in Zante for only one day), but certainly the 'Byronic icon', so sophisticatedly constructed around the Greek cause, must have been particularly inspiring for the young Zakynthian. It is not surprising that on the death of the British poet one year later, Solomos composed an *Ode on the Death of Lord Byron* (written out in parallel columns of Greek and Italian), which he sought in vain to publish in London and Paris.

If the tumultuous experience of the Greek revolution and the waves of European philhellenism occasioned by it had a major impact on Solomos's decision to transform himself into a Greek national poet, this metamorphosis was further advanced by his encounter with Spyridon Trikoupis (1788–1873), a key figure during the revolution, a poet, historiographer, and later Prime Minister of Greece. Trikoupis arrived in Zante towards the end of 1822 at the invitation of Guilford and—if we are to take his claims at face value—with the mission to initiate Solomos into the national cause. He had just published in Paris a poem in Greek (*Dimos, a Klephtic poem*)—*written for the people and in the language of the people*, as a footnote in the first page explained. Solomos, who expressed regret that he did not know the Greek language sufficiently well to write in it, accepted Trikoupis's offer to assist him. So, they began studying the extant Greek poetic traditions: medieval literature written in vernacular Greek (Cretan and Zakynthian), Phanariot poetry, and folk songs. Solomos also read the *Lyrical Works* of Christopoulos and the radical linguistic theories of Yianis Vilaras on the phonetic grammar of the Greek vernacular, which had been published only a few years earlier.[11] One story has it that Trikoupis advised the young poet as follows: *Your poetic genius reserves you a special place in the Italian Parnassus. But the first places there are already taken. The Greek Parnassus has not yet found its Dante.*[12] Whether Trikoupis really uttered these words matters little. What matters is the fact that the Greek nation offered a signal opportunity for a career in poetry, as Solomos was quick to realize. His 'recruitment' by Trikoupis into the Greek national cause showed its first (and most enduring) sign in the *Hymn to Liberty*, a 158-stanza Greek patriotic and philhellenic poem, which Solomos composed in 1823. The poem—first published between two sieges in Missolonghi in 1824 with an Italian prose translation on the opposite page, and then in 1825 in English and

[11] Athanasios Christopoulos, *Ta lyrika* (The lyrical works) (Vienna, 1811); Yiannis Vilaras, *I romeiki glosa* (The romaic language) (Corfu, 1814).
[12] See Iakovos Polylas, 'Prolegomena' (Preface), in Dionysios Solomos, *Ta ebriskomena* (The found works), edited by Iakovos Polylas (Corfu, 1859), p. ιζ'. Polylas's text was based on a letter that he received from Trikoupis, now in Octave Merlier, *Exposition du centenaire de Solomos* (Athens, 1957), pp. 187–91 (quote on p. 190). On Trikoupis's influence on Solomos see also Giorgos Veloudis, *O Solomos ton Ellinon. Ethniki poiisi kai ideologia: mia politiki anagnosi* (Solomos of the Greeks. National poetry and ideology: a political reading) (Athens, 2004), pp. 73–6.

French translations—won Solomos international recognition as a philhellene and Greek poet. In reality—save for some poetic fragments published in local Ionian journals—this was the only completed Greek work that Solomos ever published. However, it was enough to establish him as Greece's national poet.[13]

Another factor weighing heavily in Solomos's decision to turn to Greek poetry was a negative criticism that he received in 1824 for his *Rime improvvisate* (which saw a second edition in 1823) in the pages of a well-respected Florentine journal, the *Antologia*. By then Solomos had, of course, turned his attention to the Greek language and finished composing his *Hymn to Liberty*, but he kept an eye on Italy also, still craving recognition from its literary luminaries. The author of the criticism was Solomos's old friend Montani. In reiterating his earlier comments to Solomos about the patriotic mission of the poet, he criticized the latter's persistence in writing Italian poems, a 'betrayal', as he said, of the poet's principles and of his expressed intention to leave Italy and to devote himself to his country's freedom and to the creation of the modern Greek poetic language.[14] Montani's criticism, which in a certain sense represented the rejection of the 'Italian Salamon' by Italy, must have been crucial in determining the path that Solomos would eventually take.

The result was that Solomos, in accordance with Montani's wishes, became not only a Greek, but also a national poet. In recent years, scholars have advanced a set of claims about how, in the universe of modern Greek literature, the very concept of the 'national poet' was coined through a process of formalization and institutionalization of poetry and of the role of the poet, which took place in the years around the mid-nineteenth century. This phenomenon was indeed first precipitated by Solomos's own attitude towards poetry as a conscious patriotic effort and duty. It was further enhanced, as we will see below, in the period after his death, when his scattered and chaotic manuscripts were edited by his follower and student Iakovos Polylas and transformed into a single and coherent corpus of 'Greek national poetry'.[15]

The consolidation of an image of Solomos as a national poet went hand in hand with the perception that he had inaugurated the field of modern Greek literature. This he did, in essence, by transforming demotic Greek into a language suitable for

---

[13] The French translation of the *Hymn*, by Stanislas Julien, was included (together with the original Greek) in Claude Fauriel, *Chants populaires de la Grèce moderne* (Paris, 1824–5), vol. II. The English one, by Charles Brinsley Sheridan, was included in his book *The Songs of Greece from the Romaic Text* (London, 1825). The second edition of Missolonghi was accompanied by an Italian translation made by Solomos's friend Gaetano Grassetti (1825).

[14] M. [Giuseppe Montani], 'Rime improvvisate dal conte Dionisio Salamon, Zacintio', *Antologia* 14 (May 1824), pp. 76–8.

[15] On the creation of the concept of 'national poet' see Alexis Politis, 'Ethnikoi poiites' (National poets), in Despoina Papadimitriou and Serafeim Seferiades (eds), *Atheates opseis tis istorias: keimena afieromena sto Yiani Yianoulopoulo* (Unseen views of history: texts dedicated to Yianis Yianoulopoulos) (Athens, 2012), pp. 227–44; Yiannis Papatheodorou, *Romantika pepromena: o Aristotelis Valaoritis os 'ethnikos poiitis'* (Romantic destinies: Aristotle Valaoritis as a 'national poet') (Athens, 2009). On the fashioning of Solomos as a 'national poet' see Veloudis, *O Solomos ton Ellinon*, pp. 81ff. and Karen Emmerich, '"A genre mixed, but valid": Dionysios Solomos's *The Free Besieged* and its Posthumous Editorial Forms' (unpublished chapter from a book in progress on editorial practice and the material construction of modern Greek poetry).

poetry. One of the most evocative accounts of the poet is to be found in *Forever and a Day*, a late film by Theo Angelopoulos in which Solomos features as a solitary figure who wanders around Zante gathering words from the mouths of the island people.[16] Indeed, Solomos's major obstacle to becoming a Greek poet was that, save for the Zakynthian vernacular, he did not know Greek. What is more, there was no established poetic tradition in Greek language to sustain his choice. So, he had to invent almost everything from scratch. He thought that the best way to do so was by studying the living elements of his country, the natural spoken language of the people. The language of the peasants, he believed, which showed itself at its finest in folk songs, expressed the unmediated substance of the soul of the nation. *The author does not teach words; he learns them from the mouth of the people*—he declared in his work *Dialogos* (Dialogue), a dialogical prose text that he composed on the Greek language question, where he attacked the archaized forms of Greek which were then being disseminated through the teachings of Adamantios Koraes and other 'pedants' (1823). As will be discussed more extensively in Chapter 12 of this book, the emergence of the very concept of 'the people' and its association with the nation and the language of popular poetry had a particular resonance in the early nineteenth-century intellectual milieus of the Ionian Islands and the Adriatic, and derived from the works of the pre-Romantic German author Johann Gottfried Herder. In Solomos's case (as in that of other Ionian authors), arguments about the Greek linguistic question were, besides, informed by contemporary Italian linguistic debates. It was by resorting to Dante that Solomos justified his use of the Greek demotic.[17]

## STAMMERING BETWEEN LANGUAGES

It has been observed that Solomos is a remarkably odd choice for 'national poet' of Greece. To begin with, he was—and he remained—bicultural and bilingual. Despite Polylas's posthumous casting of him as a Greek national icon by heavily editing his works, by isolating the Greek verses from their Italian context, and by composing a coherent biography that served as a preface (*Prolegomena*) to the volume

---

[16] *Forever and a Day* (1998). On this see also Spyridon De Biasi, 'Apo ton bion kai ta erga tou Solomou' (From the life and works of Solomos), *Panathinaia* 84 (Mar. 1904), p. 367.

[17] Dionysios Solomos, 'Dialogos' (Dialogue), in idem, *Apanta* (The omnibus work), vol. 2: *Peza kai italika* (Prose and Italian works), edited by Linos Politis (Athens, 1955), pp. 11–30. Similar the arguments of Solomos's friend, the Zakynthian author Antonios Matesis, in his treatise on the demotic language (1824–5), published by Theodosis Pylarinos in his 'I pragmateia tou Antoniou Matesi gia ti dimotiki glossa', *Tekmirion* 9 (2010), pp. 73–103. See also Peter Mackridge, *Language and National Identity in Greece, 1766–1976* (Oxford, 2009), p. 157. On this issue see K. Th. Demaras, 'Simeioseis ston *Dialogo* tou Solomou' (Notes on the *Dialogue* of Solomos), in idem, *Ellinikos romantismos* (Greek Romanticism) (Athens, 1982), pp. 130–40; Dimitris Arvanitakis, 'Scholia gia tis proypotheseis tou solomikou *Dialogou*' (Comments on the prerequisites of Solomos's *Dialogue*), in Giorgos K. Myaris (ed.), *Dionysios Solomos (150 chronia apo ton thanato tou poiiti)* (Nicosia, 2011); Karen Van Dyck, 'The Language Question and the Diaspora', in Roderick Beaton and David Ricks (eds), *The Making of Modern Greece: Nationalism, Romanticism, and the Uses of the Past (1797–1896)* (London, 2009), p. 194.

of his *Found Works*, Solomos never actually abandoned the Italian language.[18] His manuscripts are full of sketches in Italian which he then laboriously translated into Greek and, more often than not, left in fragments. As one of his Ionian contemporaries noted, Solomos is *most inspired, and I would say unrivalled, in his capacity to impart a Greek guise to Italian concepts.*[19] Solomos's usual working method was to embark upon a first draft of the poem (or a stanza perhaps) in Italian prose, and then to proceed by gradually eliminating the Italian prose and replacing it with more and more Greek verse, although the latter might well be simply a word-for-word rendering of the Italian.[20] The bulk of Solomos's poems are, indeed, Greek fragments embedded within Italian prose drafts. What is more, the margins of these Greek poetic fragments overflow with thoughts and reminders to himself written in Italian, which comment upon the future revision of his Greek work, which is thus always a work in progress. It has been demonstrated, in addition, that even when they were finished, Solomos's Greek verses remained full of Italianisms. It was not by writing *either* in Italian *or* in Greek that Solomos proceeded, scholars say; it was by writing both in Italian *and* Greek, merging both languages inseparably together. This 'promiscuous interpenetration' of the two languages often ended up producing a third, hybrid language composed of elements from both idioms, which were used in the same sentence or phrase. The following extract, a mixture of Zakynthian Greek and Venetian-tinged Italian, is a case in point: *Ma zà κάνω ogni sproposito | Μέρα νύχτα... Μπά! a proposito, | Vostra madre τί μου κάνει;* (But now I make every kind of gaffe/all day and all night...Ah! by the way,/how is your mother doing?). Sometimes, Italian and Greek elements were merged in the same word (i.e. 'Grekιας', 'τρεmavano') or produced totally new hybrid words (e.g. 'ντισερτατσιόνες' (dissertations)).[21] Indeed, most scholars describe Solomos's march toward Greek culture as a tormented and conscious transition from one language to another, as a 'tyrannical' passage which felt as if it were doomed to remain incomplete. One of them finds a metaphor for this passage in the image of a stammering Zakynthian woman, who appears in one of Solomos's most intriguing and most paradigmatically fragmentary works, *The Woman of Zakynthos*: *Truly, in the-the-the name of Holy Mary, listen here, Tru-tru-tru-ly in the-the name of Saint Nicholas, listen here, tru-tru-tru-ly in the name of Saint Spi-spi-spi-ridon, truly in the name of the im-mac-mac-mac-culate*

---

[18] On Polylas's styling of Solomos see Vassilis Lambropoulos, *Literature as National Institution: Studies in the Politics of Modern Greek Criticism* (Princeton, 1988), pp. 66–99; Vangelis Calotychos, *Modern Greece: A Cultural Poetics* (Oxford and New York, 2003), pp. 73–87; Emmerich, '"A genre mixed, but valid": Dionysios Solomos's *The Free Besieged* and its Posthumous Editorial Forms'.

[19] Spiridione Veludo, *Breve ricordo di Dionigi Solomos* (Venice, 1857), p. 5.

[20] Mackridge, 'Dionisio Salamon/Dionysios Solomos', p. 61.

[21] The extract from Mackridge, 'Dionisio Salamon/Dionysios Solomos', p. 68. On this see also Giannis Dallas, 'O Solomos anamesa se dyo glosses: i amfidromi dokimasia tis poiitikis ideas' (Solomos between two languages), *I lexi* 142 (Nov.–Dec. 1997); Vincenzo Rotolo, 'Dionisios Solomòs fra la cultura italiana e la cultura greca', *Italoellinika* 1 (1988), pp. 87–110; Afroditi Athanasopoulou, 'To problima tis diglossias: i periptosi tou Solomou' (The problem of diglossia: the case of Solomos) (Ph.D. dissertation, University of Crete, 1999).

*mysteries of God*—the stammering voice appears to say, evoking Solomos's own difficulty in achieving a national language.[22]

Not only did Italian remain as the interlanguage of Solomos's Greek poetry, but it became the main—and even exclusive—language of his poetry again at the end of his life. While, as we have seen, at the beginning of the 1850s Greek was being applied as the official language in every sphere of Ionian public life, Solomos, now in his mid-fifties, turned to writing Italian poems again. What is more, from approximately 1854 onwards he completely abandoned Greek as a language of poetic composition. This ostensibly surprising turn of events has been characterized as a 'regression', as Solomos's return to his initial, more natural, and easier poetic language. Greek was not, after all, the language of his 'unprocessed' self. A creator of Greek language, Solomos had always nevertheless stood outside it, moving on the fringes of both linguistic universes. His friend Niccolò Tommaseo, himself an in-between figure and frontier intellectual, gave an accurate description of Solomos's transnational position: *There are nations that God places as a link between one civilisation and another; there are men that perform this office between one nation and another, whether they are conscious of it or no. One such nation was for a long time Greece; Dionysios Solomos at present is (or rather could be if Greece so wills it) one such man. And whenever there was a need to defend Italians, Solomos did so . . . Nor however is he any the less Greek; for he has devoted his intelligence to singing the praises of his patria.*[23] Solomos lived much of his life on the fringes not only of the Greek language, but also of Greece itself. It remains still something of a mystery why the poet who so devotedly sang the glories of this country never felt any desire to visit the Greek mainland, even after the end of the revolution and the founding of the Greek state. *Why do you never cross over to Greece when you love it so dearly?*—he appears to have been asked by a Zakynthian friend. *I am afraid*—the poet supposedly answered.[24]

---

[22] Van Dyck, 'The Language Question and the Diaspora', p. 195. The extract in Dionysios Solomos, *The Free Besieged and Other Poems*, translated by Peter Thompson, edited by Peter Mackridge (Nottingham, 2015), p. 77.

[23] In Niccolò Tommaseo, *Il secondo esilio: scritti di Niccolò Tommaseo concernenti le cose d'Italia e d'Europa dal 1849 in poi* (Milan, 1862), vol. II, p. 446. On Solomos's in-between position see Dallas, 'O Solomos anamesa se dyo glosses'; Rotolo, 'Dionisios Solomòs fra la cultura italiana e la cultura greca'; Mackridge, 'Dionisio Salamon/Dionysios Solomos'; Athanasopoulou, 'To problima tis diglossias'.

[24] De Biasi, 'Apo ton bion kai ta erga tou Solomou', p. 675.

# Conclusions
## Transnational Patriotism in the Adriatic

These three chapters together attempted to answer an ostensibly simple question: why did these three poets and intellectuals, born on the same little island and within a few years of each other, become the 'national poets' of two different countries? What does this tell us about the world in which they lived, about the wider issues of their epoch? By reframing their biographies and by highlighting aspects that have been overlooked, I have tried to show how these three microhistories, viewed together, tell us something about the macrohistorical processes unfolding in the Adriatic at the end of the eighteenth and during the first decades of the nineteenth century. These processes involved the transition from the old Venetian Empire to the new empires which by turns appeared and disappeared from the region (the Napoleonic, the Austrian, the Russian, and the British), as well as to the emerging nationalisms and the resulting nation-states. This transition did not signify only the slow and uneven passage from empire to nation-state. It also marked the radical transformation of the concept of 'patria', from a cultural and local community into a political and national entity. It meant the gradual reconceptualization of language that was transformed from an index of social mobility into an attribute of national identity, as well as of poetry, which was now reconfigured as committed and national. What is more important, this transition amounted to the dissolution of the common Adriatic space and to the shattering of its Venetian cultural continuum. It meant a shift in political and cultural geographies—in the case of the Ionians, loyalties shifted from the centre that Venice used to be to the centre that Athens was now becoming, while there was an in-between moment when the statelet of the Ionian Islands was configured as an autonomous space. Overall, these processes led to the total restructuring of space and to the tracing of new boundaries between homelands and languages: in the world that was now emerging, a world of mutually exclusive nationalisms, the Adriatic Sea was slowly being transformed from a bridge into a border.

I consider these three biographies to exemplify the three stages of this transition. The reconstruction of these lives under a new light allows the historian to tell a markedly different story about the way national literatures and histories were founded. By viewing Italian and Greek history through the lens of this shifting maritime periphery, from the 'in-between' space of the Ionian Islands and through the lives of these frontier and itinerant intellectuals, I hope I have managed to instil some doubts as to what 'Italian' and 'Greek' really mean and to question some of the teleologies of the national literary canons.

In sum, these chapters' argument resembled a reverse pyramid: if I started by pointing to the divergent routes that these poets eventually took, my effort was to trace these lines backward toward the single point where the three of them initially converged. I tried to re-imagine the open-endedness of this transitory period and to reconfigure a moment when all choices were still possible, all patrias attainable, and all roads open. Despite their different courses, in the interconnected lives of these people I see some common characteristics, the most significant among them being their transnational patriotism—their loyalties suspended between or across Venice, Italy, the Ionian Islands, and Greece—and at the same time their constant feeling of estrangement from these patriotisms and their sense of incompletion and defeat. Overall, though I started by showing these men as 'national poets', my approach was to see them as individuals located at the crossing point between two centuries and two cultures, as intellectuals trying to reinvent themselves and adjust to a changing world. If the dead bodies of these poets were politically so plain and stark, their lives reveal a more complex and intriguing picture.

# PART II

# IMPERIAL NATIONALISM BETWEEN RELIGION AND REVOLUTION

*Bisogna pure avere una Patria, un paese, un punto di appoggio*

(We need to have a Patria, a country, a foothold)

—Ioannis Kapodistrias to his father, Vienna, 1812[1]

*Quant à nous, mon cher et digne ami, nous avons fini; car à un certain âge, on ne commence plus rien*

(As to us, my dear and worthy friend, we are done; because from a certain age onwards, you do not start anything)

—Ioannis Kapodistrias to Mario Pieri, Ancone 1827[2]

## INTRODUCTION

In the Monastery of Platytera (Our Lady of the Sign), north-west of the city of Corfu, there are two icons which depict a somewhat unusual iconographic theme (see Figures 5, 6): a young man, his leg entangled in ropes, is violently dragged along the ground by a horse, while he is observed from the skies by the Virgin Mary (in the first icon) and by Saints Spyridon and Sophia (in the second icon). The man in question is Ioannis Kapodistrias (1776–1831), the first governor of the Greek state and so-called 'Founder of Greek Independence', certainly one of the most celebrated figures in modern Greek history and national memory.[3] According to the local Corfiot tradition, in 1792, when Kapodistrias was still a teenager, he fell from his horse and, caught as he was in the straps of his saddle, he was on the point of being killed, if a monk of the Platytera Monastery (which was near to the Kapodistrias family's summer house) had not seen a vision while he

---

[1] Kostas Dafnis (ed.), *Archeion Ioannou Kapodistria* (Archive of Ioannis Kapodistrias) (Corfu, 1976–86), vol. III, p. 190.

[2] BRF: Lettere originali a Mario Pieri, vol. II [Ricc. 3522], 117–25.

[3] The label 'Founder of Greek Independence' refers to the book by C. M. Woodhouse, which bears the same title: *Capodistria: The Founder of Greek Independence* (Oxford, 1973).

**Figure 5.** Icon depicting the miracle of Kapodistrias's salvation in 1792. Platytera Monastery, Corfu.

was praying and had not rushed from his cell to save the young man. The event was considered a miracle, and was immortalized in the two anonymous icons.[4]

Almost forty years later, the Platytera Monastery would indeed become the eternal resting-place of that same man. There was no miraculous intervention to save the governor of the Greek state, who was by then 55 years old, when, on the early morning of 27 September 1831, while he was walking to another church, the Saint Spyridon Church in Nafplio on the Peloponnese (the first capital of the new state), he was brutally assassinated by his political opponents. His brother Augustinos, who succeeded him in power for some months, was no doubt aware of Ioannis's profound wish to be buried in his native Corfu—*I told his Majesty the Tsar that I would never exchange my burial in Corfu with any establishment in the world*, the latter had written to his father in 1814 from Zurich, when he was still the rising star of Russian diplomacy and shortly to be the Tsar's Foreign Minister.[5] Indeed, on Augustinos's initiative, six months after the assassination, Ioannis's embalmed corpse was borne to Corfu on a Russian ship, arriving on the island early in the

---

[4] Konstantinos Thymis, *I Iera Moni Yperagias Theotokou Platyteras Kerkyras* (The Holy Monastery of Our Lady of the Sign in Corfu) (Corfu, 2002) and Dafnis (ed.), *Archeion Ioannou Kapodistria*, vol. III, p. 472.

[5] Dafnis (ed.), *Archeion Ioannou Kapodistria*, vol. III, p. 253.

**Figure 6.** Icon depicting the miracle of Kapodistrias's salvation in 1792. Platytera Monastery, Corfu.

morning of 12 April 1832. At the request of the British High Commissioner, however, the corpse was not transferred to the monastery until late that same night. Mindful of how Kapodistrias was idolized and worshipped after his death as much as he had been during his lifetime, the British authorities wished to avoid upsetting the crowds.[6] Indeed, supernatural powers were ascribed to the murdered man, and many flocked to the crime scene in order to sponge and collect his blood, which was considered to be miraculous. These beliefs survived for some time since, as late as 1837, there was a prophecy that Kapodistrias would rise from the dead to save Greece.[7]

Kapodistrias's whole life—and afterlife, for that matter—would seem in fact to have been ringed by miracles, churches, and religion. Chapters 4–7 will explore

---

[6] A. S. Vrokinis, *Syntomos afigisis tou biou tou Ioannou Kapodistriou* (A short narration of the life of Ioannis Kapodistrias) (Corfu, 1886), p. 30.

[7] Captain T. A. Trant, *Narrative of a Journey through Greece* (London, 1830), pp. 179–80; [Ioannis Filimon], *Epistoli tou Kyriou A.D. Dimitriou pros ton eis Triestion Kyrion* (A letter of Mr A. D. Demetriou to a gentleman in Trieste) (Nafplio, 1831), p. 36; Christina Koulouri and Christos Loukos, *Ta proposa tou Kapodistria: o protos kybernitis tis Elladas kai i neoelliniki ideologia (1831–1996)* (The faces of Kapodistrias: the first governor of Greece and the neohellenic ideology (1831–1996)) (Athens, 1996), p. 29.

his life in conjunction with a set of other biographies, devoted to his friends and collaborators in the Ionian Islands and Russia during the first three decades of the nineteenth century (namely Bishop Ignatius, Giorgio Mocenigo, Andrea Mustoxidi, Spiridione Naranzi, Alexandre Stourdza, Demetrios Mostras, and Spyridon Destunis). Their aim is to unravel a particular intellectual geography that was formed between Italy, the Ionian Islands, the Danubian Principalities (today's Romania), and Russia, and to show the peculiar brand of Orthodox Enlightenment, imperial nationalism, and conservative liberalism that these lives in conjunction forged. The basic premise here is that Russia's political and military conduct in the Mediterranean, and particularly in the Ionian Adriatic during the first decades of the nineteenth century, had a strong impact on the way Enlightenment, liberal, and national ideas were developing in the area and created trends of thought to which historians have paid scant attention.

The conventional view about the origins of Greek national consciousness assumes that it was born out of a binary opposition between secular and religious values, western Enlightenment and eastern Orthodoxy, the ecumenism of the Church and a parochial nationalism. The anticlerical and radical ideals of a significant number of late eighteenth-and early nineteenth-century Greek Enlightenment thinkers, as well as the stubborn resistance of the Ecumenical Patriarchate of Constantinople to the ideas of nationalism and liberalism—especially after 1798, when anxieties in the Orthodox East over Napoleon crossing the threshold of the Ottoman world were at their height—certainly offered convincing enough evidence to interpret the development of Greek nationalism in terms of a clash between religion and secularism and East and West. The scheme and genealogy of the 'Neohellenic Enlightenment', which dominates Greek intellectual historiography, connects the birth of Greek nationalism and the Greek state with the ideas of the Paris-based intellectual Adamantios Koraes, attributing a central place in it to the heritage of the French Revolution and the radical and secular Enlightenment tradition.

However, as this and other parts of the book will show, this is only a partial reading of the phenomenon. A new interest in the relationship between religion and the Enlightenment has led scholars in recent years to realize that this relationship was far more complex and interesting than had traditionally been supposed. The Enlightenment is no longer described as a single and unified francophone phenomenon with anti-Christian and anti-Church characteristics. Scholars over the past few years have been 'pluralizing' the phenomenon, discovering its regional and national variations across Europe and beyond. The Enlightenment, they argue, was not at war with Christianity, but rather *within* it. It was, in most cases, a 'Christian Enlightenment'.[8] Whereas in Italy Franco Venturi had, since the 1960s,

---

[8] Helena Rosenblatt, 'The Christian Enlightenment', in Stewart J. Brown and Timothy Tackett (eds), *The Cambridge History of Christianity*, vol. 7: *Enlightenment, Reawakening and Revolution 1660–1815* (Cambridge, 2006), pp. 283–301; Mark Curran, '*Mettons toujours Londres*: Enlightened Christianity and the Public in Pre-revolutionary Francophone Europe', *French History* 24/1 (2009), pp. 40–59; James E. Bradley and Dale K. Van Kley (eds), *Religion and Politics in Enlightenment Europe* (Notre Dame, Ind., 2001), esp. pp. 1–45; Knud Haakonssen, *Enlightenments and Religions*

been at pains to portray the Church as a far from monolithic universe and thus 'both a conditioning factor and an obstacle' for Enlightenment thinkers, it is only recently that the complexity of the phenomenon has been acknowledged in the context of the 'Neohellenic Enlightenment' and of Greek nationalism, thus revising a long tradition in Greek scholarship of maintaining the opposite.[9]

The same observations apply to the understanding of liberalism. The generous share of attention that the tradition of radical Enlightenment and its main representative Koraes has received in Greek intellectual history has led scholars to view this history in terms of a neat opposition between revolution and reaction, liberalism and conservatism. In this scheme, Kapodistrias and his circle were placed on the 'authoritarian' and 'conservative' side of the political scale. Compared to radical democrats such as Koraes, Kapodistrias was seen, at best, as a bearer of the tradition of 'Enlightened despotism'.[10] Nevertheless, this perspective loses sight of recent studies on liberalism, which point out that during the first half of the nineteenth century the term most often implied a centrist doctrine that opposed the revolutionary spirit in all its forms and promoted gradual political reforms. Scholars now argue that during the first half of the nineteenth century, especially in southern Europe, rather than rejecting religion, liberals strove to find accommodation between constitutional culture and enlightened forms of religiosity. These studies draw attention to the internal diversity of liberal thought and argue for the replacement of the concept of 'liberalism' by that of 'liberalisms'.[11]

As Chapters 4–7 will show, the study of an intellectual environment that developed within a geographical and cultural zone spanning the Ionian Islands, the Danubian Principalities, and Russia reveals that there was a trend of thought in the post-Napoleonic years which was deeply religious and counter-revolutionary, devoted nonetheless to philhellenism and to the Greek revolution. There was a certain form of liberalism which was consistent with all things conventionally

---

(Athens, 2010); David Sorkin, *The Religious Enlightenment: Protestants, Jews, and Catholics from London to Vienna* (Princeton, 2008); Ulrich L. Lehner, *The Catholic Enlightenment: The Forgotten History of a Global Movement* (Oxford, 2016); Francesca Bregoli, *Mediterranean Enlightenment: Livornese Jews, Tuscan Culture, and Eighteenth-Century Reform* (Stanford, Calif., 2014).

[9] Giuseppe Ricuperati, 'The Enlightenment and the Church in the Work of Franco Venturi: The Fertile Legacy of a Civil Religion', *Journal of Modern Italian Studies* 10/2 (2005), pp. 168–82. Paschalis M. Kitromilides, 'Orthodoxy and the West: Reformation to Enlightenment' and 'The Legacy of the French Revolution: Orthodoxy and Nationalism', in Michael Angold (ed.), *The Cambridge History of Christianity*, vol. 5: *Eastern Christianity* (Cambridge, 2006), pp. 202–6, 229–30; idem (ed.), *Enlightenment and Religion in the Orthodox World* (Oxford, 2016); Effi Gazi, 'Revisiting Religion and Nationalism in Nineteenth-Century Greece', in Roderick Beaton and David Ricks (eds), *The Making of Modern Greece: Nationalism, Romanticism, and the Uses of the Past (1797–1896)* (London and New York, 2009), pp. 95–106; Lucien J. Frary, *Russia and the Making of Modern Greek Identity, 1821–1844* (Oxford, 2015), esp. pp. 8–9.

[10] K. Th. Demaras, 'Prologos' (Prologue), in Dafnis (ed.), *Archeion Ioannou Kapodistria*, vol. I, p. ιζ΄; Paschalis M. Kitromilides, *Enlightenment and Revolution: The Making of Modern Greece* (Cambridge, Mass., and London, 2013), pp. 315–18.

[11] Lucien Jaume, *L'Individu effacé ou le paradoxe du libéralisme français* (Paris, 1997), 'Introduction'; Aurelian Craiutu, *Liberalism under Siege: The Political Thought of the French Doctrinaires* (Lanham, Md, 2003), pp. 287–91; Maurizio Isabella, 'Citizens or Faithful? Religion and the Liberal Revolutions of the 1820s in Southern Europe', *Modern Intellectual History* (published online: Jan. 2015), pp. 1–24: <http://dx.doi.org/10.1017/S147924431400078X>.

understood as 'reactionary'. These were people attuned to the nascent nationalist feelings of the period, but frightened by the French Revolution and the Napoleonic Wars. The excesses of those events left them, like many other European moderate liberals in the 1820s, with an intense distaste for democracy, Jacobinism, and secret societies and instilled in them the need to reorganize human relations on conservative and moral grounds. By offering a different geographical and intellectual trajectory, which places Greece in a Mediterranean context, viewing it in relation to the Ionian Islands as well as to the Russian Empire, these chapters will argue indeed that there was a circle of diasporic intellectuals who perceived the Greek nation not as incompatible with the Christian ecumene and the traditional world of the empires, but as part of it.[12]

---

[12] A concise version of Part II appeared as 'Imperial Nationalism and Orthodox Enlightenment: A Diasporic Story between the Ionian Islands, Russia and Greece, ca. 1800–1830', in Maurizio Isabella and Konstantina Zanou (eds), *Mediterranean Diasporas: Politics and Ideas in the Long Nineteenth Century* (London, 2016), pp. 117–34.

# 4

## The Russian Adriatic

### RUSSIA AND THE MEDITERRANEAN

Our story in this part of the book begins in the second half of the eighteenth century, when Russia first turned its attention towards the Mediterranean. Until that time, the Russians had not shown any ambition to become a naval power, still less a Mediterranean naval power. Their navy, created only at the end of the seventeenth century, had been far too weak to operate in seas other than the Baltic. However, during the last three decades of the eighteenth century, there was an ever-growing sense that Ottoman decline, along with the increasing debility of Venice, had left a power vacuum in the Mediterranean. The Tsarina Catherine II, reviving Peter the Great's (1689–1725) bold notion of transforming his empire from an Asiatic into a European enterprise, thought that Russia had every right to fill that vacuum. This plan was lent further credence by the outcome of the Russo-Ottoman war of 1768–74 (one of many conflicts between the two powers in the course of the eighteenth and nineteenth centuries), which ended in the utter humiliation of the Ottomans, ratified by the Treaty of Küçük-Kaynarca. The treaty recognized Russian control of the Crimea and of a number of fortresses on the Black Sea coast, and secured the right of Russian merchant ships (often manned by Greek officers and Albanian sailors) to travel through the Bosporus into the Ottoman waters of the Aegean, raising thus the prospect of the revival of the ancient trade routes linking the northern shores of the Black Sea to the Mediterranean. For that reason, Russia was now permitted to appoint consuls in the Ottoman Empire, a position usually filled by ethnic Greeks. Another clause of the treaty—symbolic, rather than substantive, and therefore subject to differing interpretations—stipulated that 'the Sublime Porte promises a firm protection to the Christian religion and to its Churches'. Along with another clause, which stated that Russia had the right to construct a 'Russo-Greek' Orthodox church in Istanbul and make representation to the Porte on its behalf, this was taken by many to mean that the Tsar had the right to intervene on behalf of the Sultan's Orthodox subjects and protect Christian worship.[1]

---

[1] Norman E. Saul, *Russia and the Mediterranean 1797–1807* (Chicago, 1970), pp. 9ff.; Thomas W. Gallant, *The Edinburgh History of the Greeks, 1768 to 1913: The Long Nineteenth Century* (Edinburgh, 2015), pp. 2–23; Nicholas Charles Pappas, *Greeks in Russian Military Service in the Late Eighteenth and Early Nineteenth Centuries* (Thessaloniki, 1991), pp. 86–8; Lucien J. Frary, 'Russian Interests in Nineteenth-Century Thessaloniki', *Mediterranean Historical Review* 23/1 (2008), pp. 15–33; idem, *Russia and the Making of Modern Greek Identity*, pp. 20–7.

During the course of the same war, the Russian fleet, under the command of Alexei Orlov—Catherine II's paramour and the principal suspect where her husband's murder was concerned—sailed for the first time in Mediterranean waters. He occupied briefly several Aegean islands—where he established a 'Russian Archipelagic Principality'—and, in 1770, with his brother Fyodor, instigated a major but unsuccessful Greek revolt in the Morea (Peloponnese), which provoked harsh reprisals from the Ottoman army and cost the lives of most of the insurgents. Among those few who managed to escape, a fair number found refuge in the Ionian Islands or further off, in southern Russia. During the same period, Catherine II's preferential treatment encouraged thousands of Greeks from the Ottoman Empire to settle along the coastline of the Sea of Azov, in the Crimea, and in Taganrog. *This privilege can be thought of as a prediction of the re-establishment of the Greek empire in Eastern Europe*, commented a contemporary Italian newspaper on what was perceived to be Russia's plan to make a new centre of Mediterranean life on the Black Sea.[2] In order to please the settlers, the Tsarina created in 1775 a new episcopal seat, to which she appointed the Ionian Eugenios Voulgaris, one of the forefathers, as we will see, of the trend of Enlightenment thought that later inspired Kapodistrias and his circle.[3]

These Russian activities formed part of a grander idea: Catherine II envisaged conquering the Ottomans—at worst only their European possessions—and founding a great Christian empire centred on Constantinople. In this plan of imagined 'recovery' of Constantinople for Orthodox Christendom—a sort of fantastical re-establishment of the Byzantine Empire under Russian control—the religiosity of the Balkan peoples played a crucial role. Luckily for the Russians, their dreams of territorial expansion were matched by the mystical exaltation of the age. Indeed, it has been argued that the eighteenth century was the 'century of oracles' and of 'apocalyptic frenzy' in the region.[4] Among the most popular 'prophecies', triggering waves of enthusiasm among the population of the Greek lands, was one concerning a 'Blond Race' that would come to the Balkans to assist the Orthodox

---

[2] Franco Venturi and R. Burr Litchfield, *The End of the Old Regime in Europe, 1776–1789*, Part II: *Republican Patriotism and the Empires of the East* (Princeton, 1991), pp. 775–6.

[3] Franco Venturi, *La rivolta greca del 1770 e il patriottismo dell'età dei lumi* (Rome, 1986); Elena Smilianskaia, '"Protection" or "Possession": How Russians Created a Greek Principality in 1770–1775', in M. Baramova, P. Mitev, I. Parvev, and V. Racheva (eds), *Power and Influence in South-Eastern Europe: 16–19th Century* (Münster, 2013), pp. 209–17; idem, 'Catherine's Liberation of the Greeks: High-Minded Discourse and Everyday Realities', in M. Di Salvo, D. Kaiser, and V. Kivelson (eds), *Word and Image in Russian History: Essays in Honor of Gary Marker* (Boston, 2015), pp. 71–89; Tassos Ath. Gritsopoulos, *Ta Orlofika: i en Peloponniso epanastasis tou 1770 kai ta epakoloutha aftis* (The Orlofika: the revolution of 1770 in Peloponnesos and its consequences) (Athens, 1967); Pantelis M. Kontogiannis, *Oi Ellines kata ton proton epi Aikaterinis B' Rossotourkikon Polemon, (1768–1774)* (The Greeks during the Russo-Turkish War of Catherine II, (1768–1774)) (Athens, 1903), pp. 64–98, 396–406; Roger P. Bartlett, *Human Capital: The Settlement of Foreigners in Russia 1762–1804* (Cambridge, 1979), pp. 130–42; Vassilis Kardasis, *Diaspora Merchants in the Black Sea: The Greeks in Southern Russia, 1775–1861* (Lanham, Md, 2001).

[4] Dionysis Tzakis, 'Rosiki parousia sto Aigaio: Apo ta Orlofika sto Lampro Katsoni' (Russian presence in the Aegean: from the Orlofika to Lambros Katsonis), in Vassilis Panagiotopoulos (ed.), *Istoria tou neou ellinismou, 1770–2000* (History of modern Hellenism, 1770–2000) (Athens, 2003), vol. 1, pp. 115–16.

Christians in their battle against the Ottomans. During the eighteenth century, this 'Blond Race' came to be identified—and there was nothing fortuitous about the identification—with the Russians. This same story was, in addition, linked to the *Vision* of Agathangelus, a pseudonymous collection of prophesies (a *prophetia post factum*), which combined the apocryphal and historical genres by putting in the mouth of a thirteenth-century monk, Agathangelus, the 'prediction' of events that had happened in the meantime. In reality, the book was written by a cleric from Mount Athos around 1751 and, despite the failure of the 1770 revolt in the Morea, it never lost its allure for the Greek masses—or not at least until the end of the Crimean War (1856), when the veracity of all these visions was dealt a fatal blow.[5]

The Russians tended to play the religious card both in Ottoman lands and in those of the Republic of Venice. In the Ionian Islands, from the beginning of the eighteenth century onwards, the Orthodoxy of the inhabitants served to differentiate them from their Venetian rulers and created links instead with their coreligionists from Russia, which started to offer Ionians career opportunities as public servants and in trade.[6] Many Ionians were actively involved in the 1770 revolt of the Morea, especially in its preparatory phase, when they were sent as secret agents to explore the shores of the Peloponnese, which they knew well.[7]

The links between the Mediterranean and Russia would be strengthened during the last decades of the century, and especially after 1783, when the Tsarina annexed the Crimea, thereby establishing a base for commercial and naval ventures in the direction of the Mediterranean. Once peace was signed with the Ottomans in 1792, Russian trade in the area was further expanded. By the time of Tsar Paul I (1796–1801) Russia could claim to have won for itself a significant role in Mediterranean affairs. Its prospects in the area had never looked so promising: it almost seemed probable that, before long, the Byzantine Empire would be reborn from its ashes in a new Russian garb.

There was only one insuperable obstacle to this dream: it went by the name of Napoleon. The Revolutionary War and the subsequent Napoleonic Wars affected the entire Mediterranean, transforming it into an exclusive theatre of conflict between Britain and France. Napoleon's expedition to Egypt in 1798 and the consequent British takeover was the last straw: the mounting anxiety of the Tsar was matched by the preoccupations of the Sultan, who could not tolerate the French landing in Ottoman Egypt. Besides, the Sublime Porte was worried by the existence

---

[5] John Nicolopoulos, 'From *Agathangelos* to the *Megale Idea*: Russia and the Emergence of Modern Greek Nationalism', *Balkan Studies* 26 (1985), pp. 41–56.

[6] Nikos Karapidakis, 'Ta Eptanisa: evropaikoi antagonismoi meta tin ptosi tis Benetias' (The Heptanese: European rivalries after the fall of Venice), in Panagiotopoulos (ed.), *Istoria tou neou ellinismou*, vol. 1, p. 155. Orthodox identity was once again invoked by the Ionians in order to draw a distinctive line between them and the British colonizers some decades later. See: Thomas W. Gallant, *Experiencing Dominion: Culture, Identity, and Power in the British Mediterranean* (Notre Dame, Ind., 2002), pp. 175–209.

[7] Up until recently the Peloponnese had still been part of the Venetian world—the Ottomans had only wrested the Morea from the Republic of Venice in 1715—and in any case Ionians continued to migrate en masse as seasonal labourers to the Peloponnese every year. See Kontogiannis, *Oi Ellines kata ton proton*, pp. 144–6.

of dangerous admirers of Napoleon and troublemakers in the Balkans, notably Ali Pasha of Yiannina (Epirus). Yet another of those who attempted to make the most of the collapse of the Venetian Empire, Ali Pasha, the so called 'Muslim Bonaparte', thought that the French revolutionary presence in the Adriatic, which upset the Ottoman authorities, gave him the ideal pretext for conquering the long-coveted cities along the Ionian shores of Epirus. Within two years of bloody warfare (1798–1800), he had managed to take control of the ex-Venetian territories of Buthrotum, Preveza, and Vonitsa and to exert threatening pressure on the still-resisting town of Parga.[8] These events and the opportunistic diplomatic games that Napoleon played with Ali Pasha in order to further his own imperialistic designs were enough to convince the two imperial powers, Russia and the Ottoman Empire, to put their historical mistrust aside and, in 1799, to enter into an alliance. Their differences apart, both powers could certainly agree on a double objective: first, to prevent the spread of revolutionary ideas in the Balkans; second, to conquer the Ionian Islands. For the Ottomans, control of the islands would reinforce the blockade of the Adriatic and prevent Napoleon from invading the Balkans. For the Russians, gaining Corfu and its neighbours meant acquiring their long-desired island base in the Mediterranean. By early March 1799, the combined forces of the two powers had taken control of the seven islands.

The outcome of this process was the 'Septinsular Republic', an aristocratic, semi-independent state on the model of Ragusa, which united the seven islands in a federation under the sovereignty of the Porte and the direct political and military protection of Russia. The republic would last only seven years (1800–7). In 1806, deep disagreements about the affairs of Wallachia led to the collapse of the Russo-Ottoman alliance and to the outbreak of a new war between the two powers. Following the reverses in Europe, the new Tsar, Alexander I, made his peace with Napoleon at Tilsit in 1807 and sealed it by ceding the Ionian Islands to imperial France. Additional British pressure convinced Russia, in due course, to give up its attempts to obtain a permanent foothold in the Adriatic and to abandon its Mediterranean ambitions. As one historian has eloquently written, 'Mediterranean intervention had cost Russia a great deal of money and in the end brought it no permanent advantage.'[9]

Very brief though Russia's presence had been in the Mediterranean, and particularly in the Adriatic, it had nonetheless left its mark on the way national and liberal ideas were developing in the region. The encounter between the post-Venetian reality of the Ionian Islands and the Russian Empire fostered a particular trend of proto-nationalism and proto-liberalism that bore its own distinctive characteristics. This was a version of Ionian patriotism, transformed later into Greek nationalism, which arose in the minds of people who were torn between old

---

[8] K. E. Fleming, *The Muslim Bonaparte: Diplomacy and Orientalism in Ali Pasha's Greece* (Princeton, 1999).

[9] David Abulafia, *The Great Sea: A Human History of the Mediterranean* (Oxford, 2011), p. 523. Information on the history of Russia in the Mediterranean is mostly drawn from: Abulafia, *The Great Sea*, pp. 518–23; Saul, *Russia and the Mediterranean*; Pierre Cabanes et al., *Histoire de l'Adriatique* (Paris, 2001), pp. 397–416.

and new empires—Venetian, Ottoman, and Russian—and the Greek nation-state; who believed that the Greek revolution was compatible with the restored order of post-Napoleonic Europe and thought that philhellenism could be built on conservative and religious foundations; who were convinced that the Enlightenment was religious in nature and that the rise of the Greek state could be explained in eschatological terms; who imagined that the Ionian state could exist within the Russian and British empires and Greek nationalism within Christian ecumenicity. It is the circle of people entertaining these beliefs that I now wish to consider. This circle included, first of all, the elite of the Septinsular Republic, the political and intellectual leaders of this short-lived polity.

## THE SEPTINSULAR REPUBLIC AND
## ITS CENTRAL CHARACTERS

Ioannis Kapodistrias probably watched from his window the last act of the long Russo-Ottoman siege of Corfu, the seizure of the islet of Vidos (just outside the island's capital) in late February 1799. He had returned from his studies in Padua no more than two years before. Some days before his final exam at the school of medicine, Napoleon had victoriously entered Venice. But unlike his Corfiot fellow-students Mario Pieri, Demetrio Arliotti, and Niccolò Delviniotti, Kapodistrias did not linger in the Veneto to witness events as they unfolded: as soon as he had obtained his degree, just one month after the fall of the Venetian Republic, he set sail for home (June 1797).[10] He arrived in Corfu almost at the same time as the French troops. The revolutionary agitation in which the islands were embroiled was certainly not to the advantage of Kapodistrias's family. His father, Antonomarias Kapodistrias, was a count registered in the *Libro d'oro* (Golden Book) of the Venetian nobility, which was now burning publicly in the central square of the city. His mother, Diamantina Gonemi, also came from a local aristocratic family. The name 'Kapodistrias' itself evoked the memories of the unified imperial Venetian sea (*Capo d'Istria* or *Capodistria* is the Italian name of Koper, a town on the present-day Slovenian Adriatic coast, to which the family apparently traced its remote origins). In fact, the history of the Kapodistrias was inextricably bound up with the existence of the Venetian Empire, and many members of the family, including Ioannis's father, had shone in the service of Venice.[11]

It is no wonder, then, that the 23-year-old Ioannis felt some relief when the Russo-Ottomans arrived. From the outset, his father emerged as one of the central figures of the transitional period—proving the local Venetian aristocracy's ability to adroitly reinvent new roles for itself. He was indeed among the sixteen local nobles who were chosen by the Russians to form the first temporary State Council,

---

[10] Grigorios Dafnis, *Ioannis A. Kapodistrias: i genesi tou ellinikou kratous* (Ioannis Kapodistrias: the birth of the Greek state) (Athens, 1976), pp. 92, 118; Christos Loukos, *Ioannis Kapodistrias* (Athens, 2009), p. 12.

[11] On the origins of the family see: S. Th. Lascaris, *Capodistrias avant la révolution grecque: sa carrière politique jusqu'en 1822* (Lausanne, 1918), p. 6; Dafnis, *Ioannis A. Kapodistrias*, pp. 25–33.

while three of his five sons, including Ioannis, were part of the wider Council of Nobles, which was summoned some days later. At the same time, the Count was appointed as one of the representatives of the Ionian Senate sent to Constantinople and St Petersburg to negotiate the terms of the Russo-Ottoman convention and to decide what type of state would issue from those same negotiations. What is more important, Antonomarias Kapodistrias was himself responsible—personally, shouldering his colleagues aside—for the actual draft of the constitution that, once approved by the two powers, would regulate the future government of the Septinsular Republic.

The 1800 Ionian constitution—which came to be known as the 'Byzantine Constitution', because it was drafted in Constantinople—resulted from the consent of two absolutist empires to create a republic. It was the first time, as one historian observed, 'that a constitution of any kind or sort was granted, with the actual tolerance of Russia, to a part of eastern Europe'.[12] Of course, if the Sultan and the Tsar agreed to create a constitutional independent state (namely a 'constitutional aristocracy'), it was not because they adhered to the principles of national independence and constitutional liberty, but for exactly the opposite reason: because they wanted to prevent these ideas from spreading further into the East. Besides, their mutual mistrust played a crucial role in determining the eventual outcome.[13] The constitution created a federal state of the seven islands governed by a Senate which was elected by the General Councils which, in their turn, were composed of the nobles of each island enrolled in the *Libro d'oro*. When Antonomarias Kapodistrias returned from Constantinople with the constitution in his pocket he was received by his fellow Ionians as a hero. Poets likened him to Moses when he delivered the Ten Commandments to the people of Israel.[14] But in reality, the narrowly aristocratic character of the new constitution, which excluded from power social classes that had won political rights during the French period, made its application problematic.[15]

After the initial withdrawal of the Russian troops (July 1801), clashes between peasantry and city dwellers, as well as rivalries between local magnates, made the turmoil on the islands almost permanent. In October 1801, an assembly representing all classes of people from the towns, villages, and countryside of Corfu—named, therefore, the 'Honourable Assembly'—assumed responsibility for drafting a new and politically more inclusive constitution. The draft which was produced, even if not particularly radical, was nevertheless opposed outright by the two imperial Protecting Powers, giving rise to a new wave of unrest on the islands.[16] *The Republic would have been dissolved into internal divisions and antagonisms had Russia not extended its arm again to protect it*, wrote a near-contemporary

---

[12] Loukos, *Ioannis Kapodistrias*, p. 14.

[13] Aliki D. Nikiforou (ed.), *Constitutional Charters of the Ionian Islands* (Athens, 2012), pp. 142ff.

[14] Ermanno Lunzi, *Della Repubblica Settinsulare* (Bologna, 1863), vol. I, pp. 54–5.

[15] Dafnis, *Ioannis A. Kapodistrias*, p. 133; *Istoria tou ellinikou ethnous* (History of the Greek nation) (Athens, 1978), vol. 11, p. 394.

[16] [N. B. Manessi], *Le tre costituzioni (1800, 1803, 1817) delle Sette Isole Jonie* (Corfu, 1849), p. 21; *Istoria tou ellinikou ethnous*, vol. 11, p. 396.

historian.[17] Indeed, before long, in August 1802, the Russian 'protective arm' reappeared on the islands in the form of five warships and 1,600 soldiers, never to abandon the region again—or, at any rate, not before the arrival of Napoleon.

These forces were headed by Giorgio Mocenigo (*c.*1762–1839), the man who became the actual 'boss' of the Septinsular Republic. A product of Russia's long-lasting flirtation with the Ionian Islands, Mocenigo was the son of a Russophile Zakynthian noble, who fell into disgrace and was imprisoned by the Venetian authorities for his involvement in the 1770 revolt in the Morea. When the Tsarina Catherine II heard about his misfortunes, she decided to save him by appointing him Russian Consul to Tuscany. By contrast with his father, the younger Mocenigo did not enjoy an exalted reputation at the tsarist court. Because of his 'frivolous nature' and his 'wasteful spending', he was soon dismissed from his (hereditary) consular duties and even banned from entering Russian land.[18] Nevertheless, his powerful connections among the local Ionian aristocracy ensured him the position of ambassador of the Septinsular Republic to the Russian court. He therefore set out for Russia and started building his career anew. This career took off when he was sent to the Ionian Islands as Russia's Imperial Proxy.

On Mocenigo's arrival, a new Legislative Body was created to draft a new charter. This time the draft won the approval of the Protecting Powers, becoming thus the first constitution to come into effect on the islands. The constitution of 1803 was remarkable for its liberal character, as it enlarged the body politic by granting political rights, not only to the members of the nobility, but to everyone *provided—* as it stated—*that they have the necessary qualifications of higher education and, especially, the ownership of substantial property, whether in real estate or commerce.*[19] In other words, it replaced the hereditary nobility with a constitutional 'nobility' (the 'notables'). It also abandoned the federal structure of the state, in favour of a unitary and indivisible power system, minimizing thus demographic and economic discrepancies between the islands.[20] What is more important, at a time when language and religion were becoming increasingly identified with the emerging national consciousness, the constitution declared Greek to be the official language of the state and Christian Orthodoxy the official religion.

Religion had indeed been the Russian besiegers' trump card: when the allied Russo-Ottoman forces arrived on the islands they were armed with an encyclical issued by the Ecumenical Patriarch of Constantinople, which urged the Ionians to accept the allies—and specifically the Russians—as their protectors and liberators from *the tyrannical yoke of impiety and atheism*, which the French, if unimpeded,

---

[17] Lunzi, *Della Repubblica Settinsulare*, vol. I, 'Preface'.

[18] Lunzi, *Della Repubblica Settinsulare*, vol. I, pp. 79–80. On the Mocenigo family, see also K. A. Palaiologos, 'Peri tou Komitos Mocenigou' (On the Count Mocenigo), *Parnassos* 6 (1882), pp. 711–20; Karapidakis, 'Ta Eptanisa: evropaikoi antagonismoi', p. 155; James Mcknight, 'Admiral Ushakov and the Ionian Republic: The Genesis of Russia's First Balkan Satellite' (Ph.D. dissertation, University of Wisconsin–Madison, 1965), p. 76; Cesare Ciano, *Russia e Toscana nei secoli XVII e XVIII: pagine di storia del commercio e della navigazione* (Livorno, 1980).

[19] [Manessi], *Le tre costituzioni*, p. 35.

[20] Sarantis C. Orfanoudakis, 'Constitutional Texts of the Ionian Islands: A Review', in Nikiforou (ed.), *Constitutional Charters*, pp. 50–1.

would have inflicted upon the islanders. One of the first measures that the commander of the Russian forces, the Admiral Fyodor Ushakov, took, once his fleet had prevailed over the French army, was to re-establish an Orthodox Greek on the episcopal throne of Corfu—thereby reversing a practice that had been followed for several centuries, and degrading still further the position of the Ionian Catholics, already weakened by the French authorities' declaration that all religions on the islands were to be regarded as equal.[21] The first decision of the freshly constituted Council of Nobles at Corfu was to enact a litany of the relic of the patron saint of Corfu, St Spyridon (only recently derided as a 'holy carcass' and a 'mummy' by the French soldiers stationed on the island).[22] But while the cult of the saint had been for centuries shared by both Christian rites on the island, now it spoke to the hearts of the Orthodox alone. The Russian presence in the Adriatic did indeed bring about a break in the centuries-old syncretic religious tradition of the islands. This 'local religious identity', which had for long permitted interaction and communication between the two rites, rearranged as it now was by Russophile propaganda, produced a new religious reality of strictly defined lines and impenetrable borders between the two dogmas.[23] As one historian has put it, Corfu, from being an 'eastern border of the Christian West' (*antemurale della Christianità*), was now becoming a 'western edge of the eastern Orthodox world'.[24]

As the Septinsular Republic was taking shape and its institutions were being created—borders were drawn, ministries were formed, the army was overhauled, the Church was reorganized, and education reformed—contemporary commentators saw it as the 'first free national Greek government after many centuries' and celebrated it as a prelude to the Greek state.[25] *I take as much interest in the Seven Islands as if it were [my] second patria*, wrote one attentive observer in Switzerland, *because I seem to see there the cradle of a new liberty and of a nation reborn*.[26] In reality, of course, the Septinsular Republic was more of a Russian protectorate than an independent state—a 'dependent autonomy,' according to a retrospective judgement.[27] In the five years that Mocenigo ruled the Ionian Islands (1802–7),

---

[21] Ermanno Lunzi, *Della Repubblica Settinsulare*, vol. I, pp. 19–28; Mcknight, 'Admiral Ushakov and the Ionian Republic', pp. 72–3, 82, 141.

[22] In Mcknight, 'Admiral Ushakov and the Ionian Republic', pp. 55–6.

[23] This change did of course come about gradually. For example, as late as 1827, the Orthodox Dionysios Solomos pronounced the eulogy on the death of Ugo Foscolo in a Catholic church, out of respect for the rite of the dead man. See Dionisio Solomos, *Elogio di Ugo Foscolo*, edited by Carlo Brighenti (Turin, Milan, and Florence, 1934), p. 28.

[24] Theodossios Nikolaidis, 'I latreia tou Agiou Spyridona stin Kerkyra, 16os–18os aionas' (The cult of Saint Spyridon in Corfu, 16th–18th centuries), *Ta istorika* 29/57 (Dec. 2012), p. 341; see also idem, '"Local Religion" in Corfu: Sixteenth to Nineteenth Centuries', *Mediterranean Historical Review* 29/2 (2014), pp. 155–68.

[25] Alexandre Stourdza, 'Notice biographique sur le comte J. Capodistrias, Président de la Grèce', in E. A. Bétant (ed.), *Correspondance du Comte Capodistrias, Président de la Grèce* (Geneva and Paris, 1839), vol. I, p. 10; André Papadopoulo-Vretos, *Mémoires biographiques—historiques sur le Président de la Grèce, le comte Jean Capodistrias* (Paris, 1837), p. 7; Lunzi, *Della Repubblica Settinsulare*, vol. I, p. 42. See also Karapidakis, 'Ta Eptanisa: evropaikoi antagonismoi', p. 173.

[26] Léonard de Sismondi to Isabella Teotochi-Albrizzi (1807). In Teresa Lodi, 'Sismondi e la *Staël veneziana*', *Civiltà moderna* 4 (1932), p. 620.

[27] Antonis Manitakis, 'The Transition, Shaped by Diplomatic Compromise, from the Old Venetian Regime of Administrative Autonomy to National and Democratic Integration', in Nikiforou (ed.),

he was vested with almost dictatorial powers. He managed to eliminate local rivalries by creating a more centralized system of government, which ensured stricter control—chiefly *his own* control. He created a new security corps, the so-called 'Sublime Police', and established his power over the judicial system. What is more important, he triggered the elections of 1806 and formed a new Legislative Body that amended the 1803 constitution, restricting participation in government and giving Russia the right to veto local decisions.[28]

Nevertheless, Mocenigo knew how to attract and incorporate into the structures of the new state the most talented individuals, creating an effective team of political and intellectual leaders. First of all, he entrusted the 27-year-old Kapodistrias with the office of the Secretary General of the Septinsular Republic, a position second only to his own in the administrative hierarchy of the new state. *The duties of this important position, however small the Ionian state was*—wrote one of Kapodistrias's first biographers—*were, unbeknownst to him, the precursors of those he would exercise ten years later as the Secretary General of a vast empire.*[29]

The Septinsular Republic found, in addition, its official historiographer in the shape of a young and promising Corfiot, Andrea Mustoxidi (1785–1860), about whom Part IV in this book will have much more to say. An avowed Russophile— he had dedicated his first book to the Tsar, and expressed a wish to see *Greece rise again, through his intervention, from the abjection to which the events of centuries have condemned it, and produce new Pindars and more Plutarchs to heap praise and blessings upon [him]*[30]—Mustoxidi would later make a name for himself on both shores of the Adriatic as an eminent philologist, translator, and archaeologist, and as one of the first historians to contribute to the construction of local Ionian and later Greek national history. In addition to this, however, he was to hold various important political positions, from attaché to the Russian consulate in Turin (with a central role in transmitting Russian policy to the 1821 revolutionary movements in Piedmont), to first Minister of Education of the Greek state in Kapodistrias's government, to member of the Ionian Senate and Parliament during the period of the British colonial administration.

Somewhat older than Mustoxidi was Spiridione Naranzi (1760–*c*.1833), another talented Ionian who was summoned to the islands to form part of the Septinsular Republics' new administration. Naranzi—who was born in Zante into the same family as Ugo Foscolo (he was his cousin)—studied law at Padua and became deeply involved in Venetian literary circles.[31] Mocenigo summoned him to Corfu so that he might apply his juridical expertise to the drafting of the republic's

*Constitutional Charters*, p. 33. On the meaning of 'independence' in the late eighteenth and early nineteenth century see David Armitage, *Foundations of Modern International Thought* (Cambridge, 2013), pp. 218ff.

[28] 'Progetto di riforma dell'atto costituzionale della Repubblica', in [Manessi], *Le tre costituzioni*, pp. 81–120. On Mocenigo's rule see *Istoria tou ellinikou ethnous*, p. 397; Karapidakis, 'Ta Eptanisa: evropaikoi antagonismoi', pp. 172–5; C. M. Woodhouse, *Capodistria*, pp. 23ff.

[29] Papadopoulo-Vretos, *Mémoires biographiques*, p. 9.

[30] Andrea Mustoxidi, *Notizie per servire alla storia corcirese* (Corfu, 1804), p. 3.

[31] Important men of letters from the Veneto dedicated books to him and spoke of him as their friend. For example: Melchior Cesarotti, *L'Iliade o la morte di Ettore, poema omerico ridotto in verso*

constitutions, but also appointed him its financial administrator. His contribution to the constitutional issues of the Septinsular Republic was so influential that many Ionians called their state the 'Naranzian Republic'. Mocenigo would, as we will see in Chapter 5, offer his help in securing Naranzi's appointment as Russian Consul to Venice when the Septinsular Republic was already a thing of the past.[32]

The last to join the cast of the principal characters of the Septinsular Republic was Bishop Ignatius (1766–1828). In terms of intellectual weight, however, he was indubitably the most important. He was born into a poor family of Lesvos, an island east of the Aegean Sea, where his parents had probably sought refuge after the suppression of the 1770 revolt in the Morea. Thanks to an uncle who was a clergyman, the young Ioannis-Ignatius pursued higher studies in the prestigious Phanar Greek Orthodox College, the so-called *Megali tou Genous Scholi* (Great School of the Nation), in Constantinople. At a very young age, the Holy Synod elected him Bishop of Arta and Nafpaktos in Epirus, a metropolitan seat within the domain of Ali Pasha. In the eleven years of his tenure (1794–1805), Ignatius came into contact with the two factors that would determine his ideological horizons thereafter: on the one hand, Ali Pasha, representative of Ottoman politics and diplomacy; on the other hand, the imperial powers that succeeded each other in the nearby Ionian Islands, the Venetians, the French, the Russians, and the British (who were covertly sailing in Adriatic waters long before 1815). Ignatius was soon asked to offer his backing to Ali Pasha's military operations against the French along the eastern shores of the Adriatic. If the Orthodox populations of the cities under attack were to be persuaded to surrender without too much resistance, Ali Pasha would have to acquire some sort of spiritual legitimization. This Ignatius willingly supplied, here performing a function that in any case coincided with his spiritual and institutional duties as designated by the official Church. In attacking the French revolutionaries, Ali Pasha did indeed embody both anti-French (that is to say, 'anti-atheist') sentiment and the Ottoman legality of the Ecumenical Patriarchate of Constantinople, which was keen to retain its role as a prominent institution within the Ottoman state. Things changed, however, when in the surrounding region the French were succeeded by the Russians. After a short period of 'acrobatic' diplomatic activity and allegiances divided between his Ottoman masters and the new Orthodox rulers of the Adriatic, Ignatius finally decided to side with the latter. In 1805, he left his metropolitan seat and moved to Corfu, committing himself unreservedly to Mocenigo's cause.[33]

*italiano* (Venice, 1805), vol. IV, p. 252; Bartolommeo Gamba, *Operette di Jacopo Morelli, bibliotecario di S. Marco, ora insieme raccolte* (Venice, 1820), vol. I, p. 1.

[32] Leonidas Zois, *Lexikon istorikon kai laografikon Zakynthou* (Historical and folkloric dictionary of Zante) (Athens, 1963), vol. I, p. 467; Artemis Xanthopoulou-Kyriakou, *I elliniki koinotita tis Benetias (1797–1866): dioikitiki kai oikonomiki organosi, ekpaideftiki kai politiki drastiriotita* (The Greek community of Venice (1797–1866): administrative and economic organization, educational and political activity) (Thessaloniki, 1978), pp. 131–2.

[33] Vassilis Panagiotopoulos, 'Ignatios Ouggroblachias' (The Bishop of Ungrovlachia Ignatius), in idem and Panagiotis Michailaris, *Klirikoi ston Agona* (Clerics in the Revolution) (Athens, 2010), pp. 49–62; Emmanouil G. Protopsaltis, *Ignatios Mitropolitis Ouggroblachias (1766–1828)* (The Bishop of Ungrovlachia Ignatius (1766–1828)) (Athens, 1961), 2 vols.

Ironically, Mocenigo made use of Ignatius's services in his attempts to confront the threat posed by the Bishop's former master, Ali Pasha. Once the Russian forces in the Adriatic had stopped him in his tracks, Ali Pasha turned his attention to the rocky area of Souli, in the Epirotic hinterland. His siege of the region in 1803 forced the Souliot warriors and chieftains to seek refuge with their families on the opposite shores of the Ionian Islands. Meanwhile, the war that broke out between Russia and the Ottoman Empire in 1806 enabled him once again to threaten Ionian territory.[34] During the first months of 1807, Mocenigo, following orders from Russia, gathered his forces in Lefkada and Parga, the two most exposed areas of the Ionian dominion, and prepared them for the imminent clash. The Souliot warriors and other deserters from the Ottoman lands (Klephts, Armatoles, etc.) were ordered to form a defensive corps in the island of Lefkada. Bishop Ignatius and Kapodistrias were together responsible for coordinating these operations. Both men would be utterly transformed by the experience, for within that motley collection of warriors, deserters, and refugees from the Ottoman lands, the two men would start to acquire a sense of patriotism that transcended the Ionian space and became more broadly, even if still vaguely, 'Greek'.[35] *Monsignor Ignatius and I . . . were surrounded by the Greek captains*—wrote Kapodistrias in his dispatch to the Ionian Senate in early July 1807—*we spent the morning listening to the most eloquent amongst them recount their exploits, and then there followed a meal that resembled in every respect the heroic banquets sung by Homer, and at the last music, song and dance. A few wise men are aware of our Republic and of the Protection that sustains it, and they are now convinced that the republic will always be their father-land, once they have given this Fatherland testimonies of their affections and once they render it in the present war signal and very important services.*[36] In political terms, while these two worlds, the mainland Ottoman and the insular Russian-Ionian, were of course still clearly distinguished, this mingling of people from different political settings who were yet seen as sharing the same cultural roots, did nonetheless create a vague sense of a wider 'Greek' world.

## SEPTINSULAR ENLIGHTENMENT AND ORTHODOX RATIONALISM

The protagonists of this story were intellectually indebted to the two major representatives of the Septinsular Enlightenment, namely, Eugenios Voulgaris (1716–1806) and Nicephorus Theotokis (1731–1800). These two Ionian clergymen, who had constructed their lives in the selfsame geographical landscape—comprising Venice, the Ionian Islands, the Ottoman Principalities, and Russia—half a century earlier, adumbrated a programme subsequently named 'Religious Humanism' (in contradistinction to 'Civic Humanism') or 'Orthodox Rationalism', which took

---

[34] Fleming, *The Muslim Bonaparte*, pp. 70–8.
[35] Panagiotopoulos, 'Ignatios Ouggroblachias', p. 59; Loukos, *Ioannis Kapodistrias*, pp. 16–17.
[36] In Karl Mendelssohn-Bartholdy, *Graf Johann Kapodistrias* (Berlin, 1864), p. 399.

the view that philosophy and religion belonged to two separate spheres of human experience and could develop along parallel lines without interfering with each other. Voulgaris went so far as to claim that anything which militated against religious doctrines could not deliver authentic philosophical knowledge. Enlightenment, in this view, was considered to be part of Divine Providence and was treated as a separate but equally valid source of knowledge, existing alongside the eschatological tradition. In accordance with this, Voulgaris believed that a revival and refinement of learning within the Orthodox Church, which would include a substantial training in the classics and greater familiarity with modern European philosophy, was necessary. Theotokis, on the other hand, advocated the creation of an 'Orthodox commonwealth' as a continuation of the 'Byzantine commonwealth', which would link the Greek to the Slavic world under the umbrella of ecumenical eastern Orthodoxy.[37] Part of the broader Adriatic Enlightenment of the Venetian imperial framework, as we will see also in Chapter 12 of this book, the Septinsular Enlightenment had as its key features not only the concern with education and the Orthodox tradition, but also history (especially local history of the Byzantine and modern periods) and folk tradition.[38]

The new imperial Russian political environment of the Ionian Islands, with its reorganization of the geopolitical realities of the area and its marked emphasis on the Orthodoxy and Greekness of its inhabitants, was thus the context within which the main characters of our story would acquire a more solid sense of a patriotism that transcended the Ionian space, thereby becoming more broadly 'Orthodox' and 'Greek'. This sense of Ionian patriotism, developing gradually into Greek nationalism (cultural and religious rather than political—at least at this stage), would be further enhanced by the meeting in Russia of these men with others with a Phanariot and *boyar* background from the Danubian Principalities. We shall see now how this encounter occurred, and what the distinctive elements of the proto-national ideology that it produced would prove to be.

---

[37] Stephen K. Batalden, *Catherine II's Greek Prelate: Eugenios Voulgaris in Russia, 1771–1806* (New York, 1982); Gregory L. Bruess, *Religion, Identity and Empire: A Greek Archbishop in the Russia of Catherine the Great* (New York, 1997); Kitromilides, *Enlightenment and Revolution*, pp. 43–53, 120–33; Eleni Angelomatis-Tsougarakis (ed.), *Evgenios Voulgaris, Conference Proceedings* (Athens, 2009); Efthymios Nicolaidis, *Science and Eastern Orthodoxy. From the Greek Fathers to the Age of Globalization* (Baltimore, 2011), pp. 151–68.

[38] Paschalis M. Kitromilides, 'Eptanisiakos diafotismos: ta oria tis idiomorfias' (Septinsular Enlightenment: the limits of its specificities), *VII Panionian Conference, Proceedings* (Athens, 2004), vol. I, pp. 241–57; Konstantina Zanou, 'Pros mia synoliki theorisi tou ethnikou chronou: pnevmatikes zymoseis ston italo-eptanisiako choro kata to a' miso tou 19ou aiona' (Intellectual activity in the Italian-Ionian space in the first half of the 19th century), *IX Panionian Conference, Proceedings* (Paxi, 2014), vol. II, pp. 319–44.

# 5

# Diasporic Lives across Empires and Nations

## IN THE BOSOM OF RUSSIA

It was not only these men's 'national feeling' that was vitally dependent on Russia; it was also their careers. So when, in July 1807, the Septinsular Republic was dissolved and Napoleon took control of the Ionian region, they were left with little choice. *I am leaving; and I am asking yours and my mother's blessing*, Ioannis Kapodistrias wrote in a short note to his father in late 1808, before embarking upon his journey, as a 'volunteer exile', to St Petersburg.[1] In spite of the offers he received from the commanders of the French forces to serve as Master in the new Council of State, Kapodistrias decided to leave, *not because he wanted to separate his destiny from that of his native land*—as a friend of his wrote—*but because his [moral] sensitivity... did not permit him to abjure his past*.[2] Actually, his father's advice and the strong anti-French feeling that permeated the whole family did not leave much leeway for thought: *I would never put myself among the ranks of those who serve Bonaparte*—he wrote several years later; *only to [the Tsar] Alexander, the real protector of Greeks, was I willing to dedicate my entire life*.[3] That is why, when in 1808 he received an invitation from the Tsar's Foreign Minister Nikolai Rumiantsev to go to Russia, everyone—not least his father—thought that Divine Providence was showing him the way.[4]

If Kapodistrias had to wait for about a year in order to quit the islands, the same was not true of the other central characters of the Septinsular Republic. Mocenigo and Ignatius left in haste as early as November 1807. They went first to Italy, the former to Naples, the latter to Livorno; from there they headed, some months later, to St Petersburg. Their fates would thereafter be inextricably linked to the Russian Empire and particularly to its presence and interests in the Mediterranean. With the passing of time, however, a second focal point of identity would be added to the above: the 'Greek nation'—still, of course, a vague cultural construction which was not associated with any clear political plan. As we shall see, the splitting

---

[1] Kostas Dafnis (ed.), *Archeion Ioannou Kapodistria* (Archive of Ioannis Kapodistrias) (Corfu, 1976–86), vol. III, p. 3. The expression 'volunteer exile' (*exilé volontaire*) belongs to Alexandre Stourdza, 'Notice biographique sur le comte J. Capodistrias, Président de la Grèce', in E. A. Bétant (ed.), *Correspondance du Comte Capodistrias, Président de la Grèce* (Geneva and Paris, 1839), vol. I, p. 13.

[2] Stourdza: 'Notice biographique sur le comte J. Capodistrias', p. 12.

[3] These words are taken from Kapodistrias's so-called 'autobiography', a report of his political career, which he sent to the Tsar in 1826, when he was officially dismissed from the Russian diplomatic service: Jean Capodistria, *Aperçu de ma carrière publique depuis 1798 jusqu'à 1822* (Paris, 1999), p. 45.

[4] Stourdza, 'Notice biographique sur le comte J. Capodistrias', p. 13.

of self between empire and nation would become ever more pronounced. Mocenigo served for many years as the Tsar's Consul in Naples and then in Turin. On his retirement in 1825 he went to Venice and became actively involved in the local Greek community and its philhellenic activities. As I have already noted, his consular role enabled him to help some of his Ionian friends obtain posts: Naranzi was appointed Russian Consul to Venice, while Mustoxidi was named attaché to Mocenigo's consulate in Turin. Mocenigo certainly had a say also in the invitation sent by Rumiantsev to Kapodistrias and Ignatius to go to St Petersburg. The latter stayed in the Russian capital for some time, until a new possibility opened up for him when, during the Russo-Ottoman war, Russia briefly annexed the Danubian Principalities (1809–12). Ignatius was then elected Bishop of Ungrovlachia (the ecclesiastical term for Moldavia and Wallachia) and, in 1810, he moved to Bucharest. He remained there for a couple of years only, since the restitution of the Danubian Principalities to the Ottoman Empire forced him to leave his metropolitan seat again. He then spent some time in Vienna—from where he witnessed the fall of Napoleon and participated in the 1814–15 Congress which 'restored' order in Europe—moving finally to Pisa, and becoming, during the years of the Greek revolution, a coordinator, after a fashion, of the European philhellenic movement.[5]

But how did the environment of St Petersburg influence this nurturing of a Greek national consciousness? Let us return to Kapodistrias. Apart from appearing at social events, which gained him access to Russian high society and allowed him to start building a political career, during the first years of his stay in the Russian capital Kapodistrias took two important steps that would leave their mark on his intellectual development thereafter: first, he learned Greek; second, he encountered the circle of *boyar* and Phanariot exiles and Ionians from a previous generation of migrants, who were employed in the Tsar's Ministry of Foreign Affairs.

## STAMMERING GREEK IN RUSSIA

*It is shameful to be a Greek and not know your mother tongue*—Kapodistrias would seem to have said to a delegation of Russian peasants of Greek extraction, when they visited him in St Petersburg some years later, in 1818.[6] Of course, had they spoken in Greek, he would have had some difficulty answering. Having received

[5] On Mocenigo's late period in Venice see: Xanthopoulou-Kyriakou, *I elliniki koinotita tis Benetias*, p. 60. On Ignatius: Emmanouil G. Protopsaltis, *Ignatios Mitropolitis Ouggroblachias (1766–1828)* (The Bishop of Ungrovlachia Ignatius (1766–1828)) (Athens, 1961), vol. I, pp. 69ff; Vassilis Panagiotopoulos, 'Ignatios Ouggroblachias' (The Bishop of Ungrovlachia Ignatius), in idem and Panagiotis Michailaris, *Klirikoi ston Agona* (Clerics in the Revolution) (Athens, 2010), pp. 62–80; idem, 'Kati egine stin Piza to 1821' (Something happened in Pisa in 1821), *Ta istorika* 5 (June 1986), pp. 177–82. Information on the philhellenic and 'suspect' activity of these men can be found in the secret reports of the Austrian police in Italy, especially of the decade 1817–27: Daniele Manin, *Carte segrete e atti ufficiali della polizia austriaca in Italia dal 4 giugno 1814 al 22 marzo 1848* (Capolago, 1851–2), vol. I, pp. 176–92.

[6] André Papadopoulo-Vretos, *Mémoires biographiques—historiques sur le Président de la Grèce, le comte Jean Capodistrias* (Paris, 1837), pp. 35–6. The episode is narrated in French, but the author specifies that the actual conversation took place in Russian.

his elementary education in a Franciscan monastery on Corfu (the only education to be had in those days), Kapodistrias had learned how to write Italian and French, Latin and maybe Ancient Greek, but had gained no knowledge of how to express himself in Modern Greek. *Δε γράφω εις την γλώσσα μας, επειδή εις αυτό το μέρος νηπιάζω περισσότερον παρά εις κανέν άλλο* (*I do not write in our language, because I am an infant in this field much more than in any other*)—he wrote to his teacher of Greek in an effort to overcome his shyness in that language.[7] His teacher was Demetrios Mostras (1774–1850), the permanent secretary of Bishop Ignatius and a man famous for his erudition.[8] During 1809 and 1810, before Ignatius's departure for Bucharest, the three of them lived under the same roof in St Petersburg and Kapodistrias's linguistic undertakings were thus closely supervised by both the Bishop and his secretary. In a rather melancholic quote from a letter to Bishop Ignatius (Feb. 1811), one of a very few written by him in Greek, Kapodistrias appears to have been in no doubts as to the symbolic weight that language was acquiring in those same years: *Let us stop our correspondence in French. The time of repentance has come. This will neither become true nor will it bring benefit if a patriotic law does not sanction it. This is, your Grace, my supplication: to order as legislators that 'if a Greek writes to another Greek in a foreign idiom, he will be proclaimed a foreigner'. I do not dare, of my own free will, to submit myself to such a violent law, because now we are not in a time of Martyrs, and when I consider the depths of my ignorance in the paternal language, the voice of my conscience assails me and torments my mind.*[9]

It seems however that Kapodistrias never managed to advance beyond the *stammering* stage in writing (and perhaps speaking) Greek, since up until the end of his life, even while he was the governor of Greece, he wrote almost everything in French and Italian. Ironically enough, he failed to apply to himself the 'patriotic law' that he had devised for others. In this he certainly resembled the constitution of the Septinsular Republic, on the drafting of which he had expended so much of his energy back in 1803. One of the articles of that constitution stated, in fact, that *From the year 1810, no one may be appointed for the first time as a public functionary if he cannot read and write in the national vulgar Greek language. From the year 1820 this language will exclusively be used in all public acts.*[10] The extraordinary contradiction of this statement lay, however, in the fact that the entire text was written in Italian and was signed by almost all of those who voted for it in the same language.[11]

[7] 15 May 1811. In Spyridon Theotokis, 'I ethniki syneidisis tou Kapodistriou kai i elliniki glossa' (Kapodistrias's national consciousness and the Greek language), *Proceedings of the Academy of Athens* 7 (1932), p. 138.

[8] Loukia Droulia, 'Logiosyni kai bibliofilia: o Dimitrios Mostras kai i bibliothiki tou' (Learned and bibliophile: Demetrios Mostras and his library), *Tetradia ergasias* 9 (1989), pp. 227–305; Liza Martini, 'Kapodistrias–Dimitrios Mostras', *Kerkyraika chronika* 9 (1962), pp. 97–132; idem, 'Anekdotes epistoles tou Dimitriou Mostra pros ton Ioannin Kapodistrian' (Unpublished letters of Demetrios Mostras to Ioannis Kapodistrias), *IV Panionian Conference, Proceedings*, [=*Kerkyraika chronika* 23 (1980)], pp. 418–35.

[9] In Theotokis, 'I ethniki syneidisis tou Kapodistriou', pp. 135–6.

[10] Peter Mackridge, 'Venise après Venise: Official Languages in the Ionian Islands, 1797–1864', *Byzantine and Modern Greek Studies* 38/1 (2014), pp. 68–90.

[11] Sarantis C. Orfanoudakis, 'Constitutional Texts of the Ionian Islands: A Review', in Aliki D. Nikiforou (ed.), *Constitutional Charters of the Ionian Islands* (Athens, 2012), p. 52.

The resemblances between Kapodistrias as a 'national individual' and the constitution of 1803 as a 'national text' did not end there, however. In the same way that Kapodistrias described himself as an 'infant' in the universe of Greek language, the constitution designated the 'Ionian peoples' as 'infants' in the world of liberty and nationalism: *Two powerful Monarchs, one the Protector of the Nation through proximity and trade, the other through religion and institutions*—read the report of the Legislative Body—*sought to be the wetnurse of the new infancy of the Septinsular Peoples.*[12] Apparently, 'national constitutions', like 'national individuals', saw themselves as being in the initial stages of their lives and needing, therefore, guidance and protection. This was one of the basic motifs, as we will see, of the Ionian proto-liberal and proto-national thought of the time.

## THE MEETING WITH THE *BOYAR*–PHANARIOT AND OLDER IONIAN ELEMENTS

One of Kapodistrias's earliest acquaintances in St Petersburg was the Stourdza family. Skarlatos Stourdza came from one of the oldest, wealthiest, and most influential *boyar* (noble) families of Moldavia. His wife, Soultana, was the daughter of the Prince of Moldavia Konstantinos Mourouzis, member of a leading Greek Phanariot family of Constantinople. The Phanariots were Ottoman Christian elites, connected with Ottoman governance as interpreters, diplomats, tax farmer-governors, and through their association with the Ecumenical Patriarchate in Constantinople, itself closely involved with the Ottoman administration.[13] In the aftermath of the Russo-Ottoman war, in 1792, the Stourdzas, like several other Phanariot-*boyar* families that had leaned towards the Russians during the war years, decided to leave the threatening atmosphere of the Danubian Principalities and seek a safe haven in Russia. They moved to the estates which Catherine II awarded them in the Belarusian campaign, where they lived for about ten years. In 1802, once Tsar Alexander I had ascended the throne, they were made to feel more welcome at court and therefore relocated to St Petersburg. It was in their famous Petersburgian salon that Kapodistrias met them. One of the daughters of the family, Roxandra (1786–1844), remembers: *Cast adrift from his family and from his country, without any prospects for the future, deprived of the resources that science and study had offered him in beautiful Italy, where he was raised, he [Kapodistrias] could not find any entertainment but in our company.*[14] Roxandra herself was, in reality, one more reason why Kapodistrias frequented their house. It seems indeed that she was the only woman who ever touched Ioannis's heart. Their story remained unfulfilled, however.[15]

---

[12] [N. B. Manessi], *Le tre costituzioni (1800, 1803, 1817) delle Sette Isole Jonie* (Corfu, 1849), p. 32.

[13] Christine M. Philliou, *Biography of an Empire: Governing Ottomans in an Age of Revolution* (Berkeley, Los Angeles, and London, 2011).

[14] Roxandra Stourdza-Edling, *Mémoires de la Comtesse Edling (née Stourdza) Demoiselle d'Honneur de sa Majesté l'Imperatrice Elisabeth Alexéevna* (Moscow, 1829), pp. 41–2.

[15] Alexandre Stourdza, 'Souvenirs de la vie de ma sœur pour ceux qui l'ont aimé', in idem, *Œuvres posthumes, religieuses, historiques, philosophiques et littéraires* (Paris, 1859), vol. I, pp. 42–59; Christos Loukos, *Ioannis Kapodistrias* (Athens, 2009), pp. 19–21; Eleni E. Koukkou, *Ioannis*

On account of Roxandra, who became lady-in-waiting to Empress Elisabeth—
Alexander I's wife—and developed a certain familiarity also with the Tsar (they
both shared the same spiritual preoccupations and an admiration for certain mystic luminaries, like Madame de Krüdener), the Stourdzas gained access to court
circles.[16] Roxandra's brother, Alexandre Stourdza (1791–1854), held various offices
in the Ministry of Foreign Affairs, eventually ascending to the position of the
Asiatic Department's specialist in Danubian matters. His multi-lingualism—he
was fluent in French, German, Italian, Russian, Greek, Latin, and Church Slavonic—
was certainly his most important asset. Alexandre soon became best friends with
Kapodistrias. With the passage of time and with Kapodistrias's entrance into the
Ministry of Foreign Affairs, the two men's careers advanced in parallel; they served
together in Bucharest, Vienna, and Paris. Stourdza worked mostly as Kapodistrias's
secretary, but also as his counsellor on Danubian and European issues. In his dual
role as a diplomat and an intellectual, Alexandre Stourdza also became known for
his published writings. His name is usually associated with the history of the Holy
Alliance (he played a major role in perceiving and drafting the treaty of the Alliance)
and of counter-revolutionary thought in general. Regarded as 'the Maistre of the
East', he is best remembered for his reactionary essay *Mémoire sur l'état actuel de
l'Allemagne* (1818), where he maintained that German universities were hotbeds of
atheism and revolution and should be stripped of their traditional autonomy and
placed under police control. On the other hand, Stourdza was also a proponent of
a certain brand of conservatism, one that aspired to marry religion with liberty,
education, and moral progress. Both he and Kapodistrias, a scholar has observed,
'typify the ambiguity of the terms *liberal* and *conservative* in the early nineteenth
century'.[17] What is more—as a recent intellectual biography has shown—he
was also a man of the Enlightenment, who tried to reinterpret and adapt the ideas
of Montesquieu and Rousseau to an Orthodox and Oriental environment.[18]
Indeed, in the activities of this circle, the Septinsular Enlightenment came to meet
the Phanariot Enlightenment of the Principalities, an intellectual tradition which
was closely connected to the reforms undertaken by the Patriarchate of Constantinople
from the seventeenth century onwards as an answer to the penetration of Catholicism
in the area. Unlike the Septinsular Enlightenment, which was mostly Italian-speaking,
the Phanariot Enlightenment endorsed Greek education and Orthodox culture and
supported the foundation of schools for the Christian populations within the political establishment of the Ottoman Empire. Its Orthodoxy notwithstanding, this

---

*Kapodistrias-Roxandra Stourdza, mia anekpliroti agapi* (Ioannis Kapodistrias—Roxandra Stourdza, an
unfulfilled love) (Athens, 1996).

[16] Andrei Zorin, ' "Star of the East": The Holy Alliance and European Mysticism', *Kritika: Explorations
in Russian and Eurasian History* 4/2 (Spring 2003), esp. pp. 315–16.

[17] Alexander M. Martin, *Romantics, Reformers, Reactionaries: Russian Conservative Thought and
Politics in the Reign of Alexander I* (DeKalb, Ill., 1997), p. 170 (but see pp. 149–96).

[18] Stella Ghervas, *Réinventer la tradition: Alexandre Stourdza et l'Europe de la Sainte-Alliance* (Paris,
2008), pp. 107–77. See also Aurelian Craiutu, 'Rethinking Modernity, Religion, and Tradition: The
Intellectual Dialogue between Alexandre Stourdza and Joseph de Maistre', *History of European Ideas*
(2013), pp. 1–13; [Anonymous], 'Notice sur la vie et les travaux d'Alexandre de Stourdza', in Stourdza,
*Œuvres posthumes*, pp. 1–33.

was an Enlightenment closely associated with the Ottoman political framework.[19] A Jacobin and republican version of the Phanariot Enlightenment would develop, in the years around the French Revolution, in the writings of Rigas Velestinlis (1757–98), too radical though it may have been for the tastes of this circle.[20]

As we will see in Chapter 6, the one matter that certainly distanced Stourdza from the Metternichian order was his opinion on the Greek revolution. It is striking in fact that, especially after the outbreak of the revolution, both he and his sister, their Romanian-Moldavian roots and their Russian nationalism notwithstanding, became not simply philhellenes but actually Greek nationalists. *All my affections were turned towards oppressed Greece*, Roxandra noted.[21] Similarly, Alexandre: *[Before 1821] I still only had a native land, but no motherland. Greece, which gave me the light of day, the Church, which conferred the sacred quality of being a Christian upon me, both living in the bottom of the tomb, estranged me time and time again from their maternal breast.*[22] The Stourdza siblings were not the only figures in Alexandrine high society to identify with the Greek cause. Their cousin, Alexandros Ypsilantis (1792–1828), an offspring of a famous Phanariot family, a senior officer in the Imperial Russian cavalry during the Napoleonic Wars, and aide-de-camp of Alexandre I, was at the same time the leader of the *Philiki Etairia*, a secret society promoting the liberation of Greece. Though others dismissed Ypsilantis as 'immature' and 'of a moderate intelligence',[23] he was the initiator of the 1821 uprising in Moldavia which triggered the Greek War of Independence.[24]

Among the 'Greek' émigrés who had been assimilated into Russian society but who nonetheless would become Greek nationalists in the years of the revolution, Spyridon Destunis (1782–1848) should also be mentioned. Nephew of a Cephalonian merchant who moved to Odessa when it was annexed to Russia in 1792, Destunis studied classics and modern languages at Moscow. By the time of Alexander I, he was working as a translator in the Asiatic Department of the Ministry of Foreign Affairs, until, in line with typical Russian practice, he was appointed Consul General in Smyrna (1818). With the outbreak of the Greek revolution and the subsequent escalation of hostilities against the Greek community of Smyrna, he sought refuge in Venice, where he stayed for five years, before returning definitively to St Petersburg. Like many of his fellow diplomats, Destunis had a dual career, both

---

[19] An earlier version of this Enlightenment coincided indeed with the Enlightenment of the Ottoman court of Ahmet III. See Harun Küçük, 'Natural Philosophy and Politics in the Eighteenth Century: Esad of Ioannina and Greek Aristotelianism at the Ottoman Court', *Journal of Ottoman Studies* 41 (2013), pp. 125–58; Molly Greene, *The Edinburgh History of the Greeks, 1453 to 1768: The Ottoman Empire* (Edinburgh, 2015), pp. 192–213.

[20] Ariadna Camariano-Cioran, *Les Académies princieres de Bucarest et de Jassy et leurs professeurs* (Thessalonica, 1974); Philliou, *Biography of an Empire*; Paschalis M. Kitromilides, *Enlightenment and Revolution: The Making of Modern Greece* (Cambridge, Mass., and London, 2013), pp. 200–29.

[21] Stourdza-Edling, *Mémoires de la Comtesse Edling*, p. 173.

[22] Alexandre Stourdza, *La Grèce en 1821 et 1822: correspondance politique publiée par un Grec* (Paris, 1823), p. 1.

[23] Stourdza-Edling, *Mémoires de la Comtesse Edling*, p. 40; Ioannis Filimon, *Dokimion istorikon peri tis Philikis Etairias* (Historical treatise on the Philiki Etairia) (Nafplio, 1834), pp. 268–9.

[24] Richard Stites, *The Four Horsemen: Riding to Liberty in Post-Napoleonic Europe* (Oxford, 2014), pp. 186–239; Polychronis K. Enepekidis, *Rigas—Ypsilantis—Kapodistrias* (Athens, 1965), pp. 108–50.

as an official in the diplomatic corps and as a publicist and translator. Amongst other things, he produced important Russian translations of Plutarch, of Byzantine historical texts, and of the Byzantine juridical text *Exavivlos*.[25]

Destunis, Stourdza, and Kapodistrias were bound not only by their friendship and their careers (they were all colleagues in the Russian Ministry of Foreign Affairs, after all), but also by their sharing the same vision of the 'regeneration' of what they more and more perceived to be their common patria, Greece. Around the years of the revolution, the three of them formed the so-called 'War party', an unofficial political lobby within the tsarist court which advocated Russian military intervention in favour of the Greek insurgents.[26] This mingling of the Ionian and Phanariot element in the chilly corridors and salons of St Petersburg would produce, as we will see, its own peculiar system of interpreting the Greek revolution and of understanding Greek nationalism in general.

## SHINING IN THE SERVICE OF THE TSAR

In October 1811, after two years of professional inactivity in the Russian capital, Kapodistrias shook off his inertia by agreeing to go as a supernumerary attaché to the Russian embassy in Vienna. Some months later, and thanks to a memoir prepared for his superiors regarding the 'present situation of the Greeks' which met with the Tsar's approval—and how could it be otherwise since it started by stating that *the Greek people owes its name, its present existence and its hopes to the magnanimous benevolence and to the honourable protection of the court of Russia?*[27]—he was appointed director of the Diplomatic Chancery of the Russian troops in the Danube. In command of those troops was Admiral Chichagov, whom Kapodistrias had met in the house of the Stourdzas.[28] He moved to the headquarters of those troops in Bucharest at the beginning of June 1812, just a few days before Napoleon's invasion of Russia. As luck would have it, the Russian response to Napoleon took the tsarist troops into the heart of central Europe, greatly enhancing the importance of the Diplomatic Chancery of Bucharest, and consequently that of Kapodistrias himself. The real twist to his career, however, was given by his meeting with the Tsar in October 1813. According to Roxandra Stourdza, Alexander I was captivated by Kapodistrias's *noble and elegant countenance, the expression of his soul as it was impressed on his perfectly balanced features;...after having talked with him awhile,*

---

[25] He also translated into Russian Adamantios Koraes's Francophile poem *Military Trumpet* (*Voennaia Truba*, 1807) slightly altering its content to chime in with the anti-Napoleonic sentiment of Russian society. Theophilus Prousis, 'The Destunis Collection in the Manuscript Section of the Saltykov-Shchedrin State Public Library in Leningrad', *Modern Greek Studies Yearbook* 5 (1989), pp. 395–452; Sonia Ilinskaya, 'Metafrastikes peripeteies gyro apo ton *Thourio* sti Rossia' (Translative adventures around the *Thourios* in Russia), in idem, *Ellinorosika synapantimata* (Greek–Russian meetings) (Athens, 2004), p. 16.

[26] Theophilus Prousis, *Russian Society and the Greek Revolution* (DeKalb, Ill., 1994), pp. 26–54.

[27] [Ioannis Kapodistrias], 'Mémoire sur l'état actuel des Grecs', in Dafnis (ed.), *Archeion Ioannou Kapodistria*, vol. VII, p. 188. For more on this memoir see Chapter 6.

[28] Papadopoulo-Vretos, *Mémoires biographiques*, p. 14.

*he was certain that he had found what he had long sought, a mind at once subtle and lofty, combined with an understanding of persons and things.*[29] It has been observed that 'Alexander's emotional reactions to individuals often had an overbearing effect on the affairs of state'.[30] As a matter of fact, from that moment on, Kapodistrias's rise was meteoric. He was immediately entrusted with an important and delicate diplomatic mission: to counter French influence upon the people of Switzerland and to ensure their unity and their backing for the allied Russo-Prussian forces in the event of their invading France. It took him several months of difficult negotiations and diplomatic manoeuvres, but in the end he was successful.[31]

Kapodistrias's achievements in Switzerland, having *surpassed [the Tsar's] expectations*,[32] earned him a ticket to one of the most impressive and important diplomatic gatherings in history, the crucial Congress of Vienna (1814–15). Recorded by historians as 'the actual moment when Europe sloughed off its cosmopolitan past and entered its national future', the Congress of Vienna re-ordered the geo-political shape and identity of the European continent and its colonial territories after the fall of Napoleon.[33] By gathering together more than 215 princely heads of Europe, diplomatic delegates, aspirants, and conspirators, the Congress also gave the principal characters in our story the opportunity to meet again and to formulate their ideas in a more concrete manner.

## IONIAN PATRIOTISM AND IMPERIAL ALLEGIANCES

Alexander I having taken such a liking to Kapodistrias, he prevailed over the other members of the Russian delegation and became the Tsar's principal collaborator throughout the Congress. From that privileged position, he was able to play an active role in mitigating the vindictive tendencies of the victorious powers against France and, as a historian recently put it, to 'make things difficult for the British in the Mediterranean' when negotiating the fate of the Ionian Islands.[34] Kapodistrias's main concern was to prevent the Ionian Islands passing to Austria, which, according to him, *would have set the Islands back a hundred years*.[35] The best option, in his opinion, was to entrust the fate of the islands to a maritime power and particularly— as he wrote to his friend Ugo Foscolo in April 1815—*England, whose sceptre is Neptune's trident*.[36] In this endeavour Kapodistrias was to prove successful. The treaty

[29] Stourdza-Edling, *Mémoires de la Comtesse Edling*, p. 135; Capodistria, *Aperçu de ma carrière publique*, pp. 48–51.

[30] Patricia Kennedy Grimsted, *The Foreign Ministers of Alexander I: Political Attitudes and the Conduct of Russian Diplomacy, 1801–1825* (Berkeley and Los Angeles, 1969), p. 40.

[31] Michelle Bouvier (ed.), *Archeion Ioannou Kapodistria* (Archive of Ioannis Kapodistrias) (Corfu, 1976–86), vol. IV.

[32] Stourdza-Edling, *Mémoires de la Comtesse Edling*, p. 146.

[33] Glenda Sluga, 'The Congress of Vienna' (part of the project 'The International History of Cosmopolitanism'): <https://sites.google.com/site/viennacon/assignments> (accessed 28 Feb. 2014).

[34] Robert Holland, *Blue-Water Empire: The British in the Mediterranean since 1800* (London, 2013), p. 29.

[35] Capodistrias, *Aperçu de ma carrière publique*, p. 57.          [36] FE, vol. 6, p. 20.

signed in Paris on 5 November 1815 handed the Ionian Islands to Britain, recognizing the legitimacy of the British forces which were already installed in most parts of the region. To this decision there was, however, a crucial Russian caveat: the islands should not be a colony, but only a British protectorate; the 'freedom' and 'independence' of the new Ionian state should, in addition, be guaranteed through the granting of a constitution.

*In England, opinions, thoughts, affections, speech, the press, are all free, the freest…* Kapodistrias wrote to his father on the eve of the agreement, as if seeking to console him for the impossibility of reviving the Russian-controlled Septinsular Republic, to which he was still deeply attached—*A government which is protected by Great Britain cannot, and should not, impose tyrannical laws.*[37] It has been said that Kapodistrias 'hated England like an Ionian'; all the more so, being 'an Ionian who had taken Russian employment'.[38] Nevertheless, to him, as to many Ionian and Italian liberals, the option of British imperialism did not appear so bad at the time. *Oh sublime, oh blessed England, … you are a great nation, unlike ugly France, which deserves to be wiped off the face of Europe*—reads an entry in the diary of Kapodistrias's compatriot and friend Mario Pieri on 27 May 1815.[39] As has been cogently argued, a liberal ideology which in the years after 1815 emerged out of a critique of the Napoleonic and Austrian empires was prepared to countenance an imperial future for some Mediterranean countries insofar as this guaranteed the extension of civil and political rights to the region.[40] For example, in a lengthy tract written in 1817, entitled *Stato politico delle isole Jonie* (Political state of the Ionian Islands), Ugo Foscolo maintained that the Ionians, being a small and peripheral nation, had no chance of becoming independent, unless they entrusted themselves to the protection of some foreign country and accepted sheltering under its wing. Like Kapodistrias, Foscolo believed that, on account of the long years of Venetian rule, which had corrupted their character, created divisions, and enhanced ignorance, the Ionian citizens were not yet ready for independence. This would be achieved only after the gradual establishment of certain preconditions, above all unity and public education.[41] In the meantime, among the imperial powers which could guarantee the 'independence' of the islands, Britain, with its constitutional traditions and freedom of the press and with its lack of restrictive laws on trade, was the best option.

It has been pointed out that Foscolo's outlook was not only 'national', but also 'imperial', insofar as he saw the Ionian Islands as part of the heritage of the Republic of Venice and argued that Britain had a moral duty to replace Venice as

---

[37] Dafnis (ed.), *Archeion Ioannou Kapodistria*, vol. III, p. 320.

[38] Holland, *Blue-Water Empire*, p. 29.

[39] BRF: Memorie di Mario Pieri, vol. II [Ricc. 3556], 132.

[40] Maurizio Isabella, 'Liberalism and Empires in the Mediterranean: The View-Point of the Risorgimento', in Silvana Patriarca and Lucy Riall (eds), *The Risorgimento Revisited: Nationalism and Culture in Nineteenth-Century Italy* (London and New York, 2012), p. 234.

[41] Ugo Foscolo, 'Stato politico delle Isole Jonie' (1817), in *Prose politiche e apologetiche (1817–1827)*, vol. I: *Scritti sulle Isole Ionie e su Parga*, edited by Giovanni Gambarin (Florence, 1964), pp. 8–25; Maurizio Isabella, *Risorgimento in Exile: Italian Emigrés and the Liberal International in the Post-Napoleonic Era* (Oxford, 2009), pp. 70–1.

the defender of European civilization in the eastern Mediterranean.[42] Likewise, Kapodistrias's Ionian patriotism was midway between an 'imperial' and a 'national' stance, insofar as his perception of the post-Venetian reality of the islands was filtered through his imperial allegiances to Russia. The binary division between 'nation' and 'empire' seems thus to be obsolete here, in that many liberals of Kapodistrias's age saw self-rule as compatible with acceptance of someone else's overlordship. Indeed, what was in question in the case of the post-Venetian Ionian Islands (in both their Russian and British phases) was some form of self-rule within larger, layered systems of imperial rule. The nation, for these Ionian proto-liberals, being in its early stages of life, could exist only as a sub-unit within an imperial, hierarchical system of rule. *Liberty and political independence could prosper... only where they are placed under the auspices of liberal and powerful protectors capable... of keeping that little state from being extinguished by the great powers*—Kapodistrias wrote to the British Foreign Secretary Lord Castlereagh in 1815.[43]

Nevertheless, the enthusiasm for Britain was not destined to last for long. The entry in Pieri's diary would be corrected some years later with a marginal comment: *Oh deception that then blurred my mind! Oh my poor Corfu!*[44] On his visit to Corfu in 1819, Kapodistrias saw with his own eyes what he had heard being whispered by his compatriots: the British High Commissioner, Thomas Maitland (1816–23), was governing in so high-handed a manner that the agreements of 1815 seemed an empty word. In addition, local families of influence which were judged to be Russophile, like the Kapodistrias, were elbowed aside by the new regime. The crowning disillusion came, in March 1819, with the cession by the British of the town of Parga to Ali Pasha. Kapodistrias witnessed the wretched mass of Pargiote exiles seeking refuge in the Ionian Islands, many ending up in shanties at the outskirts of Corfu town, where they stayed for decades.[45] The orders he had from the Tsar not to nurse hopes of an imminent Russian intervention left him with no option but to advise his fellow Ionians to trust *Divine Providence, which is the sole arbiter of nations.*[46] Nonetheless, the private activity that he undertook in coordination with Foscolo and Andrea Mustoxidi, in writing texts and delivering memoranda denouncing the authoritarian rule of the British in the Ionian, transformed the cession of Parga, an otherwise minor event in diplomatic history, into one of the first and most powerful symbols of European political philhellenism.[47]

[42]  Eugenio Biagini, 'Liberty, Class and Nation-Building: Ugo Foscolo's "English" Constitutional Thought, 1816–1827', *European Journal of Political Theory* 5/34 (2006), pp. 36–9.

[43]  In Patricia Kennedy Grimsted, 'Capodistrias and a "New Order" for Restoration Europe: The "Liberal Ideas" of a Russian Foreign Minister (1814–1822)', *Journal of Modern History* 40/2 (June 1968), p. 189. See also Grigorii Arsh, *O Ioannis Kapodistrias sti Rosia* (Ioannis Kapodistrias in Russia) (Athens, 2015), pp. 107–11.

[44]  BRF: Memorie di Mario Pieri, vol. II [Ricc. 3556], 132.

[45]  Holland, *Blue-Water Empire*, pp. 33–9.

[46]  [Ioannis Kapodistrias], 'Observations sur les moyens d'améliorer le sort de Grecs' (6/18 Apr. 1819, Corfu), in George Waddinghton, *A Visit to Greece in 1823 and 1824* (London, 1825), p. xxxvi.

[47]  Kostas Kairofilas, 'Kapodistrias kai Foskolos' (Kapodistrias and Foscolo), *Imerologion tis Megalis Ellados* 8/8 (1929), pp. 161–86; FE, vol. 8, pp. 105–6, 122–3, 143–7; idem, 'On Parga', *Edinburgh Review* (1819), in *Prose politiche e apologetiche*, vol. I, pp. 65–102; [Andrea Mustoxidi], *Exposé des faits qui ont précédé et suivi la cession de Parga* (Paris, 1820). On the issue of Parga see also Isabella, *Risorgimento in Exile*, pp. 71–5 and Natale Caccia, 'L'episodio di Parga in alcuni componimenti poetici francesi e inglesi', in *Studi sul Berchet, pubblicati per il primo centenario della morte* (Milan, 1951), pp. 389–417.

The diasporic itineraries that the principal characters of the Septinsular Republic were forced to follow after its dissolution, and the meetings in Russia they promoted with others from the Danubian Principalities with a Phanariot and *boyar* background, nurtured their belief in Enlightened Orthodoxy and fostered forms of nationalism and proto-liberalism which creatively combined the empire and the nation. Small nations, for these Ionian proto-liberals, could exist only if protected by great empires. We shall see now how these ideas found ample room for expression given the mystical atmosphere created by the Holy Alliance and by Tsar Alexander I's allegedly liberal and constitutional venture.

# 6

## Conservative Liberalism and Pan-Christian Utopianism in Post-Napoleonic Europe

### POST-NAPOLEONIC MODERATE LIBERALISM AND THE TSAR

So, if back in 1815 Kapodistrias's avowedly Russophile father could not find any consolation in words promising freedom of expression while binding the fortune of the Ionian Islands to the British Empire, he could certainly derive great solace from the fact that his son emerged from the Congress as the new Minister of Foreign Affairs of the Tsar (he served jointly with Nesselrode from 1815 to 1822). The new order of things in 'restored' Europe appeared indeed to be on Kapodistrias's side. The messianic atmosphere that took hold after the fall of the Napoleonic Empire, which led to the creation of the Holy Alliance; the mystic dimensions that this Alliance assumed, perceived as it was to be a holy pact binding all Christians together in mutual respect and everlasting peace; Alexander I's personal sense that it was his divine mission to save the Christians from the sufferings that revolutionary ideas had brought down on their heads; his abstract endorsement of Enlightenment ideals and the belief in man's capacity to improve and be morally elevated through education; even his conservative liberalism, which seemed at first to prevail over Metternich's zeal to restore absolutist order; all these looked to be in perfect sympathy with Kapodistrias's world view.[1]

Like many European moderate liberals of his time, Kapodistrias nursed, of course, an intense distaste for Jacobinism and the revolutionary ideology. The excesses of the French Revolution and Napoleon led many of his contemporaries, within the spectrum of liberal politics, to seek to discredit the experiment of 'democracy'.[2] Figures such as François Guizot (and other influential *doctrinaires*), Victor Cousin, Madame de Staël, Pellegrino Rossi, Giuseppe Pecchio, and Santorre

[1] Patricia Kennedy Grimsted, *The Foreign Ministers of Alexander I, Political Attitudes and the Conduct of Russian Diplomacy, 1801–1825* (Berkeley and Los Angeles, 1969), pp. 39, 57–9, 46–9, 60–1, 226–8; idem, 'Capodistrias and a "New Order" for Restoration Europe: The "Liberal Ideas" of a Russian Foreign Minister (1814–1822)', *Journal of Modern History* 40/2 (June 1968), pp. 166–92; Andrei Zorin, '"Star of the East": The Holy Alliance and European Mysticism', *Kritika: Explorations in Russian and Eurasian History* 4/2 (Spring 2003), pp. 313–42.

[2] Joanna Innes and Mark Philp, 'Introduction', in idem (eds), *Re-imagining Democracy in the Age of Revolutions: America, France, Britain, Ireland (1750–1850)* (Oxford, 2013), p. 2.

di Santarosa—authors with whom Kapodistrias and his Ionian friends were in contact and whose books they read[3]—were primarily preoccupied with *preventing* revolution, rather than promoting it. It has been convincingly argued that theirs was 'a liberalism of fear', haunted by the spectre of the French Revolution returning again and again.[4] What was of greater interest to the liberal world of the post-Napoleonic period was the stability of the post-revolutionary order and the prospect of gradual political progress. Kapodistrias was indeed similar to many of the liberal aristocrats of his day when he espoused evolutionary politics, hoping that social change could come about peacefully, gradually, and without revolutionary cataclysms. On the other hand, he believed that liberal reforms were necessary for the maintenance of order and disagreed with the reactionaries who thought that they would prevent revolution through repressive measures. *Since 1815*—he complained to a fellow diplomat in 1820, after Metternich's policies had dominated international affairs—*the cabinets have obstinately failed in their judgement of men and events of our time...It is as if the events of the past twenty-five years had not transpired. Such is undoubtedly the principal source of all the misfortunes with which the world is stricken...We made peace [in 1815]. One might as well say that we signed treaties stipulating, not the intention of constructing a social order anew, but of reproducing the ancient one.*[5] In fact, it was not the concern of moderate liberals to turn the clock back and restore the Old Regime, but 'to end' the Revolution by building representative institutions. What they wanted was to achieve the *juste milieu*, to provide a moderate answer between Revolution and Reaction.[6]

Besides, Kapodistrias was attuned to the national preoccupations of his day and realized that the nation had replaced the monarch as the focus of the people's loyalty in the nineteenth century. Those who fought against Napoleon were—he wrote in 1820—*called to arms in the name of the fatherland, and not in the name of the sovereign.*[7] He was also abreast of contemporary constitutional debate. In recommending a new government for Naples in 1820, for example, he remarked that unlike *the Emperor of Austria [who] has always professed the principles of absolute monarchy...Russia...has looked to the proper mixture of liberty and constitutional rights, that affords a more extended and better basis for government.*[8] Constitutions, he believed, were the bulwarks against revolution and against despotic rule. *It is this constitutionality...wise, frank, and voluntary, which is the only weapon to combat the*

---

[3] On Kapodistrias's and Mustoxidi's relations to Cousin and to the circle of Coppet see Part IV of this book. For more: Konstantina Zanou, 'Expatriate Intellectuals and National Identity: Andrea Mustoxidi in Italy, France and Switzerland (1802–1829)' (Ph.D. dissertation, University of Pisa, 2007), pp. 104–17. The catalogue of Kapodistrias's library includes books by de Staël and Guizot: <http://kapodistrias.digitalarchive.gr/biblio.php?type=1>.

[4] Aurelian Craiutu, *Liberalism under Siege: The Political Thought of the French Doctrinaires* (Lanham, Md, 2003), p. 283.

[5] In Kennedy Grimsted, 'Capodistrias and a "New Order" for Restoration Europe', p. 177.

[6] Aurelian Craiutu, 'Moderation and the Group of Coppet', in Karyna Szmurlo (ed.), *Germaine de Staël's Politics of Mediation: Challenges to History and Culture* (Oxford, 2011), pp. 109–24; Maurizio Isabella, *Risorgimento in Exile: Italian Émigrés and the Liberal International in the Post-Napoleonic Era* (Oxford, 2009), pp. 26–30.

[7] In Kennedy Grimsted, 'Capodistrias and a "New Order" for Restoration Europe', p. 181.

[8] In Kennedy Grimsted, 'Capodistrias and a "New Order" for Restoration Europe', p. 183.

*enemy from right and left*—he wrote to the French Foreign Minister Richelieu in defending the policy of establishing a constitutional monarchy in Naples and Spain after the revolutions of 1821.[9] Of course, constitutional regimes, for Kapodistrias, varied considerably from one country to another. Although he believed that republicanism was the ideal form of government (*The Swiss find me somewhat according to their way of thinking and a good republican*—he told Roxandra Stourdza in 1814),[10] he thought that the principle of representative government depended largely on the degree of 'enlightenment' of the population.

In this Kapodistrias was clearly following the ideas developed by the Neapolitan philosopher Vincenzo Cuoco in his influential *Saggio storico sulla rivoluzione di Napoli* (Historical Treatise on the Revolution of Naples, 1801). In attempting to learn theoretical and political lessons from the failed Neapolitan revolution of 1799, Cuoco argued that the historical specificities of a place should be taken into serious consideration if institutional reforms were to be successful. Any political change, he claimed, should be set upon a firm foundation: 'one could only establish political liberty if one had first managed to create free men'.[11] Cuoco's position became a dominant motif in nineteenth-century moderate liberal thought, influencing among others Foscolo. In his aforementioned tract on the political state of the Ionian Islands, Foscolo maintained that full political rights should be limited exclusively to landowners, who were the only persons to be non-dependent and thus to have free will.[12] This was a position likewise endorsed by Kapodistrias. Several years later, when he was the governor of Greece, and had to defend himself against the accusations of the political opposition for being anti-constitutional, he claimed that Greece would be ready for the constitution only when a solid class of small landowners was formed, substantial loans from foreign countries were secured, and an effective educational system was established. When people had been freed from their various *yokes of slavery*—he wrote in September 1830—they would be able to vote with their own free will, disregarding the interests of the local magnates; until that time, he continued, *every constitution would simply favour individual interests, and found the power of the strongest upon the ignorance and debasement of the masses*.[13] As a matter of fact, Kapodistrias calculated that this process would take Greece about five to six years, a period in which he would continue to govern under a 'provisional' non-constitutional regime, embodied in his own person.[14]

---

[9]  In Kennedy Grimsted, 'Capodistrias and a "New Order" for Restoration Europe', p. 183.

[10]  In Kennedy Grimsted, 'Capodistrias and a "New Order" for Restoration Europe', pp. 185–6.

[11]  Bruce Haddock, 'Between Revolution and Reaction: Vincenzo Cuoco's Saggio storico', *European Journal of Political Theory* 5/22 (2006), p. 28.

[12]  Ugo Foscolo, 'Stato politico delle Isole Jonie' (1817), in *Prose politiche e apologetiche (1817–1827)*, vol. I: *Scritti sulle Isole Ionie e su Parga*, edited by Giovanni Gambarin (Florence, 1964), p. 32; Eugenio Biagini, 'Liberty, Class and Nation-Building: Ugo Foscolo's "English" Constitutional Thought, 1816–1827', *European Journal of Political Theory* 5/34 (2006), pp. 43–4.

[13]  E. A. Bétant (ed.), *Correspondance du Comte Capodistrias, Président de la Grèce* (Geneva and Paris, 1839), vol. IV, p. 133. See also Alexandre Stourdza, 'Notice biographique sur le comte J. Capodistrias, Président de la Grèce', in Bétant (ed.), *Correspondance*, vol. I, p. 102.

[14]  Letter to Nesserlode (17/25 Dec. 1830). In Christos Loukos, *I antipolitefsi kata tou kyberniti Io. Kapodistria* (The political opposition against the governor Ioannis Kapodistrias) (Athens, 1988), p. 276.

It is a truism of Greek historiography that Kapodistrias forgot his so-called 'liberal principles' once he had set foot in Greece. During the 1980s, vigorous works chiefly designed to criticize the hagiographic image of Kapodistrias constructed through the nationalistic rhetoric of the junta period attempted to study (and appraise) the period of his government by giving voice to the claims of the political opposition.[15] It goes well beyond the scope of the present book to examine Kapodistrias's rule of Greece (1828–31) and to decide just how autocratic it really was. It should be noted however that, no matter how conservative, Kapodistrias's political outlook fell within—and not outside—the spectrum of liberal politics as these were understood in Europe in the post-Napoleonic period. His apparent political fluctuations were nevertheless grounded in what remained a moderate liberal outlook: it was consistent with his principles to suppose that the Greeks he found on the mainland were unprepared for participatory, constitutional government.

One reason why Kapodistrias has been perceived as an 'autocrat' by Greek historiography is his affinity with the Tsar and the system of the Holy Alliance—at least in its initial stages. Nevertheless, Alexander I represented one thing in the eyes of liberal Europe in the immediate post-Napoleonic years and something altogether different subsequently. *From 1819 to 1822, the sphere of moral influence that Russia possessed was really immense*, Stourdza wrote, reflecting the prestige and symbolic role of the Tsar within European liberal circles in the immediate post-war period.[16] Praised as the peaceful counterpart to Napoleon, whose language of liberal ideas he had largely adopted, the Russian Emperor appeared to be both on the side of 'humankind' and on the side of 'small nations'. From Finland to Italy and from Poland to the Ionian Islands, progressive intellectuals everywhere saw in the Tsar's constitutional concerns an impressive testimony to a new era, when liberal ideas would no longer be associated with revolution and catastrophe—little did they know that 'constitutionalism' for Alexander I merely meant an orderly system of government and administration, with no connection whatsoever to the concepts of popular sovereignty and representation.[17] In Italy particularly, Russia's sympathetic attitude towards conspiratorial and liberal activities whipped up waves of enthusiasm among patriots, who believed that the Tsar would not only help the Italian national movement but also guarantee the establishment of a liberal government in an eventually independent state. At a time when no less a figure than Madame de Staël addressed a letter to Alexander I, asking him to turn his eyes towards *Italy, at once so rich and so poor* (Feb. 1816), and Foscolo wrote that Russia would help contain Austrian ambitions in the peninsula, everyone within the spectrum of

---

[15] See, for example, Loukos, *I antipolitefsi kata tou kyberniti*, pp. 35–7 and idem, 'I antipolitefsi kata tou kyberniti Ioanni Kapodistria: epanexetasi kapoion proseggiseon' (The political opposition to the governor Ioannis Kapodistrias: reappraisal of some approaches), in Giorgos Georgis (ed.), *O kybernitis Ioannis Kapodistrias: kritikes proseggiseis kai epibebaioseis* (The governor Ioannis Kapodistrias: critical approaches and confirmations) (Athens, 2015), pp. 54–67.

[16] Stourdza, 'Notice biographique sur le comte J. Capodistrias', p. 39.

[17] Marc Raeff, *Michael Speransky, Statesman of Imperial Russia, 1772–1839* (The Hague, 1957), pp. 29–48; Jussi Kurunmäki, 'Political Representation, Imperial Dependency and Political Transfer: Finland and Sweden 1809–1819', *Journal of Modern European History* 15/2 (2017), pp. 243–60.

Italian liberalism—from moderate liberals and federalists to democrats, radical republicans, and even carbonari—placed their hopes in the 'liberal Tsar'.[18] In this sense, men like Kapodistrias, Stourdza, and Mustoxidi were not an exception.

Where the principal characters of our story differed from the rest of the European liberal world of the time was their particular affinity with the Holy Alliance and their reluctance to view the Restoration system—at least in its early years—as an anti-liberal settlement. I shall now try to explain just why that was.

## THE HOLY ALLIANCE AND PAN-CHRISTIAN UTOPIAN VISIONS

The framework for the development of a liberal society based on the solid foundations of religion was offered, for these men, by the Treaty of the Holy Alliance (1815). Expressing the Tsar's pietistic perception of international relations, the Holy Alliance was meant to be—as Kapodistrias and Stourdza wrote in their apology of 1817—*the surest guarantee of a well-ordered liberty, the true safeguard of law, and the most implacable enemy of arbitrary power.*[19] Combining the traditions of Christianity and international law, the Holy Alliance represented the application of a political theology based on the principle of 'Christian fraternity'. *Thanks to a sublime conception of [the Tsar] ... Europe has become almost one Republic, the various parts of which are governed through mutual vigilance and alternate harmony, and are sustained and conserved independent under the auspices and the empire of Our Lord Jesus Christ*— reads a note found among Kapodistrias's papers, which bears the handwriting of Mustoxidi (probably a result of collaborative endeavour between the two men in 1824, when Mustoxidi visited his friend in Geneva).[20] What is more interesting, though, is the second part of the note, where the two friends maintain that the states of the Holy Alliance should turn their attention towards Greece: *But there is still a portion of the children of this Christ who stretch out their hands to their brothers, and yearning to be joined to this family, recall that the Religion of the Man-God has spoken their language.* The allied powers should turn towards Greece, not to suppress the revolution, but to uphold it. For the two men, the Greek revolutionary cause was not incompatible with the spirit of the Restoration. Greece should be liberated, they believed, in order to join the system of the Holy Alliance.

This belief was founded upon the idea that the Holy Alliance, contracted as it was by three monarchs of different Christian dogmas (Russian/Eastern Orthodox, Austrian/Roman Catholic, and Prussian/Reformed), represented the first step

[18] Giuseppe Berti, *Russia e stati Italiani nel Risorgimento* (Turin, 1957), pp. 366, 374–5, 486–9; *Edizione nazionale delle opere di Ugo Foscolo*, vol. 8: *Prose politiche e letterarie dal 1811 al 1816*, edited by Luigi Fassò (Florence, 1972), p. 258.

[19] The apology was written, at the Tsar's request, as an explanation of the treaty and an answer to its critics. Kapodistrias was instructed to write it, but its drafting was in fact due to Stourdza. In Kennedy Grimsted, 'Capodistrias and a "New Order" for Restoration Europe', p. 190. See also Stella Ghervas, 'La Sainte-Alliance: un pacte pacifique européen comme antydote à l'Empire', in Sylvie Aprile et al. (eds), *Europe de papier: projets européens au XIXe siècle* (Lille, 2015), pp. 47–64.

[20] BM: Ioannis Kapodistrias Archive, 41, 130–1.

towards a future of fraternity between European Christian peoples. It was an act of utopian ecumenism.[21] This pan-Christian utopian vision does indeed often feature in the writings of this circle. In the same note from Kapodistrias's papers, this vision is presented as a plan to reunify the European Churches, with Orthodoxy mediating between the Catholics and the Protestants. In the reunified Christian family of Europe, Oriental Orthodoxy would become the third power that would balance the other two. Then, according to the authors, *one sole faith and one sole law will unify the souls of all peoples; and the European Republic will become also a Christian Republic.*[22] Since the Congress of Vienna, the aspiration to make of Europe a 'Corpus Christianum' that would embrace and protect all its children, whether Catholic, Protestant, or Orthodox, had indeed been a widespread motif among conservative philhellenes.[23] It found its most evocative expression in a text entitled *Mémoire sur l'importance religieuse et politique de réunir les deux Églises grecque et latine et sur les moyens d'y parvenir* (Memoir on the religious and political importance of reunifying the two Churches Greek and Latin and on the means to achieve this), which was written in 1814 by the French Abbot Henri Grégoire, a hugely important figure, noted for his role during the French Revolution, his battles for the emancipation of slaves, the Jews, and all oppressed peoples, and for his close affinity with the *idéologues*.[24] The memoir—which, as Grégoire acknowledged, was inspired by Ignatius's historical account of *The current state of the Orthodox Oriental Church* (1809)[25]—was delivered through Kapodistrias's mediation to Alexander I during the proceedings of the Congress. In addressing the Tsar, Grégoire argued that the union of the two Churches, Catholic and Orthodox, would not only guarantee the liberation of Greece but would also benefit Europe as a whole: *Religion and politics solicit the reunion of the two Churches, Greek and Latin. Religion, because the truth is one, so unity is an essential characteristic of*

[21] Georges Florovsky, 'The Orthodox Churches and the Ecumenical Movement prior to 1910', in Ruth Rouse and Stephen Charles Neill (eds), *A History of the Ecumenical Movement, 1517–1948* (London, 1967), p. 193; Zorin, '"Star of the East": The Holy Alliance and European Mysticism', pp. 313–42.

[22] BM: Ioannis Kapodistrias Archive, 41, 130–1.

[23] Angelo Tamborra, 'Aspetti di universalismo cristiano nell'età della Santa Alleanza', *Il pensiero politico* 2 (1970), pp. 234–44.

[24] P. Grunebaum-Ballin, *Henri Grégoire, l'ami des hommes de toutes les couleurs* (Paris, 1948); Yves Bénot and Marcel Dorigny (eds), *Grégoire et la cause des Noirs (1789–1831): combats et projets* (Paris, 2000). p. 139; Michele Lascaris, 'L'Abbé Grégoire et la Grèce', *La Révolution française* 3 (1932), pp. 1–16.

[25] [Bishop Ignatius], 'Synopsis istoriki peri tis enestosis katastaseos tis Orthodoxou Anatolikis Ekklisias', *Athina* 1 (Jan. 1831), pp. 6–11 and 26–32; 2 (Feb. 1831), pp. 40–6 and 55–62; 3 (Mar. 1831), pp. 71–7. This is the Greek translation of the memoir 'Précis historique sur l'état actuel de l'Église orthodoxe (non réunie) d'Orient', which Ignatius presented in 1809 to Rumiantsev. Kapodistrias informed his father that the memoir was in reality written by him. See Grigorios Dafnis, *Ioannis A. Kapodistrias: i genesi tou ellinikou kratous* (Ioannis Kapodistrias: the birth of the Greek state) (Athens, 1976), pp. 239–40 and Kostas Dafnis (ed.), *Archeion Ioannou Kapodistria* (Archive of Ioannis Kapodistrias) (Corfu, 1976–86), vol. III, p. 117. On the memoir see also *Logios Ermis* (15 Feb. 1811), pp. 61–2; Henri Grégoire, 'Précis historique sur l'état actuel de l'Église orthodoxe (non réunie) d'Orient', présenté par Monseigneur Ignace, métropolitain d'Arta, à S. Exc. Monseigneur le chancelier de l'empire de Russie, compte de Romanzof, à St.-Pétersbourg, l'an 1809', in idem, *Chronique religieuse* (Paris, 1819), vol. III, pp. 529–48.

*Christian society... Politics likewise demands this reunion because religious identity strengthens the bonds between the government and the people, but also between governments themselves.*[26]

For its part, Stourdza's version of a pan-Christian utopia did not include the whole of Europe. It was instead a pan-Orthodox utopia. Stourdza envisaged the creation of a 'post-Byzantine Orthodox commonwealth' that would include all Balkan peoples, with Russia having the leading role. It was a vision of an 'Oriental Christian ecumene' based on the Byzantine tradition. Unlike the Byzantine Empire, however, Stourdza's 'Orthodox ecumene' was not *a-national*, but *multi-national*. It was an ecumene constituted by nation-states. He clarified, of course, that there was a hierarchical relationship that should be maintained between the supra-national Church and the national states: *It is the state that is part of the Church, and not the Church of the state.*[27] As I have already noted, Stourdza's idea of an 'Orthodox commonwealth' was the intellectual heritage of an older generation of thinkers, namely Voulgaris and Theotokis, who had preceded Kapodistrias and his friends in constructing their lives in the same geographical landscape between Venice, the Ionian Islands, the Ottoman Principalities, and Russia.

It has been argued that Ecumenism was an ideological system bound to the empire and thus incompatible with the ideology of nationalism.[28] As the writings by the characters in our story show, this claim is in fact unfounded. There was clearly a contingent of European conservative liberals who, in the years around the Congress of Vienna and inspired by the mystical atmosphere of the Holy Alliance, believed that nationalisms could exist within the ecumene, and that the religious and traditional world could be combined with the reality of the Europe of nations. It was through this combination of the 'familiar' with the 'unfamiliar' that these figures faced the Greek revolution and tried to make sense of it.


## DISAPPOINTMENT WITH THE TSAR

Regrettably, the idyllic relationship between the liberals and Alexander I did not endure. All too soon the 'enigmatic Tsar's' conservative liberal phase ended, and he came down to earth—to Metternich's earth, to be precise. From 1820 onward, and as revolutionary movements broke out one after the other in Europe (Spain, Naples, Portugal, Piedmont, and finally Greece), Alexander I could no longer play the part of the Russian despot 'speaking vaguely of the rights of man and of nations'. He became increasingly convinced that his own conservative liberal solutions to the political problems of the period—supported as they were by Kapodistrias—had to be sacrificed to the preservation of the Alliance system. If peace and order were to be maintained in Europe, constitutions, national self-determination, and any other

---

[26] In Henri Grégoire, *Histoire des sectes religieuses* (Paris, 1829), vol. IV, p. 111.
[27] Alexandre Stourdza, *La Grèce en 1821 et 1822: correspondance politique publiée par un Grec* (Paris, 1823), p. 90.
[28] George Mavrogordatos, 'Orthodoxy and Nationalism in the Greek Case', *West European Politics* 26/1 (2003), p. 127.

'Enlightenment project' had to be temporarily set aside.[29] By 1822—and following the Congresses of Troppau, Laibach, and Verona, at which the powers decided to send troops and suppress the revolutionary movements in Spain and Italy—whatever 'holiness' there had been in the Holy Alliance disappeared under the militaristic and anti-spiritualistic shadow of Metternichian politics.

Only in its attitude toward the Greek revolution did the Russian government vacillate for a moment. As regards this issue, in particular, matters were much more complicated. On the one hand, the revolution of the Greeks was connected to a basic component of Russian politics from the times of Catherine II, the promise, that is, of a Russian crusade to restore Orthodoxy throughout the Near East. In addition, the eventual defeat of the Greeks' Ottoman oppressors would allow Russia to pursue a number of strategic goals in the Balkans and the Mediterranean. On the other hand, Russia at that juncture was committed to the support of the status quo in Europe. Any dismantling of the Ottoman Empire along ethnic lines would pose a dangerous precedent for the breakup of the Tsar's own multi-ethnic domains and encourage other assaults against the stability of Europe. As one historian concisely put it, 'the 1821 crisis tested the Tsar's balancing act between legitimacy and Orthodoxy, between the Concert of Europe and Russian national interest, and between the currents of absolutism and enlightened reform'.[30] Torn between these two options—whether to intervene in support of the Greeks or to declare his neutrality and denounce them as insurgents—Alexander I wavered for some time, trying to maintain an illusory balance. In the end, he chose the second option, dashing the hopes of his Greek entourage. *The uncertainty of the Prince in whose service fortune has placed me does however render me unhappy, hesitant, wretched,* wrote Mustoxidi, expressing their feelings in those days.[31]

Caught between his Greek patriotism and his personal loyalty to the Tsar, Kapodistrias chose nationalism over his imperial allegiances, resigning in August 1822 (officially in 1826). *I have made up my mind never to abandon the interests of my country...*, he had written in a letter to a fellow diplomat as early as January 1820; *of what use to me is the high favour with which Emperor Alexander honours me, if I did not seize the opportunity to come to the help of those people to whom at heart I belong exclusively?*[32] In any case, the prevailing mood in the Russian court was no longer favourable to him. He therefore retired to the more welcoming ambience of Geneva where he applied himself to supporting the Greek revolution by writing and organizing political activity, until the moment he was elected governor of the newly established Greek state (1827). His example was followed by his friend Alexandre Stourdza who, in 1822, likewise resigned from the Russian diplomatic service (officially in 1829) and relocated to Odessa, where he lived until the end of his life, pursuing a career as an independent intellectual and philhellene.[33] By the

---

[29] Kennedy Grimsted, *The Foreign Ministers of Alexander I*, p. 62.
[30] Theophilus Prousis, *Russian Society and the Greek Revolution* (DeKalb, Ill., 1994), p. 26.
[31] Letter to Beatrice Trivulzio. HMC: MP, III/1/29.
[32] In Kennedy Grimsted, 'Capodistrias and a "New Order" for Restoration Europe', p. 176.
[33] Stella Ghervas, *Réinventer la tradition: Alexandre Stourdza et l'Europe de la Sainte-Alliance* (Paris, 2008), pp. 74–6, 82, 84.

same token, the revolution had a major impact on refashioning Bishop Ignatius's loyalties. During the last years of his life, he abandoned his faith in Russia and reshaped his 'regenerative' vision for Greece within an Anglophile framework. He was the only one from this circle to do so.

These lives caught between empire and nation and the mixing that they occasioned between the Ionian, Phanariot, and Russian elements led to the creation of a peculiar system of interpreting the Greek revolution and of understanding nationalism in general. Despite its bitter conclusion, the Russian moment in the Adriatic would have a long-standing impact on the way ideas about nation and history were shaped in the area.

# 7

# The Greek Revolution through the Eyes
## of Orthodox Enlightenment

## IN SEARCH OF LEGITIMACY

For these servants of the Tsar who became attuned to the nascent nationalist feelings of the period, the outbreak of the revolution signified an almost existential dilemma: how was it possible to adhere to the principles of national liberation and, at the same time, remain loyal to the tsarist order? How could one be a philhellene without contesting the European Congress system?

One solution was to invert the concept of 'legitimacy', the most emblematic concept pertaining to the current system of international law. In a period of counter-revolution and anti-Napoleonic ardour, when it was evident that morality was no longer based on a divine foundation, there was a pressing need to found international obligations on a new basis: 'Where does legitimacy reside, if not in God?' was the question that tortured diplomats and statesmen alike. It has been convincingly argued that the modern conception of international law was born out of the need 'to stigmatise the French Revolution, and especially the Napoleonic imperial system, as unlawful in terms of the "traditional" principles of European public law and order'.[1] The Greek revolution, with its ambition to overthrow Ottoman rule, appeared indeed to be contesting these principles. How was this incompatibility to be resolved? The answer was found in an elaborate argument which inverted the terms of the equation: it was not the revolt of the Greeks that was 'illegitimate', Kapodistrias and his friends argued, it was Ottoman authority. The Greek revolution was not threatening the legitimate order. On the contrary, it was defending it from a 'distortion'. This 'distortion' lay in the fact that the Ottomans were abusing the authority which had been granted to them by Divine Providence. *Legitimacy does not reside only in the authority's origin*, Stourdza explained; *it has to be sanctioned also by the exercise of power.* And in exercising power the Ottomans exceeded the limits of legitimacy: *An authority that respects neither the religion, nor the life, nor the dignity, nor the property of those it governs, can it ever claim for itself the sacred character of legitimacy?*[2] Destunis, on the other hand, argued that the *degenerate and barbaric* nature of Ottoman rule raised doubts about the *political legitimacy* of the Ottoman

---

[1] David Armitage, *Foundations of Modern International Thought* (Cambridge, 2013), p. 41.
[2] Alexandre Stourdza, *La Grèce en 1821 et 1822: correspondance politique publiée par un Grec* (Paris, 1823), pp. 15, 17–18.

government and exonerated the Greeks from the charge that they were rebelling against their legitimate ruler.[3] 'Ottoman barbarism' was indeed the argument more often put forward by political leaders of the time to explain the empire's exclusion from the international legal order.[4]

These intellectuals claimed, besides, that, since the Greeks had never surrendered their rule by 'formal agreement', they were not 'true subjects' of the Sultan, but only his slaves. Their relationship was established exclusively by an act of conquest and not through a contractual process. Yet another note among Kapodistrias's papers (bearing again Mustoxidi's handwriting) explains how: *With the passing of time, the* acceptance *of a people which has been* unjustly *conquered may render* legitimate *an Empire whose origin was* illegitimate. *But the Greeks never* sanctioned *this conquest. No convention ever ratified their surrender to a Conqueror. It was only by a series of persistent and unprovoked wars that they were deprived of their estates and blockaded in their capital… There can never be friendship between the* master *and the* slave.[5] Bishop Ignatius, on the other hand, accepted the existence of an initial 'legitimate pact' which, nonetheless, was breached by the Ottoman authorities at a later stage. *The Turkish government*—he wrote in 1822—*having violated the treaties, which it had itself concluded with the Greeks, and the laws of the Koran, according to which life, dignity, exercise of cult and property were guaranteed for non-Muslim subjects, the Turkish government, by these manifest violations, not only forfeited its right over its Christian subjects, but also drove them to revolt. All those mercenary publicists, who try their utmost to prove to Europe the legitimacy of the Turkish government, can say nothing in its favour, because, by violating the pact with which it had acquired rights over its subjects it forfeited its alleged legitimacy.*[6]

According to these men, the European powers, and particularly Russia, had a 'moral responsibility' to intervene in order to save the Greeks and protect Europe from the 'subversion of legitimacy' committed by the Ottoman authorities. They were no different, in that sense, from many European and especially Italian liberals, who refashioned Emmerick Vattel's famous formulation of the idea of balance of

---

[3] Spyridon Destunis, 'Defense of the Contemporary Greeks: A Note' (n.d.), in Theophilus Prousis, 'The Destunis Collection in the Manuscript Section of the Saltykov-Shchedrin State Public Library in Leningrad', *Modern Greek Studies Yearbook* 5 (1989), p. 422.

[4] Davide Rodogno, *Against Massacre: Humanitarian Interventions in the Ottoman Empire, 1815–1914* (Princeton, 2012), pp. 36–7.

[5] BM: Ioannis Kapodistrias Archive, 41, 124 (emphasis in the original). Similar arguments were framed by Kapodistrias during the Congress of Vienna in regard to the issue of the Serbs. He argued that since the Serbs were Christians, they could not swear an oath of loyalty to the Sultan and, therefore, they could not become his subjects, but only his 'tributaries'. See C. M. Woodhouse, *Capodistria: The Founder of Greek Independence* (Oxford, 1973), p. 114.

[6] [Bishop Ignatius], 'Grèce, Causes de sa révolution et son état actuel' (1/13 Oct. 1822, Pisa–Memoir delivered to Nesserlode). In Emmanouil G. Protopsaltis, *Ignatios Mitropolitis Ouggroblachias (1766–1828)* (The bishop of Ungrovlachia Ignatius (1766–1828)) (Athens, 1961), vol. II, p. 336. See also Vassilis Panagiotopoulos, 'Ignatios Ouggroblachias' (The bishop of Ungrovlachia Ignatius), in idem and Panagiotis Michailaris, *Klirikoi ston Agona* (Clerics in the Revolution) (Athens, 2010), p. 75. Similar arguments can be found in the work of another intellectual and political man from Ignatius's circle in the Danubian Principalities and then Pisa, the Phanariot Alexandros Mavrocordatos. See idem, 'Coup d' œil sur la Turquie' (1820), in Anton Fr. Von Prokesch-Osten, *Geschichte des Abfall der Griechen vom türkischen Reich im Jahre 1821* (Vienna, 1867), vol. III, pp. 1–54.

power—as expressed in his influential treaty *Le Droit des gens* (1758)—to make it fit with a 'liberal' international order against the Congress system.[7] For example, in his *Difesa dei Piemontesi inquisiti a causa degli avvenimenti del 1821* (Defence of the Piedmontese who were investigated on account of the events of 1821), the philhellene Alerino Palma di Cesnola, quoting Vattel, upheld a people's right to rise up against a despotic government or absolute king, and to request military assistance from a foreign power.[8]

Calling for the intervention of European powers raised, however, an additional difficulty. How could the European rulers breach the treaties of peace they had signed with the Sultan? These treaties were invalid—Kapodistrias and his friends claimed. Actually, they said, they were not even treaties, they were simply truces. For a legitimate agreement between Christians and Muslims was impossible. Another note among Kapodistrias's papers in fact reads: *Who can claim that a Despotic Government is legitimate? Is it not, on the contrary, a government that goes against the laws of nature?*[9] Historians have argued indeed that the European conception of international law was that of a specifically Christian civilization, which could not easily be extended to non-Christian nations. And despotism was among the most frequently invoked factors that European legal scholars, diplomats, and political leaders put forward to explain why they saw the Ottoman Empire as a regime 'against nature' which should be excluded from the 'Family of Nations'.[10] Besides, another argument put forward by Bishop Ignatius recalled that, even in cases in which pacts were agreed between Christians, the Allied Powers did not hesitate to break them if it was a question of defending Europe from a 'subversion of legitimacy': *This same Europe had also contracted treaties with Napoleon; but he did not respect legitimacy, until he lost his forces in the glaciers of Russia.*[11]

## CONSERVATIVE PHILHELLENISM AND RELIGIOUS NATIONALISM

After resolving the problem of legitimacy, Kapodistrias and his friends attempted to come to grips with another critical issue. They sought to contest the prevailing view which associated the Greek revolution with the other revolutionary movements that upset Europe in 1820–1. In international diplomatic circles, especially during the Congresses of Laibach and Verona, the Greek insurgents were seen as no different from the rest of the 'revolutionary troublemakers' in Europe.

[7] Emer de Vattel, *The Law of Nations*, edited by Béla Kapossy and Richard Whatmore (Indianapolis, 2008). See also Richard Tuck, *The Rights of War and Peace: Political Thought and the International Order from Grotius to Kant* (Oxford, 1999), pp. 191–6; Maurizio Isabella, *Risorgimento in Exile: Italian Émigrés and the Liberal International in the Post-Napoleonic Era* (Oxford, 2009), pp. 99–100.

[8] Isabella, *Risorgimento in Exile*, p. 100.

[9] BM: Ioannis Kapodistrias Archive, 41, 127. See also BM: Ioannis Kapodistrias Archive, 41,125–7. The same argument in Stourdza, *La Grèce en 1821 et 1822*, p. 77.

[10] Armitage, *Foundations of Modern International Thought*, p. 41; Rodogno, *Against Massacre*, pp. 38ff.

[11] [Bishop Ignatius], 'Grèce, Causes de sa révolution', p. 336.

This association placed the Greek insurrection within a genealogy of radical movements that went back to the French Revolution and which were related to the carbonari and other secret societies. If philhellenism (the international mobilization in support of the Greeks) was generally associated with radical liberalism and revolution, these people wanted to show that it was also related to a thread of thought which was moderate liberal and counter-revolutionary.[12]

Bishop Ignatius thought that one way to do this would be to re-examine the relationship of the Greeks to the French Revolution. The latter, he argued, was never considered as an example to imitate by the Greeks, who detested the French because of their alliance with the Ottomans. As he said, *the Greeks always saw the French as their enemies, because of the Alliance which France had contracted with the Turks during the reign of Francis I.* It was not the Greeks, Ignatius continued, that the French Revolution influenced, but the Ottomans. Islam contains elements which are republican and democratic—for example, *all believers are equal before God, before the law and before the authorities*—and therefore resemble the French republican system. This similarity created, according to the Bishop, a seedbed of revolutionary ideas among the Muslims of the Ottoman Empire. Thus, the influence of the French Revolution on the Greeks, if there was any, was only collateral and it passed through the Ottoman channel. It was an Ottoman product, for whose consequences the Greeks were now paying.[13] The same line of argument was developed some years later by another scholar, who had some connections with Kapodistrias's circle. In his treatise, *Tableau synoptique de administration turque suivant les principes de la religion mahometane qui en est la base* (1827), the Phanariot linguist and scholar Panagiotis Kodrikas expressed the view that Islam and Jacobinism shared the same roots, being inspired as they both were by the distasteful and destructive ideas of equality and fraternity.[14] Besides, as has been recently argued in relation to eighteenth-century Radical Protestantism and the English Enlightenment, the reading of Islam in republican and constitutional terms (the so-called 'Islamic republicanism') was not so incongruous a phenomenon.[15]

The most effective response to the association of the Greek revolution with the revolutionary movements in Spain and Italy was, however, to maintain that the Greeks—unlike the Jacobin-influenced carbonari, who were rebelling against Christian legitimate rulers—were fighting a religious war against slavery and tyranny

[12] Stella Ghervas, 'Le Philhellénisme d'inspiration conservatrice en Europe et en Russie', in *Peuples, états et nations dans le sud-est de l'Europe* (Bucharest, 2004), pp. 98–110. On the plurality of philhellenisms see also Michel Espagne and Gilles Pécout, 'Introduction', in eidem (eds), *Philhellénismes et transferts culturels dans l'Europe du XIX^e siècle* [=*Revue Germanique Internationale* I–II (2005)], pp. 5–7. On the anti-philhellenic views of the Austrian diplomacy see: Ioannis Dimakis, *O Oesterreichischer Beobachter tis Biennis kai i Elliniki Epanastasis, 1821–1827: symboli eis tin meletin tou evropaikou antiphilellinismou* (The Oesterreichischer Beobachter of Vienna and the Greek revolution, 1821–1827: contribution to the study of European anti-philhellenism) (Athens, 1977).

[13] [Bishop Ignatius], 'Grèce, Causes de sa révolution', p. 333.

[14] Alexandra Sfoini, 'Fotismenes afthenties se grafeiokratika periballonta: o Panagiotis Kodrikas kai i glossa ton evgenon' (Enlightened experts in bureaucratic environments: Panagiotis Kodrikas and the language of the nobles), *Ta istorika* 59 (2013), p. 362.

[15] Humberto Garcia, *Islam and the English Enlightenment, 1670–1840* (Baltimore, 2012), pp. 4–12.

imposed upon them by non-European infidel rulers.[16] The Greek revolution, these intellectuals argued, was an event of an altogether different historical quality. Stourdza's assertions are very interesting in this regard. In his long exposition, which mixes historical and apocalyptic elements, Stourdza claimed that the Greek revolution was an event that transcended history, touching the sphere of theology. In his interpretative scheme, the survival of the Greeks and their regeneration was considered to be a miracle, the only historical event with messianic dimensions after the Jewish exodus. *With the exception of the people of Israel . . .*—he wrote—*whose future renaissance is foreseen at the end of time, history does not furnish any other example like the miraculous event that is today accomplished on the soil of Greece.*[17] So, the Greek revolution was comparable only to the fall and the predicted resurgence of the people of Israel and had nothing to do with the other revolutionary movements, which were restricted to the sphere of mundane history. In Greece it was God who spoke through the insurgents. The revolution was not displacing God's plans but, on the contrary, it was the first step towards their realization: *We have nothing to do here with a constitutional charter at war with an absolute authority*—Stourdza claimed—*it is religion . . . it is God himself . . . it is the Lord who deigns to use the awakening of the Greeks as the first impulsion towards an even nobler goal.*[18] Besides, in a note among Kapodistrias's papers (written again by Mustoxidi), the Greeks are presented as enduring a plight still more terrible than that of the Israelites: *The Greeks renew the example of the children of Israel, who were groaning under the Egyptian yoke . . . The cause of the Greeks is yet more just . . . because it is not in the land of the Pharaohs that they groan, but in their own land, the heritage of their fathers.*[19]

The comparison of the Greeks with the people of Israel appears sporadically in texts of the years around the revolution.[20] Biblical comparisons are also present in other nationalisms of the time.[21] If there is one source where the references to Hebrew and Jewish history abound it is the aforementioned *Vision* of Agathangelus. As we have seen, in prophesying the deliverance of Eastern Orthodoxy through a

---

[16] See, for example, Destunis's argument in this regard, in Prousis, 'The Destunis Collection', p. 422. The same argument appears prominently in an apologia published in 1824 by the brothers Alexandre and Georgios Cantacuzino, sons of a *boyar*–Phanariot family from the Danubian Principalities, Russian officers, Greek revolutionaries, and members of the Philiki Etairia. See Vassilis Panagiotopoulos (ed.), *Dyo prigkipes stin Elliniki epanastasi: epistoles aftopti martyra kai ena ypomnima tou prigkipa Georgiou Kantakouzinou* (Two princes in the Greek revolution: letters of an eyewitness and a memoir by Prince Georgios Cantacuzino) (Athens, 2015), pp. 181–2.

[17] Stourdza, *La Grèce en 1821 et 1822*, p. 7.

[18] Stourdza, *La Grèce en 1821 et 1822*, p. 8. See also Stella Ghervas, *Réinventer la tradition: Alexandre Stourdza et l'Europe de la Sainte-Alliance* (Paris, 2008), p. 103.

[19] BM: Ioannis Kapodistrias Archive, 41, 125–7.

[20] See, for example, Spyridon Trikoupis, *Logoi epikidioi kai epinikioi ekfonithentes eis epikoon tou laou epi tis Ellinikis epanastaseos* (Eulogies and orations of victory pronounced during the Greek revolution) (Aegina, 1829), pp. 15–27. See also K. E. Fleming, 'O Herzl stin Akropoli, megales istories, mikra krati: Ellada, Israil kai ta oria tou ethnous' (Herzl on the Acropolis, great histories, small states: Greece, Israel and the boundaries of the nation), *The Athens Review of Books* 1/8 (June 2010), pp. 32–7. A negative comparison between the Greeks and the Jews was made instead by Giuseppe Compagnoni as early as 1792 in his *Saggio sugli ebrei e sui greci* (Venice).

[21] Francesca Sofia, 'The Promised Land: Biblical Themes in the Risorgimento', *Journal of Modern Italian Studies* 17/5 (2012), pp. 574–86.

crusade led by the Russians, Agathangelus compared the Ottoman domination of Greece to the Babylonian captivity of the people of Israel. This biblical parallel furnishes the essential framework for a narrative in which the fall of the Byzantine Empire is viewed as the result of Christianity's sins and the Ottomans are interpreted as an instrument of God's will. The explanation of the past in apocalyptic terms gives Agathangelus the ground to predict the future with considerable accuracy: if it is all prescribed in God's plans, then the end of the story, the restoration of the Byzantine Empire, is already known.[22]

In a somewhat similar way, Kapodistrias believed that historical developments, and particularly the events in Greece, are prescribed in the plans of Divine Providence and, for that reason, they can be fully predicted. Another note among his papers (bearing his own handwriting on this occasion), entitled *De la Grèce en 1823* (On Greece in 1823), reads: *The Restoration of Greece is in God's will. And because of that, time, Politics, and everything, will be in favour of it, and they are in favour of it, despite the malevolence and the egoism of human affairs.*[23] The conviction that history moves with the mediation of the invisible hand of God does indeed often appear in Kapodistrias's writings. It is traceable, for example, in a long and important letter to Bishop Ignatius in April 1823, where he unfolded his proposal to write a history of Greece—a proposal which was attached, some years later, to a draft by the Phanariot historian Jacovaky Rizos Neroulos, producing eventually a book signed only by the latter.[24] In describing the aim of such a book to Ignatius, Kapodistrias remarked that he wanted *to demonstrate that the current situation of Greece is the inevitable consequence of all the situations through which Greece passed from the fall of the [Byzantine] Empire to the present stage.*[25] This 'inevitability' interpreted the revolution and the foundation of the Greek national state as the product-culmination of a deterministic process. It was not only a matter of historical determinism, however. It was a 'divine determinism', a sort of 'cosmic conspiracy' which transcended the mundane nature of human life.[26]

---

[22] Marios Hatzopoulos, 'Oracular Prophesy and the Politics of Toppling Ottoman Rule in South-East Europe', *The Historical Review/La Revue historique* 8 (2011), pp. 95–116. See also Antonis Liakos, *Apokalypsi, outopia kai istoria: oi metamorfoseis tis istorikis syneidisis* (Apocalypse, utopia and history: the transformations of historical consciousness) (Athens, 2011), pp. 77–8, 113–15, 126–7; Nikos Theotokas, 'I epanastasi tou ethnous kai to Orthodoxo genos: scholia gia tis ideologies tou eikosiena', (The revolution of the nation and the Orthodox race: comments on the ideologies of the 1821 revolution), in idem and Nikos Kotaridis, *I oikonomia tis bias: paradosiakes kai neoterikes exousies stin Ellada tou 19ou aiona* (The economy of violence: traditional and modern values in 19th century Greece) (Athens, 2006), pp. 11–57.

[23] BM: Ioannis Kapodistrias Archive, 41, 27.

[24] Jacovaky Rizos Neroulos, *Histoire moderne de la Grèce depuis la chute de l'Empire d'Orient* (Geneva, 1828).

[25] HMC: MP, IX/1/280. See Konstantina Zanou, 'O Ioannis Kapodistrias, o Iakobakis Rizos Neroulos kai i *Neoteri istoria tis Elladas*' (Ioannis Kapodistrias, Jacovacy Rizos-Neroulos and the *Histoire moderne de la Grèce*), *Mnimon* 30 (2009), pp. 141–78; Ioannis Koubourlis, *Oi istoriografikes ofeiles ton Sp. Zampeliou kai K. Paparrigopoulou (1782–1846)* (The historiographical debts of Sp. Zampelios and K. Paparrigopoulos (1782–1846)) (Athens, 2012), pp. 222–60.

[26] Niccolò Tommaseo, 'Rizo Jakovaky, Storia della Grecia moderna', in idem, *Dizionario estetico*, vol. II: *Parte moderna* (Milan, 1860), p. 334.

## ORTHODOX ENLIGHTENMENT

The effort to arrive at an accommodation between religious values and the language of the nation can be traced also in the way this milieu endorsed certain approaches to Greek history. For example, they argued that the preservation of the Greek nation had been primarily due to its religion. *Only the religious sentiment preserved the Greek people and made it feel free, despite its slavery*—Bishop Ignatius wrote in 1809. *Only religion united the dispersed, desolate and persecuted peoples into one nation,* he added.[27] Kapodistrias wrote similar thoughts in another note among his papers: *By conserving the Greek Church, and through the Patriarch of this Church a representative and a public organ of the Nation, Mohamed II preserved from degeneration the essence of their nationality. Thanks to their Religion, the Greeks did not mix with other human species and conserved unaltered the purity of their origin and of their race. Thanks to their Church, they all spoke uninterruptedly the same language, the language of their Fathers.*[28] These ideas were indeed repeated in the book that Kapodistrias co-authored with Rizos Neroulos.[29]

Furthermore, in their efforts to harmonize the Orthodox tradition with that of the Enlightenment, these men claimed that 'enlightenment' among the Greeks was diffused by the Church. *The cloisters of the Churches were transformed into temples of philosophy*—in the words of Bishop Ignatius.[30] Stourdza in particular asserted that if the 'regeneration' of Greece came from the western Enlightenment, it was no less true that it was, first and foremost, the result of Phanariot activity in the Principalities, of contacts with Russia, and of an 'eastern Enlightenment' coming from the Church.[31] This circle was not so much hostile to the tradition of the Enlightenment as receptive to its teachings. They attempted to negotiate with it and adjust its messages to their own traditional and mystical understanding of society.[32] *[The nation] is beyond any doubt naturally devoted to its Church*—Kapodistrias wrote in a letter to Mustoxidi in November 1827—*but it is so only through sentiment, and, if I may put it like this, through instinct. In the era in which we are living, something more is needed; it needs to be religious also by reason and, consequently, by a little bit of Enlightenment.*[33] In order to grasp this circle's understanding of Enlightenment ideas, we need, indeed, to bear in mind the concept of 'Reasonable religiosity', as it had been developed by the representatives of the Septinsular Enlightenment, Voulgaris and Theotokis, at the end of the eighteenth century.

[27] [Bishop Ignatius], 'Synopsis istoriki', *Athina* 1 (Jan. 1831), p. 29.
[28] BM: Ioannis Kapodistrias Archive, 41, 24.
[29] Rizos Neroulos, *Histoire moderne de la Grèce*, p. 13.
[30] In Protopsaltis, *Ignatios*, vol. I, p. 29.      [31] Stourdza, *La Grèce en 1821 et 1822*, p. 38.
[32] Ghervas, *Réinventer la tradition: Alexandre Stourdza*, p. 141.
[33] E. A. Bétant (ed.), *Correspondance du Comte Capodistrias, Président de la Grèce* (Geneva and Paris, 1839), vol. I, pp. 297–8.

## THE *PHILOMOUSOS ETAIRIA*

Nowhere can this concept be more convincingly traced than in the programme of the *Philomousos Etairia* (Society of the Muses). Co-founded by Kapodistrias, Ignatius, and the Stourdza siblings on the margins of the Vienna Congress, when there was still hope that the Tsar would stand by the Greek cause, the *Philomousos* was the project that brought together all the principal characters of our story, becoming the most enduring bearer of this circle's ideology, the hallmark, it might be said, of their intellectual milieu. It was born as a 'charitable' association which aimed particularly at giving financial assistance to those Greeks who were studying in Europe. In the long term, however, the association aspired to lay the basis for the creation of a Greek intellectual elite, which would be ready to govern Greece when, *after a happy coincidence of factors*, it would be liberated. The list of subscribers was headed by the name of the Tsar, who contributed with 200 Dutch ducats per year, followed by that of the Empress and of several other sovereigns and their ministers.[34]

The *Philomousos* epitomized this circle's profound concern with education. It was only through *an extended and invigorated education system*, rather than through political activism and revolution, that, according to these intellectuals, hopes for the *progressive amelioration* of society lay.[35] *Without men you can make no government—* Kapodistrias wrote to the Archimandrite of the Greek Church of Trieste in 1827— *and if the current generation does not receive reinforcement from men who are educated in excellent schools, and especially according to the principles of our holy religion and our customs, I doubt if it will be able to live up to the destiny that Providence has reserved for it.*[36] Only when the cultural and moral level of the population had been raised through an appropriate educational system, Kapodistrias believed, would the nation be ready to form a popular government. Only then, in this 'enlightened' future, would a republican regime be capable of functioning properly.[37] That is why pedagogical matters, and particularly religious education, were among his primary concerns during his periods of office both as Secretary General of the Septinsular Republic and as governor of the Greek state.[38]

[34] Capodistrias, *Aperçu de ma carrière publique*, pp. 57–8; C. W. Crawley, 'John Capodistrias and the Greeks before 1821', *Cambridge Historical Journal* 13/2 (1957), p. 174; Eleni Koukkou, *O Kapodistrias kai i paideia, 1803–1822* (Kapodistrias and education, 1803–1822) (Athens, 1958), vol. I, pp. 37ff; Grigorii Arsh, *O Ioannis Kapodistrias sti Rosia* (Ioannis Kapodistrias in Russia) (Athens, 2015), pp. 160ff.
[35] [Ioannis Kapodistrias], 'Observations sur les moyens d'améliorer le sort de Grecs' (6/18 Apr. 1819, Corfu), in George Waddinghton, *A Visit to Greece in 1823 and 1824* (London, 1825), p. xxxviii.
[36] Bétant (ed.), *Correspondance*, vol. I, p. 255.
[37] Patricia Kennedy Grimsted, *The Foreign Ministers of Alexander I: Political Attitudes and the Conduct of Russian Diplomacy, 1801–1825* (Berkeley and Los Angeles, 1969), pp. 237–8 and idem, 'Capodistrias and a "New Order" for Restoration Europe: The "Liberal Ideas" of a Russian Foreign Minister (1814–1822)', *Journal of Modern History* 40/2 (June 1968), pp. 184–5.
[38] One of his first concerns was to create good religious books for the citizens. For the Septinsular Republic he ordered the translation of an Orthodox Catechesis, while as governor of Greece he charged the clergyman Bartolommeo Cutlumusiano with the writing up of a prayer book. See Koukkou, *O Kapodistrias kai i paideia*, vol. I, pp. 1–15; K. Th. Demaras, 'Kapodistrias-Moustoxidis-Koutloumousianos (bibliografikes kai alles anazitiseis)' (Kapodistrias-Mustoxidi-Cutlumusiano (bibliographical and other researches)), *Thysavrismata* 1 (1962), pp. 14–62; Konstantina Zanou, 'O Andreas Moustoxidis, o Bartholomeos Koutloumousianos kai to *Ypomnima istorikon peri tis nisou Imbrou*' (Andrea Mustoxidi,

The same belief in the elevating power of education was sustained by Bishop Ignatius. A precursor of the *Philomousos* was the *Graikoblachiki Philologiki Etairia* (Greek-Vlach Philological Society), a literary society which the Bishop had founded in Bucharest in 1810 with the support of the mother of the Tsar and Alexander I himself. The society formed part of Ignatius's 'enlightening programme' in the Danubian Principalities, which, during the two years of his term as Bishop of Ungrovlachia (1810–12), led him to restore the old Greek School of the city (the so-called *Ellinikon Lykeion*—Greek Lyceum), to contribute financially to the studies of needy students, and to play a part in founding the first Greek literary journal (*Logios Ermis*—Literary Mercury, published in Vienna from 1811 to 1821).[39]

More than anywhere else, however, the educational vision of this circle was reflected in the programme of the *Philomousos Etairia*. Redirecting its activities during the Greek revolution towards the relief of the refugees who arrived in Europe and to the construction of schools and orphanages for their children, the *Philomousos* became extremely important in the years 1827–9. Soon after his election as governor—and with the collaboration of Ignatius, Mostras, Mocenigo, Naranzi, and Mustoxidi—Kapodistrias brought into effect an ambitious plan for the hospitalization and education of all the orphan and refugee children from Greece found in the cities of Venice, Trieste, and Ancona. He believed that the reorganized schools of these cities ought to function as a model for the establishment of similar schools in other places of the Greek diaspora. They were to represent the beginning of a broader system of national education, inspired by the principles of a 'religiously grounded Enlightenment'.[40]

Despite their disappointment at Russia's stance as regards the Greek revolution, these men continued thus to understand politics within the religious and ecumenical framework they had endorsed in the previous two decades. The Russian Empire was perhaps by that date politically out of the picture, but intellectually it was still there.

Bartolommeo Cutlumusiano and the *Historical Memorial on the Island of Imbros*), *Mnimon* 31 (2010), pp. 286–9.

[39] Protopsaltis, *Ignatios*, vol. I, pp. 88–120; Arsh, *O Ioannis Kapodistrias sti Rosia*, pp. 298–300.

[40] Bétant (ed.), *Correspondance*, vol. I, pp. 184–8, 292–303, 317–18, 360–2; Andrea Papadopulo-Vrettò, *Biografia del cavaliere Andrea Mustoxidi scritta e pubblicata in Venezia nell'anno 1836 da Emilio Tipaldo, corretta dallo stesso Mustoxidi in Corfù nell'anno 1838: annotata e continuata sino alla sua morte da Andrea Papadopulo Vreto Leucadio* etc. (Athens, 1860), pp. 32–6.

# Conclusion

The reconstruction of these diasporic intellectual trajectories, which developed far from the Parisian nuclei of Greek thought and the democratic ideological tradition of the French Revolution, allows the historian to tell a markedly different story about the Greek diasporas and their Enlightenments, one which, in terms of the circulation of ideas, is less obviously derived from the West and offers a more polycentric account, geographically and intellectually, of the origins of Greek nationalism and of the Greek revolution. Part II has shown how multilevelled Mediterraneans and their extensions—the small patria of the Ionian Islands, the big patrias of the Venetian, Russian, and Ottoman empires, and the emerging new patria of the Greek state—coexisted in the consciousness of a circle of intellectuals who were gradually becoming 'Greek' through their diasporic experience. The sense of nationalism cultivated by these figures embraced all of these smaller and greater patriotisms and was engendered by their previous cultural and political affiliations.

By describing the epoch in which these figures lived as a transitional period with an unknown future, when empires and nation-states were not yet mutually exclusive, and when the nation-state was not the most obvious solution either, this story also challenges teleological narratives of the emergence and triumph of nation-states. Like most of their contemporaries, Kapodistrias and his friends were trying to make sense of the changes they were living through by experimenting with new forms of imperial nationalism and transnational patriotism. If they were forced by Russia's last-minute disavowal of the Greek revolution to choose nationhood over their imperial allegiances, they nonetheless never abandoned the ecumenical and religious framework of their political world view and remained loyal to Orthodoxy as the foundation of their national agenda.

Overall, by presenting this panorama of lives and ideas spanning Europe, the Balkans, the Adriatic, the Aegean, and Russia, this part of the book has tried to show that Greece, rather than being the result of the (incomplete) diffusion of Enlightenment ideals from western Europe to its south-eastern periphery, was the product of a Mediterranean geography of the 'in-between', where different traditions met and conversed, producing new local realities at every turn.

# PART III

# MEMOIRS OF LIVES SUSPENDED BETWEEN PATRIAS

*L'uomo senza patria é peggio di bestia*

(The man who has no patria is worse than an animal)

—Mario Pieri, Private diary, Florence, July 1833[1]

*Vorrei l'impossibile, cioè d'essere in un istesso tempo in Corfù e in Firenze*

(I would like the impossible, that is to be at one and the same time in Corfu and in Florence)

—Ibid., Corfu, Jan. 1837[2]

## INTRODUCTION

### Narrating the Self in Times of Crisis

One summer evening in 1804, while on a visit to a friend's house in Corfu, Mario Pieri (1776–1852) overheard something that would change his life. There was talk in passing of a woman who *every evening before going to bed used to write her Diary, describing her Day, keeping a register, that is, or keeping a memory of what came into her head or of what she had read, or written, or thought, or dealt with, or encountered in the course of the day.* So deep an impression did this notion make on the young Pieri that, as he confessed, *that same evening, no sooner had I returned home than I took a piece of paper and I tried to note down what had happened to me during that day.*[3] This would be the beginning of a voluminous account of approximately 7,000 pages, which that man kept faithfully, day in day out, for over forty-eight years, from the age of 27 to his death at the age of 76. Perhaps it was the promise of a memorable life, perhaps only a feeling of curiosity and experimentation, that first motivated Pieri to record his days. With the passage of time, however, and as he traversed different places and cultures, that pile of densely written pages became a methodical archive of the self, a steady point in an unsteady life, and an essential

---

[1] BRF: Memorie di Mario Pieri, vol. V [Ricc. 3559], 240.
[2] BRF: Memorie di Mario Pieri, vol. VI [Ricc. 3560], 286.
[3] Mario Pieri, *Della vita di Mario Pieri corcirese scritta da lui medesimo* (Florence, 1850), vol. I, p. 86.

psychotherapeutic escape. *I intend to go on writing these memoirs for the whole of my life, solely for my own satisfaction and above all in order to give a necessary expression to my deepest feelings*—noted Pieri in 1812, eight years after that fateful evening; *The pen is my tongue and the paper the friend to whose bosom I confide them.*[4] His was a life lived across empires, nations, and states although without his ever setting foot in lands beyond the Adriatic Sea and northern Italy. Indeed, geographically speaking, Pieri did not move a great deal. It was the world around him which was moving instead. In the course of his life this man experienced some of the momentous upheavals that marked the birth of the modern world. As he was born, American independence was being declared on the other side of the globe (he might not have experienced it at first hand, but as a young man he had read the memoirs of Benjamin Franklin and the histories of the American Revolution which were then immensely popular in Italy). When he was 13, the French Revolution erupted, and some years later it brought the Jacobins to his small homeland, Corfu, thus ending the centuries-old Venetian domination of the Adriatic. At the age of 24, it was the turn of the Russians to arrive in his Ionian neighbourhood. Six years later, in 1806, while in Padua, Pieri had first-hand experience of the creation and expansion of the Napoleonic Kingdom of Italy, while after nine more years he chanced to witness from his balcony in Venice the fall of Napoleon and the annexation of the former lands of the Venetian Republic to the Habsburg Empire. During this same period, he saw the British Empire spreading its wings in the Mediterranean, extending its sway over the Ionian Islands and over many other polities too. At the age of 44, he witnessed the great wave of the liberal and national revolutions in southern Europe, the Balkans, and Latin America, some of which (in Piedmont, Naples, and Greece) he observed at first hand, yet others (in Portugal and Spain) as a distant but interested spectator. Finally, Pieri would live to see the creation of an independent Greek state and the beginning of the end of another long-lived imperial authority in the Mediterranean, the Ottomans. Few scholars would disagree, indeed, that this man's life spanned an era of profound change. In such a fragmented, estranging, and turbulent world, some sense of continuity could perhaps be found in the movement of a pen on blank paper—the 'unifying utopia' of the diary, to use a telling phrase.[5]

As well as representing a strategy for coping with a changing reality, the diary became also the most memorable work of a man otherwise absent from the historical record. For all the young man's dreams of literary glory at the outset, when Pieri had started his journal with such high hopes, the intimate account of his unfulfilled life was in fact, sad to say, the greatest work that he ever produced. It seems that he realized this when, in later years, approaching death and seeing his loftiest hopes dashed, he decided to rewrite his diary in a more concise form and to publish it in the guise of an autobiography. By comparison with the nine volumes of the diary, the autobiography, now entitled *La vita di Mario Pieri scritta da lui*

---

[4] Mario Pieri, *Memorie II*, edited by Claudio Chiancone (Ariccia, 2017), pp. 68 and 69.
[5] Jeremy D. Popkin, 'Philippe Lejeune, Explorer of the Diary', in Philippe Lejeune, *On Diary*, edited by J. D. Popkin and Julie Rak (Hawaii, 2009), p. 2.

*medesimo* (The life of Mario Pieri written by himself), consisted of only two volumes—including also an entirely new section covering the first twenty-seven years of his life, which had been missing from the diary. Published in 1850, this work is, in reality, the only reason why anyone would still, in the twentieth and twenty-first centuries, pause to talk about this man. Considered to be an important source of information on the Italian intellectual scene of the first half of the nineteenth century, this memoir is why Pieri's name occasionally appears as an inglorious footnote in books of Italian literature. For the rest, nobody ever calls this insignificant character to mind.

Seventeen years after Pieri's autobiography was published, another Ionian intellectual, old and half-blind after a life of ceaseless displacement and perpetual transformation, while on a visit to Paris, sat down a young woman and dictated to her his memoirs, the *Memorie biografiche e storiche* (Biographical and Historical Memories). It was apparently a sense of history and a feeling of having lived through stirring times that motivated the author in question, Andrea Papadopoulo Vretto (1800–76), to take this step: *I was born on the 2nd/14th August 1800, in other words at the beginning of the nineteenth century, the century that has been more fertile in political events and scientific discoveries than all of those preceding it*—was how his autobiography began. Having spent his life in three different states (Naples, the Ionian state and Greece) and in five different empires (Napoleonic, British, Russian, Ottoman, and Habsburg), Papadopoulo Vretto had no doubts that he had something of interest and significance to say. Perhaps he also felt that he needed to make sense of a life of incessant movement and transformation. Nobody knows why his autobiography was left incomplete (reaching only as far as 1834) and buried forever on the obscure shelves of some archive.

This part of the book is about forgotten lives and their memories. It is also about the intimate experience of change, about people trying to give a meaning to their lives in times of perpetual crisis. Based on two specific examples of autobiographical writing in the Ionian space, it brings to light a set of obscured biographies, thereby reinforcing the attempt made in this book to address history on a human scale. Unlike, however, the rest of my narrative, which looks at stories of people who, in one way or another, managed to reinvent themselves in an age of constant reconfiguration of the political and cultural landscape, Chapters 8 and 9 recount the stories of those who simply failed to adjust to a rapidly changing reality between empires and nation-states.

## THE AGE OF THE *JOURNAL INTIME*

It was precisely in such a conjuncture, at the end of one world and the beginning of another, when all values were contested and the individual wondered as never before about his destiny and discovered what we today call anxiety, that the genre of the private diary (*journal intime*) first appeared. Scholars locate its emergence at the end of the eighteenth and the beginning of the nineteenth century, especially in western Europe, and link it to the development of bourgeois individualism, the democratization of the notion of the self, and the secularization of consciousness. The idea of the 'unitary self' as a structuring principle of society was born precisely in post-revolutionary France. When God lost his privileges over the human psyche and corporate society broke down, private introspection was born.[6] Treating the diary as a literary genre, which can be seen both as a historical document and as a fictional work, most such scholars distinguish it from the other autobiographical genres, the autobiography and the historical memoir. The distinction addresses in particular issues of time, spontaneity, narrative coherence, and intimacy. It is argued that while the autobiography and the historical memoir are written long after the events to which they refer (the first focusing on a person's life, the second on the historical context), the diary is more of an immediate and spontaneous act. In addition, the actual writing of a diary is seen as discontinuous, while the opposite is the case in the other two genres, which require a narrative thread and a basic interpretative line. Finally, the diary is viewed as an everyday intimate practice, the autobiography and the historical memoir as texts intended for publication. Be that as it may, all these genres of autobiographical writing were developed simultaneously at the dawn of the modern period and reflected a single phenomenon: the need to delve into the historical dimension in the life of each and every person, the quest for the historical meaning of human existence.[7]

These distinctions are of little importance, however, when it comes to an actual case of a long-term diarist who also became an autobiographer, namely Pieri. True though it may be that during the first years of his diary Pieri's writing appears spontaneous and careless, it is no less the case that, as time went by, and as the author slowly became aware of the importance of this document for his personal self-remembering and self-fashioning, the style became increasingly elaborate and the narration more selective. From a certain point onwards, the diary fills up with corrections, marginal annotations, retrospective judgements, and even—especially once the option to transform it into an autobiography appeared on the horizon— with tables of contents. Furthermore, much of the privacy of this document had already been lost prior to its publication as an autobiography, since Pieri acquired the habit of reading parts of it to his friends. Needless to say, the published version of his autobiography did in time lend greater coherence to, and render more public, his diary self, but it also incorporated lengthy, unabbreviated passages from it. So, Pieri's diary, which in many ways may be said to stand for the genre to which it belongs, was not the autonomous document of immediacy, spontaneity, and intimacy it ought theoretically to have been and was often amalgamated with his autobiography.[8]

---

[6] Jan Goldstein, *The Post-Revolutionary Self: Politics and Psyche in France, 1750–1850* (Cambridge, Mass., and London, 2005); Charles Taylor, *Sources of the Self: The Making of the Modern Identity* (Cambridge, Mass., and London, 1989), pp. 177, 184.

[7] Béatrice Didier, *Le Journal intime* (Paris, 2002); Giuseppe Nicoletti, *La memoria illuminata: autobiografia e letteratura fra Rivoluzione e Risorgimento* (Florence, 1989); Alain Girard, 'Le Journal intime: un nouveau genre littéraire?', *Cahiers de l'Association Internationale des Études Françaises* 17 (1965), pp. 99–109 and idem, *Le Journal intime* (Paris, 1963).

[8] On this issue see also the introduction in Mario Pieri, *Memorie*, edited by Roberta Masini, vol. I (Rome, 2003), pp. xxvii–xxx.

What is more important, both the diary and the autobiography were constructed in an intertextual context, through a continuous process of comparison with the works of other memorialists (be they diarists or autobiographers). First and foremost, with the *Confessions* of Jean-Jacques Rousseau (1782–9), the founding text, or so the argument runs, of modern, non-religious autobiography. *I am commencing an undertaking, hitherto without precedent, and which will never find an imitator*— Rousseau stated in the first lines of his memoir, unable apparently to predict the sea of autobiographical writing which would flood the century in imitation of his example.[9] From Casanova to Carlo Goldoni, from Lorenzo Da Ponte to Alfieri, from Byron to Goethe and to Walter Scott, few indeed of the great men of Pieri's time failed to leave a sort of autobiographical record behind. Pieri himself read almost all of them, commenting upon them in turn in the pages of his own diary. *I have found there nothing that I have cause to envy, nor anything to make me ashamed of my own Diary*—he noted after having read about the journal of Scott in 1837, while some years earlier he had derived some satisfaction from telling his diary that it was better than that of Goethe.[10]

Nothing could come close, though, to what he felt when reading the autobiography of Alfieri (*Vita di Vittorio Alfieri da Asti scritta da esso*, written between 1790 and 1803, but published posthumously in 1806).[11] As we have seen also in Part I of this book, Alfieri, and especially the portrait that he drew of himself in his *Vita*, deeply influenced the Ionian intellectuals of Pieri's generation. We need therefore to pause for a moment in order to grasp just who that writer was. Admired by Italian patriots as the man who had restored civil and political conscience to Italian culture and as the author who had reinvented Italian tragedy-writing after a lull of many centuries, Alfieri (1749–1803) was in reality a troubled soul. After a period of restless and desultory study in the military academy of Turin, he left his native Piedmont in an attempt to flee his own anxiety and discontent and to find something which would provide a meaning and justification for his turbulent existence. He roamed, or rather raced over Italy and Europe for many years, before finally settling in Florence and dedicating himself to the discovery of the Italian language and drama. As a Piedmontese aristocrat, he had been entirely educated in French and till late in his life he could hardly speak Italian at all. The myth elaborated in his autobiography of a writer desperate for glory but ignorant of Italian, struggling for years to acquire first a language and then a style, had strong resonances with Pieri's and his compatriots' own battles to conquer their national language. It is probable, indeed, that the metaphor of 'stammering', which became so dear to them, was taken from Alfieri's famous *Il Misogallo* (The French-Hater, 1793–9), where he deplored those Italians, who *due to a total lack... of knowledge of and respect for the value of their own true written language, debase themselves by... stammering the*

---

[9] Jean-Jacques Rousseau, *The Confessions* (London, 1996), p. 3.

[10] The comment on Scott is in Pieri, *Della vita*, vol. II, p. 330, which also contains (p. 153) a comment on the memoirs of Byron. The reference to the memoir of Goethe in BRF: Memorie di Mario Pieri, vol. IV [Ricc. 3558], No. 170 (16 Jan. 1824).

[11] Translated into English by Charles Edwards Lester: *The Autobiography of Vittorio Alfieri, the Tragic Poet* (New York, 1845).

*very ugly language of a very ugly people [the French].*[12] In addition, Alfieri's aristocratic liberalism—the convictions of a man who had championed liberty but was disappointed by what seemed to be the monstrously aberrant nature of modern politics—could speak to the heart of several disillusioned Ionians of his generation.[13] One of them, Ioannis Zampelios (1787–1856)—yet another who attempted to compose an autobiography—wrote when he saw on stage one of Alfieri's most famous tragedies, *Timoleon* (published in 1783, but staged later): *I cannot find words to express my joy, my exhilaration, my excitement, my emotions, nor the agitation of my soul for many days and nights afterwards… until that moment I had loved and admired the past only of my country. But since then… I love eagerly and passionately the present and the future of my patria.* Such was Zampelios's enthusiasm that he went to Florence explicitly to make the acquaintance of the author (*my heart pounded and my legs trembled when I saw his figure*, he remembered). On his return to his native Lefkada he set out to become the Alfieri of Greece by composing tragedies in the same manner, starting indeed with his own Greek *Timoleon* (1818).[14]

More than a literary practice and a fictional form then, this part of the book examines autobiographical writing as a historical document, as a testimony (with its own narrative strategies, of course) of the intimate craving of individuals to find stability and belonging in a period when all social, political, and cultural certainties were shifting like tectonic plates beneath their feet. By zooming in on the modest lives of these diarists and autobiographers, Chapters 8 and 9 attempt to zoom out on the massive changes occurring in their febrile age.

Chapter 8 tells the story of Mario Pieri and of a number of other Ionian and Greco-Italian diaspora intellectuals with whom he was connected (namely, Maria and Spiridione Petrettini, Constantine Polychroniades, Andrea Mustoxidi, and Angelica Palli), by drawing from both his manuscript diary and his published autobiography—and sometimes also by juxtaposing them. It narrates the adventures of a man who felt that he was living his life 'out of place', of an individual who embodied 'geographical and cultural dislocation', remaining perpetually suspended between Italian and Greek culture.[15] Accompanying his steps from Russian-controlled Corfu to Napoleonic and Habsburg Padua, Treviso, and Venice, and from there to Restoration Florence and back to British-controlled Corfu, Pieri's diary attests to the sense of dislocation and fragmentation occasioned by the reframing of identities in the rapidly transforming post-Venetian Adriatic. The diary reveals how it was that Pieri refashioned himself from a Venetian subject

---

[12] Vittorio Alfieri, *Il Misogallo*, in idem, *Scritti politici e morali*, edited by C. Mazzotta (Asti, 1984), vol. III, pp. 312–13.

[13] Christian del Vento, 'Alfieri, un homme de lettres entre réformes et Révolution', *Laboratoire italien* 9 (2009), pp. 109–33; Peter Brand and Lino Pertile (eds), *The Cambridge History of Italian Literature* (Cambridge, 2008), pp. 387–96.

[14] Spyridon De Biasi, 'Ioannis Zampelios', *Apollon* 64 (1890), pp. 990–1.

[15] The quotations are from Francesca Trivellato, 'Is There a Future for Italian Microhistory in the Age of Global History?', *California Italian Studies* 2/1 (2011): <https://escholarship.org/uc/item/0z94n9hq>, and A. Woollacott, D. Deacon, and P. Russell (eds), *Transnational Lives: Biographies of Global Modernity, 1700–Present* (London and New York, 2010).

into an Ionian diaspora person and later into a Greek exile through his distant experience of the Greek revolution and of the forging of the Ionian and then of the Greek state. The chapter studies the way this ex-Venetian subject and transnational patriot came to see himself as a Greek through his involvement in Italian, and more specifically Tuscan philhellenism, investigating at the same time some of the major tropes of this movement. It hopes thus to tell something about the perceptions of the war at one remove from the theatre of battle, as well as of the impact that the Greek revolution and the European philhellenisms had on the peoples of the 'Greek diasporas', reshaping even the very meaning of this notion.

Chapter 9 retraces the life of another forgotten individual, Andrea Papadopoulo Vretto (Ithaca, 1800–Athens, 1876), through his autobiographical manuscript which, written in Paris in 1867, narrated his life up until 1834. A student of medicine in Naples, a man of letters and archaeologist in Lefkada, a librarian and bibliographer in Corfu, a pharmacist and entrepreneur of culture in Nafplio, a diplomat and translator in St Petersburg, a Greek consul in Ottoman Varna and later in Venice, Papadopoulo Vretto lived, to say the least, a mobile existence. His memoirs, more succinct and less dramatic than those of Pieri, reflect the 'big' geopolitical changes that affected the lives of the Ionians of his generation. They also attest to the intricate interconnectedness of these geopolitical phenomena through the trajectories of people who traversed the Mediterranean and the Balkans, between East and West. By illuminating the predicament of this itinerant and adventurous man, the chapter studies the way national consciousness was created as a transitional, transnational, and diasporic phenomenon. In exploring Papadopoulo Vretto's dispersed activities, it also hopes to offer a contribution to certain debates in intellectual history, for example, regarding the creation of Albanian nationalism in the diasporic centres of southern Italy, the rise of interest in archaeology in the British Mediterranean, as well as the emergence of the modern Greek bibliographic tradition. It also furnishes insights into the links between Greece and Russia that were consolidated throughout the 1830s and illustrates the way that Orthodox ecumenism was reshaped within the Greek kingdom.

# 8

## A Life in Absence
### Mario Pieri

### A (POST-)VENETIAN SUBJECT

#### Anxieties and Longings in a Venetian and Post-Venetian Province

Those few historians who have been familiar with Mario Pieri's diary have not known quite what to do with it other than to mine it for information regarding the prominent figures who feature in its pages. A number of scholars have now and then made programmatic declarations, promising to publish and study in depth the nine volumes of this document, but none, to my knowledge, has done anything more than transcribe and arrange for the publication of the first two volumes of the diary or of certain passages related to specific places and events.[1] There is no synthetic or analytical work about the life of Pieri, which would transform this modest individual from purveyor of information regarding others into the central hero of a story. None, apart of course from the work of Pieri himself, namely his autobiography.

Every self-respecting autobiography should, in theory at any rate, include a substantial section on the years of childhood seen as formative of the life to follow. This is perhaps what Pieri thought when he sat down in 1850 and wrote the part which was missing from his diary about the first twenty-seven years of his life. We are, therefore, informed that he was born in 1776 in Corfu to an aristocratic but impoverished family. Like most of his fellow Ionians, he learned his first letters, Italian and Greek, alongside Orthodox and Catholic priests. He was a disobedient and dissatisfied child, but also inclined to melancholy and introspection. During the long afternoons that he spent in his room, in a state of reverie, he discovered that there was indeed one thing that gave him satisfaction, namely, reading.

---

[1] The most valuable work on Pieri's diary has been the transcription and publication of its first two volumes: Mario Pieri, *Memorie*, edited by Roberta Masini; Mario Pieri, *Memorie II*, edited by Claudio Chiancone. Several years earlier an article announced that a team of students from the University of Pisa was transcribing and studying the diary, but it is unclear what happened to their work: Roberto Bizzocchi and Kostas Soueref, 'Gia ton Mario Pieri, Kerkyra 1776–Florentia 1852' (On Mario Pieri, Corfu 1776–Florence 1852), *Deltion Anagnostikis Etairias Kerkyras* 17 (1980), pp. 117–27. Another attempt to undertake a serious study of the diary was made at the end of the nineteenth century by Filippo Orlando, who published selected passages in the pages of the *Giornale di erudizione* (1892–3), while two other authors of the time published certain passages relating to Pieri's stay in Verona: Tommaso Casini and Salomone Morpurgo, *Mario Pieri a Verona (1805–1821): dal suo diario. Per nozze Fraccaroli–Rezzonico Della Torre* (Prato, 1895).

One of the first books to fall into his hands was the seventeenth-century Cretan romance *Erotokritos*, which he read again and again, by turns shivering with fear and weeping.[2] At the age of 12 or 13 he also read Metastasio, an initiation into the magic universe of poetry that instilled in his heart a passion for letters. His subsequent discovery of the classics of Italian and ancient Latin and Greek literature—Dante, Petrarch and Tasso, Homer and Virgil—would only make this passion stronger.[3]

In 1796, Pieri, like several of his Corfiot friends, packed his bags and set out for Venice and Padua in order to pursue higher studies. There he entered the circle of Isabella Teotochi-Albrizzi (about whom I spoke in Chapter 1) and met all the important Italian Neoclassicists and pre-Romantics: Foscolo, Pindemonte, Monti, and especially Cesarotti, who would later become his teacher and mentor.[4] It was in their company, conducting poetic experiments and engaging in philological debate, that Pieri witnessed, in 1797, the fall of the Serenissima to the French army and the end of the world that he had known. He danced with Foscolo around the Tree of Liberty in Venice, although, as he admitted, *I little understood that revolution, and perhaps loved it because I loved the French, nor could I love the Venetians, who had allowed my patria to languish in such ignorance; and I hoped that through the new state of things I would come to see it rise again, and flourish through new studies, and customs, and institutions, and arts, and professions.*[5] His enthusiasm would be checked only by a peremptory letter from his father who, in that tumultuous moment for the whole of the Adriatic, ordered his son to obtain his diploma and hurry back home.

It was thus from his family home in Corfu that Pieri witnessed the arrival of the Jacobins on the Ionian Islands and the subsequent siege of the city by the Russo-Ottoman army in 1799. It was from there also that he witnessed the founding of the Septinsular Republic one year later. The new political dispensation, which offered, as we have seen, posts to a number of people of his rank, did not leave him dissatisfied either. In 1803, on the recommendation of his good friend Kapodistrias, Pieri became the Vice-Secretary of State (meaning, in all likelihood, the secretary of Kapodistrias himself). *The Septinsular Republic, with its first Constitution, albeit somewhat modified and corrected*—he wrote in his autobiography in 1850—*under the limited protection of Russia, could ensure the true happiness of the Ionian Islands.*[6] He struck a different note, however, in his diary, which he started to keep precisely in those days. *How ever could I carry out with any conviction*—young Pieri noted in June 1804—*my official duties as Vice-Secretary of State, when I saw daily that this liberty of my patria is a fable, it is a mask that tyranny assumed in order in utter silence to trample us?*[7] It seems to me that the past would take on a different complexion when viewed through the lens of what followed, namely British colonialism.

---

[2] Pieri, *Della vita*, vol. I, p. 18.      [3] Pieri, *Della vita*, vol. I, p. 23.
[4] On Italian pre-Romanticism see Brand and Pertile (eds), *The Cambridge History of Italian Literature*, pp. 393–5.
[5] Pieri, *Della vita*, vol. I, p. 46.      [6] Pieri, *Della vita*, vol. I, p. 82.
[7] In Pieri, *Memorie*, p. 6.

Pieri's political unhappiness regarding the Septinsular Republic was secondary to his personal dissatisfaction. The truth was that the little island of Corfu could not offer what he really wanted, namely, a literary career. He and his close friends (that is, Mustoxidi, Arliotti, Delviniotti, and Kapodistrias and his brother Augustinos) had admittedly created the *Società degli Amici*, a literary circle that met to read poems and discuss books. For a short while he and Mustoxidi even published a local literary journal, the *Gazzetta Urbana* (1802). But all this was not enough. Burning with the *ardent desire and faint hope for glory*, Pieri wanted more. *I feel myself born to raise my head high above my own century*, he immodestly declared. *I loved letters above all else, indeed, they were all I loved, and with a genuine and exclusive passion.*[8]

In truth, it was not only letters that he loved. He also loved women. And in that period particularly, he loved Maria Petrettini. In the landscape of Pieri's diary, which is populated mostly by characters whom the reader has already met, Maria and her brother Spiridione now made their appearance. Likewise typifying the lost intellectual generation of the Ionian post-Venetian world, Maria and Spiridione belonged to a local aristocratic family that had fallen on hard times. Distantly related in fact to Pieri, they spent their lives between the Ionian Islands and Venice, in what once used to be the great 'Venetian gulf'. Spiridione (1777–1833) set up in business as a merchant, but was, in reality, a man of letters. A Latinist of some repute, he translated Tacitus, Paterculus, and the Emperor Julian into Italian.[9] His elder sister, Maria (1772–1851), occupies a noteworthy place among the *femmes savantes* of her time. A cousin of Teotochi-Albrizzi, she can be compared to her in terms of the progressive nature of her ideas (she too was divorced, not once but twice), as well as in the extent of her education and intellectual sociability. Her philological work includes a biography of the fifteenth-century scholar Cassandra Fedele, a translation from English into Italian of the letters of Lady Mary Wortley Montagu, as well as a translation from Greek of a part of the *Images* of Philostratus of Lemnos, a sophist of the Roman period. Her papers also contain unpublished translations from Spanish into Italian of Cervantes.[10] *This extraordinary woman*, Pieri confessed, *had a great part to play in the so wise and yet so ill-advised doings of*

---

[8] Pieri, *Della vita*, vol. I, pp. 376, 378, and 384 respectively.

[9] Mara Nardo, *Maria e Spiridione Petrettini. Contributi allo studio della cultura italo-greca tra fine del dominio veneto e Restaurazione* (Padua, 2013); Mario Pieri, 'Vita di Spiridione Petrettini, corcirese', Appendix to idem, *Della vita*, vol. II, pp. 381–94; Emilio Tipaldo, 'Pettretini Spiridione', in idem (ed.), *Biografia degli Italiani illustri nelle scienze, lettere ed arti nel secolo XVIII e dei contemporanei* (Venice, 1834–45), vol. V, pp. 476–80; Girolamo Dandolo, *La caduta della Repubblica di Venezia ed i suoi ultimi cinquant' anni: studii storici* (Venice, 1855), pp. 344–5. Spiridione Petrettini, *Istoria romana di Vellejo Patercolo* (Venice, 1813); idem, *Le opere scelte di Giuliano imperatore, per la prima volta dal Greco volgarizzate con note, e con alcuni discorsi illustrativi* (Milan, 1822); idem, *Saggio di traduzione delle Aringhe di Cajo Cornelio Tacito* (Venice, 1806).

[10] Nardo, *Maria e Spiridione Petrettini*; A. Pasquali-Petrettini, *Lettere inedite a Maria Petrettini* (Padua, 1852); Agathi Nikokaboura, 'Maria Anastasia Petrettini', *Kerkyraika chronika* 13 (1967), pp. 128–36. Maria Petrettini, *Vita di Cassandra Fedele* (Venice, 1814); idem, *Lettere a lady Maria Wartley Montague tradotte dall'inglese* (Corfu, 1838); idem, *Alcune immagini di Filostrato tradotte dal greco da Maria Petrettini corcirese* (Treviso, 1825).

*my youth.*[11] His diary includes delirious descriptions of his love for her. No less passionate was their correspondence, which, exchanged over the years 1805–13 between the two shores of the Adriatic, reveals the anxieties and longings of a youth which, they feared, was destined to be wasted in a neglected corner of the post-Venetian world. *I feel myself to be separated from humankind*, Maria protested in a characteristic passage to be found in one of her letters from Corfu.[12] It was perhaps why, in 1804, Pieri decided to leave his little island behind and set out in her company for the magic universe of Venice, never to return to what to him could not help but seem a veritable backwater.

## Freedom and Nostalgia in Napoleonic Italy

Life was certainly more interesting in Italy for the young Corfiot. Napoleon's victories had driven the Austrians out of most of the Italian peninsula and led to the organization of the north-central part of it as a free and independent state ruled by its own constitutional nobility, known as the 'Italian Republic' (1802–4). As old exiles and Jacobins, convinced that a new phase of the Revolution was about to begin, poured into Milan, the capital of the new state, from all parts of Europe, Italian patriots saw in the defeat of the Austrians at the Battle of Marengo (1800) the harbinger of the collapse of the *anciens régimes* everywhere on the peninsula and the creation of a unitary Italian state. These hopes were, paradoxically enough, further bolstered when Napoleon was crowned Emperor of France in 1804 and King of Italy in 1805. Italian national enthusiasm was once again enhanced by the French triumph at Austerlitz and the subsequent Treaty of Pressburg (1805), which obliged Austria to cede the greater part of the former Venetian territories to the Italian Republic, now renamed the 'Kingdom of Italy' (1805–14). It was the first time that something resembling an Italian national state had been created in the northern part of the peninsula.[13]

Pieri was completely attuned to the mood of the times. *Italy*, he wrote in his autobiography, *beautiful Italy wholly united in a single state, this splendid dream moved my soul more deeply than any other thing, and my imagination caught fire. And yet*, he specified, *I was not Italian!*[14] The diary recorded this selfsame moment quite differently. In place of the last specification, it contained an enthusiastic and patriotic invocation of Petrarch. *O my beloved Petrarch, incomparable soul, would that you could see what was the eternal wish, the eternal sigh of your beautiful heart!*[15] It was precisely to the Renaissance poet that the young Corfiot dedicated one of his first poems, infused with the feverish patriotic fervour of those days, entitled *Canzone*

[11] Pieri, *Della vita*, vol. I, p. 52.

[12] Mara Nardo, 'Fra Russi e Francesi, fra Venezia e Corfù: Il contrastato amore e il carteggio segreto di Mario Pieri e Maria Petrettini', *Atti dell'Istituto Veneto di Scienze, Lettere ed Arti* 163 (2009–10), p. 208.

[13] Antonino De Francesco, *L'Italia di Bonaparte: politica, statualità e nazione nella penisola tra due rivoluzioni, 1796–1821* (Milan, 2011), pp. 35–92; Desmond Gregory, *Napoleon's Italy* (London, 2001); Carlo Capra, *L'età rivoluzionaria e napoleonica in Italia, 1796–1815* (Turin, 1978), esp. pp. 239–72.

[14] Pieri, *Della vita*, vol. I, p. 126.     [15] In Pieri, *Memorie*, p. 82.

*al Petrarca per la Restaurazione del Regno d'Italia* (Song to Petrarch for the Restoration of the Kingdom of Italy, 1805). The poem was well received in Venetian intellectual circles and this, along with Pieri's well-connected circle of friends and acquaintances in Padua, helped him, in 1808, to obtain an appointment as professor of philology and history at the lycée of the neighbouring town of Treviso.

Yet, mobility, then as now, had its price. Pieri endured a constant, gnawing sense of nostalgia. *Far from the patria my soul shrinks, and I suffer from the same malady that afflicts the Swiss when in a foreign land*—he told his diary in 1805 (nostalgia was first coined as a medical condition to describe the sufferings of seventeenth-century Swiss mercenaries fighting away from home).[16] He knew that what he felt was incurable. *Yet if I were in my homeland, a longing to take my leave would immediately return*, he wrote in February 1805; *yet when I am in Padua and arm in arm with my beloved Cesarotti…I am still not content, and wish always to be where I am not.*[17] This feeling of 'dislocation', of being always 'elsewhere', would become a leitmotif in his life thereafter, acquiring, as we shall see, a dramatic intensity in later years. Sometimes it was not only Corfu that Pieri was nostalgic for, but the whole of the lost Venetian Mediterranean world. *I was born beside the sea and it seems to me that there cannot be genuine contentment if one is far from the sea*, he wrote in December of 1813, while on a visit to Milan; *Wherever can one hope to find in Mediterranean countries the variety of different prospects, the…liveliness, the indefinable quotient of both voluptuousness and magnificence to be had in countries situated on the sea? For me, then, the word* Venice *and the adjective* Venetian, *which are all but brothers to the words* Greece *and* Greek, *and still more of the words* Corfu *and* Corfiot, *have a great power over my soul and will have it for so long as these eyes of mine are open.*[18] Born and raised as a subject of an empire which had united for centuries the two shores of the Adriatic now in the process of separating and facing divergent political fates, Pieri would be haunted by a vague sense of longing for something irremediably lost—not concretely the Venetian Empire itself, but rather the wider cultural geography that was dissolving as it fell.

## AN IONIAN PATRIOT

### Gaining and Losing a New Patria

Pieri was in Milan when, in April 1814, the Kingdom of Italy faced its rapid and inglorious end, provoked by the defeat of Napoleon in the distant steppes of Russia and his subsequent fall from grace in Paris, as well as by the political manipulations of the old Lombard aristocracy, eager to regain its local power.[19] The fall of Napoleon meant yet another end to a familiar order of things and left people

---

[16] Pieri, *Memorie*, p. 52. On the history of nostalgia see Svetlana Boym, *The Future of Nostalgia* (New York, 2001); Rolf Petri (ed.), *Nostalgia: memoria e passaggi tra le sponde dell'Adriatico* (Rome, 2009); Thomas Dodman, *What Nostalgia Was: War, Empire and the Time of a Deadly Emotion* (Chicago, 2018).
[17] Pieri, *Memorie*, p. 34.      [18] BRF: Memorie di Mario Pieri, vol. II [Ricc. 3556], 73.
[19] De Francesco, *L'Italia di Bonaparte*, pp. 143–52.

everywhere in Europe bewildered about their fates—*some wept, some laughed, some did not know what to say about it, nor what to do about it, but all were astounded by it*, wrote Pieri.[20] The collapse of the Napoleonic Empire, sealed by the Congress of Vienna (1814–15), marked the end of one period and the beginning of another, which in due course came to be known as the Restoration. Having recorded the turmoil that followed the collapse of the Napoleonic government in Milan and the arrival of the Austrian army, Pieri went to Venice. There, in May 1815, he witnessed the swearing of the oath by the Austrian princes, who were by now the new masters of the territory.[21] The whole region of Veneto and Lombardy (named now 'Kingdom of Lombardy-Veneto') thus passed under the jurisdiction of the Habsburg crown and Pieri mourned the vanished dreams of Italian independence. *Oath! Kingdom! Unhappy Italy! This is how you regain your independence! Passing from one set of chains to another.*[22] Yet, the new situation filled him also with some hope. *I derive not a little comfort from the idea of universal peace, free communications with all of Europe, and the liberation of my patria*—he wrote.[23] On a more personal level, the new political settlement brought with it an unexpected promotion, since, as a result of the reorganization of schools by the new authorities, he was released from the sad town of Treviso and was transferred to Padua to teach at its prestigious university.

Meanwhile, on the other side of the Adriatic, the Ionian Islands, which had been ceded by the Russians to Bonaparte in 1807, were by now (excepting Corfu, which would fall soon thereafter) under the control of the British navy. Pieri shared the enthusiasm of a number of his fellow Ionians, who saw in the creation of the British-controlled United States of the Ionian Islands the occasion to make of their little patria a free and national statelet within a liberal empire. *We spent the evening in the company of various Greek scholars, waxing enthusiastic over our new Ionian republic*, he wrote in August 1815; *a republic that is indeed about to send me into raptures, and cause me to desert Italy. It is above all the freedom of the press, which will probably be established there, that whets my appetite. It is a great and a beautiful thing to be able to write and print whatever occurs to you or whatever you please.*[24] It seemed, in addition, that the locals' national feeling, and especially their demand for the adoption of the Greek language, would be taken into serious consideration by the new masters of the region. Much as this news filled the young Corfiot with joy, it also put him in an awkward position regarding his own linguistic abilities and cultural formation. In December 1816, when the British authorities announced a competition for the best work written by Ionians in Greek, Pieri wrote somewhat melodramatically: *But I no longer have a patria, because as a man I am Greek but as a man of letters I am Italian.*[25] It was the first time that he was forced to confront so directly the problem of belonging. In the years that followed he would be plagued by it, indeed with the passage of time it came more and more to haunt him. At that moment, however, the more he thought about the potential of this

---

[20] Pieri, *Della vita*, vol. I, p. 296.
[21] Pieri, *Della vita*, vol. I, pp. 296–301 and Pieri, *Memorie II*, pp. 203–10.
[22] Pieri, *Della vita*, vol. I, p. 271.    [23] Pieri, *Della vita*, vol. I, p. 207.
[24] Pieri, *Della vita*, vol. I, p. 315.    [25] Pieri, *Della vita*, vol. I, pp. 382–3.

new patria, the more the idea of returning preoccupied him. As is always the case, political and personal motives were intertwined: in 1817, his post at the University of Padua was about to be thrown open to public competition and Pieri, who lacked qualifications, was about to lose it.

Nevertheless, while the young Corfiot was pondering the idea of repatriation, the first rumours reached his ears about the actual situation on the Ionian Islands. In April 1818, the new constitution of the Ionian state fell into his hands and immediately dampened his enthusiasm. Drafted at the behest of the notoriously authoritarian first British High Commissioner, Thomas Maitland, it was actually a document providing in semblance only democratic, republican rule, while in reality it vested all power in the hands of the British colonial administration (1817). *At present I am reading…the constitution of the United States of the Ionian Islands, which makes me shudder and sigh at the thought of the new servitude of the patria. But what am I doing talking of patria? The Greeks (unfortunately) do not have a patria. We are forever lost!*—Pieri wrote in utter dismay.[26] The feeling of losing his newly won homeland became more pronounced as he encountered fellow Corfiots who visited Italy bringing news from home. After one such meeting, in July 1818, he noted: *Poor Greece, which is simply passing from one yoke to another! Alas, the Greeks no longer have a patria!* Nos patriam fugimus, et dulcia linquimus arva, *and perhaps forever!*, he added, paraphrasing Virgil.[27] It was probably then that he also started correcting his earlier enthusiastic diary entries, by adding small comments in the margins: *Oh, how we deluded ourselves then?—Now what more infamous tyranny [could there be] than the English tyranny?*[28] The turning-point as regards Pieri's attitude towards Britain, however, like that of most of his liberal Ionian friends, came in 1819, when news about the concession of the town of Parga to Ali Pasha reached his ears. The wretched mass of Pargiote exiles in flight from the notorious Ottoman butcher and seeking refuge in the Ionian Island made Pieri *swear eternal hatred* to Britain.[29] The prospect of a new and free patria in the Ionian state was completely lost for Pieri by the time he met Kapodistrias on his way back from Corfu in 1819. After having vividly portrayed the *lamentable state* of their homeland and the *horrendous tyranny of its protectors*, Kapodistrias advised his friend to forever forget the prospect of repatriation. *Goodbye, then, Corfu and forever, I'll no longer call you patria since you are no longer worthy of me*—Pieri wrote on that fateful day.[30]

---

[26] Pieri, *Della vita*, vol. I, p. 467.

[27] Pieri, *Della vita*, vol. I, p. 487. The actual phrase by Virgil is 'nos patriae finis et dulcia linquimus arva. | Nos patriam fugimus' (We leave our country's bounds, our much-lov'd plains, || We from our country fly), (Virgil, *Eclogues*, I, 3–4). See *The Works of Virgil in Latin and English* (London, 1778), vol. I, pp. 76–7.

[28] Pieri, *Memorie II*, pp. 315–16.

[29] BRF: Memorie di Mario Pieri, vol. III [Ricc. 3557], 83 and Pieri, *Della vita*, vol. I, pp. 405–6.

[30] BRF: Memorie di Mario Pieri, vol. III [Ricc. 3557], 55. Kapodistrias's visit also in Pieri, *Della vita*, vol. I, pp. 381–2.

## A TRANSNATIONAL REVOLUTIONARY

### In the Wave of the 1820–1821 Liberal Revolutions

More dedicated now to his Italian 'there and now', Pieri decided in 1820 to undertake a journey through the major cities of the Italian peninsula. He had, at the beginning of that year, lost his job at the University of Padua (which did however compensate him with a good pension) and published a book containing various treatises from his teachings and lectures (*Operette varie in prosa*, 1820), which nevertheless sank without trace. He was still in Padua, preparing for this journey, when news of a revolt in Naples broke. *Great news! A revolution having broken out in Naples, the king is obliged to grant his peoples a liberal constitution resembling that of Spain. May the same happen throughout all of Europe!*—he wrote in his diary on 17 July 1820.[31]

It is only recently that historians have approached the constitutional revolts of 1820 and 1821 in southern Europe and the Balkans as connected and interrelated phenomena. They argue that it was not only the reactionary powers, Metternich and those of a like mind, who saw the Neapolitan, Piedmontese, Portuguese, and Greek revolts as direct continuations of the Spanish rising, but also liberals and revolutionaries throughout Europe and the Mediterranean.[32] The transnational nature of patriotism and liberalism in the 1820s, and the conviction that the fight for freedom was a collective endeavour that transcended the boundaries of existing states, led many revolutionaries to believe that the Spanish events had ushered in a new era which would spread the revolutionary impulse all over the Continent.[33] Notions of international solidarity were reinforced by the hundreds of volunteers, mostly refugees and exiles from the Neapolitan and Piedmontese revolutions, who went directly or via Spain and Portugal to fight in Greece. This sea of 'revolutionary nomads' formed the living link between the Mediterranean uprisings and sometimes even with contemporary revolutions in South America.[34] Pieri's diary exemplifies how a contemporary liberal perceived these Mediterranean and transatlantic connections. But before delving more deeply into this matter, we need to flesh out the historical context.

---

[31]   BRF: Memorie di Mario Pieri, vol. III [Ricc. 3557], 145.

[32]   Richard Stites, *The Four Horsemen: Riding to Liberty in Post-Napoleonic Europe* (Oxford, 2014); see also the earlier contribution by Marion S. Miller, 'A Liberal International? Perspectives on Comparative Approaches to the Revolutions in Spain, Italy, and Greece in the 1820s', in R. W. Clement, B. F. Taggie, and R. G. Schwartz (eds), *Greece and the Mediterranean* (Kirksville, Mo., 1990), pp. 61–8.

[33]   Maurizio Isabella, *Risorgimento in Exile: Italian Émigrés and the Liberal International in the Post-Napoleonic Era* (Oxford, 2009); idem and Konstantina Zanou (eds), *Mediterranean Diasporas: Politics and Ideas in the Long Nineteenth Century* (London, 2016); Gilles Pécout, 'Pour une lecture méditerranéenne et transnationale du Risorgimento', *Revue d'histoire du XIXe siècle* 44 (2012), pp. 29–47.

[34]   Maurizio Isabella, 'Entangled Patriotisms: Italian Liberals and Spanish America in the 1820s', in Matthew Brown and Gabriel Paquette (eds), *Connections after Colonialism: Europe and Latin America in the 1820s* (Tuscaloosa, Ala., 2013), pp. 87–107; Gilles Pécout, 'The International Armed Volunteers: Pilgrims of a Transnational Risorgimento', *Journal of Modern Italian Studies* 14/4 (2009), pp. 413–26; Gianni Korinthios, *I liberali napoletani e la rivoluzione greca 1821–1830* (Naples, 1990).

In 1820, a military uprising took place in Spain and its leader, Colonel Rafael del Riego, delivered a *pronunciamento* calling for the reintroduction of the Spanish constitution of 1812 (which had been adopted by the Cortes, Spain's first National Assembly, in beleaguered Cadiz during the Napoleonic invasion), the most liberal of the existing constitutions of its day. Having succumbed to the recent, successful revolts of the Spanish colonies in the Americas, which had deprived the country of an important source of revenue, the Bourbon King of Spain, Ferdinand VII, was forced in March of that same year to accept the constitution, thus ushering in a period of liberal rule, the so-called 'Trienio Liberal' (1820–3). Events in Spain precipitated parallel developments in Portugal, where a liberal revolution likewise erupted in 1820, introducing a period of constitutional rule in the course of which it readjusted its colonial relationship with Brazil.[35]

Developments in the Iberian peninsula inspired events in another Bourbon kingdom, Naples, which, along with southern Italy, had for nearly ten years (1806–15) formed part of Napoleon's continental enterprise, and was returned with the latter's fall to the Bourbon crown. The restored King Ferdinand I of the Two Sicilies (as the united kingdoms of Naples and Sicily were now called), though he had by and large maintained the sweeping reforms that had been introduced during the Napoleonic period—and especially under Joachim Murat's rule (1808–15)—reigned as an absolute monarch. The suppression of liberal opinion, the expansion of ecclesiastical censorship and control over much of civic life, the sidelining of those who had served or supported the French regime (the so-called 'Muratists'), and the suffocating Austrian surveillance, exacerbated social discontent and intensified the activities of secret societies, particularly the carbonari, who infiltrated the army. In July 1820 carbonari members, along with more moderate liberal elements among Murat's former army officers, led by General Guglielmo Pepe, provoked a bloodless revolt and obliged the terrified King to sign a constitution. The latter was modelled on the 1812 Spanish constitution of Cadiz. Press freedom followed automatically in Naples, and in September elections led to the formation of a parliament.[36] Whereas in the Iberian peninsula the revolutionary regimes lasted for about three years (being eventually crushed by a French military intervention in Spain and a civil war in Portugal), that in Naples survived a mere nine months. The powers of the Holy Alliance, who met in 1820 in a conference at Laibach, feared—and rightly so—that its subversive message would inevitably spread to other countries, provoking a domino effect, with one successful liberal revolt precipitating another. They had no difficulty in persuading the Neapolitan monarch to forget his oaths in front of the parliament and allow an Austrian army to march into his kingdom and 'restore order'. *My soul is steeped in bitterness*, wrote Pieri in February 1821. *It seems that the Austrian troops are on their way to invading and sullying the*

---

[35] On Spain see Stites, *The Four Horsemen*, pp. 28–120; On Portugal see Gabriel Paquette, *Imperial Portugal in the Age of Atlantic Revolutions: The Luso-Brazilian World, c.1770–1850* (Cambridge, 2013), esp. chapter 2.

[36] George T. Romani, *The Neapolitan Revolution of 1820–1821* (Westport, Conn., 1950); John A. Davis, *Naples and Napoleon: Southern Italy and the European Revolutions (1780–1860)* (Oxford, 2006), pp. 275–316; Stites, *The Four Horsemen*, pp. 121–85.

*most beautiful country in the world, the earthly paradise of Naples, and an imbecile and scoundrel of a king wishes to perjure and dishonour himself in the face of all Europe, he wishes to see his kingdom devastated and his people ruined, he wishes to turn himself into a child under the tutelage of the other monarchs of Europe rather than give his people a liberal constitution.*[37] By the end of March 1821 the revolution in Naples was already a thing of the past.

But just as the Neapolitan revolt was at death's door, a new revolution erupted on the other side of the Italian peninsula, Piedmont. Pieri felt reinvigorated. *I am in raptures,* he wrote on 14 March 1821; *Great news! The revolution has broken out throughout Piedmont. All the troops united asked the king for the constitution… Oh my Italy, if this is a dawn that promises a most beautiful day, I am beside myself!*[38] At the beginning of that month, indeed, a group of officers, nobles, carbonari, and students, led by the Count Santorre di Santarosa, forced the Savoy King of Sardinia-Piedmont, Vittorio Emanuele I, to abdicate. Forming a provisional committee, they proclaimed the Spanish constitution of 1812 in the garrison town of Alessandria, near to the kingdom's capital, Turin. The new King, Carlo Felice, emulating Ferdinand of Naples, appealed to the powers at the Laibach conference to intervene. While the powers, each for its own reasons, were still reluctant to approve a military intervention, and the Russian embassy in Turin was trying to mediate between the King and the revolutionaries (with Mocenigo and Mustoxidi playing leading roles in this endeavour, as we will see in Chapter 10), the agony of the patriots only increased.[39] On receiving the news from Turin, Pieri wrote on 8 April 1821: *Oh, to think of the many generous efforts, the great outpouring of national feeling, the boundless love for Italic liberty, that will come to nothing! To think of the many illustrious victims! Fifty or so students from Pavia, all Lombards, are to go and shut themselves in the citadel of Turin in order to aid the cause of Italian independence; and many other Milanese, including some of the most lordly, will make their way to Turin for the same reason… but after the Neapolitan display of cowardice what hopes can there be for a good outcome?*[40] Unfortunately for him, the day before, the Austrian and royal forces had already defeated the revolutionary army and brought about the collapse of the constitutional government and the dissolution of the revolutionary forces in Turin and Alessandria. News arrived in Padua with some days of delay and plunged Pieri into despair. *At last the infamy of Italy is consummated*—he confided to his diary on 13 April 1821. *It is said for a certainty that Alessandria, at the approach of the Austrian forces, threw open its gates. After having made such a commotion… after having denied the mediation of the Russian Ministry, whoever would have expected so swift and shameful a humiliation?… Oh Italy, I am ashamed to have adopted you as my second patria. Whatever shall I do between Greece and Italy, between the two slaves? I feel anguish in my heart.*[41]

---

[37]  BRF: Memorie di Mario Pieri, vol. III [Ricc. 3557], 201.

[38]  BRF: Memorie di Mario Pieri, vol. III [Ricc. 3557], 210.

[39]  Carlo Torta, *La rivoluzione piemontese nel 1821* (Rome and Milan, 1908), pp. 94–157; Narcisso Nada, *Metternich, la diplomazia russa, Francesco IV di Modena ed i moti piemontesi del 1821* (Rome, 1972).

[40]  BRF: Memorie di Mario Pieri, vol. III [Ricc. 3557], 218.

[41]  BRF: Memorie di Mario Pieri, vol. III [Ricc. 3557], 219.

Yet, while Piedmont's fate was still undecided, another piece of news, about an eruption of a Greek revolt in Wallachia, reached Pieri's ears. *At a time when Spain, Portugal, cowardly Naples, Piedmont are in revolution, and the despots of Europe are in Laibach*—he wrote in his diary—*what do we find but another revolution in Wallachia.*[42] The view of the 1820 and 1821 revolutionary movements as a chain of events bound inextricably together and linked to contemporary developments in South America does indubitably feature in Pieri's diary. For example, in 1823 he noted the news of the suppression of the revolution in Spain and feared that a similar outcome would ensue in Greece. Likewise, in 1824 he recorded with pleasure the establishment of a constitutional empire in Brazil, while, at the same time, he read the works of the Abbot de Pradt, an influential French analyst who compared the fates of the Americas and Greece in order to reflect upon Europe's future.[43] Pieri himself set out to compare the Greek revolution with the North American context when in 1821 he read the history of the American Revolution by Carlo Botta and the memoirs of Benjamin Franklin.[44]

Pieri was certainly not alone among Ionians and diaspora Greeks in perceiving the Greek revolution within a Mediterranean and transatlantic framework. In August 1821, a group of Greek intellectuals in Paris (Adamantios Koraes, Constantine Polychroniades, Alexandros Vogorides, and Christodoulos Clonares), led by the renowned French activist and intellectual the Abbot Grégoire, sent an appeal to the *President and to the Citizens of the Republic of Haiti*, in order to ask for arms and men in aid of the revolution in Greece, based on the principle of solidarity between the peoples. *History will repeat to future generations that the flag of Haiti floating over the Mediterranean was united with that of Greece resuscitated. It will be a glorious epoch for the two nations and one of the most beautiful triumphs of justice and humanity*—the appeal read, perfectly encapsulating the view of a fraternal revolutionary world in Pieri's day.[45]

## The Greek Revolution from the Italian Shores

*So it was then, just as I was hesitating over my destiny, and over that of Italy my second and adoptive patria*, Pieri recalls in his autobiography, *that I was taken by surprise by the initial outbreak of the Greek revolution, which, having occurred in times that were hardly propitious, indeed were wretched as can be, could not help at first glance but bring only scant satisfaction.*[46] In March 1821, when Ypsilantis and his multi-ethnic

[42] BRF: Memorie di Mario Pieri, vol. III [Ricc. 3557], 216.

[43] On Brazil: BRF: Memorie di Mario Pieri, vol. IV [Ricc. 3558], 214. Pieri claims to have read de Pradt's, *Parallèle de la puissance anglaise et russe relativement à l'Europe, suivi d'un aperçu sur la Grèce* (Paris, 1823) [in BRF: Memorie di Mario Pieri, vol. IV [Ricc. 3558], 147]. De Pradt also elaborated these ideas in his *L'Europe et l'Amérique en 1821* (Paris, 1822) and especially in his *Vrai système de l'Europe relativement à l'Amérique et à la Grèce* (Paris, 1825).

[44] BRF: Memorie di Mario Pieri, vol. III [Ricc. 3557], 236–7, 244. Carlo Botta, *Storia della guerra d'Indipendenza degli Stati Uniti d'America* (Paris, 1809).

[45] BnF-BA: Autographes abbé Grégoire, MS 15145/3. See P. Grunebaum-Ballin, *Henri Grégoire, l'ami des hommes de toutes les couleurs* (Paris, 1948), pp. 240–5.

[46] Pieri, *Della vita*, vol. I, p. 455.

army of volunteers raised the banner of revolt against the Ottoman Empire in Wallachia, neither Pieri nor indeed anyone else at that time could ever have imagined that this would be the start of a war of independence that would last for nearly ten years, leading eventually to the creation of the Greek nation-state. Absorbed as he was by the Italian revolutions, the Corfiot began seriously to reflect upon Greek affairs only in May 1821, when the crushing of the revolution in Piedmont was by then a fait accompli. Like the hundreds of disappointed Italian revolutionaries who were faced with exile, and now started to make their way to Spain, Portugal, and Greece, in his mind's eye Pieri now forsook Italy for the promise of liberty which he saw being born in the Balkan peninsula. *Goodbye, base Italy. Here am I in your fond embrace, O my dearest Greece*—he wrote in his diary on 1 May 1821.[47] By mid-May, and after hearing the news of the launch of the revolution in the Peloponnese, he was ready to say, *O my own Greece, if you restore your freedom I will come to kiss your sacred earth and I shall die in your bosom.*[48] Utterly disillusioned by the turn of events in Italy, he started to re-evaluate his national belonging. *What a difference there is between the Greeks and the Italians!*—he wrote on 27 May 1821. *I confess that I am baffled by them since I no longer believe my nation to be equipped to do as much and it seems to me that it has even lost a sense of grief about its downfall. Are my Greeks then still Greeks?*[49] Angered, moreover, by the illiberal character of the British administration in the Ionian Islands, only a month would pass before Pieri concluded that it was Greece that was in fact his true homeland. *If God crowns with success the efforts of my Greeks*, he wrote on 15 June, *then Greece will become my homeland. Greece, Greece, and not Corfu, and assuredly not English Corfu.*[50]

While Pieri was pondering the idea of donning the traditional Greek costume, in the guise of the fustanella skirt (which was however expensive and hard to find in Venice), in July he heard the first rumours regarding the defeat of Ypsilantis and the Ottoman reprisals against the Greeks in Constantinople. He read the account of the funeral and the obituary of the executed Patriarch of Constantinople and burst into tears.[51] But despite Ypsilantis's disaster in the Danubian Principalities, events in the Greek peninsula progressed unexpectedly well. In the initial phase of the rebellion, the Greek forces were able to capture many of the major Turkish strongholds in the Peloponnese and to establish a strong presence in central Greece as well. *I can now breathe again*, wrote Pieri on 22 July 1821. *The newspaper reports a defeat of the Turkish fleet by the Greeks, and other good news... Hope is reborn!*[52] By the end of 1823, the revolutionaries had conquered and brought under their control all the major garrisons and fortresses in central and southern Greece. As several

[47] BRF: Memorie di Mario Pieri, vol. III [Ricc. 3557], 223.
[48] BRF: Memorie di Mario Pieri, vol. III [Ricc. 3557], 226.
[49] BRF: Memorie di Mario Pieri, vol. III [Ricc. 3557], 234.
[50] BRF: Memorie di Mario Pieri, vol. III [Ricc. 3557], 238–9.
[51] BRF: Memorie di Mario Pieri, vol. IV [Ricc 3558], 37. Konstantinos Oikonomou, *Epitafios logos eis ton aeimniston Patriarchin Konstantinoupoleos Grigorion, ekfonitheis en Odisso etc.* (Obituary to the lamented Patriarch of Constantinople Grigorios, pronounced in Odessa etc.) (Moscow, 1821).
[52] BRF: Memorie di Mario Pieri, vol. III [Ricc. 3557], 249.

of the Aegean islands also threw their lot in with the insurrection, victories on land were soon complemented by successes at sea. Despite the political rifts and local antagonisms between the various revolutionary factions, the insurgents managed to assemble for a National Congress (Epidaurus, December 1821), where they promulgated a constitution and established a republican government.[53]

It has been argued that the experience of this lengthy and bloody war was crucial in transforming a motley assortment of Ottoman subjects, peasants, brigands, clerics, and notables into Greek soldiers and potential citizens.[54] If, then, participation in battles, the experience of killing or suffering violence, and the possession of things that were material, such as spoils, arms, and land, was what essentially crafted a new Greek national consciousness, what about those Greeks who, like Pieri, 'were not there', who did not so directly take part? What did the Greek revolution mean for those Greeks who never set foot in the soil that was now, through the experience of the war, becoming Greece? It is this question I will now explore. I will do so by following Pieri and certain other Ionian and diaspora Greeks in their endeavours in philhellenic Tuscany. I will argue, first of all, that the people of the Greek diasporas perceived the revolution and their new Greek homeland through the eyes of Italian philhellenism; and, second, that the revolutionary experience produced, in the case of the Greek and especially the Ionian diasporas, a new national consciousness which was constructed around absence, exile, and estrangement.

## AN ITALIAN PHILHELLENE OR A DIASPORA GREEK?

### In the Embrace of Tuscan Philhellenism

Stirred by the events on the Greek mainland and upset by the way these were depicted in the hostile Habsburg press of the Veneto, Pieri found consolation in the burgeoning philhellenic literature. It was in September 1822 that he read one of the first eye-witness accounts of the revolution, Claude Denis Raffenel's *Histoire des événements de la Grèce, depuis les premiers troubles jusqu'à ce jour* (1822). *I received a sudden electric shock from something new I had read, which did indeed reinvigorate me, casting me into a new world*—he noted in his autobiography. *It showed me that my nation had achieved wonders of valour and patriotism.*[55] Imbued with an intense feeling of philhellenism and Greek patriotism, and encouraged by an agreement between the Habsburg Empire and the Grand Duchy of Tuscany which would permit him to keep his pension, Pieri decided, in August 1823, to move to Florence, where he could be better informed as to what was happening on the other side of the Adriatic. Thanks to the reformist rule of Ferdinand III (1814–24)

---

[53] Thomas W. Gallant, *The Edinburgh History of the Greeks, 1768 to 1913: The Long Nineteenth Century* (Edinburgh, 2015), pp. 51–106.

[54] Apostolos Bakalopoulos, *Ta ellinika stratevmata tou 1821: organosi, igesia, taktiki, ithi, psychologia* (The Greek army of 1821: organization, leadership, tactic, ethos, psychology) (Thessaloniki, 1948).

[55] Pieri, *Della vita*, vol. I, pp. 507–9.

and of his son Leopold II (1824–59), the Grand Duchy of Tuscany was blessed with the mildest of the Restoration regimes in all of Italy. Many of the Napoleonic laws and institutions were maintained, and the state personnel preserved; there were no persecutions, and censorship was lighter than in the other Italian states. This made Florence an attractive destination for liberal thinkers and exiled patriots, who flocked to the city from all over Italy and the Mediterranean in search of intellectual freedom, tranquillity, and up-to-date and reliable information.[56]

The most liberal of all the liberal institutions in Florence was the so-called *Gabinetto Vieusseux* (Vieusseux's reading room). *I frequented the Cabinet and Signor Vieusseux's salon*—wrote Pieri—*where, thanks to the sheer quantity and variety of Newspapers that arrived from all parts, and thanks also to the foreigners from every country that took refuge there, I was confident of being able to gather the most reliable news.*[57] Created in 1820 by the Genevan merchant and cultural entrepreneur Gian-Pietro Vieusseux (1779–1863), the reading room was 'the most open and intellectually refined, the least provincially Tuscan and the most European space in all Florence', as one scholar put it.[58] In addition to the Cabinet, Vieusseux also launched a journal, the *Antologia* (1821–33). This celebrated journal attracted the most important names in the Italian intellectual world, justifiably earning its editor a name for himself as the chief coordinator of culture on the Italian peninsula at that date. It has been argued indeed that it was largely thanks to this Genevan merchant's activities that a series of intellectuals managed to overcome their personal travails and vexatious municipal divisions, so as to create a nationwide, moderate liberal opinion. To be sure, his journal became the favoured channel of expression of the most progressive, international, and liberal-patriotic aspects of the Italian intelligentsia of the period. 'Sincerely liberal'—wrote one historian—'Vieusseux and his friends kept their eyes fixed on every corner of the earth in which a fight for liberty was being waged. They were friends to all oppressed peoples.'[59]

One of these corners was, of course, Greece. Vieusseux's circle not only received news, talked, and wrote about Greece. They also practised militant philhellenism. Through his links with the Swiss banker Jean-Gabriel Eynard—a renowned philhellene and perhaps Greece's most significant financial supporter—and a group of wealthy Livornese merchants, the indefatigable Vieusseux created a genuine 'philhellenic infrastructure' in Tuscany which, especially in the period 1825–8, organized the transfer of goods, arms, money, and volunteers to the beleaguered country. Thanks to his coordinating role, the port of Livorno became the essential bridge for the shipping of aid from the various European philhellenic committees to Greece. Along with Bishop Ignatius's activities in neighbouring Pisa and the support

[56] Antonio Chiavistelli, *Dallo stato alla nazione: costituzione e sfera pubblica in Toscana dal 1814 al 1849* (Rome, 2006).

[57] Pieri, *Della vita*, vol. II, p. 38.

[58] Ernesto Sestan, *La Firenze di Vieusseux e di Capponi*, edited by Giovanni Spadolini (Florence, 1986), p. 12.

[59] Raffaele Ciampini, *Gian Pietro Vieusseux: i suoi viaggi, i suoi giornali, i suoi amici* (Turin, 1953), p. 162.

of the liberal students of that town's university, Vieusseux's operations made of Tuscany the centre of philhellenic activism on the Italian peninsula.[60]

This was the ideal place, then, for someone like Pieri to be. As soon as he had settled in Florence, the Corfiot became an integral part of Vieusseux's circle and an assiduous habitué of his reading room. At the Cabinet he could keep abreast of all the very latest news about the revolution, read philhellenic books, discuss and dispute with other intellectuals, dream, and at times perhaps shed bitter tears. Among the numerous philhellenic books that arrived every week to fill the Cabinet's shelves—from the account of the revolution by Edward Blaquiere and the life of Byron by Pietro Gamba to the odes of Kalvos and the collection of Greek folk songs by Fauriel—François Pouqueville's *Histoire de la régénération de la Grèce* made the most profound impact upon this circle's meetings.[61] *Prior to dining with Vieusseux I read in Pouqueville of the death of Marco Bozzari*—wrote Pieri in a diary entry from October 1824, referring to the death in battle of the most famous Greek guerrilla captain—*and we all wept out of compassion and wonderment.*[62] This was the reason perhaps that Pieri decided to translate the book into Italian, winning finally some recognition as an author and the prestigious prize of the Crusca Academy.[63]

The philhellenic concerns of Vieusseux's group were reflected, naturally enough, in the pages of the *Antologia*. Indeed, the journal became a powerful tool for the propagation of the idea of Greek independence. The long-running debate that unfolded in its pages in favour of Greece, involving numerous important intellectuals, be they Italians (such as Gino Capponi, Enrico Mayer, Giuseppe Montani, Luigi Ciampolini, Niccolò Tommaseo) or Greco-Italians or diaspora Greeks, was not always overt. More often than not, even the 'light' censorship of the Tuscan regime—which, despite its 'lightness', eventually forced the journal to shut down in 1833—obliged the authors to hide their patriotic connotations behind more 'acceptable' pretexts. Thus, otherwise 'innocent' articles, such as book reviews, translations of the classics, discussions on linguistic themes, travel accounts, or presentations of archaeological findings, were usually transformed into passionate expressions of philhellenic propaganda.[64]

[60] Olivier Reverdin, 'La Toscane, les philhellènes genevois et l'envoi des secours à la Grèce', in *Le relazioni del pensiero italiano risorgimentale con i centri del movimento liberale di Ginevra e Coppet: colloquio italo-elvetico* (Rome, 1979), pp. 63–75; Raffaele Ciampini, 'Filellenismo e liberalismo nel 1826', *Nuova antologia* 87/1815 (1952), pp. 280–95; Cosimo Ceccuti, 'Risorgimento greco e filoellenismo nel mondo dell'*Antologia*', in *Indipendenza e unità nazionale in Italia ed in Grecia* (Florence, 1987), pp. 79–104; Aloi Sideri, *Ellines foitites sto panepistimio tis Pizas (1806–1861)* (Greek students at the University of Pisa, 1806–1861) (Athens, 1989), 2 vols.

[61] Pieri attests to have read these books at Vieusseux's Cabinet: Blaquiere and Gamba (BRF: Memorie di Mario Pieri, vol. IV [Ricc. 3558], 237), Kalvos (BRF: Memorie di Mario Pieri, vol. IV [Ricc. 3558], 245), Fauriel (BRF: Memorie di Mario Pieri, vol. IV [Ricc. 3558], 226).

[62] BRF: Memorie di Mario Pieri, vol. IV [Ricc. 3558], 213.

[63] [Mario Pieri], *Compendio della storia del Risorgimento della Grecia dal 1740 al 1824, compilato da M. P. C.* (Florence, 1825), 2 vols.

[64] A catalogue of all articles of Greek subject in the *Antologia* can be found in Enrica Lucarelli and Caterina Spetsieri Beschi (eds), *Risorgimento greco e filellenismo italiano: lotte, cultura, arte* (Rome, 1986), pp. 438–46.

## The Greeks of the *Antologia*

It was through the lens of Tuscan (and more specifically, *Antologia*) philhellenism that a group of Ionian and Greco-Italian collaborators who published in the pages of the journal perceived what was now, on the opposite shore of the Adriatic, being born as 'their homeland'. Before exploring the brand of philhellenism (which these 'Greeks' both helped shape and by which they were in turn shaped), we need to take a moment to see who these people actually were. Pieri was, of course, one of the company. He might have produced only a single article for the *Antologia*, but his regular presence at the discussions held in the reading Cabinet helped to consolidate the philhellenic leanings of the circle.[65] A more substantial contribution, however, was made by Andrea Mustoxidi. The reader will already be familiar with this Corfiot intellectual, whom we encountered in the guise of 'Official Historiographer' of the Septinsular Republic and about whom Part IV will have still more to say. Mustoxidi wrote frequently for the journal, participated in the activities of the circle whenever he happened to be in Florence, and maintained a correspondence with Vieusseux and others from this same milieu—for example, with the Tuscan historian and later Italian statesman Gino Capponi, and the celebrated philologist and liberal intellectual Pietro Giordani. These exchanges persisted even after the creation of the Greek state, when Mustoxidi became the Minister of Education in Kapodistrias's government. Vieusseux and his circle were interested in keeping a channel open with the newly liberated country and in extending journalistic collaborations and press exchanges.[66]

A still more prolific essayist for the *Antologia* was Constantine Polychroniades (d. 1826), 'a veritable representative in Italy of insurgent Greece', as one scholar has put it.[67] A native of Epirus, Polychroniades, who lived in Bucharest and Paris before settling in Pisa to work as a private tutor in the house of a Russian count, was Vieusseux's most trusted informant on developments in Greece.[68] He was in direct contact with the philhellenic nuclei of Pisa, Livorno, and Florence and served as a link between them. Under the pseudonym 'Filalithis' (Friend of the truth), Polychroniades produced several articles for the *Antologia*, the most important being his 'I Greci e i Turchi' (The Greeks and the Turks). There he argued that religion had been essential to the preservation of Greek identity and doubted whether any further coexistence between the two peoples would be possible.[69] In 1824 Polychroniades was summoned to Greece in order to assume a post in the educational administration of the revolutionary government. From there he sent long reports to Vieusseux on the course of events, as well as on the

[65] M. P. [Mario Pieri], 'Degli scrittori Greci e delle italiane versione delle loro opere, etc.', *Antologia* 30 (Apr.–June 1828), pp. 131–3.

[66] Correspondence with Vieusseux (1825–49): BCNF: cart. Vieuss., 73, 75–108 and HMC: MP, XI/140–6. Capponi: Alessandro Carraresi (ed.), *Lettere di Gino Capponi e di altri a lui* (Florence, 1887), vol. I, p. 259. Giordani: HMC: MP, X/8/355.

[67] Ceccuti, 'Risorgimento greco', pp. 86–91.

[68] His correspondence with Vieusseux in BCNF: cart. Vieuss., 83, 114–37.

[69] Filalithis, [Constantine Polychroniades], 'I greci e i turchi', *Antologia* 12 (Nov. 1823), pp. 101–16; 13 (Mar. 1824), pp. 83–108 and 14 (Apr. 1824), pp. 57–73.

state of the Greek educational system and the press. Motivated by a cultural project he had in all likelihood elaborated and discussed with Vieusseux, Polychroniades was inspired to propose a measure of cooperation between the *Antologia* and certain Greek journals and even to invite its director to leave Italy for Greece: *Your efforts will be better employed there [in Greece] than in old and inert Italy*—he told him.[70] His premature death in Nafplio in 1826 was destined, however, to leave these projects unfulfilled.

Another Greco-Italian intellectual closely connected to Vieusseux's circle was, finally, Angelica Palli (1798–1875). Born in Livorno, to Greek parents, Palli was one of the most dynamic female figures of the cultural and political life of nineteenth-century Italy. Her father, Panagiotis Pallis, a highly literate and wealthy merchant, a banker prominent in Livornese public life, was appointed in 1833 the first Greek Consul to the city and in 1835 General Consul of Greece to Tuscany and Lucca. Angelica grew up in a profoundly patriotic and liberal environment: her brothers, Giovanni and Michele, were involved in secret societies, and her family home often hosted political meetings. She was an ambitious poetess and author in her own right, and her works, like the philhellenic historical novel *Alessio ossia gli ultimi giorni di Psara* (Alessio or the last days of Psara, 1827), received glowing reviews in the pages of the *Antologia*.[71] Her literary salon at Livorno welcomed many intellectuals who were also her friends, such as Giovan Battista Niccolini and Enrico Mayer, and became, especially from 1824 to 1826, the centre of Livornese philhellenic and liberal-patriotic propaganda.[72]

These Ionian, Epirotan, and Italo-Greek intellectuals played, as I have said, a vital role in shaping the philhellenic ideology of the *Antologia*—which, in its turn, as we will shortly see, helped mould their own self-awareness as 'Greeks'. It is to this ideology that I will now turn, focusing specifically on its most pronounced characteristic, namely, the belief that Italy and Greece were sister nations.

## Sister Nations: Italy and Greece

To be sure, here too, as throughout the length and breadth of Europe, the philhellenic recipe included the usual ingredients: faith in the cultural continuity between ancient and modern Greece, the belief that Europe was indebted to Greece, assumed to be its cultural matrix, the idea of the 'degeneration' and 'regeneration' of modern Greece, and the representation of the Greek revolution as a battle between civilization and barbarism and as a war for the preservation of the Christian character of the Mediterranean. Nonetheless, Italian philhellenism in

---

[70] Quoted in Ceccuti, 'Risorgimento greco', p. 91.

[71] [Giuseppe Montani], 'Alessio o gli ultimi giorni di Psara romanzo storico d'Angelica Palli etc.', *Antologia* 27 (Aug. 1827), pp. 88–94.

[72] Alessandra d'Alessandro, *Vivere e rappresentare il Risorgimento: storia di Angelica Palli Bartolomei, scrittrice e patriota dell'Ottocento* (Rome, 2011); Francesco Ghidetti, 'Il filellenismo a Livorno tra il 1820 e il 1830', *Rassegna storica del Risorgimento* 3 (1994), pp. 291–310; Despina Vlami, *To Fiorini, to sitari kai i odos tou kipou: Ellines emporoi sto Livorno, 1750–1868* (The forin, the wheat and the garden road: Greek merchants in Livorno, 1750–1868) (Athens, 2000).

general, and its Tuscan and *Antologia* version in particular, was distinguished by its notion of a special relationship existing between Greece and Italy, a Mediterranean partnership of sorts based on cultural, historical, geographical, and climatic contiguities. This view—introduced in the journal in the years 1828–30 through the writings of Niccolò Tommaseo—was based on a series of presumed analogies between the two countries. The glorious ancient past, the 'degeneration' of culture, the continuing oppression, and the aspiration for freedom and independence were elements, our philhellenes argued, that characterized both Mediterranean nations. In this sense, the Greek revolution represented not an end in itself, but a model for all the oppressed peoples of the Mediterranean.[73] It has been observed indeed that Italian philhellenes, and not only those aligned with the *Antologia*, saw the relationship between the two nations through a set of metaphors borrowed from the realm of family ties. As the Piedmontese revolutionary and philhellene Alerino Palma di Cesnola put it, *we Italians must look upon [Greece] as our mother country*.[74] Similar sentiments were uttered by Santorre di Santarosa, the leader of the Piedmontese revolutionaries, who would in due course sacrifice his life to the Greek cause, becoming then almost as famous as Byron. *In every age, the destinies of Italy and Greece have been inextricably intertwined and, being now unable to do anything at all for my patria, I consider it almost a duty to devote to Greece the few years of vigour that still remain to me*—he wrote to his friend, the eminent French liberal intellectual Victor Cousin.[75] With his death in battle on the Greek island of Sfacteria, Santarosa became, in 1825, the embodiment of the relationship of fraternity between the two countries.[76] The idea of Italy and Greece as sister nations not only outlived the end of the revolution, but would survive for many years to come, until indeed the beginning of the twentieth century, being subsequently invoked by Italians and Greeks at various moments in their respective histories.[77]

## Becoming Greeks in Italy

Much as the Ionian, Epirotan, and Italo-Greeks helped model the philhellenism of the *Antologia*, they were also themselves largely shaped by it. 'Being Greek' became

[73] Teresa D'Anna, 'Il filellenismo sulle pagine dell'Antologia' di Gian Pietro Vieusseux (1821–1832)' (MA dissertation, University of Pisa, 2001–2), esp. pp. 53–9, 83, 92.

[74] In Isabella, *Risorgimento in Exile*, p. 83.

[75] In Salvo Mastellone, 'Santorre di Santarosa combattente per la Grecia', in *Indipendenza e unità nazionale in Italia e in Grecia*, pp. 37–8.

[76] Isabella, *Risorgimento in Exile*, pp. 82–91; Arnaldo Di Benedetto, 'Le nazioni sorelle: momenti del filellenismo letterario italiano', in Francesco Bruni (ed.), *Niccolò Tommaseo: popolo e nazioni, Italiani, Corsi, Greci, Illirici* (Rome and Padua, 2004), vol. II, pp. 435–58. On the Italian volunteers in the Greek revolution see Spyros Loukatos, *O italikos philellinismos kata ton agona tis ellinikis anexartisias, 1821–1831* (Italian philhellenism in the Greek War of Independence, 1821–1831) (Athens, 1996).

[77] Antonis Liakos, *L'unificazione italiana e la Grande Idea: ideologia e azione dei movimenti nazionali in Italia e in Grecia, 1859–1871* (Florence, 1995); Gilles Pécout, 'Amitié littéraire et amitié politique méditerranéennes: philhellènes français et italiens de la fin du xixe siècle', in idem and Michel Espagne (eds), *Philhellénismes et transferts culturels dans l'Europe du XIX<sup>e</sup> siècle* (Paris, 2005), pp. 207–8; idem, 'Philhellenism as a Political Friendship: Italian Volunteers in 19th-Century Mediterranean', *Journal of Modern Italian Studies* 9/4 (2004), pp. 405–27.

fashionable in Vieusseux's circle, as everywhere else in philhellenic Europe, thus giving Pieri and his friends a new self-awareness and self-respect. 'At the reading cabinet', a scholar wrote, 'when those attending for the first time hear that Pieri is Greek, they throng around him, acclaiming him; they honour in him the insurgent people.'[78] Greek intellectuals were appreciated not only for their role as channels of information on the beleaguered country. What mattered also was their perceived 'natural supremacy' in the field of classical studies. Being the descendants of the ancient Hellenes meant being able to understand the classics more profoundly and with less effort. In an era of boundless fascination with Neoclassicism, this was not a minor detail. A satirical text published many years after Pieri's death (1896), where the Corfiot is ridiculed for his habit of appending his native place to his name, is telling: *Do you know what that 'Corfiot' means? It means: 'Admit it, I, Mario Pieri, am Greek, I have a Greek soul, I have a Greek heart in my breast; the red blood cells that flow through my veins are not like those of all of you; they have a feeling for art, for the great, the divine classical art, of which I am made heart and soul. You have had day and night to turn the pages of Greek models whereas I learned how to spell using these same models, for me they are stuff made at home, they are family bric-à-brac.'*[79]

This new appreciation of Greekness, a product both of a novel sociability built up around the Greek cause and of philhellenic books, as well as of the re-evaluation of classical studies, created for Pieri (and for many other Greco-Italians like him) a new ground to develop yet another patriotic consciousness. *[My Greek patriotism was] inspired by [the] poetic books which were published in those days on Greece*—he admitted in his autobiography.[80] Philhellenism opened up for Pieri also a new space for a career. *I hope to vindicate my patria and thereby to become illustrious*, he wrote in his diary while he was preparing his translation of Pouqueville in 1824.[81]

At around the same time, many other diaspora intellectuals—who, like Pieri, shared a dual Greco-Italian consciousness—reinvented themselves as Greeks and were acknowledged as such in the literary space of philhellenism and Neoclassical studies. The case of Antonio Papadopoli (1802–44), another of Vieusseux's Greco-Italian friends, is instructive. A son of a noble Corfiot family that had moved to Venice at the end of the eighteenth century, a modest classical philologist but an ambitious cultural mediator and entrepreneur, Papadopoli became in the 1820s particularly concerned with his 'degree of Greekness'. Upon sharing these concerns with Mustoxidi, the latter reassured him that if he continued to occupy himself with classical letters and to socialize with the other Greeks of Venice, he would avoid the danger of fully Italianizing himself. *You were indeed born in Italy*, he said, *but in a city where a colony of Greeks has settled, whom we would call* Italiots, *but not* Italians. *And just as Callimachus and Apollonius are Greeks though born in Egypt and in Libya,...so too Antonio Papadopoli will one day be a Greek writer and not an*

[78] Ciampini, *Gian Pietro Vieusseux*, p. 165.
[79] Guido Biagi, *Aneddoti letterari* (Milan, 1896). Quoted in D'Anna, 'Il filellenismo', p. 113.
[80] Pieri, *Della vita*, vol. II, p. 163.
[81] BRF: Memorie di Mario Pieri, vol. IV [Ricc. 3558], 206.

*Italian.*[82] Angelica Palli, who during the years of the Greek revolution filled her vague sense of a Greek origin with cultural and philological content, is another case in point. *Would God that upon us . . . who are given to calling ourselves at one and the same time Greeks and Italians*—she wrote to Pieri in a late letter of 1851—*there should smile at least the hope of dying having seen one of our patrias [occupy] a beautiful and dignified place [in the world].*[83]

## AN EXILE

### Becoming an Exile

*E fino a quanto vorrò io vivere* εἰς τὴν ξενιτεία? (And for how long will I chance to live in exile?), Pieri asked his diary in a despairing Italo-Greek when in 1827 news of the declaration of Greek independence was on everyone's lips.[84] If the creation of the Greek state gave him a new patria, it also reminded him that he was someone who lived outside the political and cultural boundaries of what was now being created as his homeland. In 1824, while news of the Greek victories flooded the newspapers, Pieri asked his diary, *But why are we other Greeks still so distant from the theatre of national glory? I do not have weapons or money with which to aid the patria, nor would I know how to assist it directly with my pen, which lacks the capacity to colour my thoughts otherwise than in Italian. Should I go there, a useless burden, and scrounge bread, amongst so many scroungers, as a foreign outlaw rather than as a citizen?*[85] The more substantial Pieri's Greekness became, the more jarring and dissonant his Italian cultural formation sounded. *My age*, he explained in his autobiography, *approaching as I was my fiftieth year, was not such as to allow me to transform myself from an Italian into a Greek writer, or to renounce letters and to devote myself entirely to arms. I therefore readied myself to serve her, being at a distance from her, in the best way that I could, namely, with my Italian pen.*[86] Whereas other Ionian intellectuals like Kalvos and Solomos had, as we have seen in Chapters 2 and 3, taken a timely and conscious decision to turn themselves into Greek poets and writers, Pieri remained forever indecisive and suspended in a liminal state. If the Greek revolution, Italian philhellenism, and the creation of the Greek state made him into a 'Greek', they also exacerbated his feeling of exile and homelessness. *I am tired now of living as an outlaw*—he wrote at some point in 1824; *I hope to lay down my weary bones in free Greece, my true patria!*[87]

---

[82] BM: Mustoxidi Papers, 603. On Papadopoli see Gaspare Polizzi, ' "Io scrivo le mie letter dove ha regno Mercurio". Antonio Papadopoli: un uomo di lettere nell'Italia del primo Ottocento', *Quaderni Veneti* 45 (2007), pp. 105–44; Gaspare Gozzi, *Lettere d'illustri Italiani ad Antonio Papadopoli* (Venice, 1886).

[83] BRF: Lettere originali a Mario Pieri, vol. III [Ricc. 3523], 1/272.

[84] BRF: Memorie di Mario Pieri, vol. IV [Ricc. 3558], 308.

[85] BRF: Memorie di Mario Pieri, vol. IV [Ricc. 3558], 210.

[86] Pieri, *Della vita*, vol. II, p. 31.

[87] BRF: Memorie di Mario Pieri, vol. IV [Ricc. 3558], 213 and 223.

The news about the assassination of Kapodistrias, the subsequent civil war, and the transformation of Greece into an absolutist Bavarian kingdom under the sceptre of Otto only made Pieri's melancholy worse. In a suicide note, which he drafted in 1832—but then quietly tidied up among his diary notes—he declared that he wanted to put an end to his life because he was *weary of this world, not hoping now for anything more, at the age of 55 years and some months, of seeing the liberty of the patria, nor that of beloved Italy, my second patria.*[88] On two trips to Corfu, in 1836 and 1837, he fared no better. *This patria of mine is more welcome to me when I think of death than when I think of life, which I lead more gladly and comfortably in Florence*—he noted in his diary in August 1836. *It would pain me to no longer live in Florence and yet it would pain me not to die in Corfu.*[89] Faced with the still harsh colonial administration of the British in the Ionian Islands and sorely afflicted now by the 'disease of exile'—as much of a tragic reality as a Romantic leitmotif uniting him to the great poets he had so much admired in his youth, Foscolo and Alfieri— Pieri preferred to 'remain an exile': *Let us flee, let us flee from this land of slavery, besmirched by so much filth. It is better to die an outlaw in a foreign land than a slave in one's own*—he wrote on one of the last pages of his diary.[90] Pieri died in Florence in the spring of 1852, his last months and years spent reading, taking the occasional walk, and immersed in melancholy reflection. His body was buried in the Greek Orthodox church of Livorno, in the only place where he ever really belonged, the world of the Greek diasporas. In a piece that he wrote as early as 1832, entitled *Sfortunato chi ha due patrie* (Unlucky are those who have two homelands), Pieri drew a mournful picture of this tragic predicament: *Someone who has two patrias, his native and his elective land,* he wrote, *ends up having none, and remains an outlaw for the whole of his life...A person with two patrias is the citizen of none... He... will always live as an outlaw, and as though embarked upon a ship... he will find neither the consolations nor the comforts of life anywhere... Thus death will seize him wherever he may be as if in a public inn; no one will accompany his coffin, nor will his tomb be watered by a single tear.*[91]

## CONCLUSIONS

In this chapter I have attempted to cast light on an intimate experience of the transition from empires to nation states, in its pre-revolutionary, Napoleonic, and post-Napoleonic moments in the Adriatic. Pieri's story tells us a number of things. First of all, it illustrates just how 'slippery' geographies were in the early nineteenth-century Mediterranean, especially for a provincial imperial subject. A recent, fascinating study has shown that for the modern reader the actual limits of 'place' and 'displacement' are hard to imagine in an era of such constant geographical

---

[88] BRF: Memorie di Mario Pieri, vol. IV [Ricc. 3558], vol. V [Ricc. 3559], 176.
[89] BRF: Memorie di Mario Pieri, vol. VI [Ricc. 3560], 256 and 285.
[90] BRF: Memorie di Mario Pieri, vol. VI [Ricc. 3560], 282 and Pieri, *Della vita*, vol. II, pp. 299, 376.
[91] BRF: Mario Pieri, 'Pensieri miei', vols I–II [Ricc. 461]; published in Pieri, *Opere*, vol. IV, pp. 359–62.

and political change as the first half of the nineteenth century.[92] In a world of vast empires, customs unions, miniature city-states, and semi-independent principalities, the frontiers of which were continually shifting, it is unclear what 'home' and 'abroad' really meant. By going to Italy and by wielding his pen in the Italian language, Pieri did very much as countless generations of Ionian islanders had done before him. He was swept along by the tides of upper-class mobility, as any well-to-do Ionian family would expect when imagining a career for a talented or promising son. Just because the Venetian Republic had ceased to exist, this did not mean that a sense of Venetian 'domestic' or 'settled' space dissolved immediately along with it. Travelling across the Adriatic was no exile for Pieri. It started becoming such, at first, with the establishment of the British-controlled Ionian state (with its supposedly 'liberal' and 'Greek' character), and latterly, with the outbreak of the Greek revolution and the creation of the Greek nation-state. In this sense, the true slipperiness of place revealed itself when Pieri's Venetian legacy geographies were buffeted by the new empires and states that had come into their own in the Adriatic after Napoleon. The delineation and consolidation of new frontiers (cultural, national, linguistic, and religious) transformed Pieri into a liminal individual, a trans-imperial and transnational subject obliged to divide his allegiance between societal units which now came to be seen as separate and distinct. The Greek revolution, with its unprecedented success in creating the first independent nation-state in the Mediterranean, might have given to some a new home, but it also transformed a good number of others into 'exiles'. Pieri's story brings to life again how these persons, who were suddenly situated outside the political and cultural boundaries of something which was now being constructed as their homeland, became the 'Greeks of the diasporas'.

But if sometimes the 'national diasporas' were created as a result of the establishment of a nation-state, the opposite was also true. The nation was often constructed as a product of reflections by individuals—in this case Greeks of the diasporas and European philhellenes—far from the patria they were heatedly imagining. Their perception of homeland was thus largely based on literature and imagination, imbued with personal nostalgia, disillusionment with other political causes, and Romantic orientalism.[93] It was grounded, as one scholar has aptly phrased it, on a discourse of 'ab-sense' safeguarded by distance.[94] Pieri's growing realization of his

---

[92] Dominique Kirchner Reill, 'Away or Homeward Bound? The Slippery Case of Mediterranean Place in the Era Before Nation-States', in Isabella and Zanou (eds.), *Mediterranean Diasporas*, pp. 135–52.

[93] Benedict Anderson, 'Long-Distance Nationalism', in idem, *The Spectre of Comparisons: Nationalism, Southeast Asia and the World* (London and New York, 1998), pp. 59–74; Stathis Gourgouris, *Dream Nation, Enlightenment, Colonization and the Institution of Modern Greece* (Stanford, Calif., 1996); Konstantina Zanou, 'Nostalgia, Self-Exile and the National Idea: The Case of Andrea Mustoxidi and the Early-19th-Century Heptanesians of Italy', in A. Aktar, N. Kızılyürek, and U. Özkırımlı (eds), *Nationalism in the Troubled Triangle: Cyprus, Greece and Turkey (New Perspectives on South-East Europe)* (London and New York, 2009), pp. 98–111.

[94] Vangelis Calotychos, *Modern Greece: A Cultural Poetics* (Oxford and New York, 2003), esp. pp. 38–53.

Greek national belonging from the distant viewpoint of his Italian 'exile' and through the philhellenic literature is a case in point.

Finally, Pieri's story is also a story of a failure. Unlike most of the characters who populate this book, and who, albeit precariously, managed to adjust by reinventing and repositioning themselves within old and new political establishments and cultural belongings, Pieri was thrown into a perpetual wandering about, a peregrination, remaining forever suspended in in-between, liminal spaces. History is full of such figures of the *no man's land*, but we tend to forget them. You merely have to look at the Balkans. In the same way that the Adriatic lost its centuries-old Venetian continuum, the shattering of the common Orthodox and Greek-speaking space of the Ottoman Balkans during the second half of the nineteenth and the beginning of the twentieth century left one of modern history's most glaring gaps, creating hundreds of dislocated, disoriented, and transnational intellectuals.[95] One of the aims of this book is, precisely, to repopulate some of these *no man's lands*, by writing back into Mediterranean history the multilayered lives of their inhabitants.

---

[95] Diana Mishkova (ed.), *We, the People: Politics of National Peculiarity in Southeastern Europe* (Budapest and New York, 2009); Theodora Dragostinova, *Between Two Motherlands: Nationality and Emigration among Greeks of Bulgaria, 1900–1949* (Ithaca, NY, and London, 2011); Vangelis Kechriotis, 'On the Margins of National Historiography: The Greek İttihatçi Emmanouil Emmanouilidis – Opportunist or Ottoman Patriot?', in A. Singer, C. Neumann, and S. A. Somel (eds), *Untold Histories of the Middle East: Recovering Voices from the 19th and 20th Centuries* (New York, 2011); Raymond Detrez, 'Pre-National Identities in the Balkans', in Roumen Daskalov and Tchavdar Marinov (eds), *Entangled Histories of the Balkans*, vol. 1: *National Ideologies and Language Policies* (Leiden and Boston, 2013), pp. 13–65.

# 9

## Andrea Papadopoulo Vretto between
## East and West

Andrea Papadopoulo Vretto's story is certainly less dramatic. The 95 manuscript sheets of his unfinished autobiography (a mere nothing against the 7,000 pages written by Pieri) narrate, however, a remarkably mobile life, one which combined old and new Mediterranean geographies and united East and West. It is truly astounding just how many different aspects of history, culture, and geopolitics a human trajectory can combine. The activities of this inventive and indefatigable man will thus turn our gaze to such different places and phenomena as Naples, its nomadic revolutionaries and Italo-Albanian diaspora, the British-controlled Ionian Islands and their bibliographic and archaeological activity, Nafplio as the Greek capital of Kapodistrias's government, Russia and its new wave of Greek immigration after the latter's assassination, and the renewed links between the Greek world and the Russian Empire in the 1830s. Despite numerous books, pamphlets, and journals and an equal number of enterprising professional activities, Papadopoulo Vretto never managed to gain a place in the memoryscape of any of the countries in which he resided. Apart from a short article which appeared in 1938 in a Greek journal, this is, so far as I know, the first time that the life of this man is being addressed in its own right.[1]

### IN NAPOLEONIC AND RESTORATION NAPLES

Papadopoulo Vretto was born within the arms of Russia. He first saw the light of day in Ithaca in 1800, twenty-four years after Pieri (the span, that is, of a generation). Upon the arrival of the Russians on the Ionian Islands, his father, a Lefkadian former officer in the French provisional democratic administration, was appointed member of the High Court of Cassation of the Septinsular Republic. So devoted did his parents now become to the Russians, that *following the example of other* Signori, *they dressed my brother and me in Russian cadet uniform.*[2] This may partly explain little Andrea's later enthusiasm for all things Russian. Spending the first years of his life between the various Ionian Islands where professional and

[1] Fanis Michalopoulos, 'Andreas Papadopoulos Brettos (1800–1876)', *Nea estia* 12/283 (1 Oct. 1938), pp. 1300–7.
[2] GSA-A: K.20, Archive of A. Papadopoulos Vrettos, Manuscripts, IA' (XI), 'Memorie biografiche e storiche', p. 3.

family obligations took his parents, Papadopoulo Vretto was at the age of 11 sent to Naples in order to follow elementary studies and to stand by his mother's side during her therapeutic sessions in the mineral waters of the city. Since the sixteenth century there had been an important Greek community in Naples, which was organized around its Orthodox, Uniate, and non-Uniate churches.[3] Even before Papadopoulo Vretto had left school, the Napoleonic Kingdom of Naples collapsed and Joachim Murat conceded his throne to the restored King Ferdinand I. The young Lefkadian observed this change of power through the eyes of a schoolboy who lost most of his classmates because their parents had been aligned with the French and were now purged from their public posts.[4] By describing the insistent efforts of his teachers to convert him to Catholicism, he also attested to the way that the Restoration regime initiated a policy of religious conversion towards the Orthodox Christian populations of the kingdom. This policy would be intensified in the years following the Congress of Verona (1822) and especially in 1829, when the King of the Two Sicilies Francesco I would issue a decree ordering the transformation of the Greek Orthodox community of Naples into a Catholic community and the dissolution thus of the centuries-old syncretism of the southern Greco-Italian diasporic world.[5]

Upon leaving school, and in order to please his mother—as he confesses in his autobiography—young Andrea enrolled in the medical faculty of the University of Naples. During the period of his studies he was confronted with three distinct but equally interesting phenomena: he encountered the Napoleonic officers and Mediterranean transnational conspirators, he was involved in the intellectual production of the Italo-Albanian diaspora, and he experienced the 1820–1 revolutions in Naples and in Greece. In 1817 young Andrea entered the house of Giuseppe Rosaroll (Naples, 1775—Nafpio 1823), a Neapolitan former Napoleonic officer, Muratist general, and author of military treatises, who took the Lefkadian boy under his wing and entrusted him with the task of tutoring his children in Greek. Indeed, Rosaroll to all intents and purposes adopted Andreas as his son. The reason for Rosaroll's affection was not only that he had served as Napoleonic officer in French-occupied Zante some years earlier, where he had met Papadopoulo Vretto's father, but also—as he secretly confessed to him—because of *a political ambition that was germinating in his thought, namely, the notion of staging a revolution in the Peloponnese in order to recover for the Greeks their independence.*[6] Rosaroll was, in

[3] Antonio Solaro, 'Italia', in I. Chassiotis, O. Katsiardi-Hering, and E. Ambatzi (eds), *Oi Ellines sti diaspora, 15os–21os ai.* (The Greeks in the diaspora: 15th–21st centuries) (Athens, 2006), p. 159.

[4] GSA-A: K.20, Archive of A. Papadopoulos Vrettos, Manuscripts, IA' (XI), 'Memorie biografiche e storiche', pp. 28–9.

[5] GSA-A: K.20, Archive of A. Papadopoulos Vrettos, Manuscripts, IA' (XI), 'Memorie biografiche e storiche', pp. 29–30. On this see Vasilios Milios, 'Oi istorikes tyches tis ellinikis koinotitas tis Barletta tis Kato Italias' (The history of the Greek community of Barletta in southern Italy) (Ph.D. dissertation, Aristotelian University of Thessaloniki, 2013), pp. 213–14; On the religious syncretism of the Greco- and Albano-Italian diaspora, see Angela Falcetta, *Ortodossi nel Mediterraneo cattolico: frontiere, reti, comunità nel Regno di Napoli (1700–1821)* (Rome, 2016).

[6] GSA-A: K.20, Archive of A. Papadopoulos Vrettos, Manuscripts, IA' (XI), 'Memorie biografiche e storiche', p. 31.

fact, one of those legendary figures participating in the Mediterranean 'Liberal International' active in the Napoleonic and post-Napoleonic years and mentioned in Chapter 8. After taking part in the Neapolitan revolution of 1820, he went as an exile and fighter to Spain and from there, upon the collapse of the Spanish revolutionary regime, he headed to the Ionian Islands, and finally to revolutionary Greece. The British Ionian Islands, along with Malta, were indeed fundamental landmarks in this revolutionary Mediterranean corridor created by exiled remnants and conspirators between Spain, Naples, Sicily, and Greece in the post-Napoleonic years.[7] According to one of the many Bourbon secret agents who kept the Neapolitan exiles under surveillance, in Corfu alone during the 1820s there were at least three masonic lodges, one 'philhellenic committee', and one 'revolutionary committee'. Rosaroll was involved in most of these secret societies, his plan being to enlist Greek volunteers for a pan-meridional anti-Bourbon insurrection. He was not alone in devising such plans. Guglielmo Pepe, the leader, as we have seen, of the 1820 Neapolitan revolution, was at the same time organizing from his exile in London (and with the help of his co-conspirators in the Ionian Islands) a Mediterranean mobilization, involving Spanish, Portuguese, Italian, and Greek volunteers who would embark in Calabria and launch a liberal revolution.[8] So, through Rosaroll, whose steps he followed until his later years, referring to him on several different occasions in his autobiography, Papadopoulo Vretto mingled with this society of Mediterranean revolutionaries.[9]

The second noteworthy event of his university years is the fact of his having written a book on the life of the fifteenth-century Balkan hero George Castriot Skanderbeg. This work, which was published in Naples in 1820 (and was actually a translation into Italian of an older biography written in Modern Greek and published in Moscow in 1812), remained a source of inspiration throughout the nineteenth century and was republished several times with corrections and different appendices (in Italian in 1845 and 1847, and in Greek in 1848, 1858, and 1884).[10] It was a biography presenting the early modern Albanian prince as Europe's 'shield of Christianity' against the Muslim Ottoman threat and as a 'proud Epirotan', descendant of the ancient King of Epirus, Pyrrhus. Even if Papadopoulo Vretto did not use the word 'Greek', his became the most influential text in shaping a long-lasting tradition in Greek letters and arts which appropriated Skanderbeg as a Greek patriot and national hero.[11] Among the many works that saw the light

[7] Gilles Pécout, 'Pour une lecture méditerranéenne et transnationale du Risorgimento', *Revue d'histoire du XIXe siècle* 44 (2012), p. 39.

[8] For all the above see Gianni Korinthios, *I liberali napoletani e la rivoluzione greca 1821–1830* (Naples, 1990), pp. 30, 82, 113–25, 127–43.

[9] GSA-A: K.20, Archive of A. Papadopoulos Vrettos, Manuscripts, IA' (XI), 'Memorie biografiche e storiche', pp. 31–2, 39–40, 51–2.

[10] Andrea Papadopoulo Vreto, *Compendio dell'istoria di Giorgio Castriotto soprannominato Scanderbeg principe dell'Albania* (Naples, 1820), 2 vols. See Francesco Scalora, 'O Andreas Papadopoulos Brettos kai i istoria tou Georgiou Kastriotou metonomasthentos Skentermpei igemonos tis Albanias' (Andrea Papadopoulo Vretto and the history of George Castriot Skanderbeg prince of Albania), in *X Panionian Conference, Proceedings*, forthcoming.

[11] On this see Tito Jochalas, *O Georgios Kastriotis Skentermpeis eis tin neoellinikin istoriografian kai logotechnian* (George Castriot Skanderbeg in Greek historiography and literature) (Thessaloniki, 1975).

of day during the same period, and in the following years, was for example a drama composed by Ioannis Zampelios. Published in 1833 (but written in 1817–18), Zampelios's *Georgios Kastriotis* was a patriotic tragedy in Greek verse, which featured Skanderbeg and his ringing declaration that *Christian and Greek, I am proud to be*.[12] If, however, in these works the Greekness of the Balkan hero was unequivocal, this was not the case in Papadopoulo Vretto's book. Indeed, in the introduction, the author stated that his purpose in writing had been to please mainly *the Albanians who live in the different provinces of this [the Neapolitan] state*.[13] In order to bolster his thesis, he also added an appendix to the book, narrating the history of the Italo-Albanian communities of southern Italy. There the terms 'Albanian', 'Greek', 'Epirotan', and 'Coronean' (from Coroni, a village port in Peloponnese and home to many European consuls) were all used interchangeably to describe the trans-Adriatic Albanian diasporas.[14] What is more, it was with certain Italo-Albanian intellectuals, like Luca de Samuele Cagnazzi (1764–1852) and Tommaso Pace (1807–87), that Papadopoulo Vretto collaborated in promoting the book in Naples and in enriching it subsequently with a new appendix on the history of the Albanian language.[15] These were the years that witnessed the consolidation of the idea of an Albanian nation. Those to the fore in shaping this idea were certain Albanian-speaking diaspora intellectuals in Sicily and Calabria, along with others based in Constantinople, their shared aim being to recover the historical and cultural features of the scattered Albanian populations. The main problem for the Italo-Albanians in the early nineteenth century was to differentiate themselves from the Italo-Greek community (with which they were often merged) in order to preserve their specific Uniate ecclesiastical-educational privileges in the Kingdom of Naples.[16] Distinguishing Albanians from Greeks more generally would remain a constant preoccupation of Albanian nationalism of the following generations, which witnessed the 'rebirth of Greece' and the expansionism of the Greek state. In their efforts to create a distinct Albanian nationality, these intellectuals built up a national pantheon, which included Philip and Alexander the Great of Macedonia, King Pyrrhus of Epirus, and, last but not least, Skanderbeg.[17] Ironically, as one historian has observed, 'the Greek intellectual networks played a considerable role in elevating the figure of Skanderbeg to the ranks of an Albanian national hero'.[18]

[12] Jochalas, *O Georgios Kastriotis*, pp. 63–76.

[13] Papadopoulo Vreto, *Compendio*, vol. I, p. xxiv.

[14] Papadopoulo Vreto, *Compendio*, vol. II, pp. 230, 243.

[15] Because of this book, Cagnazzi, who was of Albanian origin, made him a member of the Pontaniana Academy, where he also presented this work. In GSA-A: K.20, Archive of A. Papadopoulos Vrettos, Manuscripts, IA' (XI), 'Memorie Biografiche e Storiche', pp. 35–6. Tommaso Pace wrote an article on the history of the Albanian language, which was added as an appendix to the first Greek edition of Papadopoulo Vretto's book.

[16] On their complex relationship see Falcetta, *Ortodossi nel Mediterraneo cattolico*, esp. pp. 243–4.

[17] Nathalie Clayer, *Aux origines du nationalisme albanais: la naissance d'une nation majoritairement musulmane en Europe* (Paris, 2007), esp. pp. 170–80; Artan Puto and Maurizio Isabella, 'Trajectories of Albanian Nationalism in the Writings of Girolamo de Rada and Semseddin Samin Frashëri, ca. 1848–1903', in Maurizio Isabella and Konstantina Zanou (eds), *Mediterranean Diasporas: Politics and Ideas in the Long Nineteenth Century* (London, 2016), pp. 171–87.

[18] Clayer, *Aux origines*, p. 191.

When we consider the fact that in this same period the deeds of Skanderbeg were read by Greek revolutionaries (like the chieftain Theodoros Kolokotronis) and were commemorated as acts of Christian and Greek national pride, then it seems that Skanderbeg was, at least in the first half of the nineteenth century, a transnational hero.[19] Papadopoulo Vretto's book stands as a testimony to this transitional moment, when nationalisms were being created and slowly consolidated and differentiated, but at the same time when the borders between the trans-Adriatic diaspora communities were still permeable and shifting.[20] The fact that a work written in Italian by a Greek Ionian could function as a reference point for the construction of two distinct and competing national mythologies provides an invaluable glimpse into the multicultural and pluri-national world of the Italian and Ottoman Adriatic in the early decades of the nineteenth century.

The third noteworthy event of Papadopoulo Vretto's university years was the fact that he experienced, in a somewhat 'inverted' fashion, the Neapolitan and Greek revolutions of 1820–1. In June 1820 he went to the Ionian Islands to meet up with his father and stock up on funds for the rest of his studies. *When I arrived in Corfu*—he wrote in his autobiography—*I was surprised to learn that a revolution had broken out in Naples and that king Ferdinand had sworn to uphold the constitution. I was sorry not to have been involved in such an event, but there was no longer enough time to return suddenly.*[21] He returned to Naples only at the beginning of spring 1821, *just when all the kingdom's forces were gathered at the frontier, threatened by an Austrian army intent upon overthrowing the revolution effected by the Carbonari.* He thus witnessed the inglorious end of the revolution, when the restored King and his ministers fanatically engaged in reprisals and punishment. *All the functionaries were obliged to give proofs of their innocence and the students even from the universities had to be purged, all those declared guilty of Carbonarism being denied the right to receive diplomas. Only then was I glad to not have been in Naples when the revolution broke out*—he commented.[22] The same 'inverted' quality is likewise discernible in his experience of the revolution in Greece: *On my arrival in Naples I learned that the revolution had broken out in Greece*—he wrote.[23] By contrast with events in Naples, however, the Greek revolution was destined to become a 'glorious' revolution, the result of which, the Greek state, Papadopoulo Vretto would have the opportunity to enjoy at first hand some years later.

---

[19]  On Kolokotronis reading Skanderbeg see Jochalas, *O Georgios Kastriotis*, pp. 21–2.

[20]  These nationalisms would not be easily disentangled. An Albanian revolt which took place in 1847, for example, would demand the unification of Albania with Greece, while as late as 1880 an intellectual of the Albano-Egyptian diaspora, writing a book in Greek, would complain about Greece not integrating Albania: Efthymios Prantis, *Albanika parapona en Minia tis Ano Aigyptou* (Albanian complaints in Minya, Upper Egypt) (Athens, 1880).

[21]  GSA-A: K.20, Archive of A. Papadopoulos Vrettos, Manuscripts, IA' (XI), 'Memorie biografiche e storiche', p. 37.

[22]  GSA-A: K.20, Archive of A. Papadopoulos Vrettos, Manuscripts, IA' (XI), 'Memorie biografiche e storiche', p. 38.

[23]  GSA-A: K.20, Archive of A. Papadopoulos Vrettos, Manuscripts, IA' (XI), 'Memorie biografiche e storiche', p. 38.

## IN BRITISH CORFU

At the end of 1821, upon his graduation from university, Papadopoulo Vretto returned with his mother to the Ionian Islands. After staying for two years in Lefkada, where he vainly attempted to set up a private school of Italian literature—a project he was obliged soon to abandon because no one was prepared to pay the fees—he moved to Ithaca. There, in 1822, he met Lord Byron, who was on his way to Greece and had seized the opportunity to tour the island of Ulysses.[24] He also had the chance to meet Lord Guilford, some months earlier, during his own tour in Lefkada. The links forged with these two prominent British philhellenes won Papadopoulo Vretto a post as a librarian at the Ionian Academy of Corfu, an institution only recently founded, in 1824, under Guilford's auspices. It was there, and amidst the piles of books which the philhellene lord had collected and brought with him from London, that Papadopoulo Vretto first formulated the idea of doing the one thing for which he is today best remembered, namely, to compile a bibliographical catalogue of all the Greek books published since the fall of Constantinople. This was an arduous undertaking, which took several years to complete, involving ongoing updates and the publication of a series of revised editions with the help of a number of his learned friends (it appeared first in 1845 and then in 1854 and 1857). As he stated in the introduction, *modern Greek philology from the disastrous fall of Constantinople to the war of Greek liberation can be considered an unknown country to the many. Very few know indeed that the Greek nation, overwhelmed by great misfortunes and worn out by a barbarian yoke, never ceased to cultivate letters—even if, because of the tyranny, only sporadically.* His aim, thus, was to show that even during the 'dark' ages of Greek history, namely the Ottoman times, the Greek intellect continued to exist and to be in contact with the *developments in sciences which happened among the free and happy peoples of Europe.*[25]

Papadopoulo Vretto's work belongs indeed to a trend of Greek intellectual production that crystallized at the turn of the eighteenth century in the diaspora centres of the Habsburg Empire and in the Venetian Adriatic and which, as we shall see in Chapter 12 of this book, reached its peak during the 1830s and 1840s in the Ionian Islands. These intellectual activities were intended to respond to, and challenge, an idea widely shared by eighteenth-century Europeans, namely the 'theory of degeneration' regarding the Greek nation. According to this theory, the modern Greeks, oppressed and uncivilized as they were, had lost their distinctive elements and, falling away from the European sphere, were associated with the oriental world.[26] The Dutch philosopher Cornelius de Pauw, the Prussian diplomat

[24] Pietro Gamba, *A Narrative of Lord Byron's Last Journey to Greece* (London, 1825), pp. 22–8.

[25] Andreas Papadopoulos Bretos, *Neoelliniki philologia itoi katalogos ton apo ptoseos tis Byzantinis Aftokratorias mechri egkathidriseos tis en Elladi basileias typothenton biblion etc.* (Modern Greek philology or catalogue of the published books from the fall of the Byzantine Empire to the foundation of the Greek Kingdom), vol. I (Athens, 1854), pp. xv–xvi.

[26] Dimitri Nicolaidis, *D'une Grèce à l'autre: représentation des Grecs modernes par la France révolutionnaire* (Paris, 1992), esp. pp. 47–8, 55–63; Giorgos Tolias, *La Médaille et la rouille: l'image de la Grèce moderne dans la presse littéraire parisienne (1794–1815)* (Paris and Athens, 1997), esp. pp. 435–51.

Jacob Ludwig Salomon Bartholdy, and the Italian intellectual Giuseppe Compagnoni, building on the theories of Voltaire and Gibbon about the political and moral decline of the Byzantine world, thus argued that the modern inhabitants of Greece could in no wise match their glorious ancestors.[27] Had not Rousseau demonstrated, after all, that mankind was prone to degeneration when enslaved?

It was in response to these 'accusations' that Greek scholars set out to examine the 'middle ages' of Greek history, not only the Byzantine and Ottoman times, but also the Macedonian, the Hellenistic, and the Roman periods. Their aim was to refute allegations about the intellectual 'inertia' of modern Greeks and to show the uninterrupted unity of 'Greek wisdom'.[28] But in so doing, they also challenged the way that Greek national consciousness and national time had been perceived up until that moment. For, even in the minds of the most devoted philhellenes, who saw the modern Greeks and their revolution as a revival of ancient classical glory, there were still several 'blank pages' of embarrassing Greek history of the in-between centuries which needed to be filled. As one historian has eloquently written, 'The present–past relationship…composed of two alternative poles, the national resurrection (the 1821 revolution and the formation of the Greek state) and Classical Antiquity…was too weak to sustain a national ideology, especially since it involved an immense time gap'.[29] The two edges of Greek history, the classical past and the Greek revolution, had thus to be united. By re-evaluating the significance of the cultural production of post-Byzantine scholars and by incorporating one of the 'less illustrious' eras into the national narrative, works such as this by Papadopoulo Vretto were therefore crucial in shifting the paradigm of Greek national history from a scheme of *revival* to a scheme of *continuity*. They contributed, in other words, to making the Greek past seem less discontinuous.[30]

It was again to underscore this continuity and similarly within the framework created by British cultural activity in the Mediterranean during the first half of the nineteenth century, that Papadopoulo Vretto wrote another interesting book in those same years, the *Memoria su di alcuni costumi degli antichi Greci tuttora esistenti nell'isola di Leucade* (Memoir on some ancient Greek customs still existing on the island of Lefkada, 1825). As the title suggests, it was an attempt to link the present inhabitants of Lefkada directly to their Homeric ancestors. According to

---

[27] Corneille de Pauw, *Recherches philosophiques sur les Grecs* (Berlin, 1787–8); J. L. S. Bartholdy, *Voyage en Grèce, fait dans les années 1803 et 1804* (Paris, 1807); Giuseppe Compagnoni, *Saggio sugli ebrei e sui greci* (Venice, 1792).

[28] See Dimitris Arvanitakis, 'Giuseppe Compagnoni: skines apo ton bio enos "katigorou tou genous"' (Giuseppe Compagnoni: moments from the life of an 'accuser of the nation'), in St. Kaklamanis, A. Kalokairinos, and D. Polychronakis (eds), *Logos kai chronos sti neoelliniki grammateia, 18os–19os aionas* (Reason and time in modern Greek literature, 18th–19th centuries) (Herakleion, 2015), pp. 373–428.

[29] Antonis Liakos, 'The Making of Greek History: The Construction of National Time', in Jacques Revel and Giovanni Levi (eds), *Political Uses of the Past: The Recent Mediterranean Experience* (London, 2001), p. 32.

[30] Konstantina Zanou, 'Pros mia synoliki theorisi tou ethnikou chronou: pnevmatikes zimoseis ston Italo-Eptanisiako choro kata to a' miso tou 19ou aiona' (Towards a holistic view of national time: intellectual activity in the Italo–Ionian space in the first half of the 19th century), *IX Panionian Conference, Proceedings* (Paxi, 2014), pp. 323–48.

the author's own words in the introduction, *Having returned to the patria, after fourteen years' absence, and enthused at seeing every day before my very eyes those customs of the ancient Greeks that the Archaeologists so carefully study and comment upon in their cabinets, I was inspired to compile a succinct Memoir, desiring that I too might offer a small tribute to the glory of the patria.*[31] The author then observed, further on, that it was true that the Ionian Islands *from the period of the Venetians, began to Italianise themselves, and lose even their own dialect, preferring that of the Gondoliers of Venice*; however, it was also true that this *total corruption of ancestral traditions* was more conspicuous in Corfu and in Zante than in Lefkada. There, and especially among the *lowest class of the people*, he claimed, one really could still discern the Homeric survivals.[32]

In reality, this work built on a literary tradition that was, by the time of Papadopoulo Vretto's publication, well established among philhellenic and Greek diaspora circles. Its beginnings can be traced to the travel literature on Greece from the last decades of the eighteenth century. Pierre-Augustin Guys, a traveller from Marseilles, was the first to claim, in his *Voyage littéraire de la Grèce, ou Lettres sur les Grecs, anciens et modernes, avec un parallèle de leurs mœurs* (1771), that the contemporary inhabitants of the country were the direct descendants of the ancient Hellenes. His assertion was based on a critical and detailed comparison between a series of ancient texts and the customs, ethos, popular practices, and superstitions of the modern Greeks. According to Guys, the rituals of the Orthodox Church were nothing less than a modified expression of pagan rites, and served as evidence for the close connection between the ancient and the modern world. But what lent further weight to his argument were his observations on language: his close examination of ancient and modern idioms convinced him that the modern, learned language of the Church and of educated Greeks contained elements that proved the uninterrupted continuity of the Hellenic heritage. Guys's ideas exercised immense influence on the subsequent generation of travellers to Greece, as well as on the Greek diaspora intelligentsia. In the first decades of the nineteenth century, it was the turn of François Pouqueville, Napoleon's consul to the court of Ali Pasha and author of various books on Greece, to show that Greece was valuable not only for its ancient, but also for its modern heritage. First in his *Voyage en Morée, à Constantinople, en Albanie, et dans plusieurs autres parties de l'Empire Ottoman* (1805) and later in the *Voyage dans la Grèce* (1820 and 1826), and especially in the four-volume *Histoire de la régénération de la Grèce* (1824), Pouqueville heralded a new attitude towards the modern Greeks, by maintaining that the continuity of Hellas was proven not so much by the educated classes, as by the popular culture of the illiterate segments of Greek society. Folk songs (and especially the songs of the klephts) were, for Pouqueville, the most powerful evidence of continuity, both at the level of language and at that of beliefs, practices, and mentality. These ideas were embraced around the same time by the French *idéologue* and

---

[31] Andrea Papadopulo Vreto, *Memoria su di alcuni costumi degli antichi Greci tuttora esistenti nell' isola di Leucade nel Mare Jonio* (Naples, 1825), p. 5.
[32] Papadopulo Vreto, *Memoria su di alcuni costumi*, pp. 4, 6.

philhellene intellectual and oriental philologist, Claude Fauriel, who published—
with the help of a group of Ionian and other Greek diaspora intellectuals, as we will
see in Part IV of this book—the first collection of Greek folk songs (1824).[33]

But Papadopoulo Vretto's book was not solely inspired by the canons set by the
philhellenic travel literature. It also owed much to the burgeoning interest in
archaeological sites within the milieu of British diplomats, aristocrats, connoisseurs, and collectors in the Italian and the Ottoman Mediterranean during the
eighteenth and nineteenth centuries. This interest was considerably reinforced by
the archaeological discoveries of the time, especially Herculaneum in 1738 and
Pompeii in 1748, through which a direct, unmediated experience of ancient classical art became for the first time possible. The British Society of Dilettanti—a
club of aristocratic connoisseurs whose aim was to promote the study of classical
antiquities and sponsor archaeological expeditions—and the German classicist
Johan Joachim Winckelmann, whose *History of Ancient Art* (1764) fixed the canons
of artistic perfection by exalting classical Greek art, played a major role in laying
the foundations of the emerging discipline of archaeology, as well as in establishing
Hellenism and Neoclassicism as cultural fashions.[34] Naples became at the time the
centre of a feverish archaeological and antiquarian activity. It was indeed during a
visit there in 1825 that Papadopoulo Vretto was inspired to write his book. As he
says in his autobiography, the enthusiasm shown by his old friend Carlo Bonucci
(1799–1880), who was by then the director of the excavations at Herculaneum
and Pompeii, instilled in him the desire *to acquaint the archaeologists, the numerous
Philhellenes of the kingdom of Naples and of Sicily, the majority of whom are of Greek
origin, with the traditions and customs of the ancient Greeks, that still exist on the
island of Santa Maura [Lefkada].*[35] More important still, Bonucci introduced
Papadopoulo Vretto to the renowned British archaeologist and topographer
Sir William Gell (1777–1836), a member of the Society of Dilettanti and author
of various books on classical Greece.[36] Gell had travelled widely in the Mediterranean
and published a topographical study of Ithaca, exploring the authenticity of the
locations on the island, with a view to shedding light on its ancient history and
Homeric descriptions.[37] At a time when these lands were being revealed for the
first time to Europeans enthralled by the putative identification of 'Homeric sites',

---

[33] On philhellenic travel literature see Fani-Maria Tsigakou, *The Rediscovery of Greece: Travellers and
Painters of the Romantic Era* (New Rochelle, NY, 1981); Robert Eisner, *Travelers to an Antique Land:
The History and Literature of Travel to Greece* (Ann Arbor, Mich., 1993); Olga Augustinos, *French
Odysseys: Greece in French Travel Literature from the Renaissance to the Romantic Era* (Baltimore, 1994);
Jean-Claude Berchet (ed.), *Le Voyage en orient: anthologie des voyageurs français dans le levant au XIXᵉ
siècle* (Paris, 1985).

[34] Suzanne L. Marchand, *Archaeology and Philhellenism in Germany, 1750–1970* (Princeton,
1996); Bruce Redford, *Dilettanti: The Antic and the Antique in Eighteenth-Century England* (Los
Angeles, 2008).

[35] GSA-A: K.20, Archive of A. Papadopoulos Vrettos, Manuscripts, IA' (XI), 'Memorie biografiche
e storiche', pp. 46–7. On Carlo Bonucci, see idem, *Pompei descritta da Carlo Bonucci, architetto etc.*
(Naples, 1827).

[36] Bonucci, *Pompei descritta*, pp. 47–8.

[37] William Gell, *The Geography and Antiquities of Ithaca* (London, 1807). See also Edith Clay (ed.),
*Sir William Gell in Italy: Letters to the Society of Dilettanti, 1831–1835* (London, 1976).

the demand for information about Greece grew ever greater. It was precisely to this demand that Papadopoulo Vretto thought to respond.

## IN THE GREEK STATE

In 1828 Lord Guilford departed this world, and in so doing he also left Papadopoulo Vretto without a job.[38] But as one door closed, another opened for the Ionian intellectual. That was the year in which Kapodistrias, newly elected as the governor of Greece, disembarked at Nafplio to set up the fledgling Greek state. On hearing the news of their compatriot's election, numerous Ionians rushed to the Greek shores in search of a better fate—including Papadopoulo Vretto's brother, who sadly lost his life during the voyage. Andrea thought to fulfil his brother's dream, by burnishing his skills as a graduate of medicine and opening a pharmacy. After a trip to Venice and Trieste, where he was supplied with the necessary drugs, he landed in Greece in March 1831. Kapodistrias—with whom Papadopoulo Vretto was on good terms, being a close friend of his brother Augoustinos—consented to the pharmacy plan, feeling especially relieved that their mutual friend was not asking for a post in government. *You are the first who, thank heaven, has come to see me without asking me for a position*, he would seem to have told him.[39] But the energetic Lefkadian was full of ideas which went beyond medical matters. *I observed*, he writes in his autobiography, *that [in Nafplio] all the officers from the garrison, the [town's] principal inhabitants and the foreigners spent the whole day and the evening in the numerous cafés concerning themselves only with political matters*. It therefore occurred to him that he should set up a reading room, a cabinet, in his own house, where *the members could at their ease read various political newspapers from Europe, not to mention voyages and other works of literature with which my own private library was supplied*.[40] We cannot help but be reminded here of what Vieusseux had done in Florence. Yet even this was not enough. In introducing to Greece another centuries-old Italian habit, Papadopoulo Vretto thought also of transforming his pharmacy into a place of political and cultural sociability by opening and attaching to it a bookshop.[41]

Time passed happily amidst these activities, until one ill-starred autumn morning of 1831. Papadopoulo Vretto remembered every detail of that fateful day: *It was a Sunday and I was still in bed when my son's nurse entered the room exclaiming: 'Master, they have killed the president!' I immediately got up, but in a daze. The fatal announcement [so disoriented me] that I could not [at first] lay hands on my*

[38] A. Papadopulo Vreto, *Notizie Biografiche-storiche su Federico Conte di Guilford etc.* (Athens, 1846).

[39] GSA-A: K.20, Archive of A. Papadopoulos Vrettos, Manuscripts, IA' (XI), 'Memorie biografiche e storiche', p. 64.

[40] GSA-A: K.20, Archive of A. Papadopoulos Vrettos, Manuscripts, IA' (XI), 'Memorie biografiche e storiche', p. 66.

[41] Filippo de Vivo, 'La farmacia come luogo di cultura: le spezierie di medicine in Italia', in M. Conforti, A. Carlino, and A. Clericuzio (eds), *Interpretare e curare: medicina e salute nel Rinascimento* (Rome, 2013), pp. 129–42.

*clothes… Count Augoustinos [Kapodistrias's brother] was sleeping in the room above my bedroom, and I could hear that he had got up and was urinating, which proves that he did not yet know of the painful loss he had suffered.*[42] In these few moments between the momentous event and its transformation into history, Papadopoulo Vretto, in a state of shock, left his nine-months pregnant wife and ran to the residence of the Russian ambassador (having in fact become his personal physician) to ascertain whether he too had been attacked. Upon his return home he was met with the terrible sight of his wife lying unconscious on the floor. Thus, from one moment to the next, the unfortunate man found himself in front of two dead bodies, that of the governor of Greece (whose autopsy he, along with another doctor, was duty bound to perform) and his prematurely born daughter.

From that point onwards, Papadopoulo Vretto became an unabashed supporter of the Kapodistrian political faction. The murdered governor's political ideology of a gradual and moderate liberalization of society, and his decision to 'temporarily' suspend the constitution and rule by executive degree, had cost him a great deal of support and split Greece's political class into two factions, one having rallied to his cause (the 'Kapodistrians') while the other contested his legacy (the 'Constitutionalists'). On his assassination, the country did in fact slide into civil war. During the wild days of anarchy that followed, Papadopoulo Vretto became involved in the ensuing press war dividing the opposed political factions. Besides preparing an apologetic biography of Kapodistrias and editing a series of other documents in support of his government, he also published a bilingual French–Greek newspaper, the *Miroir grec* (Nafplio, 1832–3), which became the mouthpiece of his party.[43] The newspaper was subtitled '*Monarchie constitutionnelle*', in order to spell out the fact that, despite the governor's 'provisional' authoritarian rule, his supporters were not the anti-constitutionalists they were made out by their adversaries to be, but advocated a constitutional monarchy for Greece.[44] A monarchical constitution was, in fact, what Augoustinos Kapodistrias—once he had been elected by a National Assembly, two months after his brother's assassination, as the second governor of Greece—attempted to bestow upon the nation. With this end in mind, he thus urged the protective powers to expedite their nomination of a sovereign prince. Augoustinos was totally unable, however, to construct a stable government and he soon fled to Corfu on board a Russian brig carrying with him his brother's mortal remains. The protective powers, Britain, France, and Russia, agreed eventually, by the London Agreement of May 1832, to install the 17-year-old Prince Otto of Bavaria as the monarch of Greece. It was not clearly declared in the agreement, however, whether Otto would govern as an absolute or as a constitutional king. What is nonetheless certain is the fact that the three-man regency consisting of Bavarian court officials, which ruled the country until Otto's coming of age (1833–5), made no mention of a constitution. Indeed,

---

[42] GSA-A: K.20: Archive of A. Papadopoulos Vrettos, Manuscripts, IA' (XI), 'Memorie biografiche e storiche', pp. 70–1.

[43] André Papadopoulo Bretós, *Mémoires biographiques-historiques sur le président de la Grèce, le Comte Jean Capodistrias* (Paris, 1837–8), 2 vols; idem, *Melanges de politique pour servir de documents à l'histoire des événements de la Grèce régénérée* (Athens, 1840).

[44] [Andrea Papadopoulo Vretto], *Le Compte rendu du Miroir grec* (Athens, 1839), p. 13.

the Kingdom of Greece ceased to be an absolute monarchy only in 1843, when a bloodless revolt in Athens forced Otto to grant a constitution.

Papadopoulo Vretto perceived the atmosphere during the first days of the regency as inimical to his faction. While Russian political actors in Greece became increasingly suspicious of the regency's attempts to modernize and westernize the state, he was personally involved in a story that further underscores the nature of foreign interference in Greek politics during those years. As the country sank into anarchy, the French *brigade d'occupation*, which had been sent to Greece by the protective powers to sweep the Egyptian army from the Peloponnese, had by now assumed the basic administrative and police functions in the region. When a group of pro-Kapodistrian senators and a body of troops from the Peloponnese gathered in Argos to form a coalition that proclaimed itself the only legitimate power, the rival faction summoned the French troops to garrison the city, involving it thus in domestic politics. Tensions escalated until in January 1833 a serious conflict erupted between the French soldiers and the local pro-Kapodistrian irregulars, resulting in 400 Greek casualties, including women, children, and the elderly.[45] The *Miroir grec* was among the first newspapers to denounce the event, and Papadopoulo Vretto, fearful of the French reaction and the threats he received, had to go into hiding for a period.[46] To add insult to injury, later that year he was also subjected to a lawsuit concocted against him by the editor of the *Athina*, the rival newspaper, who accused him of defamation.[47] *It was then*—he wrote in his auto-biography—*that I decided to leave Greece once and for all, hoping to find in Russia the compensation owed me for all that I had done for the so-called Russian, that is, the Kapodistrian party.*[48]

## NEW RUSSIAN TRAJECTORIES

So, in late 1833, Papadopoulo Vretto ventured forth to make a new life for himself using the decades-old Russian networks available in abundance to any aspiring person from his home islands. He embarked on a boat captained by P. I. Ricord, the commander of the Russian fleet in the Aegean. Ricord's involvement in Greek politics had rendered him a deeply controversial figure. (Such, indeed, was the extent of his involvement that during the war between the 'Kapodistrians' and the 'Constitutionalists' in 1832 he had been awarded Greek citizenship and nominated by the former camp as provisional governor of Greece, an offer which he declined.)[49]

[45] Lucien J. Frary, *Russia and the Making of Modern Greek Identity, 1821–1844* (Oxford, 2015), pp. 56–9, 65; Davide Rodogno, *Against Massacre: Humanitarian Interventions in the Ottoman Empire, 1815–1914* (Princeton, 2012), pp. 84–7.

[46] GSA-A: K.20, Archive of A. Papadopoulos Vrettos, Manuscripts, IA' (XI), 'Memorie biografiche e storiche', p. 73 and [Vretto], *Le Compte rendu du Miroir grec*, pp. 36–40.

[47] [Vretto], *Le Compte rendu du Miroir grec*, pp. 42–8.

[48] GSA-A: K.20, Archive of A. Papadopoulos Vrettos, Manuscripts, IA' (XI), 'Memorie biografiche e storiche', p. 76.

[49] [Andrea Papadopoulo Vretto], 'O antinabarchos Rossos Ricord ypopsifios kybernitis tis Ellados' (The Russian vice-admiral Ricord as a candidate governor of Greece), *Ethnikon imerologion* 3 (1863), pp. 153–8; K. K. Papoulides, 'Eggrafa Ellinon diplomatikon ypallilon tou 19ou ai. apo ti bibliothiki

*I approve of your decision to go to Russia*, Mustoxidi told his friend upon hearing of his imminent departure. *You will not want for protection, and in that country you will be able, I hope, on your own initiative to pursue an honourable career.*[50] Indeed, upon his arrival in Odessa, Papadopoulo Vretto encountered members of his own family who had settled at an earlier date in Russia and were employed as diplomats in the service of the Tsar. He also socialized with the community of wealthy Greek merchants and, what was more important, made the acquaintance of the Stourdza siblings. It was with their help that he was soon able to move to St Petersburg, where he managed to obtain a post, presumably as a translator, in the Asiatic Department of the Ministry of Foreign Affairs (where, indeed, Stourdza and Destunis had formerly been employed). His autobiography breaks off at around this point. However, from a letter that he sent to Mustoxidi a couple of years later, we learn that in Russia the Lefkadian adventurer did not really achieve much and shortly afterwards he left, proposing to seek his fortune westwards. In 1836 he moved to Paris, where he reinvented himself once more. This time he presented himself to the world as a scientist and inventor, creating armour made of a non-metal bulletproof material, which he tried to sell or at least to patent, but to no avail.[51]

In 1838, Papadopoulo Vretto made his way back to Athens, where he resumed his old political activities. It was not long before he found himself implicated in one of the major scandals that shook the political life of the young state, the so-called 'Philorthodox conspiracy' of 1839. The factionalism that had developed during the revolution and under Kapodistrias continued during the Othonian period but in a modified form. The old factions now formed 'parties'—not exactly in the modern sense of the term, since they were loose coalitions united by family ties and general interests—each of which looked to one of the representatives of the Great Powers for support and protection. The main parties were, consequently, the Russian, the French, and the English.[52] The Russian party, which was descended from the old Kapodistrian faction and included in its ranks the Greeks involved with Russia's rule in the Ionian Islands and all those who had relatives in Russia or had benefited from the economic opportunities and patronage of the Tsar since the 1770s, was at the heart of this episode. The whole story was about the unmasking by the Othonian government of a secret society, which aimed to foment an uprising against Ottoman rule in the 'unredeemed lands' of Thessaly, Macedonia, and Epirus. Organized by prominent members of the Kapodistrian faction, among them the deceased governor's younger brother Georgios, the 'Philorthodox Society'

Lenin tis Moschas' (Documents by 19th century Greek diplomats in the Lenin Library of Moscow), *Ellinika* 31 (1979), p. 146.

[50] *Corrispondenza del Cav. Andrea Mustoxidi col suo amico Andrea Papadopulo Vreto* (Athens, 1860), p. xxiii.

[51] HMC: MP, X/1/27. On his invention see Dimitris Arvanitakis (ed.), *Carteggio 1822–1860: Andrea Mustoxidi ed Emilio Tipaldo* (Athens, 2005), pp. 512, 544, 814, 856.

[52] John Anthony Petropoulos, *Politics and Statecraft in the Kingdom of Greece 1833–1843* (Princeton, 1968); Gunnar Hering, *Die Politischen Parteien in Griechenland 1821–1936* (Munich, 1992), 2 vols.

presumably sought also to replace King Otto—who was a Catholic—with a Christian Orthodox ruler. In reality, the story of the 'Philorthodox conspiracy' had less to do with an actual conspiracy than with the high degree of foreign involvement in Greek politics and with the competing national ideologies which ensued from such an involvement. Indeed, even after the establishment of a regular administration in Athens, the three protecting powers, wishing to use the young state as a vantage point from which to promote their wider interests in the Mediterranean, continued to pursue policies of constant meddling in its domestic affairs. Recent research has shown that, in this case, the 'Philorthodox conspiracy' was largely an invention of the agents of the rival powers, who repeatedly accused the Russians of direct participation in intrigues and plots against the King.[53] The British government and its local representatives, in particular, used the agitation caused by the discovery of a limited number of compromising documents to advance a series of demands and attempt to oust their rivals in the Greek state and the Ottoman Empire, culminating in the deposition in 1840 of the Patriarch Gregorius VI who had acted in opposition to British desires in other matters.[54] The event also had repercussions in the British Ionian Islands, where the colonial authorities laid an embargo on all traffic with Greece, made a number of arrests, and placed prominent Russophiles under surveillance—diminishing thus the power of the local opposition.[55]

This is not to say that these documents did not actually exist, or that they did not reflect a reality of Russian policy and especially of its local agents in the Kingdom of Greece. The episode of the 'Philorthodox Society' is indeed important because it illustrates how a brand of Greek national ideology continued to be forged under the auspices of Russian protection and within the imperial and ecumenical framework of Eastern Orthodoxy of previous years. This ideological framework was seriously challenged when a separate Greek national Church emerged in 1833. The establishment of the Greek autocephalous (strongly approved by Britain because it was thought to control possible Russian influence exerted through Constantinople) created deep dissatisfaction, especially among the Russophile segments of Greek society, regarding the break with the Patriarchate. Voices calling for a reconciliation and even a reunion of the Greek Church with the Patriarchate and the conversion of the King became more numerous and louder by the end of the 1830s. Unlike their opponents, who advocated a national Orthodox Church unfettered by the

---

[53] Frary, *Russia and the Making of Modern Greek Identity*, pp. 167–92; see also the older Barbara Jelavich, 'The Philorthodox Conspiracy of 1839: A Report to Metternich', *Balkan Studies* 7 (1966), pp. 89–102.

[54] Christos Loukos, 'Gyro apo tin pafsi tou Patriarchi Grigoriou tou St: nees martyries' (Around the deposition of the Patriarch Gregorius VI: new evidences), *Eranistis* 21 (1997), pp. 326–36.

[55] Among others, they placed Mustoxidi under investigation. Papadopoulo Vretto argued that the High Commissioner used the 'Philorthodox conspiracy' in order to eliminate him from the opposition in Parliament. See idem, *Biografia del cavaliere Andrea Mustoxidi scritta e pubblicata a Venezia nell'anno 1836 da Emilio Tipaldo e continuata sino alla sua morte da Andrea Papadopulo Vreto* (Athens, 1860), p. 13. See also Panagiotis Chiotis, *Istoria tou Ioniou Kratous apo systaseos aftou mechris enoseos, 1815–1864* (The history of the Ionian state from its creation to the unification with Greece, 1815–1864) (Zante, 1874), vol. II, pp. 117–18.

canonical strictures of the Ecumenical Patriarchate, which was still under the control of the Sultan, these people saw the autocephalous and the restricted boundaries of the Greek state as impeding the dream of the reunification of all Orthodox Greeks under a revived Byzantine Empire centred in Constantinople. For example, in a pamphlet that saw the light of day in 1854, Papadopoulo Vretto argued that the ultimate aim of the Greek revolution had been the liberation of Constantinople and the restoration of the Byzantine Empire.[56] These activities fortified the links between Greeks and Russians, which were further strengthened throughout the period. But the discussions around the autocephalous and the 'Philorthodox conspiracy' marked also a nascent rift within the bounds of Greek national ideology between those who believed that the new state belonged to the East and those who thought it a part of the West.[57]

As an avowed supporter of the Kapodistrian faction, at the outbreak of the 'Philorthodox scandal', Papadopoulo Vretto was immediately rendered suspect in the eyes of the King, who issued an order for his arrest (which, however, after some pleading on the part of common acquaintances, he later retracted).[58] We do not really know what he did after that date, although he would seem to have travelled for a period between the Ionian Islands and Greece. At any rate, in 1849 he was appointed Greek Consul in the Ottoman city of Varna, present-day Bulgaria, where he devoted his time to archaeological excavations and to writing one of the very first histories of Bulgaria.[59] The last traces we have of him are as a consul in Venice, where he served, intermittently, between 1850 and 1855. Later he returned to his native island of Lefkada, where he allegedly attempted to publish a newspaper.[60] It seems that death found him there, only four years after he had, in the most tragic of circumstances, buried his son.[61]

[56] André Papadopoulo-Vretos, *De l'idée dominante des Grecs sur la conquête de Constantinople* (Athens, 1854).

[57] Paraskevas Matalas, *Ethnos kai Orthodoxia: oi peripeteies mias schesis: apo to 'elladiko' sto boulgariko schisma* (Nation and Orthodoxy: the adventures of a relationship: from the Greek to the Bulgarian autocephalous) (Herakleion, 2003), p. 50.

[58] [Anonymous], 'Papadopoulos Bretos, Andreas', *Ethnikon imerologion* 3 (1866), pp. 369–70.

[59] In *Corrispondenza del Cav. Andrea Mustoxidi*, pp. xxxvii–xxxviii. See Andrea Papadopulo Vreto, *Su la scoperta di Tomi, città ellenica nel Ponto Eusino e su la bilingue iscrizione ritrovata in Varna* (Athens, 1853); idem, *La Bulgarie, ancienne et moderne* (St Petersburg, 1856).

[60] Arvanitakis (ed.), *Carteggio 1822–1860: Andrea Mustoxidi ed Emilio Tipaldo*, pp. 772, 821.

[61] Andrea Papadopulo Vretto, *Biografia Marinou Papadopoulou Bretou: syntachtheisa apo tou atychous patros tou* (Biography of Marino Papadopoulo Vretto, composed by his unfortunate father) (Athens, 1872).

# Conclusion

By entering history through the life of an individual, I hope I have illustrated some of its complications. Chapter 9 has shown how different phenomena in the sphere of geopolitics and culture were intricately interconnected and could form part of a single individual trajectory. Historical developments in Naples, the Ionian Islands, the British and the Ottoman Mediterranean, Greece, and Russia appeared here to be components of the same story, which could not have been told otherwise than in their intersection. Whereas during the first half of the nineteenth century in the sphere of high politics most of these links were slowly breaking (consider the separation of Adriatic nationalisms, the disentangling of the trans-Adriatic diasporic communities, the creation of the Greek state, and the establishment of a separate national Church outside the ecumenical and imperial framework of Eastern Orthodoxy), at the level of personal experience and intimate politics these connections continued to be vital and formative. Lives like that of Papadopoulo Vretto, extending from Nafplio and Athens in the south to St Petersburg in the north, from Naples and Paris in the west to Odessa in the east, illustrate how traditional systems of exchange within the Venetian and generally Italian trans-Adriatic universe and the Orthodox imperial world of the Ottoman and Russian empires could well coexist with the modern founding of nation-states and their political ideologies. When all is said and done, Papadopoulo Vretto's biography not only offers us tantalizing glimpses of intimate experience and personal conduct in times of tumult and change. It also invites us to rethink the reductive and antinomic categories between 'East' and 'West' by which we have learned to read our history in this part of the world.

# PART IV

# INTELLECTUALS AS 'BRIDGES' ACROSS THE SEA

*Ad A. Mustoxidi, ultimo anello fra due patrie e due lingue madri di civiltà*

(To A. Mustoxidi, the last link between two patrias and two mother tongues of civilization)

—Niccolò Tommaseo to Andrea Mustoxidi (1838)[1]

*Egli non è nè ben del secolo passato nè bene del nostro*

(He belongs neither to the past century nor to our own)

—Idem on Andrea Mustoxidi (1860)[2]

## INTRODUCTION

### Living in a dying world

Two sons belonging to two of the last illustrious patrician families of Venice, both passionate lovers of their native city, decided, in the latter half of the nineteenth century, to pick up their pens and defend the memory of the long-dead Venetian Republic. Against a swelling chorus of voices that portrayed the Republic in its closing centuries as decrepit, mummified, and ruled by a decadent oligarchic class, depicting Venice as dead long before its actual death at the hands of Napoleon's troops, the two historiographers, Girolamo Dandolo and Filippo Nani Mocenigo, celebrated the good government and the cultural productivity of the Republic's later years. In their books, documentary zeal was reinforced by a strong sense of nostalgia and the desire to evoke past glory.[3] At a time when Venice was losing its local distinctiveness to the absorbent power of the Italian state and its maritime

---

[1] Manuscript dedication on the title page of his book *Nuovo dizionario de' sinonimi della lingua italiana*. Quoted in Michele Lascaris, 'Niccolò Tommaseo ed Andrea Mustoxidi', *Atti e memorie della Società Dalmata di Storia patria* 3 (1934), p. 36.

[2] Niccolò Tommaseo, 'Andrea Mustoxidi', *Archivio storico italiano* 12/2 (1860), p. 41.

[3] Girolamo Dandolo, *La caduta della Repubblica di Venezia ed i suoi ultimi cinquant'anni: studii storici* (Venice, 1855); Filippo Nani Mocenigo, *Della letteratura veneziana del secolo XIX* (Venice, 1901 [1891]).

superiority to the rising port of Habsburg Trieste, a feverish rummaging in local archives and a systematic reorganization of the city's past seemed the best way to preserve a present that appeared to fade even as it occurred.[4] In cultivating Venice's regional imperial memory, these two works were joined by a similar book that saw the light of day in the same period on the Ionian Islands. Its author, Lavrentios Vrokinis, an apologist for the old Venetian local aristocracy, sought to stress the intellectual contribution of the Ionian nobles to the former metropole's greatness.[5] These three books are in essence the only printed sources where one can find information on the characters who populate Chapters 10–12. Figures whose names never entered the historical record except in that fleeting moment of nostalgic contemplation of a long-fallen empire, these were intellectuals who, born during the last years of the Venetian Republic or on the cusp of the new century, belonged precisely to that dying world. Venetian-Ionian, -Greek, or -Dalmatian men of letters (namely Andrea Mustoxidi, Spiridione Vlandi, Bartolommeo Cutlumusiano, Emilio Tipaldo, Anthimo Masarachi, Giovanni and Spiridione Veludo, Pier Alessandro Paravia, and the most famous of them all, Niccolò Tommaseo), the characters who process through the following pages were the last representatives of a species that was soon to face extinction: the Venetian Adriatic intellectual. As Tommaseo's words in the epigraphs at the beginning of this chapter suggest, these were people who 'bridged' two centuries and two (or more) cultures. Having experienced the Napoleonic Wars and feeling as if they lived between past and future, 'these figures participated in a world so different from that of the parents who raised them and from that of the children they would raise that we can see them as members of a unique generation'—as a scholar studying the post-Venetian Habsburg Adriatic has aptly commented.[6] But it was not only time that these figures bridged; it was also space. Even though the Venetian Republic had been erased from the map, these people continued to move within a geography that was haunted by a pre-Napoleonic legacy and that united the two shores of the Adriatic in a centuries-old intellectual dialogue. To borrow the words of another scholar, these were the last 'links' of a Greco- (or Dalmato-) Italian cultural 'chain' which was now dissolving under the shadow of the recently developed national identifications

---

[4] Giovanni L. Fontana, 'Patria veneta e stato italiano dopo l'unità: problemi di identità e di integrazione', in G. Arnaldi and M. P. Stocchi (eds), *Storia della cultura veneta*, vol. 6: *Dall'età napoleonica alla Prima Guerra Mondiale* (Vicenza, 1986), pp. 553–96; Claudio Povolo, 'The Creation of Venetian Historiography', in John Martin and Dennis Romano (eds), *Venice Reconsidered: The History and Civilization of an Italian City-State, 1297–1797* (Baltimore and London, 2000), pp. 491–519; Anastasia Stouraiti, 'Geografie del trauma e politiche di lutto: racconti sulla perdita delle Isole Ionie a Venezia', in Konstantinos Dimadis (ed.), *The Greek World between the Age of Enlightenment and the Twentieth Century* (Athens, 2007), vol. II, pp. 159–68.

[5] Lavrentios Vrokinis, *Biografika schedaria ton en tois grammasin, oraies technes kai allois kladois tou koinonikou biou dialampsanton Kerkyraion etc.* (Biographical sketches of Corfiots distinguished in letters, arts and other social fields since the mid-eighteenth century etc.) (Corfu, 1884), 2 vols. See Dimitris Arvanitakis, 'Un viaggio nella storiografia neogreca: immagini della Dominante e degli ordini sociali delle città Ionie (secoli XVI–XVIII)', in Chryssa Maltezou and Gherardo Ortalli (eds), *Italia-Grecia: temi e storiografie a confronto* (Venice, 2001), pp. 101–2.

[6] Dominique Kirchner Reill, *Nationalists Who Feared the Nation: Adriatic Multi-Nationalism in Habsburg Dalmatia, Trieste, and Venice* (Stanford, Calif., 2012), p. 32.

and of the new distances that these created.[7] *We are at one and the same time Italians and Greeks*, the Italo-Dalmatian Tommaseo wrote as late as 1840 to another child of the ruins of the Venetian Adriatic, his Greco-Italian friend Markos Renieris.[8]

But just as every bridge spans a void, so too did these intellectuals. *Never exactly Italians or exactly Greeks in intelligence and in language*, to quote the words of Tommaseo again, or *Homines schismatici et sine nomine* (Schismatic men without a name), to use Foscolo's sarcastic jibe about Mustoxidi, these intellectuals lived on the outer fringes of their nations.[9] The fact that they wrote mainly in Italian made them unsuited to feature in the Greek (or Croatian) national narrative. On the other hand, their espousal of Greek and other nationalisms meant they were expunged from Italian national history too. They thus fell victim to an interpretative gap which opened up when historical writing was separated into national schools from the late nineteenth century onwards. If we exclude the case of Tommaseo, who earned himself a supporting role in Italian political and literary history, all the other figures from this intellectual milieu slipped into oblivion. Some of them— chiefly Mustoxidi, Tipaldo, and Tommaseo—were unearthed or revisited under a new light only recently thanks to the brilliant work of a new generation of scholars inspired by the transnational turn in intellectual history.[10] It is on these works that this part of the book builds, hoping to enrich this tradition with unfamiliar figures, new geographical parameters, and fresh insights.

I therefore wish now to turn my attention to this intellectual universe, oscillating as it did between the world of the former imperial Venetian realm and the world of nations that was dawning. The leading figure here was undoubtedly Andrea Mustoxidi (1785–1860). Chapter 10 provides insight into his biography, focusing in particular on the way this largely forgotten Corfiot, who was famous in his own lifetime, inserted himself into the Italian and European intellectual scene with works on philology and history inspired by Neoclassicism and philhellenism. It also unearths the unknown adventure of this man's involvement in Russian diplomacy and the 1821 revolution in Piedmont, as well as his subsequent transformation from a Russian diplomat into a Greek minister (the first 'Ephor' for culture and education in Greece) and into a liberal politician on the British Ionian Islands. By so doing, the chapter also studies the educational programme of Kapodistrias's government, as well as the adventure of liberal politics in the British Mediterranean Empire.

In following Mustoxidi's gradual transition from Italian to Greek letters, Chapter 11 adds to the story the endeavours of a group of Ionian and Dalmatian

[7] Dimitris Arvanitakis (ed.), *Carteggio 1822–1860: Andrea Mustoxidi ed Emilio Tipaldo* (Athens, 2005), pp. 97–106 (introduction).

[8] Quoted in Caterina Carpinato, 'La corrispondenza inedita tra Niccolò Tommaseo e Markos Renieris', in Francesco Bruni (ed.), *Niccolò Tommaseo: popolo e nazioni, Italiani, Corsi, Greci, Illirici* (Rome and Padua, 2004), vol. II, p. 523.

[9] Niccolò Tommaseo, *Colloqui col Manzoni*, edited by Teresa Lodi (Florence, 1928 [1855]), p. 108 [He refers to Mustoxidi]. Ugo Foscolo, *Didymi Clerici prophetae minimi Hypercalypseos liber singularis* (Pisa, 1815), p. 8 (Clavis, Vs. 19–21).

[10] Reill, *Nationalists Who Feared the Nation*; Arvanitakis (ed.), *Carteggio 1822–1860: Andrea Mustoxidi ed Emilio Tipaldo*, esp. the introduction.

intellectuals who were enfolded in the decrepit embrace of the Greek community of Venice during the first half of the nineteenth century. By mapping out their lives, the chapter examines these men's bicultural existence and transnational patriotism, and investigates their intellectual work. Orchestrated largely by Mustoxidi, as Chapter 12 shows, these people pursued an ambitious programme to rehabilitate those aspects of culture and history that had been most grievously neglected by the Greek national ideology of the time, namely, the 'dark' centuries of Byzantine and medieval history and popular tradition (especially folk songs). This Greco-Venetian milieu placed the emphasis on the historical 'continuity'—rather than the 'revival'—of Greece, thereby creating a more coherent concept of national time, which paved the way for the composition of all-encompassing Greek histories in the second half of the nineteenth century. Shedding light on this neglected component of the Greek and Adriatic diaspora means enriching our understanding of the nineteenth-century Greek, Italian, and more broadly Mediterranean intellectual landscape.

# 10

## An Unknown 'Miracle'
### Andrea Mustoxidi

### INTRODUCTION: IN HISTORIOGRAPHY'S
### *NO MAN'S LAND*

In a letter to a friend written from Geneva on 30 August 1809, the renowned Swiss-French writer and political activist Benjamin Constant noted: *At one point I saw here one of your Greek friends called Mustoxidi;... he struck me as educated and charming, and I have been told that he was regarded, in Paris, as one of the most distinguished men from his nation.*[1] He was not alone among the famous men of his day in acknowledging Mustoxidi's moral stature. Alessandro Manzoni too, perhaps Italy's most celebrated author, appears to have said that Mustoxidi, soon after the publication of his first book, *pareva allora un miracolo* (seemed at the time to be a miracle), while Giacomo Leopardi, one of Italy's very greatest poets and an eminent philologist, dedicated one of his works to him.[2] It is something of a mystery then why this man, who had gained so lofty a reputation during his lifetime, has been so neglected by contemporary historians. Mustoxidi's personal archive, a voluminous mass of poorly catalogued papers filling until recently three cupboards in a dark corner of a payroll office in the diocese of Corfu, stands indeed as a sad relic of an unacknowledged past.[3] To be precise, the question is not why Mustoxidi is altogether absent from the memoryscape of Greece and Italy. Because he is not. Biographical accounts and obituaries by his contemporaries aside, plenty of twentieth-century writings exist on this eminent Corfiot, in Greece at least. There is even a street named after him in central Athens. But these texts, in their overwhelming majority, serve merely to inform or else are blatantly hagiographical accounts.[4]

---

[1] Quoted in Victor Glachant, *Benjamin Constant, sous l'œil du guet* (Paris, 1906), p. 122.

[2] Manzoni's words in Niccolò Tommaseo, 'Andrea Mustoxidi', *Archivio storico italiano* 12/2 (1860), p. 33. Leopardi's dedication in idem, *Saggio sopra gli errori popolari degli antichi* (Florence, 1846 [1815]), pp. 1–2.

[3] The archive is currently inaccessible, due to the renovation of the diocesan buildings. See Konstantina Zanou, 'Storia di un archivio: le carte Mustoxidi a Corfù (con due lettere inedite di Manzoni e Foscolo)', *Giornale storico della letteratura italiana* 183/604 (2006), pp. 556–76.

[4] For example: Evangelos Manis, 'Andreas Moustoxydis (1785–1860): o epistimon, o politikos, o ethnikos agonistis' (Andrea Mustoxidi (1785–1860): the scholar, the politician, the national fighter) (Ph.D. dissertation, University of Athens, 1960); Agathi Nikokaboura, *O Andreas Moustoxydis kai i paideia* (Andrea Mustoxidi and education) (Corfu, 1965); Th. Moustoxydis, *Andreas Moustoxydis: bios kai erga* (Andrea Mustoxidi: life and deeds) (Athens, 1963).

The question is rather why Mustoxidi is absent from critical historiography, from the academic agenda of nineteenth-century intellectual and political history.

The mystery has been partly answered by the recent contributions of one scholar in particular. Historian Dimitris Arvanitakis claimed that there was a major lack of comprehension between, on the one hand, the culture of mainland and Aegean Greece and, on the other, that of the Ionian Islands, especially as regards the two sides' experience of their acquisition of Greek national consciousness. The leading figure in Greek letters in Mustoxidi's time, Adamantios Koraes (1748–1833), a native of the Aegean island of Chios but a diaspora Greek based in Paris, epitomized this incomprehension when during an epistolary exchange with Mustoxidi he observed: *You cannot imagine... how sad I feel when I receive letters from Greeks not in the Greek language. They have praised you, young man, in the newspapers, that you write the Italian language perfectly; and they are right to have praised you. But, be careful that this praise does not divert you from the right path, which rules that the mother tongue should be the first and most necessary lesson for everyone, as only the study of his language distinguishes the race of the writer and the measure of his love for his patria... I warn you not to write to me again in another language. I understand nothing but Greek.*[5] Defining national patriotism in linguistic terms fostered an unsympathetic attitude towards all those individuals who felt Greek but spoke Italian, namely the Italian-educated Ionian elite. But it was not only language that disturbed Koraes. It was the whole post-Venetian reality of the Ionian Islands: the Ionian double culture, the survival of Venetian aristocratic titles, and the existence of a *petite noblesse* which despite political upheavals had preserved its integrity. It was the regional peculiarity then of the Ionian Islands in its entirety, whether cultural, social, or political, that an Ottoman diaspora Greek like Koraes could not understand—a fact which accounted, indeed (along with his Russophobia), for his late tirade against Kapodistrias's government and particularly against its minister Mustoxidi, whom he ironically called a *Jesuit*, a *Cavaliere*, and a *foreigner*.[6] To return to Arvanitakis's argument, Koraes's vision of the nation, and particularly the principle according to which Greek nationality constituted above all a linguistic unity, eventually prevailed over all other possible ways of being Greek. This monolithic affirmation of the national idea, as it was subsequently perpetuated by literary and other historians, instead of initiating a dialogue between the various components of what came to be called the 'Neohellenic society', excluded and expelled from its master narrative all 'different paths to the nation'—to borrow the title of a recent collection.[7] There is little wonder then that Mustoxidi and his like are

---

[5] Adamantios Korais, *Allilografia* (Correspondence), edited by K. Th. Demaras, A. Aggelou, E. Koumarianou, and E. Fragkiskos (Athens, 1964–84), vol. III, pp. 205–6.

[6] In G. Pantazidis [Adamantios Koraes], *Ti symferei eis tin eleftheromenin apo tous Tourkous Ellada na praxei eis tas parousas peristaseis dia na mi doulothei eis christianous tourkizontas: dialogos defteros* (What is best for the liberated Greeks to do under the circumstances in order not to be enslaved again by some Turkish-like Christians: dialogue two) (Paris, 1831), p. 28. See Apostolos Daskalakis, *Koraes kai Kapodistrias: oi kata tou kybernitou libelloi* (Koraes and Kapodistrias: the libels against the governor) (Athens, 1958).

[7] Laurence Cole (ed.), *Different Paths to the Nation: Regional and National Identities in Central Europe and Italy, 1830–70* (Basingstoke and New York, 2007).

absent from the academic historiographical panorama. Abandoned by mainstream historians, it was not long before this figure came to be endorsed by a number of apologetic historiographers, who considered it their mission to defend Mustoxidi's 'Greekness', patriotism, and national characteristics.[8]

It seems to me, however, that this is not the only reason why Mustoxidi and most of the Ionian intellectuals of his generation have remained historiographically homeless. The overall direction that intellectual history has taken in Greece is also in large part to blame. The founder of Greek intellectual history studies is generally considered to be K. Th. Demaras. In a series of hugely influential works, produced from the late 1940s to the late 1980s, this outstanding scholar forged a wholly new research field, so-called 'Neohellenic Enlightenment' studies, which explored the history of modern Greek intellectual production, especially in the centres of the diaspora during the eighteenth and nineteenth centuries, and of its connection to the emergence of Greek national consciousness. These studies, which informed an entire generation of intellectual historians in Greece, creating what one could label 'a school of Demaric thought', focused upon the eminent figure of Koraes in order to create a genealogy of men of letters—Koraes's predecessors, his contemporaries (friends or enemies), and his successors—who constituted the edifice of the 'Neohellenic Enlightenment' and of its adversaries (the latter being usually located in the circles of the Ecumenical Patriarchate of Constantinople). The geography of this scheme is centred, naturally enough, in Paris, but it extends to include the centres of the Greek diaspora in central Europe and the Balkans (principally Vienna and Bucharest), as well as the nuclei of educational activity in the Ottoman Empire. Adopting almost wholesale Koraes's own vision of the 'regeneration of Greece', this field has been chiefly engaged with the questions that occupied the Chiot-Parisian scholar himself: the linguistic battles between purists and demoticists, the westernization and secularization of Greek society, its 'reconnection' with its ancient classical heritage, and the radical democratization of the new state's institutions according to the principles of the Radical Enlightenment and the French Revolution.[9] As one would expect, in this panorama of modern Greek intellectual history, the literary environments of the post-Venetian Adriatic, with the geographies that they generated between Italy, the Ionian Islands, and Russia, and with their own questions regarding transnational affiliations, bicultural and bi-linguistic belonging, moderate liberalism and religious Enlightenment, found little place. To put it succinctly, intellectual history in Greece has shone an intense light upon a single aspect of this history, while leaving much else languishing in an ill-lit hinterland. It is hoped therefore that the attention paid to Mustoxidi and the circle of Greco-Venetian intellectuals in Chapters 10–12 will enrich this history's landscape and introduce new elements and new questions into its agenda.[10]

---

[8] Arvanitakis (ed.), *Carteggio 1822–1860: Andrea Mustoxidi ed Emilio Tipaldo*, pp. 22–5, 97–106.

[9] By way of illustration see K. Th. Demaras, *Neoellinikos diafotismos* (Neohellenic Enlightenment) (Athens, 1977); Paschalis M. Kitromilides, *Enlightenment and Revolution: The Making of Modern Greece* (Cambridge, Mass., and London, 2013).

[10] Konstantina Zanou, 'Dianooumenoi-"gefyres" sti metabasi apo tin proethniki stin ethniki epochi' (Intellectuals-'bridges' at the transition from the pre-national to the national era), *Ta istorika* 58 (2013), pp. 3–22.

Needless to say, moreover, if the figure of Mustoxidi is still stranded on the outermost margins of academic historiography in Greece, in Italy he fares no better. The fact that the Corfiot scholar passed half his lifetime in Italy and wrote mainly in Italian does not necessarily imply that he won a place in Italian literary history. Save for a few scattered references, which are encountered in histories of classical philology in Italy or in biographies of famous Italian men of letters with whom he was connected, Mustoxidi's name is absent from Italian historiography too. Unlike Foscolo, who was Italianized early enough to pass muster, the Corfiot scholar failed to relinquish, in the eyes of Italian historiography, his quality as a 'Greek'. Overall, Mustoxidi, like so many of his fellow Ionians, gives the impression of having lived in a sort of historiographical *no man's land*. It is this shimmering, evanescent zone that I will now attempt to inhabit.[11]

## IN THE LAND OF ITALIAN AND EUROPEAN NEOCLASSICISM

Mustoxidi was born in Corfu in 1785 to a local family of aristocratic background. Like every talented son of the Ionian Islands, when he reached the age of 17 he was sent to Italy to embark upon a course of higher studies. He studied law at the University of Pavia, outside Milan. At the age of 19, before even finishing his studies, he published a book which was praised for its exceptional historical and philological erudition, a local history of ancient Corfu.[12] Dedicated to the Tsar, the work served to win him (as we saw earlier in this book) his appointment as 'Official Historiographer of the Ionian Islands'. It was the golden age of the Septinsular Republic and the young Russophile Corfiot was invited to go back and deploy his intellectual capacities in the service of his patria. The fact that he was Kapodistrias's best friend certainly helped. His return to Corfu in 1805, where he taught in the newly founded public school of the island, was to prove short-lived, however. In 1808, with the dissolution of the Septinsular Republic and the passing of the islands into the hands of Napoleon, Mustoxidi returned to Italy. He went, more specifically, to Milan.

At that time, the city was flourishing. Capital of the Napoleonic Kingdom of Italy, Milan attracted to its newly founded institutions *la crème de la crème* of Italian society. Its academies, libraries, and literary salons overflowed with talented youth, eager to display their intellectual abilities, collaborate with new and prestigious journals, and meet the great masters of Neoclassical letters. Mustoxidi shone in this milieu, earning the esteem and affection of the Marquis Giangiacopo Trivulzio, a wealthy connoisseur and patron of the arts, and winning the heart of

---

[11] This chapter is heavily based on my unpublished Ph.D. dissertation, 'Expatriate Intellectuals and National Identity: Andrea Mustoxidi in Italy, France and Switzerland (1802–1829)' (University of Pisa, 2007).

[12] Andrea Mustoxidi, *Notizie per servire alla storia corcirese dai tempi eroici fino al secolo XII* (Corfu, 1804). He published a more complete version of this work some years later under the title *Illustrazioni corciresi di Andrea Mustoxidi istoriografo dell'Isole dell'Ionio* (Milan, 1811–14), 2 vols.

his wife Beatrice, with whom he in fact had an affair. The young Corfiot thus became an assiduous visitor to the best situated salon in the city.[13] Before too long he had made the acquaintance of a number of distinguished Italian men of letters. Mention might be made here of Carlo Rosmini (1758–1827), the celebrated author of a *History of Milan* and a fervent advocate of Neoclassicist ideals;[14] Felice Bellotti (1786–1858), an accomplished Hellenist, translator of the *Odyssey* and of the tragedies of Aeschylus, Sophocles, and Euripides;[15] Luigi Lamberti (1759–1813) and Angelo Mai (1782–1854), both librarians and distinguished classical philologists, the former an acclaimed Homerist, the latter the inventor of a method of reading palimpsests.[16] Mustoxidi met, of course, Ugo Foscolo, and indeed on equal terms, but also Alessandro Manzoni (1785–1873), Italy's most revered novelist and poet, with whom he became close friends.[17] The young Corfiot soon made a name for himself by contributing to Milan's most respected journals, for example, to the *Poligrafo* (1811–14), founded by the senator of the Napoleonic government and president of the *Istituto Italiano* Giovanni Paradisi, and to the *Giornale italiano*, promoted on the initiative of the Vice-President of the Italian Republic Gaetano Melzi.[18] But Mustoxidi's trump card in the universe of Italian letters was Vincenzo Monti (1754–1828). Perhaps the most representative figure of Italian Neoclassical and Napoleonic culture, at the time of their first meeting Monti was already considered to be the greatest Italian poet of the day. He was the Corfiot's professor at the University of Pavia but with the passing of time he turned out to be much more: in a cherished relationship that lasted for more than twenty-five years, Monti became for Mustoxidi a mentor, a trusted ally, and a devoted friend. *If nothing remains of us after death, I assure you that even among the departed I shall love you with the love that holds tight and binds the heart of a father to his son*—the celebrated poet wrote to him some months before leaving this world.[19]

---

[13] Gio. Ant. Maggi, 'Trivulzio Gianiacopo', in Emilio Tipaldo (ed.), *Biografia degli Italiani illustri nelle scienze, lettere ed arti nel secolo XVIII* (Venice, 1834), vol. II, pp. 470–8. Correspondence between them and Mustoxidi in HMC: MP, X/10/486–94, III/1/57–83 and III/1/23, 27–9, 31, 34, 42, 48–9, 51.

[14] Carlo Rosmini, *Dell'istoria di Milano* (Milan, 1820). See B. Gamba, 'Rosmini Carlo De', in Tipaldo (ed.), *Biografia degli Italiani illustri*, vol. I, pp. 98–102. Correspondence with Mustoxidi in HMC: MP, X/7/294–307.

[15] Carlo Tenca, 'Cenno commemorativo intorno a Felice Bellotti', *Il crepuscolo* 9/8 (1858), pp. 126–8; Giovanni Antonio Maggi, *Della vita e degli scritti di Felice Bellotti* (Milan, 1860). Correspondence with Mustoxidi in HMC: MP, III/3/161 and X/9/417–34, and BAM: Fondo Bellotti, L122 sub., 514–67.

[16] Luigi Lamberti, *Osservazioni sopra alcune lezioni della Iliade di Omero* (Milan, 1813); Vittorio Fontana, *Luigi Lamberti (Vita—scritti—amici)* (Reggio Emilia, 1892); Gianni Gervasoni, *Angelo Mai* (Bergamo, 1954). Correspondence between them and Mustoxidi in HMC: MP, X/8/349–50 and V/181.

[17] FE, vol. 2, p. 122; vol. 3, pp. 399–400, 542–3; Zanou, 'Storia di un archivio', pp. 566–76; Arvanitakis (ed.), *Carteggio 1822–1860: Andrea Mustoxidi ed Emilio Tipaldo*, pp. 87–96, 221–3; Alessandro Manzoni, *Carteggio*, edited by G. Sforza and G. Gallavresi (Milan, 1912), vol. I, pp. 4–7, 298–9; idem, *Tutte le lettere*, edited by Cesare Arieti (Milan, 1970), vol. I, pp. 12–15, 90, 92, 135.

[18] Claudio Chiancone, 'Il circolo Paradisi e il "Poligrafo"', in E. Brambilla, C. Capra, and A. Scotti (eds), *Istituzioni e cultura in età napoleonica* (Milan, 2008), pp. 232–50; Rita Chini, 'Il *Poligrafo* e l'*Antipoligrafo*: polemiche letterarie nella Milano napoleonica', *Giornale storico della letteratura italiana* 149 (1972), pp. 87–105.

[19] Vincenzo Monti, *Epistolario*, edited by Alfonso Bertoldi (Florence, 1928–31), vol. VI, p. 331. Indicatively on Monti, Raffaele Morabito, 'Vincenzo Monti', in N. Borsellino and W. Pedullà (eds),

It was Monti who introduced the promising Corfiot to the world of Greek classical philology. And it was, to be sure, a flourishing world during the first decades of the nineteenth century. Scholars were possessed by the mania of rediscovering ancient authors, Greek and Latin. Hordes of historians, philologists, archaeologists, epigraphists, and Hellenists and Latinists of every persuasion ransacked library shelves and archives in search of lost manuscripts, or translated, re-edited, and wrote commentaries on what was already found. These were the years of the 'unconditional admiration for the Greeks', as a scholar has appropriately remarked, and of the establishment of Hellenism as an artistic and literary trend.[20] Thanks largely to the Prussian archaeologist J. J. Winckelmann, who in his *History of Ancient Art* (1764) had fixed the rules of artistic perfection, exalting classical Greek art and launching the Neoclassical fashion, the imitation of the ancients became an imperative both in art and in literature, 'the only way to be great and, if possible, inimitable'—as Winckelmann himself declared.[21] In addition, the same period witnessed, especially in Germany, the development of classical philology into a methodologically circumscribed, autonomous scientific field. F. A. Wolf's lectures at the University of Halle (1783) are reckoned to be its foundation stone. Besides, the same author's *Prolegomena ad Homerum* (1795) served to recast and reinvigorate the Homeric question, which would dominate European letters for at least the following half-century.[22] These developments were to have a decisive effect on the next two generations of literati, not only in Germany and France, but also in Italy where, over a period of forty years (1785–1825), the *Iliad* and the *Odyssey* were translated more than eight and four times respectively.[23] Monti, although not an expert on classical philology nor a great connoisseur of ancient Greek, decided to venture into this field. With the assistance of Mustoxidi (and a number of other Hellenists), in 1809 he started working on a translation of the *Iliad*, the first volume of which saw the light of day one year later.[24] It did extremely well. *We have four or five versions [of the Iliad] published by Italian scholars of Greek and no one can read them; Monti's version by contrast is read and studied throughout Italy*—a contemporary commentator remarked.[25] An impressive work that outshone

---

*Storia generale della letteratura italiana*, vol. VII: *L'Italia romantica il primo Ottocento* (Milan, 2004), pp. 71–102.

[20]   Giuliana Nuvoli, 'La letteratura dell'età neoclassica', in Borsellino and Pedullà (eds), *Storia generale della letteratura italiana*, p. 54.

[21]   Quoted in Hugh Honour, *Neo-Classicism* (Harmondsworth, 1968), p. 61.

[22]   Honour, *Neo-Classicism*, pp. 62–7; Gianni Gervasoni, *Linee di storia della filologia classica in Italia*, vol. I: *Sino ai filologi settentrionali della prima metà dell'800* (Florence, 1929), p. 78.

[23]   Fortunato Federici, *Degli scrittori greci e delle italiane versioni delle loro opere* (Padua, 1828), pp. 20–8.

[24]   Andrea Mustoxidi, 'Lettera ed osservazioni sull'Iliade, volgarizzata dal Cavaliere Vincenzo Monti', in idem, *Prose varie del Cavaliere Andrea Mustoxidi, con aggiunta di alcuni versi* (Milan, 1821), pp. 173–210. See Giovanni Setti, 'Il Monti traduttore d'Omero', *Atti dell'Accademia Scientifica Veneto–Trentino–Istriana* 3–4 (1906–7), pp. 1–47; Iginio de Luca (ed.), *Osservazioni sulla Iliade del Monti di Ennio Quirino Visconti e Andrea Mustoxidi* (Florence, 1961).

[25]   Pietro Borsieri, *Avventure letterarie di un giorno o consigli di un galantuomo a vari scrittori*, edited by William Spaggiari (Modena, 1986 [1816]), p. 61.

all previous Homeric versions by placing its emphasis on the harmonious adaptation into contemporary poetry rather than on the original, Monti's *Iliad* continues to this day to be seen as a masterpiece of Italian Neoclassical literature and to be included in school curricula.

Monti's Homeric venture thus served to launch Mustoxidi's career in Italian and European Neoclassical studies. He was not slow to make a name for himself in his own right. In 1812, after diligent and scrupulous research in the Laurenziana library of Florence and the Ambrosiana of Milan, he discovered and published an important passage from Isocrates' oration *Antidosis (Peri tis Antidoseos)*.[26] In times of obsessive love and veneration for all ancient manuscripts, this was considered an enormous achievement. The oration was soon translated into Latin and German and Mustoxidi saw his name featured on the pages of international philological journals and on the membership lists of distinguished literary academies all over Europe (including the prestigious Parisian *Académie des Inscriptions et Belles Lettres* and the Prussian Royal Academy).[27] *Among those young Greeks who do honour to their patria through their learning, their zeal and their published works, M. Mustoxidi does indeed occupy a distinguished place. He has rendered his compatriots and all the Hellenists of Europe a very important service, by bringing to light these famous fragments of Isocrates, awaited for so long and with the greatest impatience*—read a contemporary French article.[28] Just as Mustoxidi was being catapulted into fame, so too his correspondence grew. Philologists, archaeologists, librarians, and epigraphists from every corner of Italy and Europe now sought his opinion on matters of Greek scholarship, sent him their works, asked for (or gave) advice, and recommended their students. Evidence of correspondence with luminaries from the philological worlds of Germany (such as August Boeckh, Christian August Brandis, and Barthold Georg Niebuhr), Tuscany (such as Francesco Del Furia, Giovanni Battista Zannoni, and Luigi Lanzi), Venice (such as Ippolito Pindemonte, Francesco Negri, Daniele Francesconi, Jacopo Morelli, Leopoldo Cicognara, Antonio Meneghelli, and Fortunato Federici) and elsewhere shows how Mustoxidi had come to occupy a prominent place within that vast and intercultural network of savants which during the first half of the nineteenth century formed the land of European Neoclassicism.[29]

---

[26] *Isokratous, Logos peri tis Antidoseos etc.* (Milan, 1812). See Pasquale Massimo Pinto, 'La riscoperta dell'*Antidosi* nel XIX secolo', in Maddalena Vallozza (ed.), *Isocrate: per una nuova edizione critica* (Florence, 2017), pp. 203–29.

[27] *Isocratis, Oratio de permutatione, etc.*, translated by Angelo Mai (Milan, 1813); *Iscratous logos peri tes antidoseos vervollständigt herausgegeben von Andreas Mustoxydes historiographen etc.*, translated by Gian Gaspare Orelli (Zurich, 1814).

[28] Constantin Nicolopoulo, 'Littérature grecque: Discours d'Isocrates sur l'Echange, rétabli dans son ancien état etc.', *The Classical Journal* 8 (Sept.–Dec. 1813), p. 124.

[29] Michel Espagne, *Les Transferts culturels franco-allemands* (Paris, 1999), p. 22. Correspondence with Boeckh: HMC: MP, X/5/157–8; Brandis: HMC: MP, X/8/365; Niebuhr: HMC: MP, X/5/155–6; Del Furia: HMC: MP, X/6/273–4 and BCNF: pal. carte del Furia, 82, 221, 1–8; Zannoni: HMC: MP, X/2/351–4; Lanzi: HMC: MP, X/14; Pindemonte: HMC: MP, X/8/344–8 and BM: Mustoxidi Papers, 23, 30, 37, 41, 45, 51, 57–9, 84; Negri: Sp. Veludo, *Lettere di Andrea Mustoxidi e di Ippolito Pindemonte a Francesco Negri* (Venice, 1864), pp. 2–7; Francesconi: HMC: MP, X/4/148–9 and

Mustoxidi's reputation as an accomplished Hellenist was further consolidated in the following years, when he started composing his magnum opus, the translation into Italian of the *Histories* (or *Nine Muses*) of Herodotus.[30] It was the first time since 1733 that the work of Herodotus had come to be published in Italian, and this publication did much to awaken Italian interest in a field, Herodotean studies, that had become highly fashionable in other parts of Europe and particularly in France.[31] Mustoxidi's Herodotus was the first of a series of ancient Greek historians translated for an Italian readership, the so-called *Collana degli antichi storici greci volgarizzati*, which the Corfiot directed at the Milanese publishing house of Sonzogno during the 1820s. A hugely ambitious venture, involving the collaboration of a throng of Italian, Greco-Venetian, and Dalmato-Venetian translators, the *Collana* included among others the works of Diodorus of Sicily, Xenophon of Athens, and Dionysius of Halicarnassus.[32] It was an operation intended to play a signal part in the general revival of ancient Greek literature.

Mustoxidi's involvement with Neoclassical letters was tinged with Greek patriotism. Indeed, he felt that he and his brethren were united in a campaign to recover modern Greece's ancient cultural heritage. In this he followed in Koraes's footsteps. The Paris-based intellectual had, by that date, edited and published more than thirty ancient texts. His series *Hellenic Library* (1805–26) and *Parerga* (1809–27) included texts by Isocrates, Plutarch, Strabo, Aristotle, Xenophon, Plato, and others, prefaced by long introductions, where Koraes disclosed his linguistic, pedagogic, and political theories on the 'regeneration' of Greece. In this project, he found a devoted follower in Mustoxidi. *Having chiefly aimed at promoting our nation, towards which now both our wishes and our hopes are directed*—the Corfiot wrote to Koraes in dedicating to him his Isocrates—*I now offer you this volume, . . . as a portion of that inheritance which in calamitous times was stolen from Greece by foreigners who were wealthy and who loved letters, and which we its sons with all solicitude should study to recover.*[33] Whether addressing a Greek, an Italian, or a French public, in the land of Neoclassical studies Greek diaspora intellectuals found a space where they could combine philology with their love for the Greek nation.

---

BTM: Fondo Acquisti e Doni, cart. 33, fasc. 23, 1–5; Morelli: HMC: MP, X/11/519–20; Cicognara: HMC: MP, XIV/3/22, 128–30; Meneghelli: HMC: MP, X/3/135; Federici: HMC: MP, X/6/279–80.

[30] *Le Nove Muse di Erodoto Alicarnasseo tradotte ed illustrate da Andrea Mustoxidi Corcirese*, vol. I (Milan, 1820) [the next four volumes were published in 1822, 1832, 1842, and, posthumously, in 1863].

[31] Amédée Duquesnel, *Histoire des lettres: cours de littératures comparées* (Paris, 1845), vol. II, p. 186.

[32] Gio. Battista Sonzogno, *Discorso intorno alla Collana degli antichi storici greci volgarizzati* (Milan, 1820); *Istoria di Diodoro, volgarizzata da B. Compagnoni* (1820–2); *Tutte le opere di Senofonte, tradotte dal greco da Marcantonio Gandini* (1821); *Le Antichità romane volgarizzate dall'ab. Marco Mastrofini* (1824); *Dionigi d'Alicarnasso, Commentarii intorno agli antichi oratori, tradotti da Spiridione Vlandi* (1827); *Dionigi d'Alicarnasso, Giudicio di alcuni tra gli antichi scrittori, tradotto da Niccolò Tommaseo* (1827); *Dionigi d'Alicarnasso, Arte rettorica, tradotta da Niccolò Tomaseo* (1827).

[33] Mustoxidi, *Prose varie*, pp. 170–1.

## IN THE LAND OF EUROPEAN PHILHELLENISM

Mustoxidi inhabited not only the land of erudite Hellenism, but also that of political philhellenism, the movement sustaining the cause of the Greek revolution. And just like the former, this was a land extending throughout the European continent. In France, he maintained the closest connection with some of the leading lights of the liberal and philhellenic world. To begin with, he was on intimate terms with the eminent historian, philologist, and publicist Claude Fauriel (1772–1844). When, in 1823, Fauriel turned his attention to Greek folk poetry, compiling the first collection of its kind and an anthology that would become a major symbol of the liberation struggle of the Greek people, it was Mustoxidi who would prove to be his most trusted collaborator.[34] *Mustoxidi, who knows everyone here and every nation*—he wrote while travelling with the Corfiot in Venice and Trieste in search of songs from the mouths of those Greek refugees who had been washed up on Italian shores during the revolution—*has been so kind as to present me to everyone; and I have let myself be led at any rate amidst the Greeks, and to their feasts, in the hope of finding the songs and the information for which I came.*[35] Through Fauriel, Mustoxidi gained access to the circle of the so-called *Idéologues*. Considered to be the last generation of Enlightenment thinkers, this was a group of French moderate liberal intellectuals who were characterized by their aversion to all kinds of political radicalism that precluded reason and reflection. Persecuted during the Terror and later condemned by Napoleon (to whose ascendancy they had initially contributed), the *Idéologues* had found their moment of glory during the years of the Directory.[36] Mustoxidi was connected with several members of this circle. The Abbot Henri Grégoire (1750–1831), already mentioned in this book for his memoir on the union of the Catholic and Orthodox Churches, as well as for his appeal to the people of Haiti to come to the assistance of the Greeks, was one of their number. Noted for his campaigns for the emancipation of slaves, the Jews, and all oppressed peoples, Grégoire was also a fervent philhellene. Much of his knowledge and views on Greece was based on information that he had gleaned from Mustoxidi and a number of other diaspora Greeks.[37] The famous philosopher Victor Cousin (1792–1867) was yet another of Mustoxidi's French contacts. Cousin had met him during his researches in the Italian libraries for manuscripts of the Neoplatonic philosopher Proclus, but what really brought them together was their common involvement in Piedmontese liberal and philhellenic circles. A convinced philhellene

---

[34] Claude Fauriel, *Chants populaires de la Grèce moderne* (Paris, 1824–5), 2 vols.
[35] Irene Botta (ed.), *Carteggio Alessandro Manzoni–Claude Fauriel* (Milan, 2000), p. 446. On the correspondence between Mustoxidi and Fauriel see Angelo De Gubernatis, *Manzoni ed il Fauriel, studiati nel loro carteggio inedito* (Rome, 1880), pp. 81–2 and Alexis Politis, *I anakalypsi ton ellinikon dimotikon tragoudion* (The discovery of Greek folk songs) (Athens, 1999), pp. 409–10.
[36] Georges Gusdorf, *La Conscience révolutionnaire: les idéologues* (Paris, 1978); Sergio Moravia, *Il pensiero degli idéologues: scienza e filosofia in Francia (1780–1815)* (Florence, 1974); J. Gaulmier, 'Gli idéologues', in Pierre Abraham and Roland Desné (eds), *Storia della letteratura francese* (Milan, 1985), vol. II, pp. 74–80.
[37] Michele Lascaris, 'L'Abbé Grégoire et la Grèce', *La Révolution française* 3 (1932), pp. 1–16. Correspondence with Mustoxidi in HMC: MP, X/9/413–14, VII/76.

himself, Cousin was the intimate friend of Santorre di Santarosa, the Piedmontese revolutionary who was martyred during the Greek War of Independence, becoming then the emblem of Italian philhellenism.[38] Through Cousin, Mustoxidi entered into contact with another *Idéologue*, the publisher Amaury Duval, who would offer in 1820 to publish the Corfiot's contribution to the debate on the affair of Parga, the *Exposé des faits qui ont précédé et suivi la cession de Parga*.[39]

In neighbouring Switzerland, Mustoxidi became closely involved with the so-called 'Coppet circle'. At her castle at Coppet, near Geneva, the celebrated author Anne Louise Germaine Necker, better known as Madame de Staël (1766–1817), gathered together during the years of her exile by Napoleon the most liberal spirits of Europe.[40] Mustoxidi, who visited Coppet in 1809 and stayed in touch with members of the circle ever afterwards, met there—as mentioned earlier—Benjamin Constant, Madame de Staël's partner and an author and political theorist of great renown. He also met the famous Genevan economist and historian Jean Charles Léonard de Sismondi (1773–1842), who had been planning to publish a collection of Greek folk songs much earlier than Fauriel, in the mid-1810s, and had asked Mustoxidi to assist him.[41] In the years that followed, the Coppet circle was actively engaged in the philhellenic movement. The founding meeting of Geneva's philhellenic committee took place at Coppet and was organized by Madame de Staël's son Auguste (1825). It was followed by Constant's pamphlet *Appel aux nations chrétiennes en faveur des Grecs*, published that same year, and by Sismondi's articles on the question of Greece and the Russo-Ottoman conflict, published between 1826 and 1829.[42] Geneva's philhellenic committee, inspired among other things by the fact of Kapodistrias having settled in the city in 1822, was one of the most active in Europe. Aiming to help the revolution by hospitalizing wounded or ailing Greek refugees and exporting arms to Greece, it employed a number of means—from the publication of pamphlets and appeals for subscriptions to the organization of concerts and art exhibitions and bazaars—in order to raise funds. Moreover, an intense collaboration with the committees of Zurich, Paris, and Marseilles and a close relationship with the centres of philhellenic activity in Tuscany, namely Vieusseux in Florence and Bishop Ignatius in Pisa, ensured the safer

---

[38] Salvo Mastellone, *Victor Cousin e il Risorgimento italiano (dalle carte dell'archivio Cousin)* (Florence, 1955), pp. 100–1; idem, 'Santorre di Santarosa combattente per la Grecia', in *Indipendenza e unità nazionale in Italia e in Grecia* (Florence, 1987), pp. 37–8. Letter by Mustoxidi to Cousin in BVC-BS: 240, 3688 (reproduced in Polychronis K. Enepekides, 'Documents et nouvelles lettres inédites d'Adamantios Coray tirées des bibliothèques et archives européennes', *Jahrbuch der Österreichischen Byzantinischen Gesellschaft* 5 (1956), pp. 121–2).

[39] [Andrea Mustoxidi], *Exposé des faits qui ont précédé et suivi la cession de Parga* (Paris, 1820).

[40] S. Balayé, 'Madame de Staël' and 'Il gruppo di Coppet', in Abraham and Desné (eds), *Storia della letteratura francese*, pp. 132–5 and 138–43 respectively.

[41] G. C. L. Sismondi, *Epistolario*, edited by Carlo Pellegrini (Florence, 1933), vol. I, pp. 40–1, 211.

[42] Benjamin Constant, *Appel aux nations chrétiennes en faveur des Grecs* (Paris, 1825); L. De Sismondi, 'On the Extermination of the Greeks', *New Monthly Magazine* (1 July 1826), pp. 90–6; idem, 'Conséquences que l'on peut désirer ou craindre pour la civilisation, de la guerre des Russes dans le Levant' [1829] and 'De la Grèce au commencement de l'anneé 1827'[1827], in idem, *Opuscoli politici*, edited by Umberto Marcelli (Bologna, 1954), pp. 101–23 and 245–58 respectively.

passage of refugees, volunteers, and arms.[43] Mustoxidi, who travelled frequently in
Switzerland (especially after Kapodistrias had settled there), was an integral part of
this philhellenic network connecting Geneva, Paris, and Florence.

In Tuscany, apart from Ignatius, with whom he was united by the venture of the
Septinsular Republic, the Corfiot maintained, as we have seen, the closest ties
with Vieusseux and the circle of the *Antologia*.[44] Mustoxidi was on intimate terms
with what were perhaps the strongest philhellenic voices on the journal, namely,
Giovan Battista Niccolini (1782–1861) and Niccolò Tommaseo (1802–74). The
former, a writer of patriotic tragedies that became immensely popular during the
Risorgimento, was concerned also with Greek politics and aroused Mustoxidi's
enthusiasm when he translated into Italian and published in the pages of the
*Antologia* the most patriotic of all Greek poems, the *Thourios* (battle-hymn) of
Rigas Velestinlis.[45] *It is sweet indeed to be able to combine and merge in a single point
several lofty sentiments, and it is sweet for me now to clasp by this means three names:
Greece, Rigas, Niccolini*—the Corfiot wrote to him ecstatically.[46] Tommaseo, for his
part, maintained with Mustoxidi, and with the Greek world in general, a strong
and multi-faceted relationship, which I will examine separately in Chapter 11 of
this book. Let me say here, though, that it was in fact he who published—years
after its original composition in 1821—Mustoxidi's Italian equivalent to Solomos's
*Hymn to Liberty*, a lengthy patriotic poem inspired by the revolution and entitled
*Inno dei Greci*, which had remained hitherto unknown.[47] For the Florentine journal
itself, the *Antologia*, Mustoxidi produced a number of articles, less overtly political
and more erudite than he would in his heart of hearts have wished, but always permeated by a philhellenic tone.[48] *I would prefer to send you something political and
moral, instead of these learned trifles*—he wrote to Vieusseux in 1826. *If only they
would let you print certain reflections on Greece…*[49] The most openly political work
he published during the years of the revolution was an account of the events that
took place in the Greek seas during its first two years, the *Précis des opérations de la
flotte grecque durant la révolution de 1821 et 1822*.[50]

[43] BpuG: MS suppl. 491 and MS suppl. 1891; Michelle Bouvier-Bron, *Jean-Gabriel Eynard
(1775–1863) et le philhellénisme genevois* (Geneva, 1963); Olivier Reverdin, 'La Toscane, les philhellènes genevois et l'envoi des secours à la Grèce', in *Le relazioni del pensiero italiano risorgimentale con
i centri del movimento liberale di Ginevra e Coppet* (Rome, 1979), pp. 63–74.

[44] Andrea Scardicchio, ' "Le vostre lettere mi riescono sempre care…": spigolature del carteggio
inedito Mustoxidi–Vieusseux (con appendice di quattro lettere)', *Studi e problemi di critica testuale*
93 (Oct. 2016), pp. 133–65.

[45] Included in Luigi Ciampolini, 'Canti popolari della Grecia moderna, raccolti e pubblicati con
una traduzione francese, schiarimenti e note da C. Fauriel', *Antologia* 26 (1827), pp. 111–13.

[46] BCNF: cart. vari, 66, 38. See Atto Vannucci, *Ricordi della vita e delle opere di G.-B. Niccolini*
(Florence, 1866), esp. vol. I, pp. 400–3, 405–7, 410–12 and vol. II, pp. 66–7.

[47] Quoted in Lascaris, 'Niccolò Tommaseo ed Andrea Mustoxidi', pp. 17–18.

[48] Andrea Mustoxidi, 'Alcune considerazioni sulla presente lingua de'Greci', *Antologia* 17 (Mar.
1825), pp. 44–73; idem, 'Notizia intorno ad un volgarizzamento inedito delle istorie di Giovanni
Ducas', *Antologia* 19 (Aug. 1825), pp. 50–7; idem, 'Sopra i due leoni posti in sull'entrata dell'Arsenale
di Venezia e sopra altri monumenti di questo genere', *Antologia* 47 (Sept. 1832), pp. 78–83.

[49] BCNF: cart. Vieuss., 73, 90.

[50] Anonymous [A. Mustoxidi], *Précis des opérations de la flotte grecque durant la révolution de 1821
et 1822 écrit par un Grec etc.* (Paris, 1822).

Among the articles that Mustoxidi wrote for the *Antologia* there was one in particular that merits closer scrutiny. This was a study on a theme dear to the *Antologia* circle, as well as to the philhellenic world in general, the issue of the modern Greek language. Following the line of Kodrikas and Kalvos (as described in Chapter 2), Mustoxidi argued that the modern Greek language was to be found in the written texts of authors, especially the Orthodox clerics and the Phanariots, who knew the ancient texts and were thus able to isolate and identify those elements of Ancient Greek that had survived in the currently spoken Greek idioms. By selecting these 'genuine' elements and by unearthing others, these authors were creating, according to Mustoxidi, a linguistic canon, which was purified, organized and understood by one and all.[51] By so arguing, Mustoxidi built on a hypothesis currently advanced also by a number of Italian intellectuals in respect to the properties of the Italian language. Notably, he elaborated upon the argument proposed by his teacher Monti and the latter's collaborator and son-in-law, Giulio Perticari, by which the Italian national language was to be found, not in the Tuscan dialect alone or in the language of the *Trecento*, but in the quintessence of all the Italian spoken idioms of the day, a thing imprinted in the works of Italian authors. The '*volgare illustre*' (illustrious vulgar tongue), which these philologists were advocating, was a sort of purified and standardized Italian which would draw from all existing dialects but elevate itself above them all; a sort of language that existed everywhere and nowhere.[52] What is interesting here is the fact that, in order to advance their argument, the Italian intellectuals built, in their turn, on Greek sources. Pieri— who also wrote a treatise on the Italian linguistic question heavily reliant on Monti's ideas—offers valuable testimony in this regard: *I spent the evening in Monti's house*—he wrote in his diary in September 1821—*where Mr Mustoxidi read some chapters, translating them into Italian, from a Greek work by one Kodrika on the Greek language, and its circumstances, and Perticari proceeded to take note of various things regarding the Greek dialects and the common Greek language, [which is] divided, according to Kodrika, into noble and plebeian… Perticari will harvest that so as to use it in his turn against the Tuscans.*[53] The activities of these transcultural intellectuals offer, therefore, a demonstration of just how transnational even the most national of historical issues, like the arenas of the nineteenth-century linguistic battles, really were.

But it was in Venice and in the heart of the city's Greek community that Mustoxidi really discovered his love for the Greek nation and was able to let his political activism flourish. From 1821—when his name appeared for the first time among the inscribed members of the community—onwards, the Corfiot

---

[51]  Mustoxidi, 'Alcune considerazioni sulla presente lingua de' Greci', esp. pp. 68–9.

[52]  Vincenzo Monti, *Proposta di alcune correzioni ed aggiunte al vocabulario della Crusca* (Milan, 1817–26), 7 vols; Giulio Perticari, *Degli scrittori del Trecento e dei loro imitatori* (Milan, 1828). See: Luca Serianni, *Storia della lingua italiana: il primo Ottocento* (Bologna, 1989), pp. 38–55.

[53]  BRF: Memorie di Mario Pieri, vol. III [Ricc. 3557], 274 and Mario Pieri, *Della vita di Mario Pieri corcirese scritta da lui medesimo* (Florence, 1850), vol. I, p. 471. Mario Pieri, 'La lingua e la letteratura italiana. Dialogo: Gasparo Gozzi, Vincenzo Monti, Antonio Cesari', in idem, *Opere* (Florence, 1852), vol. III, pp. 5–99.

strengthened his ties with the city.[54] This is not surprising. Among the people who populated the Greek colony of Venice, mostly Ionian migrants, Mustoxidi could find a home in which he might share his anxiety and enthusiasm during the years of the revolution. *I'll leave you now in order to dress and run to Divine Providence, which is what my Greeks' Café is called*—he wrote to a friend in July 1821. *Everyone flocks there, the leading lights, merchants, artists, sailors, with moustaches and without, with red berets or with caps, and everyone with tears in their eyes as caught between hopes and fears we devote our affections and our discourses to our unhappy but noble Patria.*[55] As his biographer, Papadopoulo Vretto, remarked, *The cry of independence finally echoed in Greece. Mustoxidi, having struggled with his own duties and with patriotic sentiment, thought good to retire to Venice in the midst of the little Greek community settled there for many centuries. Tormented by the desire to be useful to his fellow citizens he devoted himself during his stay in Venice to presiding over and reforming that community's schools, and he particularly concerned himself with the fate of the unhappy refugees.*[56] So deep did Mustoxidi's philhellenism run that in 1826 he took one of these 'unhappy refugees' as his wife. Her name was Pezouna Charta (later Italianized into 'Colomba Carta' and later again, when Mustoxidi went to Greece, Hellenized into 'Peristera Charta') and she was the daughter of a Cypriot chieftain who had been executed by the Ottomans when the island rose up in 1821. *I am marrying a girl who with her mother, grandmother, a brother [who is my] pupil and six other sisters have been saved here from the Turkish tyranny*—Mustoxidi wrote. *She is noble because her father's blood was spilt for the salvation of the patria, and my marriage is thus bound up with the events surrounding the Greek Palingenesis.*[57] His wife aside, Mustoxidi was particularly active in offering relief to the Greek refugees who, since the commencement of the revolution, were arriving in great numbers on the shores of the western Adriatic. As he confessed to a friend, *most of my hours are spent with my fellow citizens…A large number of these poor wretches, who have escaped fires and massacres, women, children and the elderly derive comfort from frequenting my rooms.*[58] And to yet another, *I am not rich, and in this period there is in the ports of Italy a people of Greek widows and orphans, who have a sacred right to be accorded preference. And you know, dear friend, that I contribute with monthly sums to their upkeep.*[59] Because of these activities, and because of his close relationship with Kapodistrias, Mustoxidi gradually became very influential within the Greek community of Venice, and especially within the milieu of the refugees.

---

[54] Artemis Xanthopoulou-Kyriakou, *I elliniki koinotita tis Benetias (1797–1866): dioikitiki kai oikonomiki organosi, ekpaideftiki kai politiki drastiriotita* (The Greek community of Venice (1797–1866): administrative and economic organization, educational and political activity) (Thessaloniki, 1978), p. 252.

[55] Anastasia Stouraiti, *La Grecia nelle raccolte della Fondazione Querini Stampalia* (Venice, 2000), p. 273.

[56] Andrea Papadopulo-Vrettò, *Biografia del cavaliere Andrea Mustoxidi scritta e pubblicata in Venezia nell'anno 1836 da Emilio Tipaldo, corretta dallo stesso Mustoxidi in Corfù nell'anno 1838. Annotata e continuata sino alla sua morte da Andrea Papadopulo Vreto Leucadio* etc. (Athens, 1860), pp. 4–5.

[57] Letter to Federico Sclopis, 2 Nov. 1825. HMC: MP, 170.

[58] Letter to Beatrice Trivulzio. Quoted in Alessandro Giulini, 'Spigolature del carteggio inedito di Andrea Mustoxidi', *Giornale storico della letteratura italiana* 89 (1927), p. 131.

[59] Letter to Cristoforo Feretti, Dec, 1824. BM: Mustoxidi Papers, 151.

An appeal addressed to Kapodistrias soon after his election as governor, drafted by the Corfiot and signed by the Cypriot refugees of Venice, by which they asked for a portion of the redistributed lands in the Greek state as a compensation for their travails, is a case in point.[60]

To be sure, behind Mustoxidi's personal initiatives for the relief of the refugees was, as mentioned in Chapter 7, his involvement with the *Philomousos Etairia*. By following Kapodistrias's orders and in collaboration with the other representatives of the *Philomousos* in Italy (Ignatius, Mocenigo, and Naranzi), Mustoxidi was the person chiefly responsible for implementing a coordinated programme for the hospitalization and education of all the orphan and refugee children from Greece adrift in the cities of Venice, Trieste, and Ancona. Between 1827 and 1829, he counted these children, enrolled them in the pre-existing Greek schools, and helped provide the latter with additional teachers and books.[61] *Where it is a matter of extending the elementary education of a few innocent orphans who have been settled here for many years now…*—he wrote apologetically to the director of the Department of Censorship in the Veneto, who kept him under surveillance, fearing the possibility of agitation in favour of the Greeks in the area—*it would be a grave and painful matter to me if it were generally to be supposed that virtually secret societies might be attempted here, and that we were considering the possibility of founding unbeknownst to the Government itself either Schools or Colleges for the children of the insurgents.*[62] As a matter of fact, since the mid-1810s, the Austrian authorities had been increasingly concerned about Russian infiltration in the Venetian lands. Indeed, Mustoxidi, under suspicion as he was on account of his close relationship with Kapodistrias, was named among *the secret agents that the Russian court maintains in Italy.*[63] A police report of 30 September 1817 called attention to this *individual for his antipolitical principles, for his liberal maxims, and for his suspicious relationships with notable persons [who are] almost all affected by the old system or interests of Russia.*[64] The Austrian and French police did not hesitate to keep him under strict surveillance during the whole of the following decade. As late as November 1827, a report from the Préfecture de Police in Paris noted that *The relations of origin, opinion and political situation aligning somewhat closely Count Mustoxidi and Count Kapodistria [are such] as to lead one to suppose that the former is destined to play a [significant] role in the affairs of Greece.*[65] In this case, the policemen were right.

---

[60] Konstantina Zanou, 'Profughi ciprioti a Venezia e Trieste dopo il 1821 (nuovi elementi provenienti dalle Carte Mustoxidi a Corfù)', in Mattia de Poli (ed.), *Giornate per Cipro* (Padua, 2007), pp. 39–62.

[61] Georgios P. Papageorgiou, 'Symboli stin istoria tis ellinikis paroikias tis Ankonas kata ton 19o aiona' (On the history of the Greek community of Ancona during the 19th century), *Dodoni* 4 (1975), esp. pp. 302–24, 331, 340; Xanthopoulou-Kyriakou, *I elliniki koinotita tis Benetias*, pp. 140–2.

[62] Letter to Francesco Brambilla, 14/26 Dec. 1827. HMC: MP, VII/43. See also Xanthopoulou-Kyriakou, *I elliniki koinotita tis Benetias*, p. 218.

[63] Daniele Manin, *Carte segrete e atti ufficiali della polizia austriaca in Italia dal 4 giugno 1814 al 22 marzo 1848* (Capolago, 1851–2), vol. I, p. 178.

[64] Manin, *Carte segrete*, p. 177.

[65] Polychronis K. Enepekidis, *Rigas—Ypsilantis—Kapodistrias* (Athens, 1965), p. 250.

## FROM A RUSSIAN DIPLOMAT TO A GREEK STATESMAN
## TO AN IONIAN POLITICIAN

Mustoxidi was not really a Russian secret agent. He was, however, at least nominally, a Russian diplomat. From 1821 to 1826 he worked as an attaché in the Russian embassy to Piedmont, which was run by his friend Mocenigo. He was hired as a historical researcher rather than as a political man and so his role was somewhat 'decorative'. But when the revolt erupted in Piedmont in 1821, the Corfiot philologist suddenly found himself, through a series of coincidences, at the heart of events. *I am the lynchpin around which the entire Holy Alliance so to speak turns*, he wrote to a friend without undue modesty during those days.[66] What transpired was that during the revolution which shook Turin in March 1821, forcing the King Vittorio Emanuele I to abdicate and Carlo Alberto the Prince of Carignano, his temporary replacement, to accept the constitution, Mustoxidi conceived the idea—and convinced Mocenigo of its merits—of seeking Russian mediation. The Russians, in other words, would bridge the gap between the King and the revolutionaries, ultimately defusing the situation. It appears that the idea came to him in the course of a conversation with Carlo Alberto.[67] It should be noted that Mustoxidi was intimately involved with the circle of Piedmontese liberal intellectuals (people like Federico Sclopis, Giuseppe Grassi, Costanzo Gazzera, Carlo Boucheron, Vittorio Peyron, Lodovico Sauli, and Luigi Cibrario), who not only had befriended the Prince of Carignano, but also saw in him the man who might finally reconcile the tradition of dynastic loyalty with constitutionalist principles.[68] As the revolution advanced, however, and Carlo Alberto lost his nerve and fled, their enthusiasm was tested—*the conviction of the revolutionaries that they had at last found the king to be in agreement with them was a great illusion, and the outcome was deplorable*, recalled one of their number years later.[69] The situation became yet more critical when the new King, Carlo Felice, from his refuge in Modena, called upon the powers of the Holy Alliance to intervene militarily, while at the same time the leader of the revolutionaries, Santarosa, became Minister of War and began to wield well-nigh dictatorial powers. It was at that moment of increased intransigence on both sides that the Russian ambassador, at Mustoxidi's prompting, and purportedly ensuring Kapodistrias's approval, decided to intervene. The terms proposed by the Russian diplomats were as follows: if the revolutionaries agreed to lay down

---

[66] In Giulini, 'Spigolature del carteggio inedito di Andrea Mustoxidi', p. 130.

[67] Narciso Nada, 'Metternich, la diplomazia russa, Francesco IV di Modena ed i moti piemontesi del 1821', *Annuario dell'Istituto Storico Italiano per l'età Moderna e Contemporanea* 19 (1967), pp. 29–31.

[68] Correspondence between Mustoxidi and Sclopis: HMC: MP, X/2/107–112 and BAST: Fondo Sclopis, cart. 27698–722; Grassi: HMC: MP, X/2/42–6 and BAST: Fondo Grassi, cart. 17709–18; Gazzera: HMC: MP, X/8/357–8 and BAST: Fondo Gazzera, cart. 23509–17; Boucheron: HMC: MP, X/4/150; Peyron: HMC: MP, X/6/284; Sauli: HMC: MP, X/3/131.

[69] Luigi Cibrario, *Notizie sulla vita di Carlo Alberto, iniziatore e martire della indipendenza italiana* (Turin, 1861), p. 31. See Giuseppe Talamo, 'Società segrete e gruppi politici liberali e democratici sino al 1848', in Umberto Levra (ed.), *Storia di Torino*, vol. VI: *La città nel Risorgimento (1798–1864)* (Turin, 2000), p. 471.

their arms, the Russians would seek to pre-empt any foreign military intervention, indeed, would act to guarantee that no such thing occurred, and Carlo Felice, on reassuming his throne, would declare a general amnesty and accept the constitution. *Among the different European powers, the only one that, in these circumstances, showed us some sign of sympathy and protection was Russia*—wrote Sauli, the Minister for Foreign Affairs of the revolutionary government and Mustoxidi's personal friend. *Count Mocenigo, one of its ministers, gave me a note wherein we were advised to desist and to return to the old obedience, and it extended the explicit promise of the Emperor Alexander that he would use effectively his good offices in regard to the king Carlo Felice, in order to induce him to grant the great majority of the rebels a general amnesty, excluding only the ringleaders and their lieutenants, who might be allowed to make their way to a foreign country, . . . and in addition to induce him to give his kingdom fairly broad institutions, in accordance with the spirit of the times.*[70] Nonetheless, the revolutionaries were not unanimous in this regard: unlike the relatively moderate Turin committee, the Alessandria committee, where the actual nucleus of the insurrection was, rejected the Russian proposals.[71] As a result, in the battle that ensued, the revolutionary army sustained a crushing defeat at the hands of the combined royal and Austrian forces. News of this disaster provoked the immediate collapse of the revolutionary government and the total dissolution of the revolutionary forces in Turin and Alessandria. As anticipated, the restoration of Carlo Felice to the throne as an absolute monarch was followed by a period of severe repression and a round of arrests: at least seventy people were condemned to death and dozens of others were imprisoned, while yet others managed to escape abroad. Mustoxidi, who was the person chiefly responsible for conducting the negotiations, was accused by several revolutionaries of having acted contrary to their interests by sowing confusion in, and thereby undermining, the revolutionary front, and by giving the Austrians time to make preparations to intervene. *I became the principal target of the hatred of the factional; anonymous letters were sent to me containing threats against my life; proclamations, pamphlets attacking me were printed*—he complained in a letter to the Tsar.[72] *They say that Mustoxidi, when he was working for Russia, betrayed the revolution of the Piedmontese and his actions led to rivers of blood being spilt*—an Ionian radical democrat, Mustoxidi's political opponent, recalled years later.[73] The opinion of the Piedmontese moderate liberal circles, nevertheless, was quite different. *We all remember*—wrote Sclopis in a letter to Mustoxidi as late as 1853—*how in the most difficult of times you endeavoured with intelligent and fond solicitude to render the destiny of Piedmont less harsh and to assist in the just advance of liberal ideas.*[74] Then as now, the truth is a matter of ideological stance and political

---

[70] Lodovico Sauli D'Igliano, *Reminiscenze della propria vita*, edited by Giuseppe Ottolenghi (Rome and Milan, 1908–9), vol. I, pp. 480–1.

[71] Luigi Carlo Farini, *Storia d'Italia, dall'anno 1814 sino a' giorni nostri* (Turin, 1859), vol. II, pp. 331–2.

[72] HMC: MP, VII/151.

[73] Georgios Typaldos-Iakobatos, *Istoria tis Ioniou Akadimias* (History of the Ionian Academy), edited by Sp. Asdrachas (Athens, 1982), p. 96.

[74] HMC: MP, X/2/108.

judgement. Be that as it may, the case of these Ionian individuals, who came to play a central role in a revolution in Italy acting on behalf of Russia, shows just how interconnected and transnational the political history of this period proved to be.

While the above events were unfolding in Piedmont, the tocsin of revolution sounded also on the opposite shore of the Adriatic. Greece was entering into a war against the Ottoman Empire, which would last for more than a decade, rewarding it eventually with its own free state. And this state would have at its head Mustoxidi's best friend. In 1828, one year after Kapodistrias had been elected governor, the Corfiot philologist-cum-Russian diplomat was summoned to assume real political duties in a country which he considered his patria, but which he barely knew outside of his Neoclassical imagination and his philhellenic books. 'Patria', indeed, was not such a straightforward concept for Mustoxidi as it may perhaps be for a modern reader. *Before being an islander, or Corfiot, I am Greek, and it is there that I find the Patria, when united with my ancestors I live with them... and be the language that I use either Chaldean, or Italian, or Greek, that does not have any bearing whatsoever in patriotic questions. Where two or three of you are, Jesus Christ said to his disciples, I shall be with you, and that is what the Patria tells me and cries out just as soon as I join with two or three of my fellow citizens no matter what climate I find myself in. And when I am alone I am nevertheless free and Greek.* These were his words to Kapodistrias as early as 1820.[75] But during the first days of the revolution, and while watching it from the Venetian shores, Mustoxidi felt otherwise. *But I am melancholic... [about] a patria of whose generous efforts I am an idle onlooker. [It is my] fear that these efforts may not be crowned with success*—he confessed to a friend.[76] And to yet another: *I cannot say that I have a patria of my own, and yet its name is so very glorious. I wander around like a leaf separated from its branch... But when I see my oppressed brothers, and I myself like a solitary plant, whose fruits, whose shadow falls upon a desert, then I lower my head on to my chest, and I am dumb.*[77]

His appointment by Kapodistrias as the Ephor of schools and other cultural institutions in the newly founded Greek state thus offered Mustoxidi a rare opportunity to set out in discovery of his own patria. And this is precisely what he did, losing no time in embarking on a boat and touring the Aegean. *I have arrived here after a month-long voyage on a Greek cutter with my family,* he wrote from the island of Aegina in 1830. *I have visited Megara, Eleusis, Salamis, Sounion, the islets of Patroculus and Helena, Andros, Kos, Tinos, Mycenae, Delos, Syros. Everywhere I visited impressive remains and admired Hellenic taste and art; I have gathered in a good harvest of antiquities for the Museum; I compared the narrative accounts of the ancients with the places described by them; and I would be amply justified in writing an account of my travels if I were not short of time.*[78] But aside from his personal *Grand Tour*— broadly based on the travel imagination of the period—Mustoxidi also had some real political responsibilities. *All of a sudden here I am director of the Orphanage,*

[75] HMC: MP, VII/162.
[76] Gaspare Gozzi, *Lettere d'illustri italiani ad Antonio Papadopoli* (Venice, 1886), p. 283.
[77] Letter to Beatrice Trivulzio. HMC: MP, III/1/23.
[78] Letter to Antonio Papadopoli. BM: Mustoxidi Papers, 259.

*which consists of almost six hundred souls, every single one of them needing the greatest vigilance. Here I am a member of two Commissions, one for setting up the Central School and the other for elementary education; here I am inspector of the two printing houses, secret editor of the French Newspaper [Le Courrier de la Grèce], [and] ephor of the National Museum,* he wrote to a friend in 1829, listing his multifarious duties.[79] Everything in the country's cultural and educational sector had to be built up from scratch. And Mustoxidi was the governor's right hand man so far as the design and implementation of state educational policy were concerned. Their educational programme drew both on the ancient Greek heritage and on the principles of a religiously grounded Enlightenment (as expounded in Part II of this book). Regarding particularly the latter, they were largely based on a proposal submitted by Stourdza to Kapodistrias in 1827, entitled 'Plan for the national rearing [of our youth] and public education in Greece', by which the Phanariot intellectual defined *Piety which is the source of every moral happiness* as the principal aim of the new state.[80] Likewise, Mustoxidi was convinced that religious education would liberate society from obscurantism and ignorance. *But in a country where one is ignorant of everything*—he wrote to Kapodistrias in 1829—*where corruption and unbelief foster superstition and barbarism, should one not explain to men the morality of the Gospel, the precepts of our Lord, the liturgy or the services that we attend every day in Church?*[81] The educational and cultural institutions which were created under his supervision—the National Orphanage, the Central School in Aegina (which provided higher education, especially for teachers), the National Library, the National Museum, and the National Printing Press (responsible mainly for school books and state newspapers)—were supposed to function as laboratories for the formation not only of a specific class of Greek functionaries who would staff the state institutions, but also of a new sense of citizenship and of a homogenizing Greek and Orthodox national consciousness.[82]

It was easier in theory than in practice. The once contemplative and solitary intellectual had to deal now with distressed, disaffected, and disobedient students, with hostile and ignorant colleagues, with a lack of funds, with complaints, incomprehension, and conflict. The most difficult thing to handle, though, was hostility from the opposition. Mustoxidi was indeed soon to come under attack from the anti-Kapodistrian camp, which was increasingly influential throughout the country. He was unfairly accused—by a hostile press and, what hurt him more, by Koraes himself and by his circle in Paris—of not doing enough by way of teaching the ancients and of censoring the liberal and democratic messages of their texts.[83]

[79] Arvanitakis (ed.), *Carteggio 1822–1860: Andrea Mustoxidi ed Emilio Tipaldo*, p. 148.

[80] Thanasis Christou, '"Schedion peri ethnikis anatrofis kai dimosiou paideias eis tin Ellada (1827)" tou Alexandrou Stourdza' (The 'Plan for the national upbringing and the public education in Greece (1827)' by Alexandre Stourdza), *Tomi 301* 6 (1993), pp. 90–7.

[81] HMC: MP, XIII/7/71–2.

[82] Giannis Kokkonas, *Oi mathites tou Kentrikou Scholeiou (1830–1834)* (The students of the Central School (1830–1834)) (Athens, 1997), p. 68.

[83] Pantazidis [Koraes], *Ti symferei eis tin eleftheromenin apo tous Tourkous Ellada*; F. Fournarakis and K. Th. Rallis, *Symmikta ellinika apo tis archis tis kyberniseos tou Kapodistria kai exis* (Miscellaneous Greek since the beginning of Kapodistrias's government) (Paris, 1831–2), 2 vols.

*No. Nobody was so naive and ungracious as to ostracise Plato from our schools*—he responded in the draft of his *Apology* to Koraes (which, nevertheless, was never finished or published). *But just like the stomach of an infant, so too lessons in the classroom should correspond to the needs of every age and intellectual susceptibility.*[84] The actual circumstances met with in the patria, which he had imagined as altogether different, gradually led to him feeling estranged. *I would never advise [anyone]... to come to Greece,* he wrote in April 1830, thus confessing to his bitter sense of disappointment. *We ought not to be seduced by the fame of the name and the illusion of history. The country is poor, and its inhabitants, although highly resourceful and wonderfully adept at every sort of cultivation, are not yet ready to understand the benefit... For a philosophical observer, for a traveller, Greece is a country deserving of contemplation, but to be settled there once and for all, when no duty compels you to, calls for a decision and a persistence worthy of an anchorite... So many centuries of tyranny, so many misfortunes, the recent frenzy of its enemies, has left this region without trees, without houses, and the ground itself is in large part arid or wild.*[85] In Kapodistrias's Greece the political clock advanced swiftly. In January 1831, a serious student riot broke out at the Central School of Aegina, apparently incited by the regime's enemies.[86] Ten months later the governor was gunned down by his political opponents. All this plunged the Corfiot intellectual into despair. *I am condemned to an exile on this rock...* he confessed to a friend soon after Kapodistrias's assassination. *The people may well be good, clever, and endowed with a certain natural judgement, but the men who raise themselves somewhat above the others are an amalgam of falsity and corruption... Every man looks to some happiness to which he directs all his actions. I now have only a single one, to extricate myself with dignity from this morass... I will shortly turn my back on Greece in order not to be buried.*[87] In April 1832 he packed his bags and left for good.

*I can breathe [again] because I have reached a civilised land*—he wrote just as soon as he had arrived in Corfu, in the British-controlled Ionian state.[88] He had been a confessed enemy of the British, it is true. *It is from the cession of Parga that the Greeks' eternal mistrust and dissatisfaction with the English dates,* he had written back in 1820.[89] But times change. In the 1830s a liberal wind blew from London and across the empire. The Tory government was replaced by the Whigs who, in 1832, passed the Reform Act which introduced wide-ranging changes to the electoral system and restricted the power of the landed aristocracy. The British Parliament now contained reformers prepared to criticize the high cost of imperial government and to advocate a more liberal foreign policy. Mustoxidi's arrival in Corfu coincided with the appointment of George Nugent, a Whig, as Lord High Commissioner of the Ionian Islands. His tenure (1832–5) marked a new era of liberal policy in the islands, where notions such as 'power-sharing' and 'representative

---

[84] Quoted in Arvanitakis (ed.), *Carteggio 1822–1860: Andrea Mustoxidi ed Emilio Tipaldo,* p. 48.

[85] Arvanitakis (ed.), *Carteggio 1822–1860: Andrea Mustoxidi ed Emilio Tipaldo,* p. 158.

[86] Kokkonas, *Oi mathites tou Kentrikou Scholeiou,* pp. 58–68.

[87] Arvanitakis (ed.), *Carteggio 1822–1860: Andrea Mustoxidi ed Emilio Tipaldo,* pp. 179–80.

[88] Arvanitakis (ed.), *Carteggio 1822–1860: Andrea Mustoxidi ed Emilio Tipaldo,* p. 211.

[89] [Mustoxidi], *Exposé des faits qui ont précédé et suivi la cession de Parga,* p. 61.

government' were introduced for the first time. Even if in practice his administration had scant impact on constitutional matters, he encouraged Ionian demands for reform, undermining the authoritarian order propped up by Maitland, his predecessor.[90] But it was not only the empire that changed; the local inhabitants did so also. The Greek War of Independence had roused Greek nationalism in the islands, encouraging many Ionians to view themselves now as Ionian/Greeks.[91] In a Europe which seemed readier now to abandon the conservative stability of the aftermath of the Napoleonic Wars in favour of more experimental liberal concepts, the establishment of the Kingdom of Greece gave rise to rumours that the Ionian Islands would be ceded. Although such hopes were dashed, young Ionians returning from their studies in France and Italy, where they had witnessed or participated in the revolutionary turmoil of 1820–1 and 1831–2, brought to the islands a new liberal and combative spirit. This was further fuelled by the arrival in the Ionian Adriatic of the first wave of political exiles from the defeated revolutionary fronts of the Italian peninsula and France.[92]

Nugent's electoral reforms gave rise to a new influx of Ionian liberals sitting in the Fourth Parliament (1833) and demanding constitutional change. Mustoxidi was among them. His involvement in politics, in and out of Parliament, during the decade 1832–42 did indeed inaugurate a new epoch in the political history of the Ionian Islands, one which, as one scholar has observed, 'bears his imprint'.[93] By founding a Liberal Club, around which clustered the progressive intellectuals, the so-called *Liberali*, advocating constitutional reforms, Mustoxidi actually organized the first Ionian parliamentary opposition to the power of the imperial High Commissioners.[94] This opposition became even more important when, in the mid-1830s, Maitland's brand of authoritarianism returned to the islands. Nugent's successor, Howard Douglas (1835–41), a conservative in matters of political reform, believed that the Ionians were morally unready for self-government and, while resuscitating the civilizing mission of the empire in the east, he also restored autocracy.[95] Not surprisingly, his policies intensified local resistance. Tired of vainly battling with him inside the Ionian state, the Ionian *Liberali* decided to take their grievances directly to London. In August 1839, Mustoxidi arrived in London with a memorandum for the Colonial Secretary, which criticized British colonial

---

[90] Maria Paschalidi, 'Constructing Ionian Identities: The Ionian Islands in British Official Discourses, 1815–1864' (Ph.D. dissertation, University College London, 2009), pp. 145–53.

[91] W. David Wrigley, 'The Ionian Islands and the Advent of the Greek State (1827–1833)', *Balkan Studies* 19 (1978), pp. 413–26.

[92] Antonis Liakos, 'I diathlasi ton epanastatikon ideon ston elliniko choro, 1830–1850' (The diffusion of revolutionary ideas in the Greek space, 1830–1850), *Ta istorika* 1/1 (1983), pp. 121–44; Maria Christina Chatziioannou, 'Oi Italoi prosfyges sta Ionia Nisia: diamorfomenes pragmatikotites kai proypotheseis ensomatosis' (Italian refugees on the Ionian Islands in the mid-19th century: lived realities and conditions of integration), in *VI Panionian Conference, Proceedings* (Athens, 2001), pp. 495–510.

[93] Arvanitakis (ed.), *Carteggio 1822–1860: Andrea Mustoxidi ed Emilio Tipaldo*, p. 50.

[94] Panagiotis Chiotis, *Istoria tou Ioniou Kratous apo systaseos aftou mechris enoseos, 1815–1864* (The history of the Ionian State from its creation to the unification with Greece, 1815–1864) (Zante, 1874), vol. II, p. 38.

[95] Paschalidi, 'Constructing Ionian Identities', pp. 153–77.

policy in the Ionian Islands in general and Douglas's administration in particular and demanded constitutional reforms, especially freedom of the press and financial control over the affairs of the state. He claimed that, as European peoples with a western language, history, institutions, and traditions, the Ionians had the right to handle their own political affairs though under the aegis of the empire. *For my country I should desire a national independence, were not such a desire Utopian. Loving it as I do, and convinced as I am of its weakness, I thank the Providence which has placed it under the protection of Great Britain... But for this protection to be truly efficacious and salutary, it is necessary for the Ionians to participate in a gradual and legal improvement of their institutions*—he stated, thereby expounding his political credo.[96] Although Mustoxidi's claims were dismissed out of hand by Douglas, who charged him with being a Russian agent, this episode precipitated the first serious crisis in the history of the colonial administration of the Ionian Islands.[97]

Mustoxidi's 'golden age' in Ionian/British politics belongs to the years in which John Seaton performed the duties of Lord High Commissioner (1843–9). Admittedly the most liberal of the islands' governors, Seaton cultivated relationships with the progressive intelligentsia of Corfu and reinstated a number of *Liberali* to government positions from which they had been dismissed by his predecessors. Thus, Mustoxidi became once again the 'Official Historiographer of the Ionian Islands', a post which he had lost in 1820. The liberals hoped Seaton understood the political deadlock of the last decade and would champion alterations to the political status quo of the islands. As a matter of fact, his reform agenda, which was inaugurated in 1843, led to constitutional reforms in 1848, such as freedom of the press, Ionian control of the state finances, and free elections.[98] By that time, though, a more radical opposition group had emerged among the Ionians. Born in Cephalonia, the largest and poorest of the seven islands, this club of political activists, who became known as the '*Rizospastai*' (Radical-Unionists), challenged the legitimacy of the British Protection altogether and favoured major internal sociopolitical changes on the basis of the right of national self-determination and the principle of popular sovereignty.[99] George Ward, Seaton's successor, infuriated by the growth of the Radical-Unionists, especially after an uprising in Cephalonia in 1849, attempted during the early 1850s to reinstate authoritarian rule. In his efforts to eradicate radicalism, he found in a new generation of moderate liberals a trusted ally. Mustoxidi, however, was not one of their number.[100] Dismissed once

[96] Andrea Mustoxidi, *Sulla condizione attuale delle Isole Ionie. Promemoria presentato in agosto 1839 etc.* (London, 1840), p. vi.

[97] *Dispaccio di Sir Edward Douglas Baronetto, G. C. S. M. G. Lord Alto Commissionario delle Isole Ionie, etc.* (Corfu, 1840). Mustoxidi denied these accusations by his *Al dispaccio dei 10 aprile 1840 da Sir Howard Douglas Lord Alto Commissionario di S. M. negli Stati Uniti del Ionio. Confutazione di Andrea Mustoxidi* (Malta, 1841).

[98] Paschalidi, 'Constructing Ionian Identities', pp. 187–221.

[99] Eleni Calligas, 'The "Rizospastai" (Radical-Unionists): Politics and Nationalism in the British Protectorate of the Ionian Islands, 1815–1864' (Ph.D. dissertation, London School of Economics and Political Science, 1994).

[100] Miranda Stavrinos, 'The Reformist Party in the Ionian Islands (1848–1852): Internal Conflicts and Nationalist Aspirations', *Balkan Studies* 26/2 (1985), pp. 351–61.

again from his post as 'Official Historiographer', he withdrew into private life, dedicating his time instead—as we will see in Chapter 12—to research and study. In 1857, only three years before his death, he accepted an appointment by Ward's successor, John Young, as the 'Archon' (Minister) of Education of the Ionian state. However, in the altered circumstances of the late 1850s, when radicalism was redefined on purely unionist lines and all demands for constitutional reform were replaced by the wish for union with Greece, accepting a post offered by the British administration was seen as collaborationism pure and simple. Mustoxidi, unable to follow the radical turn in Ionian politics and unwilling to take the conservative path of his old liberal companions, breathed his last in 1860. His funeral was paid for out of public funds and was attended by all official authorities, British and Ionian. *Political passions fell silent before the tomb of Andrea Mustoxidi*, his biographer wrote.[101] He was buried, fittingly, next to Ioannis Kapodistrias.

[101] Papadopulo-Vrettò, *Biografia del cavaliere Andrea Mustoxidi*, p. 23.

# 11

# The Greco- and Dalmato-Venetian Intellectuals after the End of the Serenissima

## INTRODUCTION: A COMMUNITY IN THE TWILIGHT, THE GREEKS OF VENICE

Of all the 'little Greeces' that the premodern Greek diasporas had established in Italy, the most important was in Venice. The city's Greek community had been created by sailors, merchants, and artisans, who settled there with their families after the fall of Constantinople to the Ottomans (1453), and was further enriched after the Ottoman conquest of Cyprus (1570), Crete (1669), and the Peloponnese (1715). Most of the migrants came from the Venetian or former Venetian lands of the Mediterranean: Crete, Cyprus, the Peloponnese, Epirus, and, above all, the Ionian Islands. The Orthodox populations of Serbian, Dalmatian, and Albanian origin likewise formed an integral part of the community. In the fifteenth century, the colony numbered around 4,000–5,000 people, but in the second half of the seventeenth century, particularly after the fall of Crete to the Ottomans, these numbers were doubled. The founding of the Greek Fraternity (*Confraternita*) in 1498, by which the Greeks obtained the right to draw up their own charter and elect their own priests, marked the community's coming of age. The Church of St George, which was completed in 1573, remained the nucleus of the Greeks of Venice for centuries to come, serving indeed to guarantee their religious autonomy. The other hub of their community was the so-called Flanginian School, the most important educational establishment of the Greek diaspora, which was founded in 1665.[1] At around the same date the community also gained its own printing house, transforming the city into a centre of Greek publishing.[2]

Paradoxically, the decline of Venetian trade and the rising competition of France and Britain in the Mediterranean during the second half of the seventeenth and the first decades of the eighteenth century favoured the Greek merchants, who made inroads into both the Ottoman and the Venetian worlds while also establishing a foothold in other ports on the Adriatic and the Tyrrhenian Seas. The Treaty of Passarowitz (1718), however, which stripped Venice of the greater part of its

---

[1] Athanasios Karathanasis, *I Flaggineios Scholi tis Benetias* (The Flanginian School of Venice) (Thessaloniki, 1975).

[2] Giorgos Veloudis, *To elliniko typografeio ton Glykidon sti Benetia (1670–1854): symboli sti meleti tou ellinikou bibliou kata tin epochi tis tourkokratias* (*The Greek printing house of Glikis in Venice, 1670–1854*) (Athens, 1987).

Mediterranean empire and marked the beginning of the Republic's economic and political decline, was a turning point also for the Greek colony, which shed much of its population. An ecclesiastical crisis which erupted within the bosom of the community in the second half of the eighteenth century, when its bishop converted to Catholicism, only made things worse. The increasing opportunities now open to the Greek Orthodox in the Ottoman Empire led many among the Venetian subjects to move there, while the disappearance in the same period of the Greek Orthodox settlements of the Illyrian coasts deprived the Greek community of Venice of some of its older components.[3] In the ensuing years, the crisis deepened. The geopolitical developments in the area towards the end of the eighteenth and the first half of the nineteenth centuries—namely the collapse of the Venetian Republic, the passing of the region back and forth between the French and the Austrians, and the loss of the Adriatic's centrality to the global economy—had a corresponding impact upon the life of Venice's Greek inhabitants.[4] Napoleon's invasion and his confiscation of the community's funds led to a catastrophic Greco-Venetian financial collapse, while the establishment of the Greek state some years later led many merchants to abandon Venice for the more appealing prospect of trading in the Greek lands. At the same time, the growth of Italian nationalism and the increasing rigidity of the boundaries between the two confessions threatened the linguistic and religious character of the community. As the Flanginian School fell gradually into decline and mixed marriages increased, fewer and fewer members of the community spoke Greek.[5] One of the cast featuring in the following pages, the classical philologist Spiridione Vlandi, a son of the community himself and teacher at the Flanginian School during the last years of the eighteenth century, was indeed prepared to admit that he had learned Greek *with a lot of effort*, while his Italian and Latin were better by far.[6] By 1852 only 270 members remained of the once flourishing Greek community of Venice, most of whom were by now exclusively Italian-speaking.

It is on Vlandi and his like that this chapter focuses. Born in 1765, he was actually the oldest of all the characters we shall meet in the following pages. Most of them were born at the turn of the century in Venice, the Ionian Islands, or Dalmatia, and were individuals who despite the fall of the Serenissima continued to live and work within the city's languishing Greek colony or within the ambit of the wider post-Venetian Adriatic. Even if not always prominent intellectuals, they were men

---

[3] Georgios Moschopoulos, *Oi Ellines tis Benetias kai Illyrias (1768–1797): i mitropoli Philadelfias kai i simasia tis gia ton ellinismo tis boreias Adriatikis* (The Greeks of Venice and Illyria, 1768–1797: the diocese of Philadelphia and its significance for the Greeks of north Adriatic) (Athens, 1980).

[4] Egidio Ivetic, 'L'Adriatico alla fine del Settecento: il rilancio mancato', in Francesco Bruni and Chryssa Maltezou (eds), *L'Adriatico: incontri e separazioni (XVIII–XIX secolo)* (Venice, 2011), pp. 23–38.

[5] Artemis Xanthopoulou-Kyriakou, *I elliniki koinotita tis Benetias (1797–1866): dioikitiki kai oikonomiki organosi, ekpaideftiki kai politiki drastiriotita* (The Greek community of Venice (1797–1866), administrative and economic organization, educational and political activity) (Thessaloniki, 1978); Chryssa Maltezou, *I Benetia ton Ellinon–Venice of the Greeks* (Athens, 1999).

[6] Triantafyllos Sklavenitis, 'O Spyridon Blantis kai i idiotiki didaskalia, Piano di Studi/Ekthesis Mathimaton: Benetia 1794' (Spiridione Vlandi and private education, Piano di Studi/ Plan of Study: Venice 1794), *Thysavrismata* 34 (2004), pp. 428–9.

of erudition who contributed with their ample philological and historical production to the flourishing of ancient and modern Greek studies and to the attempt made to produce a systematic record of the Venetian, Ionian, Italian, and Greek pasts. Living in a dying world, these people, all former subjects of the Venetian Empire, strove to sustain the centuries-old dialogue between the two opposite sides of the Adriatic. Some of them, like Tommaseo, sought to transform this dialogue into a sustainable political programme for a new order of fraternal nations. These intellectuals were 'bridges' who, as one scholar has put it, 'represented the continuation, or the august survival, of the civilizing sway of the Republic over the other Adriatic shore'.[7]

## GREEKS [AND DALMATIANS] FORMED BY ITALIAN LETTERS: THE TRANS-ADRIATIC INTELLECTUALS AND THEIR PATRIOTISMS

Forming a separate milieu of their own, the intellectuals brought to the fore in the course of this chapter shared some common characteristics. To begin with, most of them spent their lives in Venice, and, more specifically, at the heart of the Greek community of the city during the last years and after the fall of the Serenissima. More often than not, they worked for the nuclei of the community—the school, the church, or the printing house—or in prominent Venetian cultural institutions, like the Marciana library. Their way of life determined their bicultural existence: these were *Greeks formed by Italian letters*—to borrow Tommaseo's words in describing Mustoxidi.[8] Second, they experienced (and sometimes even as active participants) the tempestuous events that engulfed the area after the fall of the Venetian Republic— the arrival of the French revolutionary armies, the Austrian occupation, the outbreak of the Greek revolution, and the creation of the Greek state. Some placed their hopes in the possibility they saw of making Kapodistrias's Greece their new home, but they were bitterly disappointed by the governor's assassination. Hopes for a new *patria* were revived when in 1848 a revolt broke out in Venice, which created for seventeen months a revolutionary state outside Austrian control, led by liberal intellectuals and activists. Most of these people were actively involved in the Venetian revolution, a fact that should serve to remind the historian of just how local and regional, as well as transnational, the various patriotisms engendered by the 1848–9 revolutionary events were.[9] However, as we shall see, these revolutions also marked the point at which nationalism and transnationalism would start to become incompatible and even to emerge as contrary poles for the militants

---

[7] Piero Treves, 'La critica letteraria, la filologia, la bibliografia', in G. Arnaldi and M. P. Stocchi (eds), *Storia della cultura veneta*, vol. 6: *Dall'età napoleonica alla Prima Guerra Mondiale* (Vicenza, 1986), p. 369; See also Dimitris Arvanitakis (ed.), *Carteggio 1822–1860: Andrea Mustoxidi ed Emilio Tipaldo* (Athens, 2005), pp. 68–9.

[8] Niccolò Tommaseo, 'Andrea Mustoxidi', *Archivio storico italiano* 12/2 (1860), p. 33.

[9] Luca Mannori, 'Tra nazioni e nazione: una riflessione introduttiva', in idem, Angela De Benedictis, and Irene Fosi (eds), *Nazioni d'Italia: identità politiche e appartenenze regionali fra Settecento e Ottocento* (Rome, 2012), p. 31.

described in the present chapter. These developments shaped their multiple patriotisms, spanning as they did Venice, the Ionian Islands or Dalmatia, Italy, and Greece. Finally, what most of these men shared was also an involvement in a trans-Adriatic intellectual programme for the regeneration of Greek letters, an endeavour orchestrated by Mustoxidi in the period from the 1820s to the 1850s and including themes hardly touched upon by other intellectuals in the realm of Greek letters up to then: the rehabilitation of local history, the reclamation of the Byzantine and Ottoman pasts, and the re-evaluation of Greek and Mediterranean folk poetry. But in order to fully comprehend this intellectual endeavour, let us focus here on biographical profiles and on the multiple journeys which, by virtue of their various modes of cultural and political belonging, these people undertook.

The oldest of these literati was, as I have said, Spiridione Vlandi (1765–1830). *Guardian of the sacred fire of Greek wisdom*, as Mustoxidi called him, Vlandi was one of the pillars of the Greek community of Venice during the difficult decades of its decline and fall.[10] Born in Venice to a poor family of Ionian migrants from the island of Cythera, he went to school at the Flanginian School, where he later worked as a teacher for more than thirty years. He spent his life between the school and the printing house of the community, the Glikis enterprise, where he tried his hand at everything—editing, translating, and composing original works. Vlandi's name does indeed appear, under one or other of these headings, on more than 145 books. Grammars, dictionaries, translations of ancient classics, travel literature, manuals of physics and mathematics, most of the books that he helped produce belong to the spirit of educational Enlightenment.[11] A prolific scholar though he was, he nonetheless always remained hard up. This was the reason why Mustoxidi, *commiserating with him for the difficult situation he found himself in, and aware on the other hand of his merit*, invited him to become the main translator of a special section of the *Collana degli antichi storici Greci volgarizzati* dedicated to the Greek minor historians.[12] Entitled *Storici minori volgarizzati ed illustrati* (Milan, Sonzogno, 1826–31), this was an important endeavour, which brought to light works hitherto unknown to the Italian public. I will discuss its intellectual implications in Chapter 12. But let me just underline here the particular significance of the very first translation into Italian of a selection of chapters from the famous *Bibliotheca* or *Myriobiblos* of the ninth-century Patriarch of Constantinople Photius. Thus, through Vlandi's translation, the works of Ctesias of Cnidus, Nicolaus of Damascus, Conon, Memnon of Heraclea, Hesychius of Miletus, Agatharchides, Olympiodorus of Thebes, and other ancient historians—viewed, of course, through the eyes of a Byzantine patriarch—saw the light of day again.

---

[10] Quoted in Girolamo Dandolo, *La caduta della Repubblica di Venezia ed i suoi ultimi cinquant' anni: studii storici* (Venice, 1855), p. 324.

[11] Veloudis, *To elliniko typografeio ton Glykidon*, pp. 61–2; Karathanasis, *I Flaggineios Scholi tis Benetias*, pp. 134–6; Sklavenitis, 'O Spyridon Blantis kai i idiotiki didaskalia', pp. 421–46.

[12] Quoted in Tipaldo, 'Blandi Spiridione', in idem (ed.), *Biografia degli Italiani illustri nelle scienze, lettere ed arti nel secolo XVIII* (Venice, 1834), vol. V, p. 386.

Vlandi's students at the Flanginian School included two other forgotten sons of the Greek colony of Venice, the brothers Giovanni and Spiridione Veludo (1811–90 and 1815–66). Born in Venice to a family of Ionian merchants, their names were strongly linked to the history of the Greek community during its last days. Giovanni taught at the Flanginian School (1834–7) and served on several occasions as the community's *Guardian Grande* (president). However, it was in the context of the Marciana library, which he entered as a casual assistant in 1850, that his career flourished. Promoted to vice-librarian in 1852 and librarian in 1873, he served, finally, as the prefect of the Marciana (1875–84). *Belonging as he did to two great nationalities, the Greek and the Italian, the former that of his origin, the latter that of his birth and life*, as his biographer remarks, Veludo followed closely political developments in Italy and Greece alike and was emotionally involved with both of his patriotisms.[13] Exulting in the liberation of Greece and confident that the election of Kapodistrias at its head would offer his Veneto-Ionian friends an asylum in the new state, the governor's assassination proved a devastating blow. *I pity Greece for being deprived of its animating genius and guardian Angel at the hands of scoundrels*, he wrote to Mustoxidi in June 1832; *I also pity myself for having had all of a sudden to shut off any hope of being able to place any of my brothers, who now with the passing of the years are becoming for me an almost intolerable burden.*[14] But if he was overwhelmed by Greek national sentiment, he was no less moved by the Italian Risorgimento. On the morrow of the 1848 revolt in Venice, Veludo wrote: *The Lord roused us from sleep, and He rose and saved us! What a quantity of stupendous events there have been in the space of a few hours! Yet it is so. The Eagle no longer shakes his wings over the crouching Lion... So, long live St. Mark! Long live Italian independence! But Italy is not yet wholly free of its oppressors... God will see the miracle through to its completion: now that He has begun it.*[15] A prolific author, Giovanni produced more than 170 sundry works, among them historical studies, brief treatises, journal articles, dictionary entries, and others. *Veludo, a learned man, combined a love of Italy and of Greece, being a perfect connoisseur of and writer in the two languages, let alone a lover of the art and literature of the two sister nations*, wrote Nani Mocenigo of him, underlining his standing as an intellectual 'bridge'.[16] Two works, in particular, have rescued Giovanni Veludo from oblivion, although even these are scarcely ever read or consulted. First of all, his translation of a number of chapters from the *Bibliotheca* of Photius, which were left untouched by Vlandi. The philological importance of this work, although overshadowed perhaps by an almost contemporary edition of Photius compiled by another Italian philologist, has been acknowledged by modern scholarship.[17] Second and more important, his historical account of the Greek community of Venice, the first of its kind and a model for future historiography on the

---

[13] Jacopo Bernardi, 'Commemorazione di Giovanni Veludo (1811–1890)', *Atti dell'Istituto Veneto* 8/38 (1889–90), p. 701.

[14] HMC: MP, X/8/174.     [15] HMC: MP, X/5/171.

[16] Filippo Nani Mocenigo, *Della letteratura veneziana del secolo XIX* (Venice, 1901 [1891]), p. 122.

[17] Giuseppe Compagnoni, *Biblioteca di Fozio patriarca di Costantinopoli tradotta in italiano etc.* (Milan, 1836), 2 vols. See Margherita Losacco, *Antonio Catiforo e Giovanni Veludo interpreti di Fozio* (Bari, 2003).

communities of the Greek diaspora.[18] The work appeared in 1847 as a chapter in a collective volume that celebrated the greatness of Venice within the context of Italian nationalism. Indeed, the volume in question was published on the occasion of the ninth National Congress of Italian Scientists, a major Risorgimento institution, which was held in Venice that year. Nevertheless, Veludo's chapter did not so much address Italian as Greek national concerns. Aiming principally at showing the value of the Greco-Venetian community within the framework of the Greek national regeneration, Veludo recounted how by its educational and printing activities in times of pervasive 'darkness', the community prepared the ground for the birth of modern Greek culture. *History will from now on tell of how it was that from the Greek colony in Venice there issued the seed that engendered modern Greek civilization*—he wrote.[19] In fact, the chapter was further revised and then published as a book in Greek in 1872. In its conclusion we read that, after the fall of Constantinople to the Ottomans, the light of the Orthodox religion was kept lit thanks to those Greeks who had found refuge in Venice, creating the Orthodox colony of the city.[20] Mustoxidi, who had encouraged Veludo to undertake this study and corrected its various versions, considered it to be *an argument that is national, and boasting copious information and some lovely observations.*[21] It was indeed in line with his own intellectual programme that, as we will see in Chapter 12, Veludo imagined this work as the first part of a greater study which would show the educational activity of the Greeks during the 'dark' ages of Ottoman domination.

Veludo's younger brother, Spiridione, was also a man of letters. Life and soul of the Greek printing house of St George (which specialized in the publication of religious Greek Orthodox books), Spiridione became involved with Italian intellectual circles beyond the boundaries of Venice. Particular note should be taken of his friendship with the important author and classical scholar Pietro Giordani.[22] His oeuvre consists of no more than a handful of journal articles but it seems that Spiridione was silently working on a more ambitious project that was left unfinished. He was gathering material in order to compose a history of modern Greek literature, which would complement and revise the only account of that kind so far attempted, the *Cours de littérature grecque moderne* by the Phanariot scholar Jacovaky Rizo Neroulos (Geneva, 1827).[23]

An 1846 article by Spiridione Veludo drew the attention of the Italian public to another pillar of the Greek community of Venice. The clergyman Bartolommeo

---

[18] Sotiris Koutmanis, 'Giovanni Veludo (1811–1890) tra la storiografia greca e veneziana dell'800', in Bruni and Maltezou (eds), *L'Adriatico: incontri e separazioni*, pp. 289–95.

[19] Giovanni Veludo, 'Cenni sulla colonia greca orientale', in *Venezia e le sue lagune* (Venice, 1847), vol. I, pp. 78–100.

[20] Giovanni Veludo, *Ellinon Orthodoxon apoikia en Benetia: istorikon ypomnima* (The colony of the Greek Orthodox in Venice: a historical account) (Venice, 1893 [1872]), p. 146.

[21] BM: Mustoxidi Papers, 498.

[22] G. S. Ploumidis, 'To benetiko typografeio tou Agiou Georgiou (1850–1882)', (The Venetian printing house of St George (1850–1882)), *Eranistis* 8 (1970), pp. 169–85; Pietro Giordani, *Lettere di Pietro Giordani a Spiridione Veludo* (Venice, 1880).

[23] Emilio de Tipaldo, *Intorno Spiridione Veludo, lettera* (Venice, 1866); Nani Mocenigo, *Della letteratura veneziana*, p. 122.

Cutlumusiano (1772–1851), a native of the northern Aegean island of Imbros (Gökçeada), had made his way through Constantinople, Mount Athos, Thessaloniki, and Marseilles, before settling in Venice and becoming for a period the Flanginian School's director (1827–33).[24] An author of ecclesiastical and educational books and a close friend of Mustoxidi, he played a role in Kapodistrias's religious educational programme for the Greek state, when he was asked to prepare an easy-to-read prayer book for Greek citizens. It was supposed to include prayers translated into Modern Greek and divided into different types reflecting the various occupations and social classes of the citizens. Although the project failed in the wake of Kapodistrias's assassination—and subsequently because the Patriarch of Constantinople refused to give his permission, suspecting Protestant influences—the episode shows once again that Kapodistrias, Mustoxidi, and their circle attempted to implement in Greece an educational programme inspired by the principles of Orthodox Enlightenment.[25] But the case of Cutlumusiano interests us here also because of his co-authored book with Mustoxidi on the history and anthropogeography of the island of Imbros (1845).[26] A fruit of the collaboration between the two friends when, on Mustoxidi's invitation, Cutlumusiano moved to Corfu in 1833 to teach at the ecclesiastical school on the island, the book encapsulates a long-standing tradition of local historiography and historical geography, which had developed within Greek letters since the beginning of the eighteenth century, but was particularly flourishing in the Ionian region during the first half of the nineteenth century. Considering geography to be a safe path when tracing history, the aim of these studies was to explore the modern Greek national space by comparison with the ancient. A basic component, indeed, of this tradition was the so-called *patridography* or *storia patria*, intended as a form of writing inspired by a patriotic concern for the homeland.[27]

Another distinguished member of the Greek community of Venice, a teacher at the Flanginian School and vicar of the Church of St George, a transnational patriot

[24] Spiridione Veludo, 'Memorie istoriche intorno all'isola d'Imbro, raccolte dal cav. Andrea Mustoxidi con supplementi del padre B. Cutlumusiano etc.', *Il vaglio* 9/33 (15 Aug. 1846), pp. 262–3.

[25] K. Th. Demaras, 'Kapodistrias—Moustoxydis—Koutloumousianos (bibliografikes kai alles anazitiseis)' (Kapodistrias-Mustoxidi-Cutlumusiano (bibliographical and other researches)), *Thysavrismata* 1 (1962), pp. 14–62; Konstantina Zanou, 'O Andreas Moustoxydis, o Bartholomeos Koutloumousianos kai to *Ypomnima istorikon peri tis nisou Imbrou*' (Andrea Mustoxidi, Bartolommeo Cutlumusiano and the *Historical Memorial on the Island of Imbros*), *Mnimon* 31 (2010), pp. 286–9; Dimitrios Stratis, *Bartholomeos Koutloumousianos (1772–1851): biografia—ergografia* (Bartolommeo Cutlumusiano (1772–1851), life and works) (Mount Athos, 2002), p. 529.

[26] Andrea Mustoxidi and Bartolommeo Cutlumusiano, *Memorie istoriche intorno all'isola d'Imbro etc.* (Constantinople, 1845). Republished recently in English: Andreas Moustoxydis and Bartholomew Koutloumousianos, *A Historical Memorandum Concerning the Island of Imbros* (Imbros/Gökçeada, 2010).

[27] Robert Shannan Peckham, *National Histories, Natural States, Nationalism and the Politics of Place in Greece* (London and New York, 2001); Giorgos Tolias, 'Choros kai istoria: archaiodifikes kai istoriografikes proseggiseis tis geografias, 19os–20os ai.' (Space and history: antiquarian and historiographical approaches to geography, 19th–20th centuries), in P. Kitromilides and Tr. Sklavenitis (eds), *Istoriografia tis neoteris kai sygchronis Elladas, 1833–2002* (Historiography in modern and contemporary Greece, 1833–2002) (Athens, 2004), vol. II, pp. 77–118; Zanou, 'O Andreas Moustoxydis, o Bartholomeos Koutloumousianos', pp. 294–8.

and author of a noteworthy *storia patria*, was Antimo Masarachi (1800/1–68). Born in Cephalonia, Masarachi studied in Constantinople and Corfu, before returning as a clergyman and teacher to his native island. An ardent patriot and liberal—he had fought in the Greek revolution—he soon became a thorn in the side of the British authorities, so much so that he was forced to abandon the Ionian Islands. In 1838, he found a safe refuge in Venice and especially in the arms of its Greek colony, which made him their teacher and vicar. There Masarachi stayed for more than ten years, dedicating himself to literary, pedagogical, and charitable activities. In 1848, he openly manifested his support for the Venetian revolt by officiating at a public prayer for the revolutionary government. This was a some-what scandalous episode in the annals of the politically cautious Greco-Venetian community. Although it counted among its members a number of students and intellectuals who were overtly liberal and revolutionary, the community had been in general conservative, or rather opportunistic, in political matters. The celebra-tory doxologies by which the Greeks had welcomed the Austrian troops when in 1798 they entered Venice are a case in point.[28] So, when Austrian rule was restored once more after the 1848–9 Venetian revolution, Masarachi was arrested, imprisoned, and condemned to death. He managed to save his skin only through the agency of the British ambassador and of some ecclesiastical intermediaries. He was, however, forced to leave Venice. The liberal clergyman spent the rest of his life on the island of Chalki (Heybeliada), near Constantinople, where he became director of the island's Holy Theological School. Two years before his death he was appointed Bishop of Seleucia and Pisidia in Asia Minor.[29] Among Masarachi's works, mostly ecclesiastical treatises, a book entitled *Vite degli uomini illustri dell'Isola di Cefalonia* (Biographies of the illustrious men of the island of Cephalonia) is of particular interest to us here. Originally published in Greek in 1843 and translated into Italian in that same year by Tommaseo, the book was a combination of two literary traditions, the *storia patria* and the biographical dictionary. As its title would suggest, the book included biographies of learned men and other illustrious personalities from Cephalonia's medieval and modern periods. It was the first systematic attempt to record and compile a miscellany of the island's recent past. Here, as elsewhere, local history was perceived in terms of its national and educational character. *The lives of worthy Greeks who flourished from the fall of the empire up until the present Resurgence*, Masarachi wrote in the introduction, *would offer our youth examples deserving of imitation; narrating the zeal of our ancestors for the regeneration of the patria, . . . would rouse the soul ever further to emulation of the good.*[30] The book was

---

[28] Xanthopoulou-Kyriakou, *I elliniki koinotita tis Benetias*, p. 125; Apostolos Papaioannou, 'Oi Ellines tis Benetias kai i benetiki epanastasi tou 1848–49' (The Greeks of Venice and the 1848–49 Venetian revolution) (Ph.D. dissertation, University of Ioannina, 1986).

[29] Ilias Tsitselis, *Kefalliniaka symmeikta: symbolai eis tin istorian kai laografian tis nisou Kefallinias* (Miscellaneous Cephalonian: contributions to the history and folkloric research of the island of Cephalonia) (Athens, 1904), vol. I, pp. 363–70; Xanthopoulou-Kyriakou, *I elliniki koinotita tis Benetias*, pp. 144, 220; Arvanitakis (ed.), *Carteggio 1822–1860: Andrea Mustoxidi ed Emilio Tipaldo*, esp. p. 747.

[30] Antimo Masarachi, *Vite degli uomini illustri dell'isola di Cefalonia etc., tradotte dal greco da N. Tommaseo* (Venice, 1843), p. xi.

actually a collective venture, not only as regards its general alignment with the intellectual programme elaborated by Mustoxidi and his circle, but also because its realization involved the collaboration of a number of Greco- and Dalmato-Venetian intellectuals.

Pier-Alessandro Paravia (1797–1857) was one of their number. Along with Tommaseo they constituted the Dalmatian component in this circle of Greco-Venetian Adriatic intellectuals. Born in Zadar (Zara), Dalmatia, to Corfiot parents who later moved to Venice, Paravia beautifully encapsulated the interconnectedness of the Adriatic world before the fall of the Serenissima. He studied in Padua and lived in Venice until 1832, when he was appointed professor of rhetoric at the University of Turin. A fervent Italian patriot, he became known for the overtly liberal tone of his lectures.[31] A modest author of philological and historical treatises, he was also preparing a biographical dictionary of contemporary Italian poets, which, nevertheless, remained unfinished.[32] Paravia was closely linked to the Ionians of Venice and contributed in various ways to their intellectual programme.

The most prominent, however, among the characters involved in this trans-Adriatic intellectual milieu was Niccolò Tommaseo (1802–74). Born in Dalmatia (*in a country midway between Greece and Italy* in his own words) when this area had just passed from Venetian into Napoleonic and then into Austrian hands, he studied in Italy and lived there, between Venice, Florence, and Turin, for the greater part of his life.[33] A prolific author, lexicographer, journalist, and political activist, Tommaseo was perhaps the nineteenth-century Adriatic's most famous son. One of the most influential voices of the Italian Risorgimento (and, notably, the second-in-command in the 1848–9 Venetian revolution), he was compelled to spend several years in exile—in Paris and Corsica during the 1830s and in Corfu one decade later. But exile was, for Tommaseo, something more than simply an experience he had to pass through. It was the lens through which he narrated his whole existence as a national and cultural 'in-betweener'.[34] During the 1840s, he became the unofficial leader of what has aptly been called the 'Adriatic multinational movement', a political programme championing a vision of nationhood which was unbordered, inclusive, and fraternal.[35] For Tommaseo, as for most of the characters we have encountered in this book, 'patria' was by no means a straightforward concept. *It is not always easy to define the word 'patria',*

---

[31] Pier-Alessandro Paravia, *Lezioni di varia letteratura* (Turin, 1852–6). See Gian Paolo Romagnani, *Storiografia e politica culturale nel Piemonte di Carlo Alberto* (Turin, 1985), pp. 372–7.

[32] Pier-Alessandro Paravia, *Memorie veneziane di letteratura e di storia* (Turin, 1850); Federico Sclopis, 'Pier-Alessandro Paravia', *Archivio storico italiano*, Nuova Serie 4 (1857), pp. ii–iv; Nani Mocenigo, *Della letteratura veneziana*, pp. 357–9.

[33] Niccolò Tommaseo, *Il supplizio d'un Italiano in Corfù*, edited by Fabio Danelon (Venice, 2008 [1855]), p. 742.

[34] Mariasilvia Tatti, 'Esilio e identità nazionale nell'esperienza francese di Tommaseo', in Francesco Bruni (ed.), *Niccolò Tommaseo: popolo e nazioni, Italiani, Corsi, Greci, Illirici* (Rome and Padua, 2004), vol. I, pp. 95–114; Dominique Kirchner Reill, 'Away or Homeward Bound? The Slippery Case of Mediterranean Place in the Era Before Nation-States', in Maurizio Isabella and Konstantina Zanou (eds), *Mediterranean Diasporas: Politics and Ideas in the Long Nineteenth Century* (London, 2016), pp. 135–52.

[35] Reill, *Nationalists Who Feared the Nation*.

he once wrote;... *love of patria has to be reconciled with love of humanity; and the common faith in the nations, and the unity of the religious association that is formed from it, should prepare the time, still far off, in which the whole of humankind shall feel itself to be one family.*[36] Tommaseo was linked to the Greco-Venetian Adriatic intellectual world in various ways: not only did he enjoy close friendships with many of the characters we have encountered in this chapter, he was also one of Mustoxidi's most assiduous collaborators in his projects for the translation of the classics. What is more, Tommaseo worked with a number of intellectuals from this circle in order to compile his anthology of folk ballads (*Canti popolari, Toscani, Corsi, Illirici e Greci*, 1841), an important statement of his sort of transnational Romantic patriotism, about which Chapter 12 will have much more to say.

One of Tommaseo's, as well as Mustoxidi's, closest collaborators and most trusted friends was, finally, Emilio Tipaldo (1798–1878), a remarkable presence in Greco-Venetian history. The figure of this *Greek by nationhood but Italian by language and by choice* would have vanished into obscurity like the rest of his Veneto-Ionian peers, had it not been for the work of two scholars who have recently published and commented on his forgotten correspondence.[37] Born in Cephalonia, Tipaldo followed his parents to Venice at the age of 12, never to leave. An assiduous presence in the affairs of the Greek community of the city, he served as its president on several occasions from the 1820s to the 1850s. *Nothing that happens in our little Colony escapes me... nothing is done without me knowing of it, and without me supervising everything,* he confessed to a friend without undue modesty; *everyone has recourse to me, knowing that my voice is of some weight if affairs are to succeed.*[38] But Tipaldo's activity extended far beyond the narrow boundaries of this Greco-Venetian microcosm. A professor of history and geography at the Maritime College of Venice, and a member and occasional president of the city's most important cultural institution, the *Ateneo Veneto*, Tipaldo was also a prolific author who published in various Venetian journals and a speaker in demand at diverse cultural events. One of his speeches, delivered in 1847 on the occasion of the ninth National Congress of Italian Scientists, which, as noted above, was held in Venice that year with Austria's reluctant permission, achieved particular renown. In listing Venice's neglected intellectual achievements during the second half of the eighteenth century, the Greco-Venetian intellectual also voiced his opinion on something else: the need to cast off the Austrian yoke and to create a federal Italy.[39] Tipaldo's share in Italy's nation-building is best exemplified, however, by a monumental work which has featured prominently on the shelves of Italian libraries for the

---

[36] Niccolò Tommaseo, 'Amore di patria', in idem, *Il secondo esilio: scritti di Niccolò Tommaseo concernenti le cose d'Italia e d'Europa dal 1849 in poi* (Milan, 1862), vol. II, pp. 19–24.

[37] Arvanitakis (ed.), *Carteggio 1822–1860: Andrea Mustoxidi ed Emilio Tipaldo*; Donatella Rasi, 'Un greco amico del Tommaseo: Emilio de Tipaldo', in Bruni (ed.), *Niccolò Tommaseo: popolo e nazioni*, vol. II, pp. 537–78 and idem, 'Storia di un'amicizia: il carteggio inedito Niccolò Tommaseo-Emilio de Tipaldo', in Adriana Chemello (ed.), *Alla lettera: teorie epistolari dai Greci al Novecento* (Milan, 1998), pp. 263–313.

[38] Rasi, 'Un greco amico del Tommaseo', p. 545.

[39] 'Discorso del Cav. Emilio de Tipaldo', in *Discorsi letti nella pubblica adunanza del giorno 11 luglio 1847 nell'Ateneo Veneto, alla IX riunione degli scienziati italiani* (Venice, 1847), pp. 7–20.

last two centuries: the voluminous *Biografia degli Italiani illustri* (Biographies of illustrious Italians, 1834–45). Written in collaboration with a number of others, this multi-volume venture constituted the first truly ambitious attempt to record the repertoire of the protagonists of Italian culture, offering, as stated in its preface, *a perspective on the past and present culture of the Italian nation.*[40] But if Tipaldo's scholarly activities were Italian in patriotic scope, they were no less Greek. In a work worthy of note, a translation of the Prussian diplomat Friedrich Schoell's *Istoria della letteratura Greca profana dalla sua origine sino alla presa di Constantinopoli fatta dai Turchi* (History of Greek literature from its origins to the fall of Constantinople to the Turks, 1827–30), which he dedicated to Mustoxidi, Tipaldo spelled out his intentions: *to pay tribute… [to] a Nation that after almost three thousand years is deservedly regarded as the teacher of all peoples, and of all times.*[41] It was not only the glories of ancient Greece that stirred his patriotic feelings. Those of the modern country, and especially the feats of the Greek revolution, held just as important a place in Tipaldo's affections. He was thus inspired by the Greek national epic to compose a collection of poems in 1821, which only saw the light of day somewhat later in his life.[42]

That Tipaldo was a transnational patriot (*in whose soul an ardent affection for Greece was never detached from his [concern] with Italian independence*—as his biographer put it) can be seen also in his political activity.[43] His participation in the 1848–9 revolutionary events in Venice is a case in point. Having by then been forced to retire from the Maritime College because of the liberal tone of his lectures (*His majesty's aim is to create a navy which is Austrian, not Italian*—was the official reasoning of the imperial authorities in 1844), Tipaldo became the Chief Inspector of Elementary Schools for the revolutionary government.[44] That he was the best friend of Tommaseo, the Minister of Education, no doubt had something to do with the appointment. At any rate, the Venetian revolution of 1848–9, like the city in which it unfolded, was an event rich in transcultural and transnational elements. As Tommaseo writes, *[many members of the] Government were Jewish in origin or from Modena, Armenian or Greek, from Bergamo or Dalmatia, but had either been born in Venice, or had Venetian relatives, or had long resided in the Veneto.*[45] The concept of the nation did not yet exclude ethnic and linguistic plurality.

Nonetheless, as Tipaldo's case illustrates, though nationalist claims and transnationalist ideals were intertwined in the revolutionary movements of Italy and central Europe in 1848, religious and political divisions did nevertheless increase.[46]

---

[40] Tipaldo (ed.), *Biografia degli Italiani illustri*, vol. I, p. viii.

[41] Federico Schoell, *Istoria della letteratura greca profana etc., recata in italiano per la prima volta con giunte ed osservazioni critiche da Emilio Tipaldo* (Venice, 1827), vol. I, p. vii.

[42] Emilio de Tipaldo, *Poesie* (Mestre, 1877).

[43] Giovanni Veludo, *Parole nei funerali del commendatore Emilio de Tipaldo, dette in S. Giorgio de' Greci il di III aprile 1878* (Venice, [1878]), p. 9.

[44] Pietro Rigobon, *Gli eletti alle assemblee veneziane del 1848–1849* (Venice, 1950), p. 220.

[45] Niccolò Tommaseo, *Venezia negli anni 1848 e 1849* (Florence, 1931), vol. I, p. 157. See also Papaioannou, 'Oi Ellines tis Benetias'.

[46] Axel Körner, 'Introduction', in idem (ed.), *1848: A European Revolution? International Ideas and National Memories of 1848* (New York, 2000), p. 5.

Tipaldo was soon forced to resign his post, if only because the Bishop of Venice and his ecclesiastical circle were reluctant to place their trust in a non-Catholic. Time once was when religious tolerance and peaceful coexistence defined relations between Catholics and Orthodox in the Venetian Adriatic. The election of Pius IX, a perceived liberal, as Pope in 1846, associated as it became with the national fervour of the Risorgimento, brought hopes not only for the renewal of the Catholic Church, but also for a change in the fate both of Italy and of humanity as a whole. In addition, increased Russian infiltration in the Balkans during the 1840s provoked suspicion among the European powers, which were led gradually to abandon the utopian ecumenism of previous years in favour of a more wary stance towards Eastern Orthodoxy. In 1848, very much to Tommaseo's satisfaction, Pius IX published the encyclical of 6 January *Litterae ad Orientales* 'In Suprema Petri Apostoli Sede', by which he invited the Orthodox peoples to 'return' to the bosom of the Catholic Church. As anticipated, the encyclical provoked much indignation among Orthodox circles in the eastern Mediterranean and Europe, an official rejoinder being issued by the Patriarch some months later. Several Orthodox intellectuals—along with Tipaldo's friends, including Mustoxidi and Stourdza—were involved in the ill-tempered and fractious debate that ensued, which would become, as we will see in the epilogue of this book, still more bitter in the ensuing years.[47] *I read with genuine pleasure your remarks on the Pope's Encyclical to the Orientals*, wrote Tipaldo to Mustoxidi on the eve of his resignation from the revolutionary government; *it is not a politician who is speaking… it is an Eastern Greek, who knows full well how much persecution, disruption and intolerance his brothers in the states of Italy have undergone and suffered. And I myself have been and am unfortunately the victim of such acts of persecution and intolerance.*[48] As religion was becoming all the more bound up with the emerging nationalisms across the Adriatic, intellectuals such as Tipaldo, who set out to be 'bridges', would become all the more alienated from their multiple patrias. *If I was concerned about the age of my father*, he observed in his letter to Mustoxidi, *by this time I would have left Italy and retired to the Islands, weary of living on a soil that will always be alien to us Greeks.*[49] Despite these declarations, Tipaldo returned to the Ionian Islands only once, and this for a relatively short stay. On that occasion, he also paid a tribute to Greece by visiting Athens for the first time, the capital of a state which he thought of as his homeland but which he had never seen. That was the year 1859, when tempestuous events engulfed the Italian peninsula. The Second Italian War of Independence, when the Piedmontese and the French forces were in an alliance in order to drive out the Austrians and unify the Italian states, was under way, and Tipaldo was eager to return to his Venetian home.[50] He might have been disappointed by the immediate result of the

---

[47] Angelo Tamborra, 'Pio IX, la lettera agli orientali del 1848 e il mondo ortodosso', *Rassegna storica del Risorgimento* 56 (July–Sept. 1959), pp. 347–67 and idem, 'Niccolò Tommaseo, il mondo ortodosso e il problema dell'Unione delle Chiese', in V. Branca and G. Petrocchi (eds), *Niccolò Tommaseo nel centenario della morte* (Florence, 1977), pp. 583–628.

[48] Arvanitakis (ed.), *Carteggio 1822–1860: Andrea Mustoxidi ed Emilio Tipaldo*, p. 905.

[49] Arvanitakis (ed.), *Carteggio 1822–1860: Andrea Mustoxidi ed Emilio Tipaldo*, p. 905.

[50] Arvanitakis (ed.), *Carteggio 1822–1860: Andrea Mustoxidi ed Emilio Tipaldo*, p. 822.

war—which ended with an armistice abandoning Veneto and other areas of the peninsula to Austrian rule—but he lived long enough to see some years later, in 1866, the realization of his youthful dream, the liberation of Venice from the Austrians and its annexation to Italy.

By unearthing a number of largely obscure biographies, this chapter has attempted to shed light on a group of Ionian and Dalmatian intellectuals who, for the most part, were enfolded in the decrepit embrace of the Greek community of Venice during the first half of the nineteenth century. Although most of their number were part of a post-Napoleonic generation born just after the Serenissima had closed its eyes, they nevertheless belonged to the cultural and memorial landscape of that Adriatic sunken world. These were individuals with multiple national patriotisms and cultural belongings, which they vainly tried to preserve in a world that—as the revolutionary events of 1848–9 made all too clear—was increasingly becoming divided and distinct in terms of culture, politics, nation, and religion. Be that as it may, these children of the ruins of the Venetian Adriatic were also actors in an ambitious intellectual programme aiming at the regeneration of Greek letters. It is to this that I will now turn my attention.

# 12

# A Trans-Adriatic Programme for the Regeneration of Greek Letters

## THE LATE SEPTINSULAR ENLIGHTENMENT

These men, who lived in between old and new patriotisms and imperial and national borders, were the protagonists of a collective intellectual enterprise aiming at the regeneration of Greek letters. The period from the 1820s to the 1850s, by and large the key decades in which this project was prosecuted, were years of intense intellectual activity in the Mediterranean and in the wider world: in this moment of late Enlightenment, national histories, archaeologies, literatures, and folklore traditions were founded, in order to fit the needs of a new and demanding political landscape, the world of the emerging nation-states. The post-Venetian intellectual programme in which our protagonists were involved was a continuation of the Venetian Adriatic Enlightenment of a previous period—and more particularly of its 'Septinsular' version, analysed in Chapter 4—and had as its key features not only the concern with education and the Orthodox tradition (which we have already explored), but also local history, with an emphasis on the Byzantine and Ottoman eras, as well as folk traditions. In a nutshell, all that has been framed by Greek intellectual historians of the 'Demaric school' as a taboo issue in the thought of the 'Neohellenic Enlightenment' scholars of the Ottoman Empire and the diaspora centres in France and central Europe, stands here, in this trans-Adriatic intellectual milieu, centre stage. To tell, then, this forgotten story means to turn our gaze away from the one, all-encompassing 'Neohellenic Enlightenment' scheme to the multiple Greek and Mediterranean Enlightenments formed on the verge of the modern world.

To be sure, like all other Greek Enlightenments, this one too had at the core of its concerns the revival of ancient Greek literature. Mustoxidi's collective *Collana degli antichi storici volgarizzati*, mentioned above, and Tipaldo's translation of Schoell's *Istoria della letteratura greca* are a case in point. But here emphasis was placed not only on the glorious classical period; texts of authors from the less-celebrated Hellenistic, Roman, and Byzantine pasts also found their way to Venetian printing houses. *The Greek unpublished manuscripts [presented here]*—read the announcement of another series launched by Mustoxidi and his Constantinopolitan friend and philologist Demetrios Schinas in 1816—*if they do not generally shine with the classical beauties of the most famous centuries, are nonetheless worthy of study and interesting as regards their own periods and the materials they contain.*[1] The series, labelled *Raccolta d'opere inedite di poeti e prosatori greci in epoche diverse* (Collection of unpublished works by Greek poets and prose writers of different times, Venice, Alvisopoli, 1816–17), consisted of five small volumes of Ambrosian *Anecdota*, which brought to light unknown manuscripts by the Byzantine medical writer Aëtius of Amida, the fourth-century Cypriot Bishop Epiphanius of Salamis, the Neoplatonic philosophers Olympiodorus the Younger (fifth century) and Georgius Gemistus Plethon (fourteenth century), the Byzantine astronomer and historian Nicephorus Gregoras, and others. Like the aforementioned collection *Storici minori volgarizzati ed illustrati* (1826–31), which was directed by Mustoxidi and comprised translations by Vlandi and Veludo of chapters from Photius' ninth-century *Biblioteca*, it shifted attention to periods which had hitherto been disregarded by European philological circles. 'When Greek scholars were still dominated by a vision of a Middle Ages of barbarism, interposed between the glorious age of classical Antiquity and modern progress, Mustoxidi popularised in Italy the greatest work of an eminent Byzantine author', observes a modern scholar.[2]

## SAVING THE SHIPWRECKS OF HISTORY

Illuminating the 'dark' centuries of the Greek past was part of Mustoxidi's programme when he set out in 1843 to publish the philological/historical journal *Hellenomnemon*. The journal's twelve volumes, published between 1843 and 1853 and written entirely in Greek, represented the first attempt in Greek historiography to examine and reassess the cultural production of the Byzantine and modern Greek eras. Their pages contain bibliographical and epigraphical catalogues, unpublished manuscripts, philological notes, historical memoirs, and, above all, a number of biographies of scholars, artists, Church Fathers, and other prominent personalities from the Byzantine, Venetian, and Ottoman periods of Greek history. By unearthing the works of Greek-speaking scholars who had fled to Europe during the centuries of the 'decline' of the Greek world, the journal placed emphasis on the interaction between Greek medieval scholarship and the West. Mustoxidi's aim was threefold: first of all, to show *what the Greeks were capable of accomplishing even during the hard times of their slavery*;[3] second, to prove that Greek scholars not only remained alive during the eras of their country's political 'death', but had also salvaged the ancient Greek wisdom and transmitted it to the West, thus contributing to the Renaissance of European letters; and, third, to offer archival material for the use of future historians, who would then be able to compose a fully integrated account of the Greek nation. In presenting the journal, Spiridione Veludo, who,

---

[1] *Gazzetta privilegiata di Venezia* (22 May 1816), pp. 3–4.
[2] Margherita Losacco, *Antonio Catiforo e Giovanni Veludo interpreti di Fozio* (Bari, 2003), pp. 32–3.
[3] From Mustoxidi's correspondence. In A. Nikokaboura, 'O Andreas Moustoxydis kai o Ellinomnimon' (Andrea Mustoxidi and the *Hellenomnemon*), *Kerkyraika chronika* 8 (1960), pp. 156–7.

along with his brother and their Greco-Venetian friends, participated actively in the enterprise by laboriously transcribing manuscripts in the Marciana library and by sending material to Corfu, summarized Mustoxidi's intentions as follows: *The illustrious Corfiot's main aim is to publish as much as he has been able to gather in his various peregrinations respecting the Greek people from the different epochs; different epochs but [united] in language, religion, memories and hopes... [With these documents] it will one day certainly be possible to weave Greek history in its entirety... We will furthermore be able to trace it down to us by a varied and continuous series of circumstances: to show how by sad events, by solemn examples of heroic virtue our own times are strictly linked with ancient [times] and form the most beautiful episode [in the history] of humanity.*[4]

It seems to me, then, that the journal's ultimate purpose was to bring about the unity of Greek history. However, as I have said elsewhere in this book, this was no easy task. In trying to connect the ancient glories of classical Greece with the modern epos of the revolution and the nation-state, one had to come to grips with another critical issue: the incorporation of medieval times and, more specifically, the Byzantine past. Any attempt to do so stumbled up against a long-standing tradition among European Enlightenment thinkers, and indeed one nurtured by *philosophe* historians of the stature of Voltaire, Montesquieu, and Gibbon, of scorning all things Byzantine. For them, Byzantium was the embodiment of everything the Enlightenment deplored and despised: despotism, corruption, religious fanaticism, ignorance. The contempt shown for the political history of Byzantium, cast as an early version of Ottoman 'oriental' despotism, made it necessary for Greek intellectuals to devise alternative ways of approaching the Greek medieval past. The best course of action seemed at that moment to be to place the emphasis on cultural history. By focusing on the cultural achievements of the Byzantine and post-Byzantine period, Greek intellectuals could thus make the claim that the Greek nation had preserved its cultural continuity, despite the successive phases of its political 'decline'. What is more, emphasis on the work of Byzantine and post-Byzantine scholars who had found refuge in the West, where they continued to cultivate Greek letters and the arts, offered the grounds to create one of the most powerful myths of modern Greek nationalism: that the Greeks had managed to keep the flame of the ancient civilization alive and to transfer it to the West, thus contributing to the European, and especially the Italian, Renaissance.[5]

Of course, this is far from saying that Mustoxidi and his circle appreciated the Byzantine and modern Greek texts for what they were, for their literary value. *In the midst of disasters and slavery, in the midst of lawlessness and ruined temples, in the midst of fire, bloodshed and devastation, one would hope in vain to find the pure, the fullest and life-giving light of wisdom*—reads a passage from the second volume of

---

[4] Spiridione Veludo, 'Andrea Mustoxidi, *L'Ellenomnemone (Greco rammentatore) o Miscellanee greche*, opera compilata da etc.', *Il gondoliere* 9/61 (2 Aug. 1843), pp. 241–2.

[5] David Ricks and Paul Magdalino (eds), *Byzantium and the Modern Greek Identity* (Aldershot and Brookfield 1998); Diana Mishkova, 'The Afterlife of a Commonwealth: Narratives of Byzantium in the National Historiographies of Greece, Bulgaria, Serbia and Romania', in Roumen Daskalov and Alexander Vezenkov (eds), *Entangled Histories of the Balkans*, vol. 3: *Shared Pasts, Disputed Legacies* (Leiden, 2015), pp. 118–273.

the *Hellenomnemon; any praise should be proportionate to the miseries of our patria [in those times] and not to the actual value of the works.*[6] As modern scholarship has pointed out, even later in the nineteenth century the rehabilitation of Byzantine texts happened not *because of,* but *despite* their presumed aesthetic value. Intellectuals took a lively interest in them not in terms of literature, but in terms of history: Byzantine sources mattered first and foremost as historical documents.[7]

This is not to say, though, that Mustoxidi aspired to compose a comprehensive account of Greek history. He believed that the moment had not yet come for such a synthesizing endeavour. His programme was only meant to collect scattered archival material which, like *shipwrecks after a storm,* had survived in European libraries in the midst of *the afflictions suffered by our common fatherland.*[8] He imagined his journal as a historian's emporium, where *the lover of local memories could find sporadic news useful to his researches.*[9] Besides, as he stated in one of the first volumes, *we believe that Greek scholars of the period between the horrible times of the [conquest of Constantinople] and the happiest [days] of the revolution cannot provide material for the composition of a literary history, but only for the writing of separate biographies.*[10] Its search for continuity notwithstanding, this milieu's view of Greek history remained fragmentary. *These researches,* we read in the *Hellenomnemon, are like the bones, which circumscribe the flesh of the historical body.*[11] The reconstitution of that body would indeed have to wait until the second half of the century, when Constantinos Paparrigopoulos, Greece's 'national historiographer', would compose his monumental *History of the Greek Nation* (1860–74).[12]

The same rationale was behind this group's exertions in the fields of local historiography, bibliography, and biography. Of course, these men were not alone in taking such an interest. Every scholar and publicist in the post-Venetian Adriatic was swept up in a wave of passion for archival documents, bibliographical lists, biographical dictionaries, and local histories. Such an activity served a number of different purposes. In Venice, it was connected to the rediscovery and reaffirmation of the glorious history of the Serenissima and to a new sort of Venetian 'municipal patriotism', which developed vis-à-vis the Austrians and within the overarching context of Italian nationalism.[13] In the former Venetian colonies of the northern Adriatic, on the other hand, archival organization served Habsburg administrative purposes, while delving into the local past by Triestine, Dalmatian, and Istrian intellectuals fostered competing regional identities. Just like the *Hellenomnemon,* the philological/historical journal *L'Istria,* published here between 1846 and 1852,

---

[6] *Hellenomnemon* 2 (1843), p. 94.

[7] Panagiotis Agapitos, 'Byzantine Literature and Greek Philologists in the Nineteenth Century', *Classica et mediaevalia* 43 (1992), pp. 231–60.

[8] 'Biografika' (On biographies), *Hellenomnemon* 2 (1843), pp. 95–6.

[9] 'Aggelia' (Announcement), *Hellenomnemon* 1 (1843), p. 2.     [10] 'Biografika', pp. 95–6.

[11] 'Peri tinon ponimaton anaferomenon eis tin istorian tis Ipeirou, etc.' (On some works about the history of Epirus, etc.), *Hellenomnemon* 4 (1843), p. 230.

[12] See Antonis Liakos, 'The Making of Greek History. The Construction of National Time', in Jacques Revel and Giovanni Levi (eds), *Political Uses of the Past: The Recent Mediterranean Experience* (London, 2001).

[13] Gino Benzoni, 'La storiografia', in G. Arnaldi and M. P. Stocchi (eds), *Storia della cultura veneta,* vol. 6: *Dall'età napoleonica alla Prima Guerra Mondiale* (Vicenza, 1986), pp. 597–623.

brought to the light of day sundry medieval documents and other local archival sources.[14] Finally, in the British Ionian Islands, local historiography and the compilation of biographical dictionaries served to empower the locals in their bid to wrest liberal reforms from a reluctant colonial administration. *What do the Ionians lack that might render them worthy of more liberal Institutions?*—asked Mustoxidi in his memorandum, which he presented to the Colonial Secretary in 1839; *What country, if we take into account its small size, its scant population, has ever achieved so much renown in letters, sciences, in warfare, in politics... Do the histories and biographical Dictionaries not already tell of it? Are the Ionians not suited to ruling themselves?*[15]

## MONUMENTS OF NATIONAL CONTINUITY: RE-EVALUATING THE GREEK FOLK SONGS

It was again to underscore the cultural continuity of the Greek nation that the intellectuals of this circle, before anybody else, took an interest in Greek folk songs, treasuring them as monuments of national history. Mustoxidi was again the life and soul of the project, but several others among the characters mentioned above— and, most significantly, Tommaseo—were engaged in collecting, studying, publishing, and translating Greek songs. The process was not always easy. *It's a long time since I went into the countryside to collect [songs] from the peasants, [who]... are somewhat intractable because they are ashamed and believe that I am out to play a joke on them*, Mustoxidi complained to Tipaldo at some point in 1842.[16] Much earlier than this, and indeed much earlier than the appearance of any published collection of the kind, the Corfiot intellectual had shown signs of an interest in such material. As mentioned in Chapter 10, in 1804 he had offered to help the Italo-Swiss scholar Sismondi, who was at the time trying to assemble a collection, although to no avail. Some years later, in 1820, in an open letter that he addressed to his friend the philologist Schinas, Mustoxidi announced his own intention to publish a collection of songs, which likewise came to nothing.[17] Four years later, the first book of Greek folk poetry finally saw the light of day. It was Claude Fauriel's two-volume *Chants populaires de la Grèce moderne* (1824–5), in which, as mentioned in Chapter 10, Mustoxidi had a hand. *[Having formed a] close friendship with Fauriel,* he recalled in a letter to Tipaldo, *I surrendered my works to him, and when he came to Italy, I went with him from house to house, and we garnered a rich harvest from the Greek women in Veneto and Trieste.*[18] Along with Masarachi, the Corfiot intellectual

[14]   Egidio Ivetic, 'Ricerca storica, archivi e sviluppo nazionale nell'Adriatico Orientale e in Croazia (1815–1914)', in Irene Cotta and Rosalia Manno Tolu (eds), *Archivi e storia nell'Europa del XIX secolo: alle radici dell'identità culturale europea* (Florence, 2006), pp. 687–704.

[15]   Andrea Mustoxidi, *Sulla condizione attuale delle Isole Ionie: promemoria presentato in agosto 1839 etc.* (London, 1840), pp. 19–20.

[16]   Dimitris Arvanitakis (ed.), *Carteggio 1822–1860: Andrea Mustoxidi ed Emilio Tipaldo* (Athens, 2005), p. 483.

[17]   Andrea Mustoxidi, 'A Demetrio Schina bizantino. Andrea Mustoxidi corcirese', in idem, *Prose varie del Cavaliere Andrea Mustoxidi, con aggiunta di alcuni versi* (Milan, 1821), pp. 213–18.

[18]   Arvanitakis (ed.), *Carteggio 1822–1860: Andrea Mustoxidi ed Emilio Tipaldo*, pp. 458–9.

would likewise assist Tommaseo, when about two decades later he published a collection of folk songs from various Mediterranean shores, including Greece.[19]

Globally, the emergence of the interest in what we know as 'folk poetry' is dated no earlier than the second half of the eighteenth century. In 1760 a young Scotsman, James Macpherson, published the *Fragments of Ancient Poetry*, a collection of folk songs attributed to the third-century Scottish bard Ossian. In reality the songs were composed by Macpherson himself (who drew to some degree on the traditional tales and ballads of the Highlands of Scotland), but the acclaim they received across Europe testified to a new thirst for all things 'primitive' and 'folkloric'.[20] In Italy, where the songs were translated by no less a figure than Cesarotti, Ossian was hailed as the Celtic Homer and one of the greatest poets of all time. Ossianism served not only to break down the established literary paradigm of strict classicism, but also to champion the cause of nascent nationalism.[21] This new taste found theoretical expression in the work of the German scholar Johann Gottfried Herder, *Correspondence on Ossian* (1773). The folk songs, Herder declared, were the *archives of their people, the treasury of their science and religion, their theogony and cosmogony, the deeds of their fathers and the events of their history.*[22] What was being created here, in reality, was the ideological concept of 'the people'. The combination of this new concept with the emerging idea of the nation is what transformed the matter into an issue of the most urgent intellectual concern, a set of intertwined beliefs that spread swiftly across Europe and beyond. It was in this new invention, 'the people', and in its 'unspoiled' songs, that the *génie de la nation* was considered to reside; the duty of the intellectual was merely to find it and display it. As Mustoxidi wrote in a 1825 article, *the proverbs that arise...among a people... merit investigation by grammarians and writers, and no less deserving in this regard are those songs which, inspired by the domestic affections, by love, by admiration, by warlike enthusiasm, contain in themselves the seed of a virgin poetic faculty, and the impressions of nature, of the climate of the Greeks, and the expression of their physical and moral condition, without otiose and artificial ornaments.*[23] Moreover, the discovery and re-evaluation of folk poetry proved to be a powerful tool to show the existence of a 'deeper essence' of a nation, which, no matter what, remained unchanged through time. *The modern Greeks*, wrote Fauriel in his introduction, *have... a popular poetry in every sense and with all the force of this term, a direct and true expression of the character and of the national spirit, which every Greek understands and feels with love, simply by dint of being Greek, of inhabiting the soil and breathing the air of*

[19] Niccolò Tommaseo, *Canti popolari, toscani, corsi, illirici e greci* (Venice, 1841–2). See also Georgios Zoras, *A. Mazarakis kai N. Thomazeos: anekdotos allilografia* (A. Masarachi and N. Tommaseo: unpublished correspondence) (Athens, 1963).

[20] Clare O'Halloran, 'Irish Recreations of the Gaelic Past: The Challenge of Macpherson's Ossian', *Past and Present* 124 (Aug. 1989), pp. 69–95.

[21] Matteo Sante, 'Ossian and Risorgimento: The Poetics of Nationalism', in Larry H. Peer (ed.), *Romanticism across the Disciplines* (Lanham, Md, and New York, 1998), pp. 27–40.

[22] Johann Gottfried Herder, 'Excerpt from a Correspondence on Ossian and the Songs of Ancient Peoples', in Burton Feldman and Robert D. Richardson (eds), *The Rise of Modern Mythology, 1680–1860* (Bloomington, Ind., 1999), p. 229.

[23] Andrea Mustoxidi, 'Alcune considerazioni sulla presente lingua de' Greci', *Antologia* 17 (Mar. 1825), pp. 54–5.

*Greece; a poetry, finally, that lives, not in books, having an artificial and often only apparent life, but in the people itself, and having all the life of the people… Such a collection, if it were complete, would be at once both the veritable national history of Greece, and the most faithful picture of the mores of its inhabitants.*[24] Fauriel, Mustoxidi, and their like claimed that in the songs of the modern Greeks there survived the spirit, the language, and the culture of the ancients. *Mustoxidi himself noted down words from the most ancient Greek among living peasants,* noted Tommaseo.[25] For these people, folk songs were not only a poetic expression of the modern rural world; they were carriers of ancient values, monuments of Greek history. *The more I have reflected upon it,* we read in Fauriel's introduction, *the more it has seemed to me that this poetry must be incomparably more ancient than all of its surviving monuments.*[26] It was, in a certain sense, another way to incorporate the peasantry into the new era of nation-states.[27]

Somewhat different was Tommaseo's philosophy regarding folk traditions. Like Mustoxidi and Fauriel, he believed that folk songs revealed the deeper moral and aesthetic values of a nation. But he also believed that folk traditions might reveal the common elements shared between different nations. Nowhere can Tommaseo's vision of the world, at the same time fraternal and national, be more clearly discerned than in his anthology of folk ballads from Tuscany, Corsica, Greece, and Illyria, which I mentioned in Chapter 11 (*Canti popolari, Toscani, Corsi, Illirici e Greci*, 1841). By putting these four corpuses of songs within one and the same anthology, he was, furthermore, arguing that fraternity among peoples would be reached, not by eliminating national distinctions, but by attaining a deeper understanding of them. In addition, by bringing out each people's connections with, and influences from its neighbours, he wanted to show just how intertwined nations really were. In a separate volume which he published in that same year, entitled *Scintille* (Sparks), he argued indeed that the greatness of a nation is seen in the way it culti-vates its bonds with its neighbours: *The true greatness of every nation would seem to me to consist in this, [namely], modestly and resolutely preserving its own nature, while also embracing its sisters with respectful affection.*[28] *Scintille* was written variously in Italian, French, South Slavic, and Greek, the aim being to show the world that diversity in language and culture did not constitute an obstacle, but should rather provide impetus for the sisterhood of Mediterranean nations. It was Tommaseo's firm conviction that no one nation was superior to any other and that each should develop by helping, supporting, and respecting the others. He would live long enough (until 1874) to see his vision utterly defeated by a version of nationalism which was exclusionary, divisive, and, at times, sanguinary and aggressive. This will indeed be the final act of our story.

---

[24]  Claude Fauriel, *Chants populaires de la Grèce moderne* (Paris, 1824–5), vol. I, p. xxv.

[25]  Niccolò Tommaseo, 'Andrea Mustoxidi', *Archivio storico italiano* 12/2 (1860), p. 43.

[26]  Fauriel, *Chants populaires de la Grèce moderne*, vol. I, p. cxii.

[27]  Michael Herzfeld, *Ours Once More: Folklore, Ideology, and the Making of Modern Greece* (Austin, Tex., 1982); Miodrag Ibrovac, *Claude Fauriel et la fortune européenne des poésies populaires grecque et serbe* (Paris, 1966); Alexis Politis, *I anakalypsi ton ellinikon dimotikon tragoudion* (The discovery of Greek folk songs) (Athens, 1999).

[28]  Niccolò Tommaseo, *Scintille* (Venice, 1841), p. 7.

# Epilogue
## The Sunken World of the Adriatic

*Chi mai s'è avvisato di mutare una rissa di taverna in rissa di nazioni?*
(Who would ever have imagined that a tavern brawl would turn into a war between nations?)

—Andrea Mustoxidi to Niccolò Tommaseo (Corfu, 1855)[1]

It was a hot evening in July 1853 on Corfu when it all started. Two Italian friends, both exiles from the 1848–9 revolutions on the opposite shore, sat at a table in a local tavern. When some Greeks who were eating and drinking at a nearby table saw them, they stood up and started singing something about the 'Cross that will shine again above Constantinople', following this with a volley of insults against Italians. It was the time of the Crimean War and rumour had it that a foreign legion, comprising Italian soldiers, was being formed in Constantinople to fight the Russians alongside the Ottomans. The news may have been refuted by the local newspapers, but that made no difference. Italians in Corfu were greeted in the streets as *dogs, and the defenders of dogs*. The tavern confrontation soon developed into a brawl and ended with a Greek man being stabbed to death and left lying on the doorstep. At the ensuing trial, which became more of a political than a legal event, the defendant, ostensibly one of the two Italians, was sentenced to death. In spite of the numerous appeals of other Italian exiles to the Ionian Senate, pleading that the death penalty not be enacted, he was eventually executed.

Shortly afterwards a long pamphlet appeared under the controversial title *Il supplizio d'un Italiano in Corfù* (The martyrdom of an Italian in Corfu). Its author was Niccolò Tommaseo. Himself an exile on Corfu since 1849, Tommaseo denounced the legal processes employed in the case, arguing that the court had evidently been swayed by the ill feeling on the Ionian Islands directed at the time towards the Italian exiles.[2] He was not entirely mistaken. The echoes of the Crimean War aside, Italian refugees were viewed with suspicion in this corner of the Adriatic. An integral part of Corfiot society since the time of the French Revolution, they, nevertheless,

---

[1] 'Open letter to Niccolò Tommaseo', *Efimeris ton eidiseon* (5 Dec. 1855). In Michele Lascaris, 'Niccolò Tommaseo ed Andrea Mustoxidi', *Atti e memorie della Società Dalmata di Storia patria* 3 (1934), pp. 12–15.

[2] Niccolò Tommaseo, *Il supplizio d'un Italiano in Corfù*, edited by Fabio Danelon (Venice, 2008 [1855]).

were never more than fifty or so in number. In 1848–9, though, and following the revolutionary events in Italy, a wave of political exiles from Calabria, the Papal States, and Venice flooded into the islands. The local liberal newspaper may have welcomed them with open arms (*Let us consider all nations, close and distant, as children of the same father* it wrote; *as members of the same body, as drops of the blood in which all mankind was baptised on the Mount of Redemption*),[3] but their numbers were now ten times greater than the islanders had been used to, and even if everyone did not stay, the mere presence of those who did was enough to disrupt local society. Most of them had difficulties in finding a job and adapting to the realities of everyday existence on the islands, thus failing to achieve a genuinely peaceful symbiosis with the local inhabitants.[4]

Be that as it may, what chiefly upset Tommaseo was the attitude of his faithful old friend and helpmate during his first days of exile, Mustoxidi. He thought that the Corfiot, who was at the time a member of the Provincial Council of the city, instead of trying to damp down the situation and intervene in order to save the Italian exile's life, did everything to make things worse. In a letter to Tipaldo written in the aftermath of the episode, he complained about Mustoxidi's participation in the events immediately following the tavern brawl and which included, among other things, a procession of the dead Greek's body through the streets. *They were not content simply to bear the slain man's body through the most frequented streets*, he said; *they made an inscription for him that said that he was dead on account of an 'Italian knife'; and they bore him to [Mustoxidi], whether on account of his forming part of the municipal government or as a scholar or as the head of a party; and he corrected it to 'treacherous knife', by which 'Italian' was understood, which everyone knows and will repeat from father to son.*[5]

Tommaseo's pamphlet was discussed all over the Ionian Island and elicited a number of polemical responses. So much so that one year later the Dalmatian intellectual was obliged to speak out publicly in his own defence. In an open letter to the 'People of Corfu', he specified that he did not consider all Corfiots responsible for what had happened. Besides, some of his local friends, like the poet Dionysios Solomos, had shown their support by opposing the death penalty and by petitioning for mercy, albeit to no avail. *The fault*, he claimed, *lies with those who, taking no care to allay people's anger, led affairs or let them be led to the wretched conclusion that we each and everyone of us deplore.*[6]

[3] In Panagiotis Chiotis, *Istoria tou Ioniou Kratous apo systaseos aftou mechris enoseos, 1815–1864* (The history of the Ionian state from its creation to the unification with Greece, 1815–1864) (Zante, 1877), vol. II, p. 178.

[4] Maria Christina Chatziioannou, 'Oi Italoi prosfyges sta Ionia nisia sta mesa tou 19ou aiona: diamorfomenes pragmatikotites kai proypotheseis ensomatosis' (Italian refugees on the Ionian Islands in the mid-19th century: lived realities and conditions of integration), in *VI Panionian Conference, Proceedings* (Athens, 2001), vol. II, pp. 495–510. See also Christos Aliprantis, 'Political Refugees of the 1848–1849 Revolutions in the Kingdom of Greece: Migration, Nationalism, and State-formation in Nineteenth Century Mediterranean', *Journal of Modern Greek Studies*, forthcoming.

[5] Niccolò Tommaseo, *Il secondo esilio: scritti concernenti le cose d'Italia e d'Europa dal 1849 in poi* (Milan, 1862), vol. I, p. 285.

[6] Niccolò Tommaseo, 'Al popolo di Corfù', *Il Diritto* (14 Oct. 1855) (reproduced in idem, *Il secondo esilio*, vol. II, pp. 174–88); Caterina Carpinato, '*Il supplizio d' un italiano in Corfù*: un caso di

It was at this point that Mustoxidi decided to take up his pen and set things right. *But to such a degree is every norm overturned*, he wrote in his 'Open letter to Niccolò Tommaseo', that *whoever does not proclaim to be unjust the sentences that fall upon a murderer, is against the offender's patria, and cares not for the honour of their own. Yet if you so believe, do at least be so kind as not to heap blame on those who feel offended by the title of your book, 'Martyrdom of an Italian in Corfu', as if to say 'Martyrdom of a Saint in Barbary', and resent the fact of witnesses, judges and supreme magistrates, their fellow citizens and friends and relatives, being with such passion abused.*[7] Tommaseo's reply was not slow in coming. From his lengthy *j'accuse* let us keep the following: *I am deeply saddened that [Mustoxidi] should by way of exculpation and out of pride have thought to correct the sign...that spoke of an 'Italian' knife, replacing the word 'Italian' with the word 'traitor'; the 'God of forgiveness' teaches us that we are all brothers; and Mr Mustoxidi's learning and the Italian names featuring on so many Corfiot houses tell us that Italy and Greece are the closest of sisters...It saddens me, as I have said, that Mr Mustoxidi,...who in his work as a translator has 'burned the midnight candle' countless times, and will do so many more in order to finish his Herodotus,... has translated 'Italian' as 'traitor', a somewhat unfaithful rendering.*[8]

The dispute dragged on for some time, leading eventually to a definitive breach between the two friends. It remains now to be seen why *a tavern brawl would turn into a war between nations* and thus precipitate the final act in our trans-Adriatic drama.

## LINGUISTIC WARS

Bearing in mind Tommaseo's multinationalism, it is not difficult to imagine what disturbed him while in the Ionian Islands. It was something more than the inimical atmosphere created on Corfu against Italian exiles, something beyond the controversial juridical process following the tavern episode. It was a phenomenon older and deeper than the events which unfolded during those troubling days. Tommaseo was profoundly troubled by what he saw as the fanatical efforts of Ionian intellectuals and politicians since the 1830s to demonize all things Italian and, more specifically, to purge the Italian language from all domains of public life in favour of Greek. *The casting away of the Italian language and memories as if the body of a shipwrecked person, would be a double barbarism if you were to do it, O Ionians, it truly would*, read another of his desperate appeals to his Adriatic 'brothers' during those years.[9]

intolleranza etnica nell'Eptaneso della seconda metà dell'Ottocento e la fallita mediazione di Dionisios Solomós', in Adriano Pavan and Gianfranco Giraudo (eds), *Integrazione, assimilazione, esclusione e reazione etnica* (Naples, 2008), vol. II, pp. 272–93; idem, 'Ancora su Niccolò Tommaseo, Dionìssios Solomòs e la lingua greca', in Christos Bintoudis (ed.), *Kalvos e Solomòs: studi e ricerche* (Rome, 2017), pp. 203–24.

[7] In Lascaris, 'Niccolò Tommaseo ed Andrea Mustoxidi', pp. 12–13.

[8] Tommaseo, *Il secondo esilio*, vol. II, pp. 455–7.

[9] Niccolò Tommaseo, 'Della civiltà italiana nelle Isole Ionie e di Niccolò Delviniotti', *Archivio storico italiano* 2 (1855), p. 79.

As discussed in Part I of this book, the linguistic reality of the Ionian Islands (and of the whole of the former Venetian Adriatic, for that matter) during the nineteenth century was a complex phenomenon. The centuries-old diglossic settlement between, on the one hand, aristocrats and city-dwellers who spoke Venetian and wrote Italian and, on the other hand, people of the lower echelons of society and peasants who conducted their day-to-day affairs in the local Greek dialect, outlasted not only the end of the Venetian rule but also the consecutive Ionian constitutions (1799, 1803, and 1817) which proclaimed Greek to be the official language of the state. To be sure, a change of a linguistic regime was not an easy thing to implement. There were three types of obstacle, social, legal, and practical. To begin with, proposals about language change were not only a way of redefining the relations of the islands with the opposite shore of the Adriatic, but also of challenging the old local Venetian social order. In other words, abandoning Italian meant abandoning one of the key elements distinguishing Ionian high from low social strata. Second, since all juridical codes were written in Italian, a change in language entailed reforming the legislative system. It comes, then, as no surprise that the very last places where Greek was adopted were the courts. Juridical codes continued, indeed, to be drafted in Italian until 1851. But what was even more difficult than all of the above was the practical aspect of the change. The great majority of Ionian intellectuals and politicians who advocated the abandonment of Italian, educated in Italy or by Italian teachers as they were, wrote their ardent pleas and declarations in that very same language.[10] Tommaseo could not have put it better: *For several years now, the cry has gone up, and rightly so, that Greek should be the language of the nation reborn to a sense of itself; and almost everyone agrees about this, and it is a thing established by laws: and yet Italian is the language that the majority can most easily write, and by very many of those who decry it… It is so difficult to root out from the human soul the intimate roots of thought that are in speech; and the desires of the learned, the trumpeting of the newspapers and the laws can do very little about this.*[11]

The situation was, of course, familiar to Tommaseo because of his native Dalmatia. During the long period of Venetian domination and for several decades afterwards, there, just as in the Ionian Islands, bilingualism was the rule. The ruling classes of the Adriatic coasts, especially in the cities, wrote in Italian, whereas the rural population of the hinterland communicated in a local Slavic idiom (Croatian). The situation became even more complex with the annexation of the area to the Habsburg Empire in 1815. Then, as one source puts it, 'in Dalmatia one would think and speak in Italian, obey in German and listen in Slavic'.[12] This multilingual settlement was,

---

[10] Peter Mackridge, 'Venise après Venise: Official Languages in the Ionian Islands, 1797–1864', *Byzantine and Modern Greek Studies* 38/1 (Mar. 2014), pp. 68–90; Theodosis Pylarinos, *Glossikos patriotismos: oi agones gia tin kathierosi tis glossas tou ellinikou laou ktl.* (Linguistic patriotism: the battles for the establishment of the language of the Greek people etc.) (Corfu, 2013); Dimitris Arvanitakis, 'Glossa kai ethniki taftotita sto Ionio kata ton 19o aiona' (Language and national identity on the Ionian Islands in the nineteenth century), *Ta istorika* 46 (2007), pp. 15–24; Tzortzis Ikonomou, 'Le Isole Ionie, la Grecia e il *Supplizio*', in Tommaseo, *Il supplizio d'un Italiano in Corfù*, pp. 277–336.

[11] Tommaseo, *Il secondo esilio*, vol. I, p. 158.

[12] In Egidio Ivetić, 'La patria del Tommaseo: la Dalmazia tra il 1815 e il 1860', in Francesco Bruni (ed.), *Niccolò Tommaseo: popolo e nazioni, Italiani, Corsi, Greci, Illirici* (Rome and Padua, 2004), vol. II,

however, challenged in the late 1840s by a new generation of nationalist intellectuals, and tensions erupted between Slavic and Italian speakers. Tommaseo was one of a handful of intellectuals who still hoped (albeit vainly) that the area's folk traditions would lead to a Slavo-Italian 'fraternal' national culture instead of frictions between its different elements.

Problems of a diglossic society vis-à-vis the rise of an exclusionary nationalism did not only appear on this side of the Italian world, however. Tommaseo and his friends knew full well the situation created in the same period in Piedmont, the leading player among the Italian states so far as Risorgimento politics was concerned. There, French was the language not only of the state's administration and justice system (a phenomenon which was reinforced during the Napoleonic period), but also of the educated elites. *In Turin*, wrote Mario Pieri in the 1820s, *everyone uses French, they read it, and they write it, and only a few learned people [use] Italian. All the Piedmontese do however have an Italian soul; but there are not any very polished Italian teachers, who can be invited into houses, and who speak their own language well.*[13] Just as the Ionians had to Hellenize their patriotic feelings, so too did the Piedmontese have to Italianize theirs. This was a difficult process, which required constant practice and unstinting effort. One of their number, Cesare Balbo, spoke about their *zeal to restore Italian language*;[14] two others, Federico Sclopis and Carlo Boucheron, planned in 1826 to publish a *Description of Piedmont* that would list its glories and stress its *italianità. A work fashioned entirely with national glory in mind, intended to serve as a guide to foreigners upon their first entering Italy*, they wrote in perfect French*, can only be written in Italian; we therefore propose to make exclusive use of this language throughout this work.*[15] And the most famous of them all, Camillo Cavour, one of the 'Fathers' of the Risorgimento and Italy's first Prime Minister, was praised for the tenacity with which he had learned Italian. *I am full of praise for the noble plan you have adopted in order to Italianize yourself*, a friend told him; *Be of good courage, Camillo!…I like the method you propose to follow in your Italian studies.*[16]

This was not so very different from what Tommaseo saw happening to his former friend, Mustoxidi. His reaction was, however, diametrically opposed. *It is to the Italian language and to his friends from Italy*, he lamented, *that he [Mustoxidi] owes the measure of fame that he enjoys; and when it was a question so far as public use in Corfu was concerned of replacing Italian with Greek, which he does not know how to write, having need therefore of a translator (and in the case of the ancient [language],*

p. 597. See also Emanuele Banfi, 'Dinamiche linguistiche nell'area Adriatica tra i secoli XVIII–XIX: tra diglossie, bilinguismi e ricerca di lingue nazionali', in Francesco Bruni and Chryssa Maltezou (eds), *L'Adriatico: incontri e separazioni (XVIII–XIX secolo)* (Venice, 2011), pp. 39–93.

[13] Mario Pieri, *Della vita di Mario Pieri corcirese scritta da lui medesimo* (Florence, 1850), vol. I, p. 436.

[14] In Gian Luigi Beccaria, 'Intellettuali, accademie e "Questione della Lingua" in Piemonte tra Sette e Ottocento', *Atti della Accademia delle Scienze di Torino* 119 (1985), p. 138.

[15] In Achille Erba, *L'azione politica di Federico Sclopis: dalla giovinezza alla codificazione Albertina (1798–1837)* (Turin, 1960), p. 57.

[16] In Claudio Mazzarini, 'L'italiano rinnegato: politica linguistica nel Piemonte francese', in Giovanna Ioli (ed.), *Atti del convegno: Piemonte e letteratura 1789–1870* (Turin, 1986), vol. I, p. 72.

*in which he spent his whole life, he does not know the prosody, and in the case of the modern he used to ask me how one would say such and such a thing, and failing to find the Greek term, he was obliged to have recourse to Italian), he would say in a scornful tone that the Venetian dialect was a language of Harlequins.* Tommaseo was profoundly hurt by Mustoxidi's leading role in what he called *a war against the Italian language*, a process in which he discerned a tendency towards xenophobia and alienation.[17] *Many decrees issued by your present government*, he declared to the Ionians, *sound like those discordant and strident attempts an orchestra makes when tuning up its instruments: but they remain dissonant.*[18] As Greek nationalism crystallized in the Ionian Islands, Tommaseo realized to his regret and sorrow that, one after the other, his Adriatic 'brothers' were slowly moving away from what he still believed was their common Venetian multinational home.

## RELIGIOUS WARS

It was not just the violent and exclusive Hellenization of the Ionian Islands that sounded to Tommaseo's ears like an instrument woefully out of tune. There was something else. *When I observe these learned men who seek to maintain and even exacerbate the division between Greece and the West,* he wrote to a friend in 1854, *I discern despite myself and with a painful sense of compassion for their arguments, for what they are saying, and for their actual mode of being, something incomplete and false, like the sound of an off-key instrument, like a piece of broken machinery.*[19] What disturbed Tommaseo in Mustoxidi and in other, like-minded intellectuals was not only their anti-Italian linguistic politics, but also their Russophile and increasingly anti-Catholic positions. The Dalmatian writer was convinced that Russia's expansionist policy constituted a grave danger for Greece, the Balkans, and the wider Mediterranean and European world. Given this threat, he thought that the integrity of the Ottoman Empire, as well as the status quo of the British protectorate of the Ionian Islands, should be safeguarded at all costs. *Which of the two peoples, the Russian or the Ottoman, is further removed from genuine civilisation?*, he asked, only to answer that Russia was more Turkish than the Turks.[20] Things took a yet more serious turn when in 1853 reports about the outbreak of a war in the Crimea poured into Corfu. It was religious controversy that served to precipitate the conflict. In deciding that it should champion the discontent felt by many Orthodox of the Ottoman Empire towards the Porte's decision to concede only to its Catholic subjects certain religious privileges concerning the Holy Lands in Palestine, Russia grasped the opportunity to pursue its expansionist policy at the expense of the Ottoman Empire. Such a policy constituted a threat for the other European Powers, which sought their share from the putative dismembering of 'the sick man' of the East. In March 1854, indeed, Britain and France declared war on Russia.

---

[17]  Niccolò Tommaseo, 'Andrea Mustoxidi', *Archivio storico italiano* 12/2 (1860), p. 46.

[18]  Tommaseo, 'Della civiltà italiana nelle Isole Ionie', pp. 79–80.

[19]  Tommaseo, *Il secondo esilio*, vol. I, pp. 321–2.

[20]  In Stefano Aloe, 'Tommaseo e la Russia', in Bruni (ed.), *Niccolò Tommaseo: popolo e nazioni*, vol. II, pp. 736–7.

The Austrian Empire and the Italian Kingdom of Sardinia (Piedmont) followed suit. Many in the Ionian Islands followed the progress of the Crimean War very closely. Most of these observers hoped that a Russian victory would lead to the total dismemberment of the Ottoman Empire and, consequently, to the creation of more favourable terms for the desired unification of the islands with Greece. It comes, then, as no surprise that the alignment of Piedmont with the anti-Russian camp provoked much indignation, which in turn gave rise to a series of conspiracy theories against Italians in general.

Religion was involved in this war in more ways than one. Tommaseo believed, not without reason, that Orthodoxy served as the major pretext for the promotion of Russian aspirations. He therefore favoured the spreading of Catholic propaganda in the Balkans and backed projects envisioning the unification of the two Churches under the ecclesiastical authority of the Pope. As a liberal Catholic, he was convinced that progress and liberty could be reconciled with the values of the Catholic Church if the Papacy abandoned its political power and focused on its spiritual regeneration. Tommaseo explained these ideas in his book *Rome et le monde*, published in 1851. The fact that the book was condemned by a papal encyclical did little to discourage him.[21]

The Crimean War was pivotal also in sharpening the differences between the Catholic and Orthodox populations of the Adriatic, thus dealing the final blow to an already shaken equilibrium between the two religious groups in the area. The tensions created in Dalmatia between Catholic Croats and Orthodox Serbs are a case in point.[22] But Tommaseo was more worried by the repercussions of the war in Corfu. *I have said to you before, I believe,* he said in a letter to a friend in 1853, ... *as in the case of those Italians however many and whoever they may be, who enrolled in a legion against Russia (but the legion vanished), the Italians from here and the Corfiots following the Latin rite, were whipped up by the press and by public words of contempt and hatred.*[23] As discussed in Chapter 4 of this book, discrimination against the Catholic inhabitants of the island started at the turn of the nineteenth century with the arrival of the Russians in the Adriatic, to become still worse in the ensuing years. The local Corfiot religious identity, a sort of syncretic 'borderland religion', which had for centuries permitted interaction and communication between the two rites, Greek and Latin, was coming slowly to an end.[24] The new balance of power in the Mediterranean following the emergence of the Russian and the British empires, along with the instrumentalization of religion for the purposes of national ideologies on both shores of the Adriatic, produced a new religious reality of strict division between the two dogmas. Things in Corfu became even more critical in 1847, when an outbreak of violence between members of the two

---

[21] Angelo Tamborra, 'Niccolò Tommaseo, il mondo ortodosso e il problema dell'Unione delle Chiese', in V. Branca and G. Petrocchi (eds), *Niccolò Tommaseo nel centenario della morte* (Florence, 1977), pp. 583–628; Antonis Liakos, *L'unificazione italiana e la Grande Idea: ideologia e azione dei movimenti nazionali in Italia e in Grecia, 1859–1871* (Florence, 1995), p. 36.

[22] Tamborra, 'Niccolò Tommaseo, il mondo ortodosso e il problema dell'Unione delle Chiese'.

[23] Tommaseo, *Il secondo esilio*, vol. I, pp. 280–1.

[24] The term 'borderland religion' is borrowed from Daphne Lappa, 'Borderland Religion in the Eastern End of the *Serenissima*: Greeks in the Venetian City of Corfu' (unpublished paper).

religious groups led the Catholics of the island to surrender their right to hold processions in the streets, thus effectively relinquishing public space to the Orthodox. As the then Orthodox Bishop of the Ionian Islands put it, ... *time, the long coexistence, the mixed marriages and the common cycle of festivals had somehow united the spirits ... [But now] the people are watching, indignant, the Latins moving away from the churches which, in the past, they visited, respected and decorated with their votive offerings; thus,* he concluded, *the religious feeling, allied with the national one, and being offended in its own country, cannot help but produce disastrous results.*[25] The gradual consolidation of Orthodoxy in this corner of the Adriatic, combined with the ossifying of Catholic religiosity in the Italian peninsula, led by the time of the Crimean War to the total disappearance of whatever remnants of the Adriatic Venetian unity still subsisted.

## THE DISSOLUTION OF THE COMMON VENETIAN SPACE OF THE ADRIATIC

Behind the apparently insignificant episode of the tavern brawl and the sentencing to death of its perpetrator, Tommaseo painfully discerned the origins of an unbridgeable gap which was now opening up between the Ionians and the Italians. Geopolitical rearrangements and the gradual 'Hellenization' and 'Orthodoxization' of the Ionian Islands led to the decisive alienation of this area from its former geographies of cultural belonging. In the final analysis, the rift between Tommaseo and Mustoxidi masked a deeper crisis which took place in the Adriatic during the first half of the nineteenth century. This concerned the dissolution of the common Venetian space of the Adriatic and the disappearance of the centuries-old links which had existed between the opposite shores of the sea. With them there vanished also the in-between space, which intellectuals like Tommaseo, Mustoxidi, and all the other characters thronging the pages of this book had carved out for themselves at the interstices of multiple societies, beyond narrow geographical, religious, and linguistic boundaries. If the 'transnational patriotism' moment in the Mediterranean saw its first signs of crisis at the beginning of the 1830s with the creation of the Greek state, it suffered a second blow in 1848 with the calcifying of nationalist politics in the Italian peninsula and the British Ionian Islands, to breathe its last in the 1850s with the new religious separations created as echoes of the Crimean War. Whereas some forms of transnational solidarity in the Mediterranean survived up to the end of the century, the times of the intellectual-as-bridge had now irrevocably passed.[26] The bridging sea and its last inhabitants were now lost, never to return.

---

[25] In Theodossios Nikolaidis, '"Local Religion" in Corfu: Sixteenth to Nineteenth Centuries', *Mediterranean Historical Review* 29/2 (2014), p. 163.

[26] Gilles Pécout, 'Philhellenism in Italy: Political Friendship and the Italian Volunteers in the Mediterranean in the Nineteenth Century', *Journal of Modern Italian Studies* 9/4 (2004), pp. 405–27; Liakos, *L'unificazione italiana e la Grande Idea*.

# Bibliography

## UNPUBLISHED SOURCES

**Archives**
Benaki Museum, Athens: Ioannis Kapodistrias Archive, Mustoxidi Papers.
Biblioteca Ambrosiana di Milano: Fondo Bellotti.
Biblioteca Nazionale Centrale di Firenze: Cart. Vieuss., Pal. carte del Furia, Cart. Vari.
Biblioteca dell'Accademia delle Scienze di Torino: Fondo Sclopis, Fondo Grassi, Fondo Gazzera.
Biblioteca Riccardiana di Firenze: Lettere originali a Mario Pieri, Memorie di Mario Pieri.
Biblioteca Trivulziana di Milano: Fondo Acquisti e Doni.
Bibliothèque nationale de France-Bibliothèque de l'Arsenal: Autographes abbé Grégoire.
Bibliothèque publique et universitaire de Genève: Département de Manuscrits.
Bibliothèque Victor Cousin-Bibliothèque de la Sorbonne.
General State Archives, Athens: K.20, Archive of A. Papadopoulos Vrettos, Manuscripts, IA' (XI), 'Memorie biografiche e storiche'.
Holy Metropolis of Corfu: Mustoxidi Papers.

## MA/Ph.D. Dissertations–Unpublished Papers
Athanasopoulou, Afroditi. 'To problima tis diglossias: i periptosi tou Solomou' (Ph.D. dissertation, University of Crete, 1999).
Calligas, Eleni. 'The "Rizospastai" (Radical-Unionists): Politics and Nationalism in the British Protectorate of the Ionian Islands, 1815–1864' (Ph.D. dissertation, London School of Economics and Political Science, 1994).
D'Anna, Teresa. 'Il filellenismo sulle pagine dell'Antologia' di Gian Pietro Vieusseux (1821–1832)' (MA dissertation, University of Pisa, 2001–2).
Emmerich, Karen. '"A genre mixed, but valid": Dionysios Solomos's *The Free Besieged* and its Posthumous Editorial Forms' (unpublished chapter from a book in progress on editorial practice and the material construction of modern Greek poetry).
Ilicak, Sukru. 'A Radical Rethinking of Empire: Ottoman State and Society during the Greek War of Independence 1821–1826' (Ph.D. dissertation, Harvard University, 2011).
Lappa, Daphne. 'Borderland Religion in the Eastern End of the *Serenissima*: Greeks in the Venetian City of Corfu' (unpublished paper).
Manis, Evangelos. 'Andreas Moustoxydis (1785–1860): o epistimon, o politikos, o ethnikos agonistis' (Ph.D. dissertation, University of Athens, 1960).
Mcknight, James. 'Admiral Ushakov and the Ionian Republic: The Genesis of Russia's First Balkan Satellite' (Ph.D. dissertation, University of Wisconsin–Madison, 1965).
Milios, Vasilios. 'Oi istorikes tyches tis ellinikis koinotitas tis Barletta tis Kato Italias' (Ph.D. dissertation, Aristotelian University of Thessaloniki, 2013).
Papaioannou, Apostolos. 'Oi Ellines tis Benetias kai i benetiki epanastasi tou 1848–49' (Ph.D. dissertation, University of Ioannina, 1986).
Paschalidi, Maria. 'Constructing Ionian Identities: The Ionian Islands in British Official Discourses, 1815–1864' (Ph.D. dissertation, University College London, 2009).
Zanou, Konstantina. 'Expatriate Intellectuals and National Identity: Andrea Mustoxidi in Italy, France and Switzerland (1802–1829)' (Ph.D. dissertation, University of Pisa, 2007).

## PUBLISHED SOURCES

Abulafia, David. *The Great Sea: A Human History of the Mediterranean* (Oxford, 2011).

Agapitos, Panagiotis. 'Byzantine Literature and Greek Philologists in the Nineteenth Century'. *Classica et mediaevalia* 43 (1992): pp. 231–60.

Alfieri, Vittorio. *Il Misogallo*. In Vittorio Alfieri, *Scritti politici e morali*, edited by C. Mazzotta (Asti, 1984), vol. III.

Alfieri, Vittorio. *The Autobiography of Vittorio Alfieri, the Tragic Poet*, translated by Charles Edwards Lester (New York, 1845).

Aliprantis, Christos. 'Political Refugees of the 1848–1849 Revolutions in the Kingdom of Greece: Migration, Nationalism, and State-formation in Nineteenth Century Mediterranean', *Journal of Modern Greek Studies*, forthcoming.

Aloe, Stefano. 'Tommaseo e la Russia'. In *Niccolò Tommaseo: popolo e nazioni, Italiani, Corsi, Greci, Illirici*, edited by Francesco Bruni (Rome and Padua, 2004): vol. II, pp. 733–56.

Anastasopoulos, Antonis, and Elias Kolovos (eds). *Ottoman Rule and the Balkans, 1760–1850: Conflict, Transformation, Adaptation* (Rethymno, 2007).

Anderson, Benedict. *Imagined Communities: Reflections on the Origin and Spread of Nationalism* (London, 1983).

Anderson, Benedict. *The Spectre of Comparisons: Nationalism, Southeast Asia and the World* (London and New York, 1998).

Andrade, Tonio. 'A Chinese Farmer, Two Black Boys, and a Warlord: Towards a Global Microhistory'. *Journal of World History* 21/4 (2011): pp. 573–91.

Angelomatis-Tsougarakis, Eleni (ed.). *Evgenios Voulgaris, Conference Proceedings* (Athens, 2009).

[Anonymous]. 'Aftobiografia Io. Zampeliou'. *Armonia* III (1902): pp. 225–37.

[Anonymous]. 'Papadopoulos Bretos, Andreas'. *Ethnikon imerologion* 3 (1866): pp. 369–70.

Anscombe, Frederick. 'The Balkan Revolutionary Age'. *The Journal of Modern History* 84 (2012): pp. 572–606.

Antona-Traversi, Camillo. *Una lettera inedita di Ugo Foscolo e una canzone inedita di Andrea Calbo* (Rome, 1884).

Arbel, Benjamin. 'Venice's Maritime Empire in the Early Modern Period'. In *A Companion to Venetian History 1400–1797*, edited by Eric R. Dursteler (Leiden and Boston, 2013): pp. 125–253.

Arliotti, Demetrio. 'Inno alla luna'. *Nuovo giornale de' letterati di Pisa* 46 (1839): pp. 174–5.

Arliotti, Demetrio. *La vita di Giovanni Conte Capodisria* (Corfu, 1859).

Armitage, David. *Foundations of Modern International Thought* (Cambridge, 2013).

Arsh, Grigorii. *O Ioannis Kapodistrias sti Rosia* (Athens, 2015).

Artusi, Pellegrino. *Vita di Ugo Foscolo* (Florence, 1878).

Arvanitakis, Dimitris (ed.). *Carteggio 1822–1860: Andrea Mustoxidi ed Emilio Tipaldo* (Athens, 2005).

Arvanitakis, Dimitris. 'Giuseppe Compagnoni: skines apo ton bio enos "katigorou tou genous"'. In *Logos kai chronos sti neoelliniki grammateia, 18os–19os aionas*, edited by St. Kaklamanis, A. Kalokairinos, and D. Polychronakis (Herakleion, 2015): pp. 373–428.

Arvanitakis, Dimitris. 'Glossa kai ethniki taftotita sto Ionio kata ton 19o aiona'. *Ta istorika* 46 (2007): pp. 15–24.

Arvanitakis, Dimitris. 'O Thiramenis tou Andrea Kalvou: ena athelito work in progress'. *Ta istorika* 29/57 (Dec. 2012): pp. 345–66.

Arvanitakis, Dimitris. 'Scholia gia tis proypotheseis tou solomikou *Dialogou*'. In *Dionysios Solomos (150 chronia apo ton thanato tou poiiti)*, edited by Giorgos K. Myaris (Nicosia, 2011): pp. 101–50.

Arvanitakis, Dimitris. 'Un viaggio nella storiografia neogreca:. immagini della Dominante e degli ordini sociali delle città Ionie (secoli XVI–XVIII)'. In *Italia-Grecia: temi e storiografie a confronto*, edited by Chryssa Maltezou and Gherardo Ortalli (Venice, 2001): pp. 91–111.

Arvanitakis, Dimitris. *Ston dromo gia tis patrides: i 'Ape Italiana', o Andreas Kalvos, i istoria* (Athens, 2010).

Augustinos, Olga. *French Odysseys: Greece in French Travel Literature from the Renaissance to the Romantic Era* (Baltimore, 1994).

Bakalopoulos, Apostolos. *Ta ellinika stratevmata tou 1821: organosi, igesia, taktiki, ithi, psychologia* (Thessaloniki, 1948).

Balayé, S. 'Il gruppo di Coppet'. In *Storia della letteratura francese*, edited by Pierre Abraham and Roland Desné (Milan, 1985): pp. 138–43.

Balayé, S. 'Madame de Staël'. In *Storia della letteratura francese*, edited by Pierre Abraham and Roland Desné (Milan, 1985): pp. 132–5.

Banfi, Emanuele. 'Dinamiche linguistiche nell'area Adriatica tra i secoli XVIII–XIX: tra diglossie, bilinguismi e ricerca di lingue nazionali'. In *L'Adriatico: incontri e separazioni (XVIII–XIX secolo)*, edited by Francesco Bruni and Chryssa Maltezou (Venice, 2011): pp. 39–93.

Banti, Alberto M. *La nazione del Risorgimento: parentela, santità e onore alle origini dell'Italia unita* (Turin, 2000).

Banti, Alberto M. *L'onore della nazione: identità sessuali e violenza nel nazionalismo europeo dal XVIII secolo alla Grande Guerra* (Turin, 2005).

Barozzi, Niccolò (ed.). *Lettere d'illustri italiani ad Isabella Teotochi-Albrizzi* (Florence, 1836).

Bartholdy, J. L. S. *Voyage en Grèce, fait dans les années 1803 et 1804* (Paris, 1807).

Bartlett, Roger P. *Human Capital: The Settlement of Foreigners in Russia 1762–1804* (Cambridge, 1979).

Batalden, Stephen K. *Catherine II's Greek Prelate: Eugenios Voulgaris in Russia, 1771–1806* (New York, 1982).

Battista Sonzogno, Gio. *Discorso intorno alla Collana degli antichi storici greci volgarizzati* (Milan, 1820).

Beales, Derek, and Eugenio F. Biagini. *The Risorgimento and the Unification of Italy* (London and New York, 2002).

Beaton, Roderick. *Byron's War: Romantic Rebellion, Greek Revolution* (Cambridge, 2014).

Beccaria, Gian Luigi. 'Intellettuali, accademie e "Questione della Lingua" in Piemonte tra Sette e Ottocento'. *Atti della Accademia delle Scienze di Torino* 119 (1985): pp. 135–61.

Bénichou, Paul. *The Consecration of the Writer, 1750–1830* (Lincoln, Nebr., and London, 1999).

Bénot, Yves, and Marcel Dorigny (eds). *Grégoire et la cause des Noirs 1789–1831: combats et projets* (Paris, 2000).

Benton, Lauren, and Lisa Ford. *Rage for Order: The British Empire and the Origins of International Law, 1800–1850* (Cambridge, Mass., and London 2016).

Benzoni, Gino. 'La storiografia'. In *Storia della cultura veneta*, vol. 6: *Dall'età napoleonica alla Prima Guerra Mondiale*, edited by G. Arnaldi and M. P. Stocchi (Vicenza, 1986): pp. 597–623.

Berchet, Giovanni. *Poesie*, edited by Egidio Bellorini (Bari, 1941).

Berchet, Jean-Claude (ed.). *Le Voyage en orient: anthologie des voyageurs français dans le levant au XIXe siècle* (Paris, 1985).

Bernardi, Jacopo. 'Commemorazione di Giovanni Veludo (1811–1890)'. *Atti dell'Istituto Veneto* 8/38 (1889–90): pp. 701–29.

Berti, Giuseppe. *Russia e stati Italiani nel Risorgimento* (Turin, 1957).

Bétant, E. A. (ed.). *Correspondance du Comte Capodistrias, Président de la Grèce* (Geneva and Paris, 1839), 4 vols.

Biagi, Guido. *Aneddoti letterari* (Milan, 1896).

Biagini, Eugenio. 'Liberty, Class and Nation-Building: Ugo Foscolo's "English" Constitutional Thought, 1816–1827'. *European Journal of Political Theory* 5/34 (2006): pp. 34–49.

Bizzocchi, Roberto, and Kostas Soueref. 'Gia ton Mario Pieri, Kerkyra 1776–Florentia 1852'. *Deltion Anagnostikis Etairias Kerkyras* 17 (1980): pp. 117–27.

Bonucci, Carlo. *Pompei descritta da Carlo Bonucci, architetto etc.* (Naples, 1827).

Borsieri, Pietro. *Avventure letterarie di un giorno o consigli di un galantuomo a vari scrittori*, edited by William Spaggiari (Modena, 1986).

Borutta, Manuel, and Sakis Gekas (eds). 'A Colonial Sea: The Mediterranean, 1798–1956'. Special issue of the *European Review of History–Revue européenne d'histoire* 19/1 (2012).

Botta, Irene (ed.). *Carteggio Alessandro Manzoni–Claude Fauriel* (Milan, 2000).

Bouvier-Bron, Michelle. *Jean-Gabriel Eynard (1775–1863) et le philhellénisme genevois* (Geneva, 1963).

Boym, Svetlana. *The Future of Nostalgia* (New York, 2001).

Bradley, James E., and Dale K. Van Kley (eds). *Religion and Politics in Enlightenment Europe* (Notre Dame, Ind., 2001).

Brand, Peter, and Lino Pertile (eds). *The Cambridge History of Italian Literature* (Cambridge, 2008).

Bregoli, Francesca. *Mediterranean Enlightenment: Livornese Jews, Tuscan Culture, and Eighteenth-Century Reform* (Stanford, Calif., 2014).

Breuilly, John. 'Hobsbawm and Researching the History of Nationalism'. In *History after Hobsbawm: Writing the Past for the Twenty-First Century*, edited by J. H. Arnold, M. Hilton, and J. Ruger (Oxford, 2018): pp. 76–95.

Broers, Michael. *The Napoleonic Mediterranean: Enlightenment, Revolution and Empire* (London, 2017).

Bruess, Gregory L. *Religion, Identity and Empire: A Greek Archbishop in the Russia of Catherine the Great* (New York, 1997).

Bruni, Francesco, and Chryssa Maltezou (eds). *L'Adriatico: incontri e separazioni (XVIII–XIX secolo)* (Venice, 2011).

Cabanes, Pierre, et al. *Histoire de l'Adriatique* (Paris, 2001).

Caccia, Natale. 'L'episodio di Parga in alcuni componimenti poetici francesi e inglesi'. In *Studi sul Berchet, pubblicati per il primo centenario della morte* (Milan, 1951): pp. 389–417.

Calbo, Andrea [Andreas Kalvos Ioannidis Zakynthios]. *I lyra* (Geneva, 1824).

Calbo, Andrea [Andreas Kalvos Ioannidis]. *Elpis Patridos: odi en ti ton nyn Ellinon dialekto* (London, 1819).

Calbo, Andrea [Andreas Kalvos]. *Allilografia*, edited by Dimitris Arvanitakis and Lefkios Zafeiriou (Athens, 2014), 2 vols.

Calbo, Andrea [Andreas Kalvos]. *Odes*, translated by George Dandoulakis (Nottingham, 1998).

Calbo, Andrea [C** de Zante]. 'Il poeta di teatro/Le Poète de théâtre. Par F. Pananti'. *Le Globe* 160 (20 Sept. 1825): pp. 829–30.

Calbo, Andrea. *Italian Lessons in Four Parts* (London, 1820).

Calotychos, Vangelis. *Modern Greece: A Cultural Poetics* (Oxford and New York, 2003).

Camariano-Cioran, Ariadna. *Les Académies princières de Bucarest et de Jassy et leurs professeurs* (Thessalonica, 1974).

Cambon, Clauco. *Ugo Foscolo, Poet of Exile* (Princeton, 2014).

Capra, Carlo. *L'età rivoluzionaria e napoleonica in Italia, 1796–1815* (Turin, 1978).

Carpinato, Caterina. 'Ancora su Niccolò Tommaseo, Dionìssios Solomòs e la lingua greca'. In *Kalvos e Solomòs: studi e ricerche*, edited by Christos Bintoudis (Rome, 2017): pp. 203–24.

Carpinato, Caterina. '*Il supplizio d' un italiano in Corfù*: un caso di intolleranza etnica nell'Eptaneso della seconda metà dell'Ottocento e la fallita mediazione di Dionisios Solomós'. In *Integrazione, assimilazione, esclusione e reazione etnica*, edited by Adriano Pavan and Gianfranco Giraudo (Naples, 2008): vol. II, pp. 272–93.

Carpinato, Caterina. 'La corrispondenza inedita tra Niccolò Tommaseo e Markos Renieris'. In *Niccolò Tommaseo: popolo e nazioni, Italiani, Corsi, Greci, Illirici*, edited by Francesco Bruni (Rome and Padua, 2004): vol. II, pp. 511–36.

Carraresi, Alessandro (ed.). *Lettere di Gino Capponi e di altri a lui* (Florence, 1882–90), 6 vols.

Casini, Tommaso, and Salomone Morpurgo. *Mario Pieri a Verona (1805–1821): dal suo diario. Per nozze Fraccaroli–Rezzonico Della Torre* (Prato, 1895).

Ceccuti, Cosimo. 'Risorgimento greco e filoellenismo nel mondo dell'*Antologia*'. In *Indipendenza e unità nazionale in Italia ed in Grecia* (Florence, 1987): pp. 79–104.

Cesarotti, Melchior. *L'Iliade o la morte di Ettore, poema omerico ridotto in verso italiano* (Venice, 1805).

Chatziioannou, Maria Christina. 'Oi Italoi prosfyges sta Ionia nisia sta mesa tou 19ou aiona: diamorfomenes pragmatikotites kai proypotheseis ensomatosis'. In *VI Panionian Conference, Proceedings* (Athens, 2001): vol. II, pp. 495–510.

Chiancone, Claudio. 'Il circolo Paradisi e il "Poligrafo"'. In *Istituzioni e cultura in età napoleonica*, edited by E. Brambilla, C. Capra, and A. Scotti (Milan, 2008): pp. 232–50.

Chiancone, Claudio. *La scuola di Cesarotti e gli esordi del giovane Foscolo* (Pisa, 2012).

Chiarini, Giuseppe. *Gli amori di Ugo Foscolo nelle sue lettere* (Bologna, 1892).

Chiavistelli, Antonio. *Dallo stato alla nazione: costituzione e sfera pubblica in Toscana dal 1814 al 1849* (Rome, 2006).

Chini, Rita. 'Il *Poligrafo* e l'*Antipoligrafo*: polemiche letterarie nella Milano napoleonica'. *Giornale storico della letteratura italiana* 149 (1972): pp. 87–105.

Chiotis, Panagiotis. *Istoria tou Ioniou Kratous apo systaseos aftou mechris enoseos, 1815–1864* (Zante, 1874), 2 vols.

Christopoulos, Athanasios. *Ta lyrika* (Vienna, 1811).

Christou, Thanasis. '"Schedion peri ethnikis anatrofis kai dimosiou paideias eis tin Ellada (1827)" tou Alexandrou Stourdza'. *Tomi 301* 6 (1993): pp. 90–7.

Ciampini, Raffaele. 'Filellenismo e liberalismo nel 1826'. *Nuova antologia* 87/1815 (1952): pp. 280–95.

Ciampini, Raffaele. *Gian Pietro Vieusseux: i suoi viaggi, i suoi giornali, i suoi amici* (Turin, 1953).

Ciampolini, Luigi. 'Canti popolari della Grecia moderna, raccolti e pubblicati con una traduzione francese, schiarimenti e note da C. Fauriel'. *Antologia* 26 (1827): pp. 111–13.

Ciano, Cesare. *Russia e Toscana nei secoli XVII e XVIII: pagine di storia del commercio e della navigazione* (Livorno, 1980).

Cibrario, Luigi. *Notizie sulla vita di Carlo Alberto, iniziatore e martire della indipendenza italiana* (Turin, 1861).

Clancy-Smith, Julia. *Mediterraneans: North Africa and Europe in an Age of Migration, c.1800–1900* (Berkeley, 2010).

Clay, Edith (ed.). *Sir William Gell in Italy: Letters to the Society of Dilettanti, 1831–1835* (London, 1976).

Clayer, Nathalie. *Aux origines du nationalisme albanais: la naissance d'une nation majoritaire-ment musulmane en Europe* (Paris, 2007).

Cole, Laurence (ed.). *Different Paths to the Nation: Regional and National Identities in Central Europe and Italy, 1830–70* (Basingstoke and New York, 2007).

Compagnoni, Giuseppe. *Biblioteca di Fozio patriarca di Costantinopoli tradotta in italiano etc.* (Milan, 1836), 2 vols.

Compagnoni, Giuseppe. *Saggio sugli ebrei e sui greci* (Venice, 1792).

Constant, Benjamin. *Appel aux nations chrétiennes en faveur des Grecs* (Paris, 1825).

*Corrispondenza del Cav. Andrea Mustoxidi col suo amico Andrea Papadopulo Vreto* (Athens, 1860).

Cortelazzo, Manlio. 'Il dialetto corcirese per Niccolò Tommaseo'. In *Daniele Manin e Niccolò Tommaseo: cultura e società nella Venezia del 1848*, edited by T. Agostini (Ravenna, 2000): pp. 323–7.

Coutelle, Louis. *Formation poétique de Solomos (1815–1833)* (Athens, 1977).

Craiutu, Aurelian. 'Moderation and the Group of Coppet'. In *Germaine de Staël's Politics of Mediation: Challenges to History and Culture*, edited by Karyna Szmurlo (Oxford, 2011): pp. 109–24.

Craiutu, Aurelian. 'Rethinking Modernity, Religion, and Tradition: The Intellectual Dialogue between Alexandre Stourdza and Joseph de Maistre'. *History of European Ideas* (2013): pp. 1–13.

Craiutu, Aurelian. *Liberalism under Siege: The Political Thought of the French Doctrinaires* (Lanham, Md, 2003).

Crawley, C. W. 'John Capodistrias and the Greeks before 1821'. *Cambridge Historical Journal* 13/2 (1957): pp. 162–82.

Curran, Mark. '*Mettons toujours Londres*: Enlightened Christianity and the Public in Pre-revolutionary Francophone Europe'. *French History* 24/1 (2009): pp. 40–59.

D'Alessandro, Alessandra. *Vivere e rappresentare il Risorgimento: storia di Angelica Palli Bartolomei, scrittrice e patriota dell'Ottocento* (Rome, 2011).

D'Ezio, Marianna. 'Isabella Teotochi Albrizzi's Venetian Salon: A Transcultural and Transnational Example of Sociability and Cosmopolitanism in Late Eighteenth- and Early Nineteenth-Century Europe'. In *Social Networks in the Long Eighteenth Century: Clubs, Literary Salons, Textual Coteries*, edited by Ileana Baird (Cambridge, 2014): pp. 175–98.

Dafnis, Grigorios. *Ioannis A. Kapodistrias: i genesi tou ellinikou kratous* (Athens, 1976).

Dafnis, Kostas (ed.). *Archeion Ioannou Kapodistria* (Corfu, 1976–87), 10 vols.

Dallas, Giannis. 'O Solomos anamesa se dyo glosses: i amfidromi dokimasia tis poiitikis ideas'. *I lexi* 142 (Nov.–Dec. 1997): pp. 688–703.

Dallas, Giannis. *Solomos kai Kalvos: dyo antizyges poiitikes tis epochis, philologika dokimia* (Athens, 2009).

Dandolo, Girolamo. *La caduta della Repubblica di Venezia ed i suoi ultimi cinquant'anni: studii storici* (Venice, 1855).

Daskalakis, Apostolos. *Korais kai Kapodistrias: oi kata tou kybernitou libelloi* (Athens, 1958).

Davis, John A. *Naples and Napoleon: Southern Italy and the European Revolutions (1780–1860)* (Oxford, 2006).

De Biasi, Spyridon. 'Apo ton bion kai ta erga tou Solomou'. *Panathinaia* 84 (Mar. 1904): pp. 364–70.

De Biasi, Spyridon. 'Eptanisioi poiitai: Antonios Martelaos'. *Nea zoi* 5/59 (1909): pp. 354–68.

De Biasi, Spyridon. 'Eptanisioi poiitai: Nikolaos Delbiniotis'. *Nea zoi* 5/58 (1909): pp. 310–17.

De Biasi, Spyridon. 'Ioannis Zampelios'. *Apollon* 64 (1890): pp. 990–1.

De Biasi, Spyridon. *I lyra tou Andrea Kalvou* (Zante, 1881).

De Biasi, Spyridon. *O Ougos Foskolos kai i elliniki epanastasis* (Zante, 1890).

De Biasi, Spyridon. *Ta apokalyptiria tis anathimatikis plakos epi tis genethliou oikias Ougou Foskolou* (Zante, 1892).

De Courtivron, Isabelle (ed.). *Lives in Translation: Bilingual Writers on Identity and Creativity* (London, 2003).

De Francesco, Antonino. *L'Italia di Bonaparte: politica, statualità e nazione nella penisola tra due rivoluzioni, 1796–1821* (Milan, 2011).

De Gubernatis, Angelo. *Manzoni ed il Fauriel, studiati nel loro carteggio inedito* (Rome, 1880).

De Luca, Iginio (ed.). *Osservazioni sulla Iliade del Monti di Ennio Quirino Visconti e Andrea Mustoxidi* (Florence, 1961).

De Pauw, Corneille. *Recherches philosophiques sur les Grecs* (Berlin, 1787–8).

De Pradt, Dominique G. F. *L'Europe et l'Amérique en 1821* (Paris, 1822).

De Pradt, Dominique G. F. *Parallèle de la puissance anglaise et russe relativement à l'Europe, suivi d'un aperçu sur la Grèce* (Paris, 1823).

De Pradt, Dominique G. F. *Vrai système de l'Europe relativement à l'Amérique et à la Grèce* (Paris, 1825).

De Sanctis, Francesco. 'Ugo Foscolo poeta e critico'. *Nuova antologia* 17/6 (1871): pp. 253–82.

De Sismondi, Léonard J. Ch. 'Conséquences que l'on peut désirer ou craindre pour la civilisation, de la guerre des Russes dans le Levant'. In Léonard J. Ch. De Sismondi, *Opuscoli politici*, edited by Umberto Marcelli (Bologna, 1954): pp. 101–23.

De Sismondi, Léonard J. Ch. 'De la Grèce au commencement de l'anneé 1827'. In Léonard J. Ch. De Sismondi, *Opuscoli politici*, edited by Umberto Marcelli (Bologna, 1954): pp. 245–58.

De Sismondi, Léonard J. Ch. 'On the Extermination of the Greeks', *New Monthly Magazine* (1 July 1826): pp. 90–6.

De Stefanis Ciccone, Stefania. *La questione della lingua nei periodici letterari del primo Ottocento* (Florence, 1971).

De Tipaldo, Emilio. 'Blandi Spiridione'. In *Biografia degli Italiani illustri nelle scienze, lettere ed arti nel secolo XVIII*, edited by Emilio de Tipaldo (Venice, 1834–45): vol. V, pp. 385–90.

De Tipaldo, Emilio. 'Discorso del Cav. Emilio de Tipaldo'. In *Discorsi letti nella pubblica adunanza del giorno 11 luglio 1847 nell'Ateneo Veneto, alla IX riunione degli Scienziati Italiani* (Venice, 1847): pp. 7–20.

De Tipaldo, Emilio. 'Pettretini Spiridione'. In *Biografia degli Italiani illustri nelle scienze, lettere ed arti nel secolo XVIII*, edited by Emilio de Tipaldo (Venice, 1834–45): vol. V, pp. 476–80.

De Tipaldo, Emilio. *Intorno Spiridione Veludo, lettera* (Venice, 1866).

De Vattel, Emer. *The Law of Nations*, edited by Béla Kapossy and Richard Whatmore (Indianapolis, 2008).

Del Vento, Christian. 'Alfieri, un homme de lettres entre réformes et Révolution'. *Laboratoire italien* 9 (2009): pp. 109–33.

Del Vento, Christian. 'Il mito di Foscolo e il modello dell'*Ortis*'. In *Il romanzo del Risorgimento*, edited by C. Gigante and D. Vanden Berghe (Brussels, 2011): pp. 13–27.

Del Vento, Christian. *Un allievo della rivoluzione: Ugo Foscolo dal 'noviziato letterario' al 'nuovo classicismo' (1795–1806)* (Bologna, 2003).

Delviniotti, Niccolò. *Poesie* (Corfu, 1809).

Demaras, K. Th. 'Kapodistrias—Moustoxidis—Koutloumousianos (bibliografikes kai alles anazitiseis)'. *Thysavrismata* 1 (1962): pp. 14–62.

Demaras, K. Th. *Ellinikos romantismos* (Athens, 1982).

Demaras, K. Th. *Neoellinikos diafotismos* (Athens, 1977).

Detrez, Raymond. 'Pre-National Identities in the Balkans'. In *Entangled Histories of the Balkans,* vol. 1: *National Ideologies and Language Policies,* edited by Roumen Daskalov and Tchavdar Marinov (Leiden and Boston, 2013): pp. 13–65.

De Vivo, Filippo. 'La farmacia come luogo di cultura: le spezierie di medicine in Italia'. In *Interpretare e curare: medicina e salute nel Rinascimento,* edited by M. Conforti, A. Carlino, and A. Clericuzio (Rome, 2013): pp. 129–42.

Di Benedetto, Arnaldo. 'Le nazioni sorelle: momenti del filellenismo letterario italiano'. In *Niccolò Tommaseo: popolo e nazioni, Italiani, Corsi, Greci, Illirici,* edited by Francesco Bruni (Rome and Padua, 2004): vol. II, pp. 435–58.

Didier, Béatrice. *Le Journal intime* (Paris, 2002).

Dimakis, Ioannis. *O Oesterreichischer Beobachter tis Biennis kai i Elliniki Epanastasis, 1821–1827: symboli eis tin meletin tou evropaikou antiphilellinismou* (Athens, 1977).

Dionisotti, Carlo. *Appunti sui moderni, Foscolo, Leopardi, Manzoni e altri* (Bologna, 1988).

*Dispaccio di Sir Edward Douglas Baronetto, G. C. S. M. G. Lord Alto Commissionario delle Isole Ionie, etc.* (Corfu, 1840).

Dodman, Thomas. *What Nostalgia Was: War, Empire and the Time of a Deadly Emotion* (Chicago, 2018).

Dragostinova, Theodora. *Between Two Motherlands: Nationality and Emigration among Greeks of Bulgaria, 1900–1949* (Ithaca, NY, and London, 2011).

Droulia, Loukia. 'Logiosyni kai bibliofilia: o Dimitrios Mostras kai i bibliothiki tou'. *Tetradia ergasias* 9 (1989): pp. 227–305.

Duquesnel, Amédée. *Histoire des lettres: cours de littératures comparées* (Paris, 1845), 2 vols.

Dursteler, Eric R. (ed.). *A Companion to Venetian History, 1400–1797* (Leiden and Boston, 2013).

Eisner, Robert. *Travelers to an Antique Land: The History and Literature of Travel to Greece* (Ann Arbor, Mich., 1993).

Enepekides, Polychronis K. 'Documents et nouvelles lettres inédites d'Adamantios Coray tirées des bibliothèques et archives européennes'. *Jahrbuch der Österreichischen Byzantinischen Gesellschaft* 5 (1956): pp. 85–126.

Enepekides, Polychronis K. *Korais—Koumas—Kalvos—An. Gazis—Ougos Foskolos... etc.* (Athens, 1967).

Enepekides, Polychronis K. *Rigas—Ypsilantis—Kapodistrias* (Athens, 1965).

Erba, Achille. *L'azione politica di Federico Sclopis: dalla giovinezza alla codificazione Albertina (1798–1837)* (Turin, 1960).

Espagne, Michel. *Les Transferts culturels franco-allemands* (Paris, 1999).

Espagne, Michel, and Gilles Pécout (eds), *Philhellénismes et transferts culturels dans l'Europe du XIXᵉ siècle.* (=*Revue germanique internationale* 1–2 (2005)).

Falcetta, Angela. *Ortodossi nel Mediterraneo cattolico: frontiere, reti, comunità nel Regno di Napoli (1700–1821)* (Rome, 2016).

Farini, Luigi Carlo. *Storia d'Italia, dall'anno 1814 sino a' giorni nostri* (Turin, 1859), 2 vols.

Fauriel, Claude. *Chants populaires de la Grèce moderne* (Paris, 1824–5), 2 vols.

Favaro Adriano. *Isabella Teotochi Albrizzi: la sua vita, i suoi amori e i suoi viaggi* (Udine, 2003).

Federici, Fortunato. *Degli scrittori greci e delle italiane versioni delle loro opere* (Padua, 1828).

Fido, Franco. 'La tragedia nell'età giacobina e napoleonica'. In *Storia generale della letteratura italiana*, edited by N. Borsellino and W. Pedullà (Milan, 2004): pp. 103–18.

[Filimon, Ioannis]. *Epistoli tou Kyriou A. D. Dimitriou pros ton eis Triestion Kyrion* (Nafplio, 1831).

Filimon, Ioannis. *Dokimion istorikon peri tis Philikis Etairias* (Nafplio, 1834).

Fleming, K. E. 'O Herzl stin Akropoli, megales istories, mikra krati: Ellada, Israil kai ta oria tou ethnous'. *The Athens Review of Books* 1/8 (June 2010): pp. 32–7.

Fleming, K. E. *The Muslim Bonaparte: Diplomacy and Orientalism in Ali Pasha's Greece* (Princeton, 1999).

Florovsky, Georges. 'The Orthodox Churches and the Ecumenical Movement prior to 1910'. In *A History of the Ecumenical Movement, 1517–1948*, edited by Ruth Rouse and Stephen Charles Neill (London, 1967): pp. 171–216.

Fontana, Giovanni L. 'Patria veneta e stato italiano dopo l'unità: problemi di identità e di integrazione'. In *Storia della cultura veneta*, vol. 6: *Dall'età napoleonica alla Prima Guerra Mondiale*, edited by G. Arnaldi and M. P. Stocchi (Vicenza, 1986): pp. 553–96.

Fontana, Vittorio. *Luigi Lamberti (Vita—scritti—amici)* (Reggio Emilia, 1892).

Foscolo, Ugo. *Didymi Clerici prophetae minimi Hypercalypseos liber singularis* (Pisa, 1815).

Foscolo, Ugo. *Edizione nazionale delle opere di Ugo Foscolo*, vol. 2: *Tragedie e poesie minori*, edited by Guido Bézzola (Florence, 1961).

Foscolo, Ugo. *Edizione nazionale delle opere di Ugo Foscolo*, vol. 8: *Prose politiche e letterarie dal 1811 al 1816*, edited by Luigi Fassò (Florence, 1972).

Foscolo, Ugo. *Epistolario*, edited by Plinio Carli, Giovanni Gambarin, Francesco Tropeano, and Mario Scotti (Florence, 1949–94), 9 vols.

Foscolo, Ugo. *Il sesto tomo dell'io*, edited by V. Di Benedetto (Turin, 1991).

Foscolo, Ugo. *Last Letters of Jacopo Ortis*, translated by J. G. Nichols (London, 2002).

Foscolo, Ugo. *Prose politiche e apologetiche (1817–1827)*, vol. I: *Scritti sulle Isole Ionie e su Parga*, edited by Giovanni Gambarin (Florence, 1964).

Foscolo, Ugo. *Sepulchres and Other Poems*, translated by J. G. Nichols (London, 2009).

Frary, Lucien J. 'Russian Interests in Nineteenth-Century Thessaloniki'. *Mediterranean Historical Review* 23/1 (2008): pp. 15–33.

Frary, Lucien J. *Russia and the Making of Modern Greek Identity, 1821–1844* (Oxford, 2015).

Gallant, Thomas W. *Experiencing Dominion: Culture, Identity, and Power in the British Mediterranean* (Notre Dame, Ind., 2002).

Gallant, Thomas W. *Modern Greece* (London, 2001).

Gallant, Thomas W. *The Edinburgh History of the Greeks, 1768 to 1913: The Long Nineteenth Century* (Edinburgh, 2015).

Gamba, Bartolommeo. 'Rosmini Carlo De'. In *Biografia degli Italiani illustri nelle scienze, lettere ed arti nel secolo XVIII*, edited by Emilio de Tipaldo (Venice, 1834–45): vol. I, pp. 98–102.

Gamba, Bartolommeo. *Operette di Jacopo Morelli, Bibliotecario di S. Marco, ora insieme raccolte* (Venice, 1820), 2 vols.

Gamba, Pietro. *A Narrative of Lord Byron's Last Journey to Greece* (London, 1825).

Garcia, Humberto. *Islam and the English Enlightenment, 1670–1840* (Baltimore, 2012).

Gaulmier, J. 'Gli *idéologues*'. In *Storia della letteratura francese*, edited by Pierre Abraham and Roland Desné (Milan, 1985): vol. II, pp. 74–80.

Gazi, Effi. 'Revisiting Religion and Nationalism in Nineteenth-Century Greece'. In *The Making of Modern Greece: Nationalism, Romanticism, and the Uses of the Past (1797–1896)*, edited by Roderick Beaton and David Ricks (London and New York, 2009): pp. 95–106.

Gekas, Sakis. *Xenocracy: State, Class and Colonialism in the Ionian Islands, 1815–1864* (New York and Oxford, 2017).

Gell, William. *The Geography and Antiquities of Ithaca* (London, 1807).

Georganta, Athina. *Ta thavmasia nera, Andreas Kalvos: o romantismos, o Byronismos kai o kosmos ton karmponaron* (Athens, 2011).

Gervasoni, Gianni. *Angelo Mai* (Bergamo, 1954).

Gervasoni, Gianni. *Linee di storia della filologia classica in Italia*, vol. I: *Sino ai filologi settentrionali della prima metà dell'800* (Florence, 1929).

Ghervas, Stella. 'La Sainte-Alliance: un pacte pacifique européen comme antydote à l'Empire', in *Europe de papier: projets européens au XIXe siècle*, edited by Sylvie Aprile et al. (Lille, 2015): pp. 47–64.

Ghervas, Stella. 'Le Philhellénisme d'inspiration conservatrice en Europe et en Russie'. In *Peuples, états et nations dans le sud-est de l'Europe* (Bucharest, 2004): pp. 98–110.

Ghervas, Stella. *Réinventer la tradition: Alexandre Stourdza et l'Europe de la Sainte-Alliance* (Paris, 2008).

Ghidetti, Francesco. 'Il filellenismo a Livorno tra il 1820 e il 1830'. *Rassegna storica del Risorgimento* 3 (1994): pp. 291–310.

Ghobrial, John-Paul A. 'The Secret Life of Elias of Babylon and the Uses of Global Microhistory', *Past and Present* 222 (2014): pp. 51–93.

Ginsborg, Paul. 'Romanticismo e Risorgimento: l'io, l'amore e la nazione'. In *Storia d'Italia*, Annali 22: *Il Risorgimento*, edited by Paul Ginsborg and Alberto M. Banti (Turin, 2007): pp. 5–67.

Giordani, Pietro. *Lettere di Pietro Giordani a Spiridione Veludo* (Venice, 1880).

Giorgetti, Cinzia. *Ritratto di Isabella: studi e documenti su Isabella Teotochi Albrizzi* (Florence, 1992).

Girard, Alain. 'Le Journal intime, un nouveau genre littéraire?'. *Cahiers de l'Association Internationale des Études Francaises* 17 (1965): pp. 99–109.

Girard, Alain. *Le Journal intime* (Paris, 1963).

Giulini, Alessandro. 'Spigolature del carteggio inedito di Andrea Mustoxidi'. *Giornale storico della letteratura italiana* 89 (1927): pp. 127–35.

Glachant, Victor. *Benjamin Constant, sous l'œil du guet* (Paris, 1906).

Goldstein, Jan. *The Post-Revolutionary Self: Politics and Psyche in France, 1750–1850* (Cambridge, Mass., and London, 2005).

Gourgouris, Stathis. *Dream Nation: Enlightenment, Colonization and the Institution of Modern Greece* (Stanford, Calif., 1996).

Gozzi, Gaspare. *Lettere d'illustri italiani ad Antonio Papadopoli* (Venice, 1886).

Greene, Molly. *The Edinburgh History of the Greeks, 1453 to 1768: The Ottoman Empire* (Edinburgh, 2015).

Grégoire, Henri. 'Précis historique sur l'état actuel de l'Église orthodoxe (non réunie) d'Orient, présenté par Monseigneur Ignace, métropolitain d'Arta, à S. Exc. Monseigneur le chancelier de l'empire de Russie, comte de Romanzof- A St.-Pétersbourg, l'an 1809'. In Henri Grégoire, *Chronique religieuse* (Paris, 1819): vol. III, pp. 529–48.

Grégoire, Henri. *Histoire des sectes religieuses* (Paris, 1829), 2 vols.

Gregory, Desmond. *Napoleon's Italy* (London, 2001).

Gritsopoulos, Tassos Ath. *Ta Orlofika, i en Peloponniso epanastasis tou 1770 kai ta epakoloutha aftis* (Athens, 1967).

Groddeck, Carl Theodor. *De la maladie démocratique, nouvelle espèce de folie* (Paris, 1850).

Grunebaum-Ballin, P. *Henri Grégoire, l'ami des hommes de toutes les couleurs* (Paris, 1948).

Gusdorf, Georges. *La Conscience révolutionnaire: les idéologues* (Paris 1978).

Haakonssen, Knud. *Enlightenments and Religions* (Athens, 2010).

Haddock, Bruce. 'Between Revolution and Reaction: Vincenzo Cuoco's Saggio storico'. *European Journal of Political Theory* 5/22 (2006): pp. 22–33.

Hatzopoulos, Marios. 'Oracular Prophecy and the Politics of Toppling Ottoman Rule in South-East Europe'. *The Historical Review/La Revue historique* 8 (2011): pp. 95–116.

Henderson, G. P. *The Revival of Greek Thought (1620–1830)* (Albany, NY, and New York, 1970).

Herder, Johann Gottfried. 'Excerpt from a Correspondence on Ossian and the Songs of Ancient Peoples'. In *The Rise of Modern Mythology, 1680–1860*, edited by Burton Feldman and Robert D. Richardson (Bloomington, Ind., 1999): pp. 228–30.

Hering, Gunnar. *Die Politischen Parteien in Griechenland 1821–1936* (Munich, 1992), 2 vols.

Herzfeld, Michael. *Ours Once More: Folklore, Ideology, and the Making of Modern Greece* (Austin, Tex., 1982).

Heyberger, Bernard, and Chantal Verdeil (eds). *Hommes de l'entre-deux: parcours individuels et portraits de groupes sur la frontière de la Méditerranée (XVIe–XXe siècle)* (Paris, 2009).

Ho, Engseng. 'Empire through Diasporic Eyes: A View from the Other Boat'. *Society for Comparative Study of Society and History* 46/2 (Apr. 2004): pp. 210–46.

Hobsbawm, Eric. *Nations and Nationalism since 1780* (Cambridge, 1992).

Hodes, Martha Elizabeth. *The Sea Captain's Wife: A True Story of Love, Race, and War in the Nineteenth Century* (New York and London, 2007).

Holland, Robert. *Blue-Water Empire: The British in the Mediterranean since 1800* (London, 2013).

Honour, Hugh. *Neo-Classicism* (Harmondsworth, 1968).

Hroch, Miroslav. *Social Preconditions of National Revival in Europe: A Comparative Analysis of the Social Composition of Patriotic Groups among the Smaller European Nations* (New York, 1985).

Ibrovac, Miodrag. *Claude Fauriel et la fortune européenne des poésies populaires grecque et serbe* (Paris, 1966).

[Ignatius, Bishop]. 'Synopsis istoriki peri tis enestosis katastaseos tis Orthodoxou Anatolikis Ekklisias', *Athina* 1 (Jan. 1831): pp. 6–11 and 26–32; 2 (Feb. 1831): pp. 40–6 and 55–62; 3 (Mar. 1831): pp. 71–7.

*I Ierousalim Eleftheromeni, Poiima iroikon tou Torkouatou Tassou…metafrasthen…para tou Dimitriou Gouzeli Zakynthiou* (Venice, 1807).

Ikonomou, Tzortzis. 'Il dialetto corcirese: dialetto veneto e lingua italiana nelle Isole Ionie'. In *Storia della lingua italiana e dialettologia*, edited by Giovanni Ruffino and Mari D'Agostino (Palermo, 2010): pp. 459–76.

Ikonomou, Tzortzis. 'In cerca della musa italiana: Niccolò Delviniotti e la poesia ionia in italiano'. In *L'Adriatico: incontri e separazioni (XVIII–XIX secolo)*, edited by Francesco Bruni and Chryssa Maltezou (Venice, 2011): pp. 221–38.

Ikonomou, Tzortzis. 'Le Isole Ionie, la Grecia e il *Supplizio*'. In Niccolò Tommaseo, *Il supplizio d'un Italiano in Corfù*, edited by Fabio Danelon (Venice, 2008): pp. 277–336.

Ilinskaya, Sonia. 'Metafrastikes peripeteies gyro apo ton *Thourio* sti Rossia'. In *Ellinorosika synapantimata* (Athens, 2004): pp. 13–26.

Innes, Joanna, and Mark Philp (eds), *Re-imagining Democracy in the Age of Revolutions: America, France, Britain, Ireland (1750–1850)* (Oxford, 2013).

Isabella, Maurizio, and Konstantina Zanou (eds), *Mediterranean Diasporas: Politics and Ideas in the Long Nineteenth Century* (London, 2016).

Isabella, Maurizio. 'Citizens or Faithful? Religion and the Liberal Revolutions of the 1820s in Southern Europe'. *Modern Intellectual History* (published online: Jan. 2015) <http://dx.doi.org/10.1017/S147924431400078X>.

Isabella, Maurizio. 'Entangled Patriotisms: Italian Liberals and Spanish America in the 1820s'. In *Connections after Colonialism: Europe and Latin America in the 1820s*, edited by Matthew Brown and Gabriel Paquette (Tuscaloosa, Ala., 2013): pp. 87–107.

Isabella, Maurizio. 'Esilio'. In *Atlante culturale del Risorgimento: lessico del linguaggio politico dal Settecento all'Unità*, edited by A. M. Banti, A. Chiavistelli, L. Mannori, and M. Meriggi (Rome and Bari, 2011): pp. 65–74.

Isabella, Maurizio. 'Exile and Nationalism: The Case of the Risorgimento'. *European History Quarterly* 36/4 (2006): pp. 493–520.

Isabella, Maurizio. 'Liberalism and Empires in the Mediterranean: The View-Point of the Risorgimento'. In *The Risorgimento Revisited: Nationalism and Culture in Nineteenth-Century Italy*, edited by Silvana Patriarca and Lucy Riall (London and New York, 2012): pp. 232–54.

Isabella, Maurizio. *Risorgimento in Exile: Italian Émigrés and the Liberal International in the Post-Napoleonic Era* (Oxford, 2009).

Isocratis, *Oratio de permutatione, etc.*, translated by Angelo Mai (Milan, 1813).

*Isocratous logos peri tes antidoseos vervollständigt herausgegeben von Andreas Mustoxydes historiographen etc.*, translated by Gian Gaspare Orelli (Zurich, 1814).

*Isokratous logos peri tis antidoseos etc.*, edited by Andrea Mustoxidi (Milan, 1812).

*Istoria tou ellinikou ethnous* (Athens, 1978), vol. 11.

Ivetic, Egidio. 'L'Adriatico alla fine del Settecento: il rilancio mancato'. In *L'Adriatico: incontri e separazioni (XVIII–XIX secolo)*, edited by Francesco Bruni and Chryssa Maltezou (Venice, 2011): pp. 23–38.

Ivetic, Egidio. 'La patria del Tommaseo: la Dalmazia tra il 1815 e il 1860'. In *Niccolò Tommaseo: popolo e nazioni, Italiani, Corsi, Greci, Illirici*, edited by Francesco Bruni (Rome and Padua, 2004): vol. II, pp. 595–624.

Ivetic, Egidio. 'Ricerca storica, archivi e sviluppo nazionale nell'Adriatico Orientale e in Croazia (1815–1914)'. In *Archivi e storia nell'Europa del XIX secolo: alle radici dell'identità culturale europea*, edited by Irene Cotta and Rosalia Manno Tolu (Florence, 2006): pp. 687–704.

Jaume, Lucien. *L'Individu effacé ou le paradoxe du libéralisme français* (Paris, 1997).

Jelavich, Barbara. 'The Philorthodox Conspiracy of 1839: A Report to Metternich'. *Balkan Studies* 7 (1966): pp. 89–102.

Jochalas, Tito. *O Georgios Kastriotis Skentermpeis eis tin neoellinikin istoriografian kai logotechnian* (Thessaloniki, 1975).

Kairofilas, Kostas. 'Kapodistrias kai Foskolos'. *Imerologion tis Megalis Ellados* 8/8 (1929): pp. 161–86.

[Kapodistrias, Ioannis]. 'Mémoire sur l'état actuel des Grecs'. In *Archeion Ioannou Kapodistria*, edited by Kostas Dafnis (Corfu, 1976–86): vol. VII, pp. 188–207.

[Kapodistrias, Ioannis]. 'Observations sur les moyens d'améliorer le sort de Grecs'. In George Waddinghton, *A Visit to Greece in 1823 and 1824* (London, 1825): pp. xxxiv–xlv.

Kapodistrias, Ioannis [Jean Capodistria]. *Aperçu de ma carrière publique depuis 1798 jusqu'à 1822* (Paris, 1999).

Karapidakis, Nikos. 'Ta Eptanisa: evropaikoi antagonismoi meta tin ptosi tis Benetias'. In *Istoria tou neou ellinismou, 1770–2000*, edited by Vassilis Panagiotopoulos (Athens, 2003): vol. 1, pp. 149–84.

Karathanasis, Athanasios. *I Flaggineios Scholi tis Benetias* (Thessaloniki, 1975).

Kardasis, Vassilis. *Diaspora Merchants in the Black Sea: The Greeks in Southern Russia, 1775–1861* (Lanham, Md, 2001).

Katramis, N. 'Ougos Foskolos'. *Pandora* 282 (15 Dec. 1861): pp. 440–4.

Katsiardi-Hering, Olga. *I elliniki paroikia tis Tergestis, 1751–1830* (Athens, 1986), 2 vols.

Kechriotis, Vangelis. 'On the Margins of National Historiography: The Greek İttihatçi Emmanouil Emmanouilidis —Opportunist or Ottoman Patriot?'. In *Untold Histories of the Middle East: Recovering Voices from the 19th and 20th Centuries*, edited by A. Singer, C. Neumann, and S. A. Somel (New York, 2011).

Kennedy Grimsted, Patricia. 'Capodistrias and a "New Order" for Restoration Europe: The "Liberal Ideas" of a Russian Foreign Minister (1814–1822)'. *Journal of Modern History* 40/2 (June 1968): pp. 166–92.

Kennedy Grimsted, Patricia. *The Foreign Ministers of Alexander I: Political Attitudes and the Conduct of Russian Diplomacy, 1801–1825* (Berkeley and Los Angeles, 1969).

Khuri Makdisi, Ilham. *The Eastern Mediterranean and the Making of Global Radicalism, 1860–1914* (Berkeley, 2010).

Kirchner Reill, Dominique. 'Away or Homeward Bound? The Slippery Case of Mediterranean Place in the Era Before Nation-States'. In *Mediterranean Diasporas: Politics and Ideas in the Long Nineteenth Century*, edited by Maurizio Isabella and Konstantina Zanou (London, 2016): pp. 135–52.

Kirchner Reill, Dominique. *Nationalists Who Feared the Nation: Adriatic Multi-Nationalism in Habsburg Dalmatia, Trieste, and Venice* (Stanford, Calif., 2012).

Kitromilides, Paschalis M. 'Eptanisiakos diafotismos: ta oria tis idiomorfias'. In *VII Panionian Conference, Proceedings* (Athens, 2004): vol. I, pp. 241–57.

Kitromilides, Paschalis M. 'Orthodoxy and the West: Reformation to Enlightenment'. In *The Cambridge History of Christianity*, vol. 5: *Eastern Christianity*, edited by Michael Angold (Cambridge, 2006): pp. 202–6.

Kitromilides, Paschalis M. 'The Legacy of the French Revolution: Orthodoxy and Nationalism'. In *The Cambridge History of Christianity*, vol. 5: *Eastern Christianity*, edited by Michael Angold (Cambridge, 2006): 229–30.

Kitromilides, Paschalis M. *Enlightenment and Revolution: The Making of Modern Greece* (Cambridge, Mass., and London, 2013).

Kitromilides, Paschalis M. (ed.). *Enlightenment and Religion in the Orthodox World* (Oxford, 2016).

Kokkonas, Giannis. *Oi mathites tou Kentrikou Scholeiou (1830–1834)* (Athens, 1997).

[Konomos, Ntinos]. 'Dyo simeiomata anekdota tou Ougou Foskolou'. *Eptanisiaka fylla* 14 (Feb. 1949): p. 222.

Konomos, Ntinos. *Eptanisiakos typos, 1798–1864*. Special issue of *Eptanisiaka fylla* 5 (1964).

Kontogiannis, Pantelis M. *Oi Ellines kata ton proton epi Aikaterinis B' Rossotourkikon Polemon, (1768–1774)* (Athens, 1903).

Koraes, Adamantios [Adamantios Korais]. *Allilografia*, edited by K. Th. Demaras, A. Aggelou, E. Koumarianou, and E. Fragkiskos (Athens, 1964–84), 6 vols.

Koraes, Adamantios [G. Pantazidis]. *Ti symferei eis tin eleftheromenin apo tous Tourkous Ellada na praxei eis tas parousas peristaseis dia na mi doulothei eis christianous tourkizontas: dialogos defteros* (Paris, 1831).

*Bibliography*

Korinthios, Gianni. *I liberali napoletani e la rivoluzione greca 1821–1830* (Naples, 1990).

Körner, Axel (ed.). *1848: A European Revolution? International Ideas and National Memories of 1848* (New York, 2000).

Koubourlis, Ioannis. O*i istoriografikes ofeiles ton Sp. Zampeliou kai K. Paparrigopoulou (1782–1846)* (Athens, 2012).

Koukkou, Eleni E. *Ioannis Kapodistrias—Roxandra Stourdza mia anekpliroti agapi* (Athens, 1996).

Koukkou, Eleni E. *O Kapodistrias kai i paideia, 1803–1822* (Athens, 1958), 2 vols.

Koulouri, Christina, and Christos Loukos. *Ta proposa tou Kapodistria: o protos kybernitis tis Elladas kai i neoelliniki ideologia (1831–1996)* (Athens, 1996).

Koutmanis, Sotiris. 'Giovanni Veludo (1811–1890) tra la storiografia greca e veneziana dell'800'. In *L'Adriatico: incontri e separazioni (XVIII–XIX secolo)*, edited by Francesco Bruni and Chryssa Maltezou (Venice, 2011): pp. 289–95.

Küçük, Harun. 'Natural Philosophy and Politics in the Eighteenth Century: Esad of Ioannina and Greek Aristotelianism at the Ottoman Court'. *Journal of Ottoman Studies* 41 (2013): pp. 125–58.

Kurunmäki, Jussi. 'Political Representation, Imperial Dependency and Political Transfer: Finland and Sweden 1809–1819'. *Journal of Modern European History* 15/2 (2017): pp. 243–60.

Lamberti, Luigi. *Osservazioni sopra alcune lezioni della Iliade di Omero* (Milan, 1813).

Lambropoulos, Vassilis. *Literature as National Institution: Studies in the Politics of Modern Greek Criticism* (Princeton, 1988).

Lane, Frederic C. *Venice: A Maritime Republic* (Baltimore and London, 1973).

Lascaris, Michele. 'L'Abbé Grégoire et la Grèce'. *La Révolution française* 3 (1932): pp. 1–16.

Lascaris, Michele. 'Niccolò Tommaseo ed Andrea Mustoxidi'. *Atti e memorie della Società Dalmata di Storia Patria* 3 (1934): pp. 1–39.

Lascaris, Michail. 'Demetrio Arliotti, 1777–1860'. *Kerkyraika chronika* 8 (1960): pp. 62–3.

Lascaris, S. Th. *Capodistrias avant la révolution grecque: sa carrière politique jusqu'en 1822* (Lausanne, 1918).

Laven, David, and Lucy Riall (eds). *Napoleon's Legacy: Problems of Government in Restoration Europe* (Oxford and New York, 2000).

Lehner, Ulrich L. *The Catholic Enlightenment: The Forgotten History of a Global Movement* (Oxford, 2016).

*Le Nove Muse di Erodoto Alicarnasseo tradotte ed illustrate da Andrea Mustoxidi Corcirese* (Milan, 1820–63), 5 vols.

Leopardi, Giacomo. *Saggio sopra gli errori popolari degli antichi* (Florence, 1846).

Letsios, Vasilis. 'Elytis, Kalvos, Solomos: mia synomilia me prosdokies'. *Ionios logos* 4 (2013): pp. 213–26.

Liakos, Antonis. 'I diathlasi ton epanastatikon ideon ston elliniko choro, 1830–1850'. *Ta istorika* 1/1 (1983): pp. 121–44.

Liakos, Antonis. 'The Making of Greek History: The Construction of National Time'. In *Political Uses of the Past: The Recent Mediterranean Experience*, edited by Jacques Revel and Giovanni Levi (London, 2001): pp. 27–42.

Liakos, Antonis. *Apokalypsi, outopia kai istoria: oi metamorfoseis tis istorikis syneidisis* (Athens, 2011).

Liakos, Antonis. *L'unificazione italiana e la Grande Idea: ideologia e azione dei movimenti nazionali in Italia e in Grecia, 1859–1871* (Florence, 1995).

Lilti, Antoine. *The Invention of Celebrity, 1750–1850* (Cambridge, 2017).

Lodi, Teresa. 'Sismondi e la *Staël veneziana*'. *Civiltà moderna* 4 (1932): pp. 604–24.

Losacco, Margherita. *Antonio Catiforo e Giovanni Veludo interpreti di Fozio* (Bari, 2003).

Loukatos, Spyros. *O italikos philellinismos kata ton agona tis ellinikis anexartisias, 1821–1831* (Athens, 1996).

Loukos, Christos. 'Gyro apo tin pafsi tou Patriarchi Grigoriou tou St: nees martyries'. *Eranistis* 21 (1997): pp. 326–36.

Loukos, Christos. 'I antipolitefsi kata tou kyberniti Ioanni Kapodistria: epanexetasi kapoion proseggiseon'. In *O kybernitis Ioannis Kapodistrias: kritikes proseggiseis kai epibebaioseis*, edited by Giorgos Georgis (Athens, 2015): pp. 54–67.

Loukos, Christos. *I antipolitefsi kata tou kyberniti Io. Kapodistria* (Athens, 1988).

Loukos, Christos. *Ioannis Kapodistrias* (Athens, 2009).

Lucarelli, Enrica, and Caterina Spetsieri Beschi (eds). *Risorgimento greco e filellenismo italiano: lotte, cultura, arte* (Rome, 1986).

Lunzi, Ermanno. *Della Repubblica Settinsulare* (Bologna, 1863), 2 vols.

Mackridge, Peter. 'Dionisio Salamon/Dionysios Solomos: Poetry as a Dialogue between Languages'. *Dialogos* 1 (1994): pp. 59–76.

Mackridge, Peter. 'Peri boulis kai gerousias: o Platon Petridis kai i "neoelliniki" metafrasi tou ioniou syntagmatos tou 1817'. In *Logos kai chronos sti neoelliniki grammateia (18os–19os aionas)*, edited by St. Kaklamanis, Al. Kalokairinos, and D. Polychronakis (Herakleion, 2015): pp. 157–70.

Mackridge, Peter. 'Venise après Venise: Official Languages in the Ionian Islands, 1797–1864'. *Byzantine and Modern Greek Studies* 38/1 (Mar. 2014): pp. 68–90.

Mackridge, Peter. *Language and National Identity in Greece, 1766–1976* (Oxford, 2009).

Maggi, Gio. Ant. 'Trivulzio Gianiacopo'. In *Biografia degli Italiani illustri nelle scienze, lettere ed arti nel secolo XVIII*, edited by Emilio de Tipaldo (Venice, 1834–45): vol. II, pp. 470–8.

Maggi, Giovanni Antonio. *Della vita e degli scritti di Felice Bellotti* (Milan, 1860).

Malamani, Vittorio. *Isabella Teotochi Albrizzi: i suoi amici, il suo tempo* (Turin, 1882).

Maltezou, Chryssa. *I Benetia ton Ellinon—Venice of the Greeks* (Athens, 1999).

[Manessi, N. B.]. *Le tre costituzioni (1800, 1803, 1817) delle Sette Isole Jonie* (Corfu, 1849).

Manin, Daniele. *Carte segrete e atti ufficiali della polizia austriaca in Italia dal 4 giugno 1814 al 22 marzo 1848* (Capolago, 1851–2): vol. I.

Mannori, Luca. 'Tra nazioni e nazione: una riflessione introduttiva'. In *Nazioni d'Italia: identità politiche e appartenenze regionali fra Settecento e Ottocento*, edited by Luca Mannori, Angela De Benedictis, and Irene Fosi (Rome, 2012): pp. 7–31.

Mantegazza, Paolo. 'Il cranio di Ugo Foscolo'. *Archivio per l'antropologia e la etnologia* 1/3 (1871): pp. 301–6.

Manzoni, Alessandro. *Carteggio*, edited by G. Sforza and G. Gallavresi (Milan, 1912–21), 2 vols.

Manzoni, Alessandro. *Tutte le lettere*, edited by Cesare Arieti (Milan, 1970), 3 vols.

Marchand, Suzanne L. *Archaeology and Philhellenism in Germany, 1750–1970* (Princeton, 1996).

Martin, Alexander M. *Romantics, Reformers, Reactionaries: Russian Conservative Thought and Politics in the Reign of Alexander I* (DeKalb, Ill., 1997).

Martini, Liza. 'Anekdotes epistoles tou Dimitriou Mostra pros ton Ioannin Kapodistrian'. In *IV Panionian Conference, Proceedings*. [=*Kerkyraika chronika* 23 (1980)]: pp. 418–35.

Martini, Liza. 'Kapodistrias–Dimitrios Mostras'. *Kerkyraika chronika* 9 (1962): pp. 97–132.

Masarachi, Antimo. *Vite degli uomini illustri dell'isola di Cefalonia etc., tradotte dal greco da N. Tommaseo* (Venice, 1843).

Mastellone, Salvo. 'Santorre di Santarosa combattente per la Grecia'. In *Indipendenza e unità nazionale in Italia e in Grecia* (Florence, 1987).

Mastellone, Salvo. *Victor Cousin e il Risorgimento italiano (dalle carte dell'archivio Cousin)* (Florence, 1955).

Matalas, Paraskevas. *Ethnos kai Orthodoxia, oi peripeteies mias schesis: apo to 'elladiko' sto boulgariko schisma* (Herakleion, 2003).

Matvejević, Predrag. *Mediterranean: A Cultural Landscape* (Berkeley, 1999).

Mavrocordatos, Alexandros. 'Coup d' œil sur la Turquie' (1820). In Anton Fr. Von Prokesch-Osten, *Geschichte des Abfall der Griechen vom türkischen Reich im Jahre 1821* (Vienna, 1867): vol. III, pp. 1–54.

Mavrogordatos, George. 'Orthodoxy and Nationalism in the Greek Case', *West European Politics* 26/1 (2003): pp. 117–36.

Mayer, Enrico [Ellenofilo]. 'Cenni sulla lingua romaica'. *Antologia* 4 (Oct.–Dec. 1821): pp. 438–54.

Mazzarini, Claudio. 'L'italiano rinnegato: politica linguistica nel Piemonte francese'. In *Atti del convegno: Piemonte e letteratura 1789–1870*, edited by Giovanna Ioli (Turin, 1986): vol. I, pp. 56–77.

Mazzini, Giuseppe. 'A chi legge'. In Ugo Foscolo, *Scritti politici inediti, raccolti a documentarne la vita e i tempi* (Lugano, 1844): pp. vii–xxxix.

Mendelssohn-Bartholdy, Karl. *Graf Johann Kapodistrias* (Berlin, 1864).

Merlier, Octave. *Exposition du centenaire de Solomos* (Athens, 1957).

Michalopoulos, Fanis. 'Andreas Papadopoulos Brettos (1800–1876)'. *Nea estia* 12/283 (1 Oct. 1938): pp. 1300–7.

Miller, Marion S. 'A Liberal International? Perspectives on Comparative Approaches to the Revolutions in Spain, Italy, and Greece in the 1820s'. In *Greece and the Mediterranean*, edited by R. W. Clement, B. F. Taggie, and R. G. Schwartz (Kirksville, Mo., 1990): pp. 61–8.

Mishkova, Diana. 'The Afterlife of a Commonwealth: Narratives of Byzantium in the National Historiographies of Greece, Bulgaria, Serbia and Romania'. In *Entangled Histories of the Balkans*, vol. 3: *Shared Pasts, Disputed Legacies*, edited by Roumen Daskalov and Alexander Vezenkov (Leiden, 2015): pp. 118–273.

Mishkova, Diana (ed.). *We, the People: Politics of National Peculiarity in Southeastern Europe* (Budapest and New York, 2009).

[Montani, Giuseppe]. 'Alessio o gli ultimi giorni di Psara romanzo storico d'Angelica Palli etc.' *Antologia* 27 (Aug. 1827): pp. 88–94.

Montani, Giuseppe [M.]. 'Rime improvvisate dal conte Dionisio Salamon, Zacintio'. *Antologia* 14 (May 1824): pp. 76–8.

Monti, Vincenzo. *Epistolario*, edited by Alfonso Bertoldi (Florence, 1928–31), 6 vols.

Monti, Vincenzo. *Proposta di alcune correzioni ed agiiunte al vocabulario della Crusca* (Milan, 1817–26), 7 vols.

Morabito, Raffaele, 'Ugo Foscolo'. In *Storia generale della letteratura italiana*, vol. VII: *L'Italia romantica il primo Ottocento*, edited by N. Borsellino and W. Pedullà (Milan, 2004): pp. 119–204.

Morabito, Raffaele. 'Vincenzo Monti'. In *Storia generale della letteratura italiana*, vol. VII: *L'Italia romantica il primo Ottocento*, edited by N. Borsellino and W. Pedullà (Milan, 2004): pp. 71–102.

Moravia, Sergio. *Il pensiero degli idéologues: scienza e filosofia in Francia (1780–1815)* (Florence, 1974).

Moschopoulos, Georgios. *Oi Ellines tis Benetias kai Illyrias (1768–1797): i mitropoli Philadelfias kai i simasia tis gia ton ellinismo tis boreias Adriatikis* (Athens, 1980).

Moustoxydis, Th. *Andreas Moustoxydis, Bios kai erga* (Athens, 1963).

Mpoumpoulidis, Faidon. *Prosolomikoi* (Athens, 1966–97), 5 vols.

Murat, Laure. *The Man Who Thought He Was Napoleon: Toward a Political History of Madness* (Chicago, 2014).

[Mustoxidi, Andrea]. 'Aggelia'. *Hellenomnemon* 1 (1843): p. 2.

[Mustoxidi, Andrea]. 'Biografika'. *Hellenomnemon* 2 (1843): pp. 95–6.

[Mustoxidi, Andrea]. 'Peri tinon ponimaton anaferomenon eis tin istorian tis Ipeirou, etc.' *Hellenomnemon* 4 (1843): pp. 204–30.

[Mustoxidi, Andrea]. *Exposé des faits qui ont précédé et suivi la cession de Parga* (Paris, 1820).

[Mustoxidi, Andrea]. *Précis des opérations de la flotte Grecque durant la révolution de 1821 et 1822 écrit par un Grec etc.* (Paris, 1822).

Mustoxidi, Andrea. 'Alcune considerazioni sulla presente lingua de' Greci'. *Antologia* 17 (Jan.–Mar. 1825): pp. 44–73.

Mustoxidi, Andrea. 'Notizia intorno ad un volgarizzamento inedito delle istorie di Giovanni Ducas'. *Antologia* 19 (Aug. 1825): pp. 50–7.

Mustoxidi, Andrea. 'Sopra i due Leoni posti in sull'entrata dell'Arsenale di Venezia e sopra altri monumenti di questo genere'. *Antologia*, 47 (Sept. 1832): pp. 78–83.

Mustoxidi, Andrea. *Al dispaccio dei 10 aprile 1840 da Sir Howard Douglas Lord Alto Commissionario di S. M. negli Stati Uniti del Ionio. Confutazione di Andrea Mustoxidi* (Malta, 1841).

Mustoxidi, Andrea. *Illustrazioni corciresi di Andrea Mustoxidi istoriografo dell'Isole dell'Ionio* (Milan, 1811–14), 2 vols.

Mustoxidi, Andrea. *Notizie per servire alla storia corcirese dai tempi eroici fino al secolo XII* (Corfu, 1804).

Mustoxidi, Andrea. *Prose varie del Cavaliere Andrea Mustoxidi, con aggiunta di alcuni versi* (Milan, 1821).

Mustoxidi, Andrea. *Sulla condizione attuale delle Isole Ionie: promemoria presentato in agosto 1839 etc.* (London, 1840).

Mustoxidi, Andrea, and Bartolommeo Cutlumusiano. *Memorie istoriche intorno all'isola d'Imbro etc.* (Constantinople, 1845).

Nada, Narciso. 'Metternich, la diplomazia russa, Francesco IV di Modena ed i moti piemontesi del 1821'. *Annuario dell'Istituto storico italiano per l'età moderna e contemporanea* 19 (1967): pp. 5–121.

Nada, Narcisso. *Metternich, la diplomazia russa, Francesco IV di Modena ed i moti piemontesi del 1821* (Rome, 1972).

Nani Mocenigo, Filippo. *Della letteratura veneziana del secolo XIX* (Venice, 1901).

Nardo, Mara. 'Fra Russi e Francesi, fra Venezia e Corfù: il contrastato amore e il carteggio segreto di Mario Pieri e Maria Petrettini'. *Atti dell'Istituto Veneto di Scienze, Lettere ed Arti* 163 (2009–10): pp. 191–233.

Nardo, Mara. *Maria e Spiridione Petrettini: contributi allo studio della cultura italo-greca tra fine del dominio veneto e Restaurazione* (Padua, 2013).

Nicolaidis, Dimitri. *D'une Grèce à l'autre: représentation des Grecs modernes par la France révolutionnaire* (Paris, 1992).

Nicolaidis, Efthymios. *Science and Eastern Orthodoxy: From the Greek Fathers to the Age of Globalization* (Baltimore, 2011).

Nicoletti, Giuseppe. *La memoria illuminata: autobiografia e letteratura fra Rivoluzione e Risorgimento* (Florence, 1989).

Nicolopoulo, Constantin. 'Littérature grecque: discours d'Isocrates sur l'Échange, rétabli dans son ancien état etc.'. *The Classical Journal* 8 (Sept.–Dec. 1813): pp. 124–6.

Nicolopoulos, John. 'From *Agathangelos* to the *Megale Idea*: Russia and the Emergence of Modern Greek Nationalism'. *Balkan Studies* 26 (1985): pp. 41–56.

Nikiforou, Aliki D. (ed.). *Constitutional Charters of the Ionian Islands* (Athens, 2012).

Nikokaboura, Agathi. 'Maria Anastasia Petrettini'. *Kerkyraika chronika* 13 (1967): pp. 128–36.

Nikokaboura, Agathi. 'O Andreas Moustoxydis kai o Ellinomnimon'. *Kerkyraika chronika* 8 (1960): pp. 151–62.

Nikokaboura, Agathi. *O Andreas Moustoxydis kai i paideia* (Corfu, 1965).

Nikolaidis, Theodossios. 'I latreia tou Agiou Spyridona stin Kerkyra, 16os-18os aionas'. *Ta istorika* 29/57 (Dec. 2012): pp. 313–44.

Nikolaidis, Theodossios. '"Local Religion" in Corfu: Sixteenth to Nineteenth Centuries'. *Mediterranean Historical Review* 29/2 (2014): pp. 155–68.

Nolan, Frederick. *A Harmonical Grammar of the Principal Ancient and Modern Languages* (London, 1822).

Nuvoli, Giuliana. 'La letteratura dell'età neoclassica'. In *Storia generale della letteratura italiana*, vol. VII: *L'Italia romantica il primo Ottocento*, edited by N. Borsellino and W. Pedullà (Milan, 2004): pp. 29–70.

O'Halloran, Clare. 'Irish Recreations of the Gaelic Past: The Challenge of Macpherson's Ossian'. *Past and Present* 124 (Aug. 1989): pp. 69–95.

Oikonomou, Konstantinos. *Epitafios logos eis ton aeimniston Patriarchin Konstantinoupoleos Grigorion, ekfonitheis en Odisso etc.* (Moscow, 1821).

Osterhammel, Jürgen. 'Nationalism and Globalization'. In *The Oxford Handbook of the History of Nationalism*, edited by John Breuilly (Oxford, 2013): pp. 694–709.

Özkirimli, Umut. *Theories of Nationalism: A Critical Introduction* (Basingstoke, 2000).

Palaiologos, K. A. 'Peri tou Komitos Mocenigou'. *Parnassos* 6 (1882): pp. 711–20.

Palmer, Eric. 'Less Radical Enlightenment: A Christian Wing of the French Enlightenment'. In *Reassessing the Radical Enlightenment*, edited by Steffen Ducheyne (London, 2017): pp. 197–222.

Panagiotopoulos, Vassilis. 'Ignatios Ouggroblachias'. In Vassilis Panagiotopoulos and Panagiotis Michailaris, *Klirikoi ston Agona* (Athens, 2010): pp. 49–62.

Panagiotopoulos, Vassilis. 'Kati egine stin Piza to 1821'. *Ta istorika* 5 (June 1986): pp. 177–82.

Panagiotopoulos, Vassilis (ed.). *Dyo prigkipes stin Ellinki epanastasi: epistoles aftopti martyra kai ena ypomnima tou prigkipa Georgiou Kantakouzinou* (Athens, 2015).

Pantazopoulos, Nikolaos. 'Ethniko fronima, glossa kai dikaio sto Ionio kratos prin tin ensomatosi'. In *To Ionio kratos, 1815–1864*, edited by Panagiotis Moschonas (Athens, 1997): pp. 359–83.

[Papadopoulo Vretto, Andrea], 'O antinabarchos Rossos Ricord ypopsifios kybernitis tis Ellados'. *Ethnikon imerologion* 3 (1863): pp. 153–8.

Papadopoulo Vretto, Andrea [André Papadopoulo Bretós]. *Mélanges de politique pour servir de documents à l'histoire des événements de la Grèce régénérée* (Athens, 1840).

Papadopoulo Vretto, Andrea [André Papadopoulo Bretós]. *Mémoires biographiques-historiques sur le président de la Grèce, le Comte Jean Capodistrias* (Paris, 1837–38), 2 vols.

Papadopoulo Vretto, Andrea [André Papadopoulo-Vretos]. *De l'idée dominante des Grecs sur la conquête de Constantinople* (Athens, 1854).

Papadopoulo Vretto, Andrea [Andrea Papadopoulo Vreto]. *Compendio dell'istoria di Giorgio Castriotto soprannominato Scanderbeg principe dell'Albania* (Naples, 1820), 2 vols.

Papadopoulo Vretto, Andrea [Andrea Papadopulo Vreto]. *La Bulgarie, ancienne et moderne* (St Petersburg, 1856).

Papadopoulo Vretto, Andrea [Andrea Papadopulo Vreto]. *Memoria su di alcuni costumi degli antichi Greci tuttora esistenti nell' isola di Leucade nel Mare Jonio* (Naples, 1825).

Papadopoulo Vretto, Andrea [Andrea Papadopulo Vreto]. *Notizie biografiche-storiche su Federico Conte di Guilford etc.* (Athens, 1846).

Papadopoulo Vretto, Andrea [Andrea Papadopulo Vreto]. *Su la scoperta di Tomi, città ellenica nel Ponto Eusino e su la bilingue iscrizione ritrovata in Varna* (Athens, 1853).

Papadopoulo Vretto, Andrea [Andrea Papadopulo-Vrettò]. *Biografia del cavaliere Andrea Mustoxidi scritta e pubblicata in Venezia nell'anno 1836 da Emilio Tipaldo, corretta dallo stesso Mustoxidi in Corfù nell'anno 1838: annotata e continuata sino alla sua morte da Andrea Papadopulo Vreto Leucadio etc.* (Athens, 1860).

Papadopoulo Vretto, Andrea [Andreas Papadopoulos Bretos]. *Neoelliniki philologia itoi katalogos ton apo ptoseos tis Byzantinis Aftokratorias mechri egkathidriseos tis en Elladi basileias typothenton biblion etc.* (Athens, 1854–58), 2 vols.

Papadopoulo Vretto, Andrea. *Biografia Marinou Papadopoulou Bretou, syntachtheisa apo tou atychous patros tou* (Athens, 1872).

Papageorgiou, Georgios P. 'Symboli stin istoria tis ellinikis paroikias tis Ankonas kata ton 19o aiona'. *Dodoni* 4 (1975): pp. 295–340.

Papatheodorou, Yiannis. *Romantika pepromena: o Aristotelis Valaoritis os 'ethnikos poiitis'* (Athens, 2009).

Papoulides, K. K. 'Eggrafa Ellinon diplomatikon ypallilon tou 19ou ai. apo ti bibliothiki Lenin tis Moschas'. *Ellinika* 31 (1979): pp. 144–58.

Pappas, Nicholas Charles. *Greeks in Russian Military Service in the Late Eighteenth and Early Nineteenth Centuries* (Thessaloniki, 1991).

Paquette, Gabriel. *Imperial Portugal in the Age of Atlantic Revolutions: The Luso-Brazilian World, c.1770–1850* (Cambridge, 2013).

Paravia, Pier-Alessandro. *Memorie veneziane di letteratura e di storia* (Turin, 1850).

Paravia, Pier-Alessandro. *Lezioni di varia letteratura* (Turin, 1852–6).

Paschalis, Michail. *Xanadiabazontas ton Kalvo: o Andreas Kalvos, i Italia kai i archaiotita* (Herakleion, 2013).

Pasquali-Petrettini, A. *Lettere inedite a Maria Petrettini* (Padua, 1852).

Pastore Stocchi, Manlio. '1792–1797: Ugo Foscolo a Venezia'. In *Storia della cultura veneta*, vol. VI: *Dall'età napoleonica alla Prima Guerra Mondiale*, edited by G. Arnaldi and M. P. Stocchi (Vicenza, 1986): pp. 21–58.

Pastore Stocchi, Manlio. 'Moralità e costume nei letterati delle province adriatiche e ioniche'. In *L'area alto-adriatica dal riformismo veneziano all'età napoleonica*, edited by Filiberto Agostini (Venice, 1998): pp. 91–101.

Pecchio, Giuseppe. *Vita di Ugo Foscolo* (Milan, 1851).

Pécout, Gilles. 'Amitié littéraire et amitié politique méditerranéennes: philhellènes français et italiens de la fin du xixe siècle'. In *Philhellénismes et transferts culturels dans l'Europe du XIXe siècle*, edited by Gilles Pécout and Michel Espagne (Paris, 2005): pp. 207–18.

Pécout, Gilles. 'Philhellenism in Italy: Political Friendship and the Italian Volunteers in the Mediterranean in the Nineteenth Century'. *Journal of Modern Italian Studies* 9/4 (2004): pp. 405–27.

Pécout, Gilles. 'Pour une lecture méditerranéenne et transnationale du Risorgimento'. *Revue d'histoire du XIXe siècle* 44 (2012): pp. 29–47.

Pécout, Gilles. 'The International Armed Volunteers: Pilgrims of a Transnational Risorgimento'. *Journal of Modern Italian Studies* 14/4 (2009): pp. 413–26.

Perticari, Giulio. *Degli scrittori del Trecento e dei loro imitatori* (Milan, 1828).

Pertici, Roberto. 'Appunti sulla nascita dell'"intellettuale" in Italia'. In Christophe Charle, *Gli intellettuali nell'Ottocento* (Bologna, 2002): postface.

Petrettini, Maria. *Alcune immagini di Filostrato tradotte dal greco da Maria Petrettini corcirese* (Treviso, 1825).

Petrettini, Maria. *Lettere a lady Maria Wartley Montague tradotte dall'inglese* (Corfu, 1838).

Petrettini, Maria. *Vita di Cassandra Fedele* (Venice, 1814).

Petrettini, Spiridione. *Istoria romana di Vellejo Patercolo* (Venice, 1813).

Petrettini, Spiridione. *Le opere scelte di Giuliano imperatore, per la prima volta dal Greco volgarizzate con note, e con alcuni discorsi illustrativi* (Milan, 1822).

Petrettini, Spiridione. *Saggio di traduzione delle Aringhe di Cajo Cornelio Tacito* (Venice, 1806).

Petri, Rolf (ed.). *Nostalgia: memoria e passaggi tra le sponde dell'Adriatico* (Rome, 2009).

Petropoulos, John Anthony. *Politics and Statecraft in the Kingdom of Greece 1833–1843* (Princeton, 1968).

Philliou, Christine M. *Biography of an Empire: Governing Ottomans in an Age of Revolution* (Berkeley, Los Angeles, and London, 2011).

[Pieri, Mario]. *Compendio della storia del Risorgimento della Grecia dal 1740 al 1824, compilato da M. P. C.* (Florence, 1825), 2 vols.

Pieri, Mario [M. P.]. 'Degli scrittori Greci e delle italiane versione delle loro opere, etc.' *Antologia* 30 (Apr.–June 1828): pp. 131–3.

Pieri, Mario. 'Elogio di Antonio Trivoli Pieri'. In Mario Pieri, *Tributo all'amicizia, con vari componimenti in verso* (Verona, 1806): pp. 7–63.

Pieri, Mario. 'Elogio di Pier Antonio Bondioli'. In Mario Pieri, *Operette varie in prosa* (Milan, 1821): pp. 289–327.

Pieri, Mario. 'La lingua e la letteratura italiana. Dialogo: Gasparo Gozzi, Vincenzio Monti, Antonio Cesari'. In Mario Pieri, *Opere* (Florence, 1852): vol. III, pp. 5–99.

Pieri, Mario. 'Vita di Spiridione Petrettini, corcirese'. In Mario Pieri, *Della vita di Mario Pieri corcirese scritta da lui medesimo* (Florence, 1850): vol. II, pp. 381–94.

Pieri, Mario. *Della vita di Mario Pieri corcirese scritta da lui medesimo* (Florence, 1850), 2 vols.

Pieri, Mario. *Memorie*, edited by Roberta Masini (Rome, 2003), vol. I.

Pieri, Mario. *Memorie II*, edited by Claudio Chiancone (Ariccia, 2017).

Pinto, Pasquale Massimo. 'La riscoperta dell'*Antidosi* nel XIX secolo', in *Isocrate: per una nuova edizione critica*, edited by Maddalena Vallozza (Florence, 2017): pp. 203–29.

Pizanias, Petros (ed.). *The Greek Revolution of 1821: A European Event* (Istanbul, 2011).

Pizzamiglio, Gilberto. 'Ugo Foscolo nel salotto di Isabella Teotochi-Albrizzi'. *Quaderni Veneti* 2 (1985): pp. 49–66.

Ploumidis, G. S. 'To benetiko typografeio tou Agiou Georgiou (1850–1882)'. *Eranistis* 8 (1970): pp. 169–85.

Politis, Alexis. 'Ethnikoi poiites'. In *Atheates opseis tis istorias: keimena afieromena sto Yiani Yianoulopoulo*, edited by Despoina Papadimitriou and Serafeim Seferiades (Athens, 2012): pp. 227–44.

Politis, Alexis. *I anakalypsi ton ellinikon dimotikon tragoudion* (Athens, 1999).

Politis, Linos. *Gyro sto Solomo: meletes kai arthra (1938–1982)* (Athens, 1995).

Polizzi, Gaspare. '"Io scrivo le mie letter dove ha regno Mercurio". Antonio Papadopoli: un uomo di lettere nell'Italia del primo Ottocento'. *Quaderni Veneti* 45 (2007): pp. 105–44.

Polychroniades, Constantine [Filalithis]. 'I greci e i turchi'. *Antologia* 12 (Nov. 1823): pp. 101–16; 13 (Mar. 1824): pp. 83–108; 14 (Apr. 1824): pp. 57–73.

Polylas, Iakovos. 'Prolegomena'. In Dionysios Solomos. *Ta ebriskomena*, edited by Iakovos Polylas (Corfu, 1859). pp. γ'–νδ'.

Popkin, Jeremy D. 'Philippe Lejeune, Explorer of the Diary'. In Philippe Lejeune, *On Diary*, edited by J. D. Popkin and Julie Rak (Hawaii, 2009): pp. 1–15.

Porfyris, K. *O Andreas Kalvos karmponaros: i mystiki diki ton karmponaron tis Toskanis* (Athens, 1992).

Povolo, Claudio. 'The Creation of Venetian Historiography'. In *Venice Reconsidered: The History and Civilization of an Italian City-State, 1297–1797*, edited by John Martin and Dennis Romano (Baltimore and London, 2000): pp. 491–519.

Prantis, Efthymios. *Albanika parapona en Minia tis Ano Aigyptou* (Athens, 1880).

Protopsaltis, Emmanouil G. *Ignatios Mitropolitis Ouggroblachias (1766–1828)* (Athens, 1961), 2 vols.

Prousis, Theophilus. 'The Destunis Collection in the Manuscript Section of the Saltykov-Shchedrin State Public Library in Leningrad'. *Modern Greek Studies Yearbook* 5 (1989): pp. 395–452.

Prousis, Theophilus. *Russian Society and the Greek Revolution* (DeKalb, Ill., 1994).

Puto, Artan and Maurizio Isabella. 'Trajectories of Albanian Nationalism in the Writings of Girolamo de Rada and Semseddin Samin Frashëri, ca.1848–1903'. In *Mediterranean Diasporas: Politics and Ideas in the Long Nineteenth Century*, edited by Maurizio Isabella and Konstantina Zanou (London, 2016): pp. 171–87.

Pylarinos, Theodosis. 'I pragmateia tou Antoniou Matesi gia ti dimotiki glossa'. *Tekmirion* 9 (2010): pp. 73–103.

Pylarinos, Theodosis. 'O *Artaxerxis* tou Petrou Metastasiou, metafrasmenos stin aploelliniki apo ton prosolomiko Ioanni Kantouni (1731–1817)'. *Parabasis* 10 (2010): pp. 377–9.

Pylarinos, Theodosis. 'O thanatos tou D. Solomou'. *Periplous* 46–7 (July 1998–Feb. 1999): pp. 203–19.

Pylarinos, Theodosis. *Eptanisiaki Scholi* (Athens, 2003).

Pylarinos, Theodosis. *Glossikos Patriotismos: oi agones gia tin kathierosi tis glossas tou ellinikou laou ktl.* (Corfu, 2013).

Pylarinos, Theodosis, and Panagiota Tzivara. 'Foskoliana ergobiografika: oi epistoles tou Spyridona de Biasi pros ton Domenico Bianchini'. In *X Panionian Conference, Proceedings*: forthcoming.

Raeff, Marc. *Michael Speransky, Statesman of Imperial Russia, 1772–1839* (The Hague, 1957).

Rallis, K.Th. *Symmikta ellinika apo tis archis tis kyberniseos tou Kapodistria kai exis* (Paris, 1831–2), 2 vols.

Rapport, Michael. *1848: Year of Revolution* (New York, 2010).

Rasi, Donatella. 'Storia di un'amicizia: il carteggio inedito Niccolò Tommaseo–Emilio de Tipaldo'. In *Alla lettera: teorie epistolari dai Greci al Novecento*, edited by Adriana Chemello (Milan, 1998): pp. 263–313.

Rasi, Donatella. 'Un greco amico del Tommaseo: Emilio de Tipaldo'. In *Niccolò Tommaseo: popolo e nazioni, Italiani, Corsi, Greci, Illirici*, edited by Francesco Bruni (Rome and Padua, 2004): vol. II, pp. 537–78.

Redford, Bruce. *Dilettanti: The Antic and the Antique in Eighteenth-Century England* (Los Angeles, 2008).

Reverdin, Olivier. 'La Toscane, les philhellènes genevois et l'envoi des secours à la Grèce'. In *Le relazioni del pensiero italiano risorgimentale con i centri del movimento liberale di Ginevra e Coppet: colloquio italo-elvetico* (Rome, 1979): pp. 63–75.

Riall, Lucy. *Risorgimento: The History of Italy from Napoleon to Nation State* (London, 2009).

Ricks, David, and Paul Magdalino (eds). *Byzantium and the Modern Greek Identity* (Aldershot and Brookfield, 1998).

Ricuperati, Giuseppe. 'The Enlightenment and the Church in the Work of Franco Venturi: The Fertile Legacy of a Civil Religion'. *Journal of Modern Italian Studies* 10/2 (2005): pp. 168–82.

Rigobon, Pietro. *Gli eletti alle assemblee veneziane del 1848–1849* (Venice, 1950).

Rizos Neroulos, Jacovaky. *Histoire moderne de la Grèce depuis la chute de l'Empire d'Orient* (Geneva, 1828).

Roessel, David. *In Byron's Shadow: Modern Greece in the English and American Imagination* (Oxford, 2002).

Romagnani, Gian Paolo. *Storiografia e politica culturale nel Piemonte di Carlo Alberto* (Turin, 1985).

Romani, George T. *The Neapolitan Revolution of 1820–1821* (Westport, Conn., 1950).

Rosada, Bruno. *La giovinezza di Niccolò Ugo Foscolo* (Padua, 1992).

Rosenblatt, Helena. 'The Christian Enlightenment'. In *The Cambridge History of Christianity*, vol. 7: *Enlightenment, Reawakening and Revolution 1660–1815*, edited by Stewart J. Brown and Timothy Tackett (Cambridge, 2006): pp. 283–301.

Rosmini, Carlo. *Dell'istoria di Milano* (Milan, 1820).

Rothman, Natalie. *Brokering Empire: Trans-Imperial Subjects between Venice and Istanbul* (Ithaca, NY, 2012).

Rotolo, Vincenzo. 'Dionisios Solomòs fra la cultura italiana e la cultura greca'. *Italoellinika* 1 (1988): pp. 87–110.

Rousseau, Jean-Jacques. *The Confessions* (London, 1996).

Sante, Matteo. 'Ossian and Risorgimento: The Poetics of Nationalism'. In *Romanticism across the Disciplines*, edited by Larry H. Peer (Lanham, Md, and New York, 1998): pp. 27–40.

Saul, Norman E. *Russia and the Mediterranean 1797–1807* (Chicago, 1970).

Sauli D'Igliano, Lodovico. *Reminiscenze della propria vita*, edited by Giuseppe Ottolenghi (Rome and Milan, 1908–9), 2 vols.

Scalora, Francesco. 'O Andreas Papadopoulos Brettos kai i istoria tou Georgiou Kastriotou metonomasthentos Skentermpei igemonos tis Albanias'. In *X Panionian Conference, Proceedings*: forthcoming.

Scardicchio, Andrea. ' "Le vostre lettere mi riescono sempre care…": spigolature del carteggio inedito Mustoxidi-Vieusseux (con appendice di quattro lettere)'. *Studi e problemi di critica testuale* 93 (Oct. 2016): pp. 133–65.

Schoell, Federico. *Istoria della letteratura greca profana etc., recata in italiano per la prima volta con giunte ed osservazioni critiche da Emilio Tipaldo* (Venice, 1827), 18 vols.

Sclopis, Federico. 'Pier-Alessandro Paravia'. *Archivio storico italiano*, Nuova Serie 4 (1857): pp. ii–iv.

Seferis, Giorgos. 'Apories diabazontas ton Kalvo'. In Giorgos Seferis, *Dokimes*, vol. I: *1936–1947*, edited by G. P. Savvides (Athens, 1981): pp. 56–63.

Seferis, Giorgos. 'Kalvos, 1960'. In Giorgos Seferis, *Dokimes*, edited by G. P. Savvides, vol. II: *1948–1971* (Athens, 1981): pp. 112–35.

Seferis, Giorgos. 'Prologos gia mia ekdosi ton Odon'. In Giorgos Seferis, *Dokimes*, vol. I: *1936–1947*, edited by G. P. Savvides (Athens, 1981): pp. 179–210.

Sensini, Francesca Irene. 'Niccolò Ugo Foscolo in Grecia: prolegomena', *Cahiers d'études italiennes* 20 (2015): pp. 201–15.

Serianni, Luca. *Storia della lingua italiana: il primo Ottocento* (Bologna, 1989).

Sestan, Ernesto. *La Firenze di Vieusseux e di Capponi*, edited by Giovanni Spadolini (Florence, 1986).

Setti, Giovanni. 'Il Monti traduttore d'Omero'. *Atti dell'Accademia Scientifica Veneto–Trentino–Istriana* 3–4 (1906–7): pp. 1–47.

Sfoini, Alexandra. 'Fotismenes afthenties se grafeiokratika periballonta: o Panagiotis Kodrikas kai i glossa ton evgenon'. *Ta istorika* 59 (2013): pp. 323–63.

Shannan Peckham, Robert. *National Histories, Natural States: Nationalism and the Politics of Place in Greece* (London and New York, 2001).

Sideri, Aloi. *Ellines foitites sto panepistimio tis Pizas (1806–1861)* (Athens, 1989), 2 vols.

Sigouros, Marinos. *Ougos Foskolos (biografiki meleti)* (Athens, 1915).

Sismondi, G. C. L. *Epistolario*, edited by Carlo Pellegrini (Florence, 1933), 4 vols.

Sklavenitis, Triantafyllos. 'O Spyridon Blantis kai i idiotiki didaskalia, Piano di Studi/Ekthesis Mathimaton: Benetia 1794'. *Thysavrismata* 34 (2004): pp. 421–46.

Sluga, Glenda. 'The Congress of Vienna' (part of the project 'The International History of Cosmopolitanism'): <https://sites.google.com/site/viennacon/assignments> (accessed 28 Feb. 2014).

Smilianskaia, Elena. 'Catherine's Liberation of the Greeks: High-Minded Discourse and Everyday Realities'. In *Word and Image in Russian History: Essays in Honor of Gary Marker*, edited by M. Di Salvo, D. Kaiser, and V. Kivelson (Boston, 2015): pp. 71–89.

Smilianskaia, Elena. '"Protection" or "Possession": How Russians Created a Greek Principality in 1770–1775'. In *Power and Influence in South-Eastern Europe: 16–19th Ccentury*, edited by M. Baramova, P. Mitev, I. Parvev, and V. Racheva (Münster, 2013): pp. 209–17.

Sofia, Francesca. 'The Promised Land: Biblical Themes in the Risorgimento'. *Journal of Modern Italian Studies* 17/5 (2012): pp. 574–86.

Solaro, Antonio. 'Italia'. In *Oi Ellines sti diaspora, 15os–21os ai.*, edited by I. Chassiotis, O. Katsiardi-Hering, and E. Ambatzi (Athens, 2006): pp. 158–63.

Soldatos, Konstantinos E. 'I ethniki glossa eis tin Eptanison'. *Kerkyraika chronika* 13 (1967): pp. 84–104.

Solomos, Dionysios [Conte Dionisio Salamon Zacintio], *Rime Improvvisate* (Corfu, 1822).

Solomos, Dionysios [Dionisio Solomos], *Elogio di Ugo Foscolo*, edited by Carlo Brighenti (Turin, Milan, and Florence, 1934).

Solomos, Dionysios. 'Dialogos'. In Dionysios Solomos, *Apanta*, vol. 2: *Peza kai italika*, edited by Linos Politis (Athens, 1955): pp. 11–30.

Solomos, Dionysios. *Allilografia*, edited by Linos Politis (Athens, 1991).

Solomos, Dionysios. *The Free Besieged and Other Poems*, translated by Peter Thompson, edited by Peter Mackridge (Nottingham, 2015).

Sorkin, David. *The Religious Enlightenment: Protestants, Jews, and Catholics from London to Vienna* (Princeton, 2008).

St Clair, William. *That Greece Might Still Be Free: The Philhellenes in the War of Independence* (Oxford, 1972).

Stavrinos, Miranda. 'The Reformist Party in the Ionian Islands (1848–1852): Internal Conflicts and Nationalist Aspirations'. *Balkan Studies* 26/2 (1985): pp. 351–61.

Stites, Richard. *The Four Horsemen: Riding to Liberty in Post-Napoleonic Europe* (Oxford, 2014).

Stouraiti, Anastasia. 'Geografie del trauma e politiche di lutto: racconti sulla perdita delle Isole Ionie a Venezia'. In *The Greek World between the Age of Enlightenment and the Twentieth Century*, edited by Konstantinos Dimadis (Athens, 2007): vol. II, pp. 159–68.

Stouraiti, Anastasia. *La Grecia nelle raccolte della Fondazione Querini Stampalia* (Venice, 2000).

Stourdza, Alexandre. 'Notice biographique sur le comte J. Capodistrias, Président de la Grèce'. In *Correspondance du Comte Capodistrias, Président de la Grèce*, edited by E. A. Bétant (Geneva and Paris, 1839): vol. I, pp. 1–128.

Stourdza, Alexandre. 'Souvenirs de la vie de ma sœur pour ceux qui l'ont aimé'. In Alexandre Stourdza, *Œuvres posthumes, religieuses, historiques, philosophiques et littéraires* (Paris, 1859): vol. I, pp. 42–59.

Stourdza, Alexandre. *La Grèce en 1821 et 1822: correspondance politique publiée par un Grec* (Paris, 1823).

Stourdza-Edling, Roxandra. *Mémoires de la Comtesse Edling (née Stourdza) Demoiselle d'Honneur de sa Majesté l'Impératrice Elisabeth Alexéevna* (Moscow, 1829).

Stratis, Dimitrios. *Bartholomeos Koutloumousianos (1772–1851): biografia—ergografia* (Mount Athos, 2002).

Tabet, Xavier. 'Foscolo et la révolution vénitienne'. In *Ugo Foscolo, l'Italie et la révolution française*, edited by Enzo Neppi (Grenoble, 2004): pp. 37–64.

Talamo, Giuseppe. 'Società segrete e gruppi politici liberali e democratici sino al 1848'. In *Storia di Torino*, vol. VI: *La città nel Risorgimento (1798–1864)*, edited by Umberto Levra (Turin, 2000): pp. 461–91.

Tamborra, Angelo. 'Aspetti di universalismo cristiano nell'età della Santa Alleanza'. *Il pensiero politico* 2 (1970): pp. 234–44.

Tamborra, Angelo. 'Niccolò Tommaseo, il mondo ortodosso e il problema dell'Unione delle Chiese'. In *Niccolò Tommaseo nel centenario della morte*, edited by V. Branca and G. Petrocchi (Florence, 1977): pp. 583–628.

Tamborra, Angelo. 'Pio IX, la lettera agli orientali del 1848 e il mondo ortodosso'. *Rassegna storica del Risorgimento* 56 (July–Sept. 1959): pp. 347–67.

Tatti, Mariasilvia. 'Esilio e identità nazionale nell'esperienza francese di Tommaseo'. In *Niccolò Tommaseo: popolo e nazioni, Italiani, Corsi, Greci, Illirici*, edited by Francesco Bruni (Rome and Padua, 2004): vol. I, pp. 95–114.

Taylor, Charles. *Sources of the Self: The Making of the Modern Identity* (Cambridge, Mass., and London, 1989).

Tenca, Carlo. 'Cenno commemorativo intorno a Felice Bellotti'. *Il crepuscolo* 9/8 (1858): pp. 126–8.

Teotochi-Albrizzi, Isabella. *Opere di scultura e di plastica di Antonio Canova* (Florence, 1809).

Teotochi-Albrizzi, Isabella. *Ritratti* (Brescia, 1807).

Terzoli, Maria Antonietta. *Foscolo* (Rome and Bari, 2000).

Theotokas, Nikos, and Nikos Kotaridis. *I oikonomia tis bias: paradosiakes kai neoterikes exousies stin Ellada tou 19ou aiona* (Athens, 2006).

Theotokis, Spyridon. 'I ethniki syneidisis tou Kapodistriou kai i elliniki glossa'. *Proceedings of the Academy of Athens* 7 (1932): pp. 130–42.

Thymis, Konstantinos. *I Iera Moni Yperagias Theotokou Platyteras Kerkyras* (Corfu, 2002).

Tolias, Giorgos. 'Choros kai istoria: archaiodifikes kai istoriografikes proseggiseis tis geografias, 19os–20os ai.' In *Istoriografia tis neoteris kai sygchronis Elladas, 1833–2002*, edited by P. Kitromilides and Tr. Sklavenitis (Athens, 2004): vol. II, pp. 77–118.

Tolias, Giorgos. *La Médaille et la rouille: l'image de la Grèce moderne dans la presse littéraire parisienne (1794–1815)* (Paris and Athens, 1997).

Tommaseo, Niccolò. 'Andrea Mustoxidi'. *Archivio storico italiano* 12/2 (1860): pp. 30–61.

Tommaseo, Niccolò. 'Della civiltà ionia e di Niccolò Delviniotti'. *Archivio storico italiano* 2/1 (1855): pp. 65–88.

Tommaseo, Niccolò. 'Rizo Jakovaky: storia della Grecia moderna'. In Niccolò Tommaseo, *Dizionario estetico*, vol. *II: Parte moderna* (Milan, 1860): p. 334.

Tommaseo, Niccolò. *Canti popolari, toscani, corsi, illirici e greci* (Venice, 1841–42).

Tommaseo, Niccolò. *Colloqui col Manzoni*, edited by Teresa Lodi (Florence, 1928).

Tommaseo, Niccolò. *Il secondo esilio: scritti concernenti le cose d'Italia e d'Europa dal 1849 in poi* (Milan, 1862), 2 vols.

Tommaseo, Niccolò. *Il supplizio d'un Italiano in Corfù*, edited by Fabio Danelon (Venice, 2008).

Tommaseo, Niccolò. *Venezia negli anni 1848 e 1849* (Florence, 1931).

Torta, Carlo. *La rivoluzione piemontese nel 1821* (Rome and Milan, 1908).

Trant, Captain T. A. *Narrative of a Journey through Greece* (London, 1830).

Treves, Piero. 'La critica letteraria, la filologia, la bibliografia'. In *Storia della cultura veneta*, vol. 6: *Dall'età napoleonica alla Prima Guerra Mondiale*, edited by G. Arnaldi and M. P. Stocchi (Vicenza, 1986): pp. 365–96.

Trikoupis, Spyridon. *Logoi epikidioi kai epinikioi ekfonithentes eis epikoon tou laou epi tis Ellinikis epanastaseos* (Aegina, 1829).

Trivellato, Francesca. 'Is There a Future for Italian Microhistory in the Age of Global History?' *California Italian Studies* 2/1 (2011): <https://escholarship.org/uc/item/0z94n9hq>.

Trivoli Pieri, Antonio. *Poesie* (Venice, 1800).

Tsatsos, Konstantinos. 'Kalvos, o poiitis tis ideas'. In Andreas Kalvos, *Omnibus Work*, edited by K. Tsatsos (Athens, 1979): introduction.

Tsigakou, Fani-Maria. *The Rediscovery of Greece: Travellers and Painters of the Romantic Era* (New Rochelle, NY, 1981).

Tsitselis, Ilias. *Kefalliniaka symmeikta: symbolai eis tin istorian kai laografian tis nisou Kefallinias* (Athens, 1904), 2 vols.

Tuck, Richard. *The Rights of War and Peace: Political Thought and the International Order from Grotius to Kant* (Oxford, 1999).

Typaldos-Iakobatos, Georgios. *Istoria tis Ioniou Akadimias*, edited by Sp. Asdrachas (Athens, 1982).

Tzakis, Dionysis. 'Rosiki parousia sto Aigaio: apo ta Orlofika sto Lampro Katsoni'. In *Istoria tou Neou Ellinismou, 1770–2000*, edited by Vassilis Panagiotopoulos (Athens, 2003): vol. 1, pp. 115–16.

Tziovas, Dimitris (ed.). *Greek Diaspora and Migration since 1700* (London, 2009).

Tzivara, Panagiota. *Scholeia kai daskaloi sti venetokratoumeni Kerkyra (16os–18os aionas)* (Kavala, 2003).

Vagenas, Nasos. 'Mia eftichis aporripsi'. *To Bima* newspaper (18 June 2006).

Vagenas, Nasos. 'Paramorfoseis tou Kalvou'. *To dentro* 71–72 (Sept.–Oct. 1992): pp. 123–39.

Vagenas, Nasos. 'Scholia ston Kalvo'. *Parnassos* 14/3 (1972): pp. 453–65.

Van Dyck, Karen. 'The Language Question and the Diaspora'. In *The Making of Modern Greece: Nationalism, Romanticism, and the Uses of the Past (1797–1896)*, edited by Roderick Beaton and David Ricks (London, 2009): pp. 189–98.

Vannucci, Atto. *Ricordi della vita e delle opere di G.-B. Niccolini* (Florence, 1866).

Veloudis, Giorgos. *To elliniko typografeio ton Glykidon sti Benetia (1670–1854): symboli sti meleti tou ellinikou bibliou kata tin epochi tis tourkokratias* (Athens, 1987).

Veloudis, Giorgos. *O Solomos ton Ellinon: ethniki poiisi kai ideologia: mia politiki anagnosi* (Athens, 2004).

Veludo, Giovanni. 'Cenni sulla colonia greca orientale'. In *Venezia e le sue lagune* (Venice, 1847): vol. I, pp. 78–100.

Veludo, Giovanni. *Ellinon Orthodoxon apoikia en Benetia, istorikon ypomnima* (Venice, 1893).

Veludo, Giovanni. *Parole nei funerali del commendatore Emilio de Tipaldo, dette in S. Giorgio de'Greci il dì III aprile 1878* (Venice, 1878).

Veludo, Spiridione. 'Andrea Mustoxidi, *L'Ellenomnemone (Greco Rammentatore) o Miscellanee greche*, opera compilata da etc.' *Il gondoliere* 9/61 (2 Aug. 1843): pp. 241–2.

Veludo, Spiridione. 'Memorie istoriche intorno all'isola d'Imbro, raccolte dal cav. Andrea Mustoxidi con supplementi del padre B. Cutlumusiano etc.' *Il vaglio* 9/33 (15 Aug. 1846): pp. 262–3.

Veludo, Spiridione. *Breve ricordo di Dionigi Solomos* (Venice, 1857).

Veludo, Spiridione. *Lettere di Andrea Mustoxidi e di Ippolito Pindemonte a Francesco Negri* (Venice, 1864).

Venturi, Franco. *La rivolta greca del 1770 e il patriottismo dell'età dei lumi* (Rome, 1986).

Venturi, Franco. *The End of the Old Regime in Europe, 1776–1789*, Part II: *Republican Patriotism and the Empires of the East*, translated by R. Burr Litchfield (Princeton, 1991).

Verdery, Katherine. *The Political Lives of Dead Bodies: Reburial and Postsocialist Change* (New York, 1999).

Vilaras, Yiannis. *I romeiki glosa* (Corfu, 1814).

Vincent, Eric Reginald. *Ugo Foscolo: An Italian in Regency England* (Cambridge, 1953).

Vitti, Mario. *Istoria tis ellinikis logotechnias* (Athens, 2003).

Vitti, Mario. *O Kalvos kai i epochi tou* (Athens, 1995).

Vlami, Despina. *To fiorini, to sitari kai i odos tou kipou: ellines emporoi sto Livorno, 1750–1868* (Athens, 2000).

Volpi, Vittorio (ed.). *Odissea di Omero: traduzione di Niccolò Delviniotti corcirese* (Iseo, 2005).

Vrokinis, A. S. *Syntomos afigisis tou biou tou Ioannou Kapodistriou* (Corfu, 1886).

Vrokinis, Lavrentios. *Biografika Schedaria ton en tois grammasin, oraies technes kai allois kladois tou koinonikou biou dialampsanton Kerkyraion etc.* (Corfu, 1884), 2 vols.

Walsh, Rachel A. *Ugo Foscolo's Tragic Vision in Italy and England* (Toronto, 2014).

Wilson, Frances (ed.). *Byromania: Portraits of the Artist in Nineteenth- and Twentieth-Century Culture* (New York, 1999).

Woodhouse, C. M. *Capodistria: The Founder of Greek Independence* (Oxford, 1973).

Woollacott, A., D. Deacon, and P. Russell (eds). *Transnational Lives: Biographies of Global Modernity, 1700–Present* (London and New York, 2010).

Wrigley, David W. 'The Ionian Islands and the Advent of the Greek State (1827–1833)'. *Balkan Studies* 19 (1978): pp. 413–26.

Xanthopoulou-Kyriakou, Artemis. *I elliniki koinotita tis Benetias (1797–1866): dioikitiki kai oikonomiki organosi, ekpaideftiki kai politiki drastiriotita* (Thessaloniki, 1978).

Zafeiriou, Lefkios. 'Charlotte Augusta Kalvo (Wadams) kai Andreas Kalvos apo tin Kerkyra sto Londino kai sto Louth: nea stoicheia'. *Porfyras* 147–8 (Apr.–Sept. 2013): pp. 43–53.

Zafeiriou, Lefkios. *O bios kai to ergo tou Andrea Kalvou (1792–1869)* (Athens, 2006).

Zampelios, Spyridon. *Pothen i koini lexis 'Tragoudo'? Skepseis peri ellinikis poiiseos* (Athens, 1859).

Zanou, Konstantina. 'Dianooumenoi-"gefyres" sti metabasi apo tin proethniki stin ethniki epochi'. *Ta istorika* 58 (2013): pp. 3–22.

Zanou, Konstantina. 'Imperial Nationalism and Orthodox Enlightenment: A Diasporic Story between the Ionian Islands, Russia and Greece, ca. 1800–1830'. In *Mediterranean Diasporas: Politics and Ideas in the Long Nineteenth Century*, edited by Maurizio Isabella and Konstantina Zanou (London, 2016): pp. 117–34.

Zanou, Konstantina. 'Nostalgia, Self-Exile and the National Idea: The Case of Andrea Mustoxidi and the Eearly-19th-Century Heptanesians of Italy'. In *Nationalism in the Troubled Triangle: Cyprus, Greece and Turkey*, edited by A. Aktar, N. Kızılyürek, and U. Özkırımlı (London and New York, 2009).

Zanou, Konstantina. 'O Andreas Moustoxidis, o Bartholomeos Koutloumousianos kai to *Ypomnima istorikon peri tis nisou Imbrou*'. *Mnimon* 31 (2010): pp. 286–9.

Zanou, Konstantina. 'O Ioannis Kapodistrias, o Iakobakis Rizos Neroulos kai i *Neoteri istoria tis Elladas*'. *Mnimon* 30 (2009): pp. 141–78.

Zanou, Konstantina. 'Profughi ciprioti a Venezia e Trieste dopo il 1821 (nuovi elementi provenienti dalle Carte Mustoxidi a Corfù)'. In *Giornate per Cipro*, edited by Mattia de Poli (Padua, 2007): pp. 39–62.

Zanou, Konstantina. 'Pros mia synoliki theorisi tou ethnikou chronou: pnevmatikes zymoseis ston italo-eptanisiako choro kata to a' miso tou 19ou aiona'. In *IX Panionian Conference, Proceedings* (Paxi, 2014): vol. II, pp. 319–44.

Zanou, Konstantina. 'Storia di un archivio: le carte Mustoxidi a Corfù (con due lettere inedite di Manzoni e Foscolo)'. *Giornale storico della letteratura italiana* 183/604 (2006): pp. 556–76.

Zois, Leonidas. *Lexikon istorikon kai laografikon Zakynthou* (Athens, 1963), 2 vols.

Zoras, Georgios. 'Andreou Kalvou, Odi eis Ionious'. *Nea estia* 21/248 (15 Apr. 1937): pp. 564–75.

Zoras, Georgios. *A. Mazarakis kai N. Thomazeos: anekdotos allilografia* (Athens, 1963).

Zorin, Andrei. '"Star of the East": The Holy Alliance and European Mysticism'. *Kritika: Explorations in Russian and Eurasian History* 4/2 (Spring 2003): pp. 313–42.

# Index

Printed and bound by CPI Group (UK) Ltd, Croydon, CR0 4YY